Studies in Regional and Local History

General Editor Nigel Goose

Previous titles in this series

Volume 1: *A Hertfordshire Demesne of Westminster Abbey: Profits, productivity and weather*
by Derek Vincent Stern (edited and with an introduction by Christopher Thornton)

Volume 2: *From Hellgill to Bridge End: Aspects of economic and social change in the Upper Eden Valley, 1840–95*
by Margaret Shepherd
(ISBN 978-1-902806-32-7, £18.95 pb)

Volume 3: *Cambridge and its Economic Region, 1450–1560*
by John S. Lee
(ISBN 978-1-902806-47-1, £35.00 hb; ISBN 978-1-902806-52-5, £18.99 pb)

Volume 4: *Cultural Transition in the Chilterns and Essex Region, 350 AD to 650 AD*
by John T. Baker
(ISBN 978-1-902806-46-4, £35.00 hb; ISBN 978-1-902806-53-2, £18.99 pb)

Volume 5: *A Pleasing Prospect: Society and culture in eighteenth-century Colchester*
by Shani D'Cruze
(ISBN 978-1-902806-72-3, £35.00 hb; ISBN 978-1-902806-73-0, £18.99 pb)

Volume 6: *Agriculture and Rural Society after the Black Death: Common themes and regional variations*
by Ben Dodds and Richard Britnell
(ISBN 978-1-902806-78-5, £35.00 hb; ISBN 978-1-902806-79-2, £18.99 pb)

Volume 7: *A Lost Frontier Revealed: Regional separation in the East Midlands*
by Alan Fox
(ISBN 978-1-902806-96-9, £35.00 hb; ISBN 978-1-902806-97-6, £18.99 pb)

Volume 8: *Land and Family: Trends and local variations in the peasant land market on the Winchester bishopric estates, 1263–1415*
by John Mullan and Richard Britnell
(ISBN 978-1-902806-94-5, £35.00 hb; ISBN 978-1-902806-95-2, £18.99 pb)

Volume 9: *Out of the Hay and into the Hops: Hop cultivation in Wealden Kent and hop marketing in Southwark, 1744–2000*
by Celia Cordle
(ISBN 978-1-907396-03-8, £35.00 hb; ISBN 978-1-907396-04-5, £18.99 pb)

Volume 10: *A Prospering Society: Wiltshire in the later Middle Ages*
by John Hare
(ISBN 978-1-902806-84-6, £35.00 hb; ISBN 978-1-902806-85-3, £18.99 pb)

Bread and Ale for the Brethren

The Provisioning of Norwich Cathedral Priory, 1260–1536

Philip Slavin

University of Hertfordshire Press
Studies in Regional and Local History

Volume 11

First published in Great Britain in 2012 by
University of Hertfordshire Press
College Lane
Hatfield
Hertfordshire
AL10 9AB
UK

© Philip Slavin 2012

The right of Philip Slavin to be identified as the author of this work has been asserted by him in accordance with the Copyright, Designs and Patents Act 1988.

All rights reserved. No part of this book may be reproduced or utilised in any form or by any means, electronic or mechanical, including photocopying, recording or by any information storage and retrieval system, without permission in writing from the publisher.

British Library Cataloguing in Publication Data
A catalogue record for this book is available from the British Library

ISBN 978-1-907396-62-5 hardback
ISBN 978-1-907396-63-2 paperback

Design by Mathew Lyons
Printed in Great Britain by Henry Ling Ltd

*For
Tanya and Yannai
With much love*

Publication grant

Publication has been made possible by a generous grant from the Marc Fitch Fund

Contents

List of figures	ix
List of tables	xi
Acknowledgements	xiii
General Editor's preface	xv
Abbreviations	xvii

1 'A puzzling economy': demesne cultivation and seigniorial autarky in the age of commercialisation — 1
- Commercialisation and marketisation of the late medieval economy — 1
- Seigniorial autarky in the age of commercialisation — 4

2 Norwich Cathedral Priory: population, food requirements and provisioning channels — 8
- The priory population, 1096–1538 — 8
- The grain requirements of Norwich Cathedral Priory — 15
- Getting grain: sources and resources — 21
- The grain supply of Norwich Cathedral Priory in a wider context — 23
- Why two channels? Economic instability, risk aversion and diversified portfolios — 24

3 Norwich Cathedral Priory's grain market, 1260–1538 — 26
- Geographic extent of the priory grain market — 26
- The grain trade: reputation and trust — 29
- Quantities of purchased grain — 33
- Frequency and seasonality of transactions — 36
- Norwich grain prices, 1264–1536: between endogenous factors and exogenous shocks — 39
- Market integration? — 44

4 Grain production on Norwich Cathedral Priory demesnes — 48
- The era of direct management — 48
- Regional and chronological trends in crop geography — 57
- Crop geography determinants: environment, markets and consumption — 63
- Annual crop disposal: chronological and regional patterns — 69
- Crop disposal in a wider context — 75
- Production costs — 77
- Food farms — 81
- Conclusions — 83

5 Shipping the produce: transportation requirements, strategies and costs — 84
- Grain transportation: sources and resources — 84
- Demesne horses — 85
- The 'Great Boat' (*magna navis*) — 87
- Transporting services: customary dues — 88
- Transporting services: harvest *famuli* — 92
- Transporting services: stipendiary *famuli* — 102
- Transporting services: priory carters and boatmen — 103
- Carting requirements and logistics — 105
- Transportation costs and savings — 109

Transportation logistics: the case of Eaton carters	113
Road versus river transportation: advantages and drawbacks	115
Conclusions	116

6 Space for grain: barns and granaries — **119**

The medieval barn and modern scholarship	119
Demesne barns: nature, layout and capacity	120
Demesne barns: storage costs	122
The Great Granary: layout and costs	126
The almoner's granary	130
Barns and granaries: a tool for insurance, speculation or practical storage?	130
Grain storage mechanisms and depletion rates	136
Conclusions	139

7 Grain into bread and ale: processing and consumption — **140**

Cathedral mills	140
Cathedral bakery and brewery	142
Annual baking patterns	145
Panis monachorum	147
Panis ponderis minoris	150
Panis militum	153
Bread consumption patterns	156
Two kinds of ale	159
Annual brewing patterns	163
Turning malt into ale: gallons and calories	163
Grain consumption in a comparative perspective	167
Bread and ale consumption in a wider perspective	169

8 Economics of charity: grain alms as poor relief — **173**

Hermits and anchorites	173
Prisoners in the castle prison	175
Almoner's soup kitchen for Norwich paupers	179
Grain alms in a wider context, theological and social	183
Conclusions	186

Conclusion: Seigniorial conservativism as an economic strategy — **188**

Appendix: Transportation costs, requirements and speed estimates — **193**

Bibliography	199
Index	211

Figures

1.1	Norfolk 'formal' markets and fairs in the fourteenth century	2
2.1	Estimated population of Norwich Cathedral Priory, 1301–1536	13
2.2	Norwich Cathedral Priory precinct	16
2.3	Market and demesne shares of grain supply, real wages and grain prices, 1261–1460	20
3.1	Grain market of Norwich Cathedral Priory, 1279–98	27
3.2	Grain market of Norwich Cathedral Priory, 1382–1538	28
4.1	Landed estates of Norwich Cathedral Priory in the early fourteenth century	49
4.2	Norwich Cathedral Priory demesne acreage and livestock units, 1261–1430	50
4.3	Canterbury Cathedral Priory demesne acreage and livestock units, 1271–1390	52
4.4	Annual Gross Crop Receipt (AGCR) components on Norwich Cathedral Priory demesnes, 1261–1430	67
4.5	Annual crop disposal patterns on Norwich Cathedral Priory demesnes, 1261–1430	68
4.6	Proportions of raw wheat and malted barley sent to Norwich, as percentage of Annual Gross Crop Receipt (AGCR) of wheat and barley, 1261–1430	70
4.7	Net annual profit from the arable sector of Norwich Cathedral Priory, 1261–1536	78
4.8	Food farm components, 1261–1536	80
5.1	Average harvest periods across the demesnes of Norwich Cathedral Priory, 1264–1424	93
5.2	Daily and harvest-period expenditure on one carter, 1264–1424	95
5.3	Relative transportation costs of crops from the demesnes to Norwich Cathedral Priory, 1261–1480	110
6.1	The 'provisioning compound' within the cathedral precinct	127

Tables

2.1	Grain supply of Norwich Cathedral Priory, 1261–1536	19
2.2	Grain-supply balance at select conventual houses, 1285–1528	21
3.1	The extent of Norwich Cathedral Priory's grain market, 1279–98 and 1382–1538	29
3.2	Sources of purchased grain supply, 1383–1536	30
3.3	Annual grain purchases (in quarters), 1261–1536	34
3.4	Frequency of crop purchases by Norwich Cathedral Priory, 1271–1536	36
3.5	Crop prices in Norwich, 1264–1536	40
4.1	Arable composition of English demesnes, *c*.1300	54
4.2	Crop specialisation on Norwich Cathedral Priory demesnes, 1261–1430	58
4.3	Exogenous and endogenous determinants of crop geography on Norwich Cathedral Priory estates, *c*.1300	62
4.4	Annual Gross Crop Receipt (AGCR) disposal, *c*.1300 and *c*.1400	74
4.5	Demesne grain production costs and grain value on Norwich market, 1261–1430	76
5.1	Annual fodder requirements on the manors of Norwich Cathedral Priory, 1261–1430	86
5.2	Total numbers of harvest *famuli* and carters, and annual expenditure on them	99
5.3	Carters and *famuli* on Norwich Cathedral Priory demesnes and other religious estates, *c*.1340 and *c*.1380	101
5.4	Annual wages of select priory employees paid jointly by the master of the cellar and the cellarer, 1261–1536	104
5.5	Amounts of grain sent to Norwich Cathedral Priory, and estimated numbers of carts, horses and boat-trips required for delivery, 1261–1480	106
5.6	Annual costs of transporting grain to Norwich Cathedral Priory, 1261–1480	108
5.7	Estimated potential transportation costs of grain, comparing the 'mixed scenario' with the inland transportation costs, 1261–1430	114
5.8	Approximate speed of grain transportation by 'mixed scenario' and by carts, *c*.1300 and *c*.1400	117
6.1	Annual storage costs on the demesnes of Norwich Cathedral Priory, 1261–1430	123
6.2	Comparative wheat storage costs, *c*.1300 and 2010	125
6.3	Annual grain storage costs in the Great Granary, 1261–1536	129
6.4	Total annual carryovers of crops stored in barns of Norwich Cathedral Priory demesnes, 1261–1430	131
6.5	Annual food rents and carryovers of barley on Norwich Cathedral Priory demesnes, 1261–1430	132
6.6	Pre-Black Death instances of excessive carryovers of grains on Norwich Cathedral Priory demesnes	133
6.7	Annual carryovers of crops stored at the Great Granary, 1261–1536	135
6.8	Estimated monthly depletion rates on Norwich Cathedral Priory crop storage facilities, *c*.1300–1500	137
7.1	Annual wages paid to the priory bakers and brewers, 1261–1536	145
7.2	The two increments of wheat, as reckoned by the master of the cellar, 1281–1343	146

7.3	Distribution of wheat and maslin for baking bread	147
7.4	Bread: extraction rates, weight and calorific value, *c.*1300	149
7.5	Annual allocation of *panis monachorum* bread, 1261–1343	151
7.6	Annual allocation of *panis ponderis minoris* bread, 1261–1343	152
7.7	Annual allocation of *panis militum* bread, 1261–1343	155
7.8	Bread consumption patterns across different groups, 1261–1343	156
7.9	The increment of barley malt, as reckoned by the master of the cellar, 1261–1343	163
7.10	Estimated levels of ale brewing at Norwich Cathedral Priory, 1261–1343 and 1495–1536	166
7.11	Annual baking and brewing patterns at select late medieval conventual houses	168
7.12	Estimated calorific values allowed to an average Norwich monk on a daily basis, 1329–30	171
7.13	Estimated calorific values allowed to an average Norwich monk on a daily basis, 1327–1530	172
8.1	Number of prisoners at Norwich Castle and the amounts of bread distributed among them, 1308–16	177
8.2	The AGCR stored at the almoner's granary, *c.*1310–54	181
8.3	Annual distribution of crops among the paupers, its calorific equivalent and hypothetical amount of people it was capable of feeding, *c.*1310–54	182
A.1	Mixed and inland routes from the demesnes to the priory precincts	196

Acknowledgements

Writing a book is, undoubtedly, a process in which the author may often appear exploitative to his colleagues and selfish (and often eccentric, if not weird) to his close friends and relatives. I was, I am sure, no exception to this rule. The acknowledgements offered below reflect my genuine thankfulness and admiration of my colleagues', friends' and relatives' kindness and forbearance.

First and foremost, my deepest gratitude goes to my mentor, PhD supervisor and now colleague and friend, John H. Munro. During my PhD studies at the Centre for Medieval Studies (CMA), University of Toronto (and beyond), his academic brilliance, erudition and personality have been a source of constant inspiration to me and his impact on my scholarly career cannot be described here. His untold generosity and encouragement of his students, shown at various occasions, including his legendary seminar on late-medieval economic history, stimulating conversations over dinner and, naturally, most detailed (and most helpful) comments on my PhD thesis drafts, will always be seen as an example of what the teacher *should* be. Above all, however, I feel deeply privileged and proud to have been his last (and hopefully, not worst) PhD student, whom he kindly agreed to accept two years after his mandatory retirement in 2003. The present book stems from my PhD thesis. Neither the thesis nor the book would have seen light without his continual and kind support. Equal thanks go to Joseph Goering, my co-supervisor, whose support and forbearance have always been exemplary, and whose expertise in all matters ecclesiastical has expanded my horizons considerably.

My cordial thanks also belong to two eminent scholars of late medieval economic history (in alphabetical order), Bruce Campbell and John Langdon. Their scholarship has been a source of great inspiration to me ever since I switched to the study of economic history in 2004: a decision I have never regretted. Professor Campbell followed the development of the current project since its very conception in February 2005 as a PhD thesis proposal. In the course of the following years he has shown a genuine interest in my work and provided many helpful comments and insights, based on his encyclopaedic knowledge of late medieval agriculture, both electronically and in person. Professor Langdon's involvement in this project started with his most meticulous reading of my dissertation in his capacity as an external appraiser, which resulted in numerous wise suggestions that slew some potentially embarrassing errors. Similarly, he kindly agreed to read parts of this book and offered most valuable critique.

As a graduate student in Toronto, I have profited from the genuinely welcoming and stimulating atmosphere, whether in a CMS classroom, or at the Pontifical Institute Library. In particular, I am grateful (again, in alphabetical order) to (the late) Virginia Brown, Grace Desa, Nicholas Everett, Father James Farge, CSB, Mark Meyerson, George Rigg and David Townsend for making my study so rewarding and rich. I would also like to thank John Geck and Tim Newfield for so many enjoyable conversations (and pints) we had together. I am genuinely happy to realise that so many common scholarly interests I share with Tim transformed our initial collegiality into a real (and not a Facebook) friendship.

The 'end of the road' feeling is, as many former and current PhD candidates can testify, a rather scary one, which makes one wonder how to find his/her daily bread. I feel extremely lucky to have been offered the prestigious post-doctoral fellowship at the Economic Growth Center at Yale shortly before the submission of my thesis, in the midst of personal and professional insecurity. The two years at Yale proved to be most fruitful and stimulating thanks to Professor Timothy Guinnane, whose genuine enthusiasm about my projects has been a source of my own academic enthusiasm. In addition, while at Yale, I was able to profit from taking a number of classes in economic theory and methodology, *sine quibus* I would have never been able to produce the numerous statistical tables throughout this book.

Going back in time to my BA and MA studies at the Hebrew University, Jerusalem, I especially wish to thank Amnon Linder, whose constant support and encouragement has been all over me since my undergraduate days. In addition, I would like to extend my thanks to Esther Cohen, Michael Heyd, Benjamin Z. Kedar, Emmanuel Sivan, Moshe Sluhovsky and Guy Stroumsa. Outside academia, I am deeply indebted to Alan Kiriev, whose lifelong and faithful friendship has been a true source of inspiration and support.

Between 2004 and 2011 I undertook 16 research trips to over 60 archives and repositories in the UK, partially for this book, partially for other projects. During the course of these trips I was able to locate, digitise and tabulate a large number of manorial documents. This would not have been possible without the generous financial support of various institutions, especially the Economic Growth Center, Yale and the Mellon Fellowship, McGill. I am equally grateful for the Marc Fitch Fund, for contributing to the costs of publishing this book. The generosity and, in many cases, exemplary forbearance of different archivists have contributed a great deal to my research. I am thankful to them all, realising, with much guilt, that I will have to abuse their kindness again and again in the future. In particular, I am grateful to the staff of the Norfolk Record Office (Norwich), where my archival adventures began in June 2004, when, as a beginning PhD student, I was both excited and confused by the incomparable sight of late medieval documents. Finally, my numerous visits to the UK would have never been so enjoyable without the boundless hospitality of my dear friends Ilia Avroutine and Maria Kozlov of High Wycombe, Buckinghamshire, who, in effect, became my English foster family.

While (constantly) roaming between the two coasts of the Atlantic, I have been able to share my insights and ideas with numerous colleagues, who have always been most generous and welcoming to me. I wish to thank (again, in alphabetical order) Richard Britnell, Stephen Broadberry, Martha Carlin, Anne and Edwin DeWindt, Christopher Dyer, Paul Freedman, George Grantham, John Hare, Paul Harvey, Richard Hoffmann, Maryanne Kowaleski, Kenneth MacKenzie, Michael McCormick, Richard Oram, Alasdair Ross, Phillipp Schofield, Maxim Sinitsyn, Nathan Sussman and Richard Unger. In addition, I would like to thank my students at Yale and McGill for not only learning from me, but also teaching me.

Last, but by no means least, I would like to express my gratefulness to my immediate family: my better and much beloved half, Tanya, and our son Yannai. Being related to a person with quite esoteric academic interests is, by no means, a picnic – and I fully realise that. My sincere apologies for making them suffer from both the Great Famine and the Black Death more than they should have. I can only hope that I can partially atone this by dedicating this book, with much love, to them.

Studies in Regional and Local History

General Editor's preface

Volume 11 of *Studies in Regional and Local History* presents a highly detailed analysis of the processes and strategies involved in the grain provisioning of an important urban, East Anglian religious fraternity between the mid-thirteenth century and the eve of its dissolution in the fourth decade of the sixteenth century. Urban grain supplies, for self-evident reasons, were potentially precarious, notwithstanding the widespread presence of local markets, the activities of cornmongers, the expansion of credit, the existence of a network of grain stores and an established international trade in grain. Despite all of this, only one major urban conventual household – Westminster Abbey – relied almost entirely upon the market for its provisions, and this was exceptional in being located in the heart of London. Instead, they depended largely up on their directly farmed demesnes. In the era of direct demesne management at Norwich Cathedral Priory, about 80 per cent of the total grain supply of the house was derived in this way.

Norwich Cathedral Priory was a Benedictine community, before the Black Death comprising about 60 monks and a further permanent staff of about 240 workers and lay brethren. At the Dissolution of the priory in 1538 there were 32 brethren and a further 100 servants and workers. The priory was one of the wealthiest landlords in East Anglia, and – like so many estates – exercised direct management of its demesnes through to the third quarter of the fourteenth century, although its last manor was not farmed out until 1431. But even then the priory community continued to rely quite heavily on its own lands for grain provisioning, for while fourteen of its manors paid cash rents, six rendered grain in lieu of cash. The enigma of this refusal to embrace the market in an era of commercialisation, and in the face of dramatically changing economic realities, is the key theme of this study.

Before the Black Death of 1348–9 and subsequent outbreaks of epidemic disease so dramatically changed the relationships between prices, wages and rents, a strategy of 'dual provisioning' on the part of seigneurial estates might be regarded as a rational response to the vagaries of nature, which produced fluctuating harvest conditions not only between years but also between different places in the same year. However, given that the share of crops purchased at local markets by Norwich Cathedral Priory was so small in this period, it would appear that this religious house adopted a particularly conservative stance, and one that indicates a pronounced aversion to risk.

From the late 1370s onwards, by which time demographic decline had caused agricultural prices to fall and wages to rise, direct demesnes management became an increasingly heavy burden, for the costs of production, transportation and storage all rose, and these costs were particularly high in the 1380s and the 1420s. This is, of course, now a familiar story to historians of the later medieval English agrarian economy. Less familiar is the fact that after the Black Death the priory authorities used their storage facilities to carry over the grain surpluses from year to year, not to profit from years of dearth but to provide a secure food supply for the brethren and other inhabitants, providing a further indication of its conservatism and failure to embrace the market. Slavin argues, however, that this should not be equated with 'irrationality', 'inefficiency' or 'backwardness', but was in fact the most beneficial strategy for the priory to adopt to ensure a secure grain supply, both before and after the Black Death.

There are other themes that play a supporting role in this study. One of these is the relative importance of environmental and institutional factors in the agrarian economy. For Norwich Cathedral Priory Slavin suggests that they complemented each other rather than constituting opposing or alternative forces. Hence the geography of crops grown on the priory estates was dictated equally by institutional and ecological factors, while the structure of grain provisioning was shaped by both monetary and natural forces, even if it was monetary forces that were of prime importance in inducing demesne leasing from the later fourteenth century. Another supporting theme is the diet of the monks in comparison with those supplied from its soup kitchen. The brethren, the accounts reveal, appear to 'have eaten and drunken in truly heroic quantities', with white bread and ale constituting about half of their daily ration, and fish and meat the other half. They ate very little dairy, and no fruit or vegetables. This contrasted with the daily menu of the paupers fed at the priory soup-kitchen, which included coarser rye bread and legume-based pottage. This is, of course, an inversion of present-day views on nutritional health, but one that finds reflection in many medieval and early modern assizes of bread, where bread of 'fine white maslin' was the premium product, with rye or horsebread – packed with healthy roughage – forming the diet of the poor. The existence of the almoner's soup-kitchen forms the final sub-theme of this study, indicating as it does the operation of late-medieval charity, and in a quantifiable form. As Slavin concludes, this is a feature of later medieval social history that deserves more attention and one where the records of other conventual households and the numerous independent hospitals provide a wealth of evidence still awaiting exploitation. Recent research, particularly through reappraisal of the *Valor Ecclesiasticus*, has done much to reinstate the importance of the charitable work of monastic institutions on the eve of the Reformation, and continued exploration of the detailed accounts of particular estates will shed further light, and help us to understand how the state was compelled to respond to the vacuum in social welfare that the Dissolution produced.

Nigel Goose
December 2011

Abbreviations

AHR	*Agricultural History Review*
CCR	*Calendar of the Close Rolls*
CFR	*Calendar of the Fine Rolls*
CPR	*Calendar of the Patent Rolls*
EcHR	*Economic History Review*
EHR	*English Historical Review*
JEH	*Journal of Economic History*
P&P	*Past & Present*

Chapter 1

'A puzzling economy': demesne cultivation and seigniorial autarky in the age of commercialisation

Commercialisation and marketisation of the late medieval economy

In the course of the twelfth and thirteenth centuries, England and other west European countries underwent a significant degree of urbanisation. Older towns grew, new ones were founded and the urban population expanded accordingly.[1] By 1300, there were between 4.75 and 6 million people living in England, about 15 per cent of whom dwelled in towns.[2] The single largest urban settlement was London, with a population of some 70,000 people.[3] London, however, was clearly exceptional in its size: Norwich, the second-largest town, was inhabited by no more than perhaps 15,000 citizens around that time.[4] Winchester, Bristol and York had between 10,000 and 12,000 burgesses each.[5] Northampton and Gloucester housed around 3000 and 4000 individuals respectively.[6] Most urban settlements, however, were even smaller: for example, the population of the abbatial town of Ramsey was most certainly less than 1000.[7] Regardless of size and population density, however, one main distinguishing characteristic of towns was their pronouncedly non-agricultural nature. This meant that the urban populations did not have a direct and ready access to food supplies, which

---

1. On late medieval urbanisation in England, see various articles in D. Palliser (ed.), *The Cambridge urban history of Britain*, vol. I (Cambridge, 2000).
2. The estimates vary a great deal. Most recently, the Warwick University-based project reconstructing the GDP of England (and later, Great Britain) and Holland in a very long run suggested 4.75 million in 1290. See S. Broadberry *et al.*, 'British economic growth, 1270–1870' (working paper, 2010), available: http://www2.warwick.ac.uk/fac/soc/economics/staff/academic/broadberry/wp/britishgdplongrun8a.pdf (accessed 11 October 2011). Richard Smith, on the other hand, suggested the ceiling of 6 million: R.M. Smith, 'Human resources', in G. Astill and A. Grant (eds), *The countryside of medieval England* (Oxford, 1992), pp. 189–91.
3. Again, estimates differ here. See B.M.S. Campbell *et al.*, *A medieval capital and its grain supply: agrarian production and distribution in the London region, c.1300* (London, 1993), p. 31; P. Nightingale, 'The growth of London in the medieval economy', in R.H. Britnell and J. Hatcher (eds), *Progress and problems in medieval England* (Cambridge, 1996), pp. 97–8.
4. E. Rutledge, 'Immigration and population growth in early fourteenth-century Norwich: evidence from the tithing roll', *Urban History Yearbook 1988* (Cambridge, 1988), pp. 15–30.
5. D. Keene, *Survey of medieval Winchester*, 2 vols (Oxford, 1985), I, pp. 352–68; E. Miller and J. Hatcher, *Medieval England: towns, commerce and crafts, 1086–1348* (London, 1995), p. 326.
6. R.H. Britnell, *Britain and Ireland, 1050–1530: economy and society* (Oxford, 2004), p. 140.
7. A.R. DeWindt and E.B. DeWindt, *Ramsey: the lives of an English fenland town, 1200–1600* (Washington, 2006), pp. 43–6. It is assumed that five out of six towns had a population of less than 2000 people. See R.H. Britnell, 'Town life', in R. Horrox and M. Ormrod (eds), *A social history of England, 1200–1500* (Cambridge, 2006), p. 145.

Bread and Ale for the Brethren

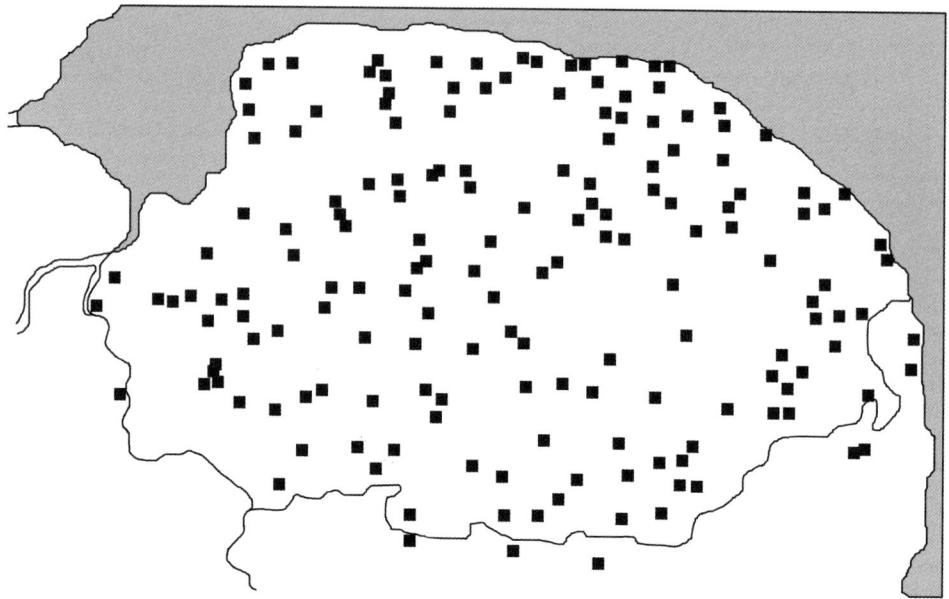

Figure 1.1 Norfolk 'formal' markets and fairs in the fourteenth century.
Source: S. Letters, *Gazetteer of markets and fairs in England and Wales*, http://www.history.ac.uk/cmh/gaz/gazweb2.html (accessed 11 October 2011).

had to come from the surrounding countryside. The growth of urban populations inevitably increased the demand from towns for various raw foodstuffs and led to an expansion of commercialisation and marketisation, especially throughout the thirteenth century.[8] On the eve of the Black Death (1348–51) there were around 2100 settlements with 'formal' markets and fairs in England, in contrast with only around 500 such places c.1200.[9] Naturally, the figures varied from county to county, indicating different degrees of regional commercialisation. Thus, in Norfolk, one of the most commercialised counties, there were 283 markets and fairs in some 175 vills (that is, some 8 per 10,000 inhabitants and 14 per ten square miles). Similarly, in neighbouring Lincolnshire there were 238 markets and fairs (around 8 per 10,000 inhabitants and 9 per ten square miles). Even in more backward Lancashire there were 82 trade hubs (about 14 per 10,000 inhabitants and 5 per ten square miles). In other words, one can boldly state that by the early fourteenth century England had achieved a remarkable degree of commercialisation, the clear manifestations of which were a proliferation of markets and fairs; a strong reliance on monetary and credit economies; a certain degree of market integration, revealed by relatively uniform or similar commodity prices; and a dependence on international trade, with wool and textiles as the chief articles of export.

---

8. See R.H. Britnell and B.M.S Campbell (eds), *A commercializing economy: England 1086 to c.1300* (Manchester, 1995).

9. Retrieved from S. Letters, Gazetteer of markets and fairs in England and Wales, http://www.history.ac.uk/cmh/gaz/gazweb2.html.

Arguably, the single most demanded product was crops (grains and legumes). In late medieval England, and especially before the Black Death, crop-based products such as bread, ale and pottage constituted the largest part (around 70 per cent) of an average commoner's diet, in both towns and villages. A daily per-capita consumption of a 2lb bread wheat loaf and some three pints of light barley ale would require the supply of 1.63 quarters of wheat and 1.42 quarters of barley on an annual basis.[10] On the eve of the Black Death the population of Norwich, which had risen by that time to around 25,000,[11] would have required at least 75,000 quarters of grain on a daily basis and some 27.4 million quarters of grain on an annual basis. The figures for the provisioning of pre-plague London were significantly higher.[12] There is no doubt that ensuring a steady supply of grain to such large urban communities, notwithstanding the well-developed network of grain markets, was a challenge for a variety of reasons. First, communication and transportation systems were relatively under-developed. Second, the ongoing warfare with Scotland in the north and France in the south tended to disrupt the supply of grain because military incursions destroyed fields and granaries and because of forced extraction of grain to provision garrisons, as well as rising transportation costs resulting from these conflicts.[13] Finally, and chiefly in bad years, some lords tended to hoard their grain either for speculation or household consumption. Speculative prices contributed to the disruption of the supply of and access to grain resources because real wages tended to be abysmally low in years with bad harvests, such as those between 1315 and 1317.[14]

To avoid potential subsistence crises, urban communities had to learn how to cope with difficulties in grain supply. A crucial role here was played by grain merchants, known as 'cornmongers', whose place and activities within the commercialised economy of the late medieval period is well documented. In effect, they were middlemen between the rural producers and the urban consumers. By 1300 there were some 50 grain traders in London: a truly striking figure given the fact that there were only four 'formal' grain markets in the city at that point.[15] This, however, does not imply that these cornmongers were serving only these four markets. It is highly likely that they also provided 'door-to-door' deliveries of their merchandise to customers such as bakers, cooks and brewers. It is known that cornmongers purchased grain both from rural marketplaces and directly from demesnes.[16] Credit-based transactions

---

10. For the conversion of grain volume into weight, see Campbell et al., *A medieval capital*, p. 41.
11. For the population of Norwich, see E. Rutledge, 'Economic life', in C. Rawcliffe and R. Wilson (eds), *Medieval Norwich* (London, 2004), pp. 157–8.
12. Campbell et al., *A medieval capital*, pp. 25–36.
13. P. Slavin, 'Food security, safety, and crises', in K. Albala (ed.), *A cultural history of food: vol. 3: the Renaissance 1300–1600* (London, 2011), pp. 63–82.
14. B.M.S. Campbell, 'Four famines and a pestilence: harvest, price, and wage variations in England, 13th to 19th centuries', in B. Liljewall, I.A. Flygare, U. Lange, L. Ljunggren and J. Söderberg (eds), *Agrarhistoria på många sätt; 28 studier om manniskan och jorden. Festskrift till Janken Myrdal på hans 60-årsdag* (Stockholm, 2009), pp. 23–56.
15. This is the average figure deriving from the London portion of 1292 and 1319 tax assessments. See Campbell et al., *A medieval capital*, p. 83.
16. Ibid., pp. 98–9.

related to the grain trade were becoming increasingly widespread in that period, too, both in towns and the countryside. In some cases lords were willing to sell their grain on credit to cornmongers, while some grain-traders were found to have served as creditors to both landlords and peasants.[17] Credit transactions were particularly crucial in years of bad harvests or economic crisis. Another measure of security against potential hazards was a sophisticated network of crop storage facilities, in the form of granaries and barns. These were found all over the country, both in the countryside and in towns. They were available for either rent or purchase and they functioned not only as space for carrying over the grain from one year to another, to avoid the risk of bad harvest and starvation, but also as intermediary stations in the process of grain delivery from producers to consumers.[18] Paradoxically, however, there was not a single public granary in English towns similar to those established in some continental cities, such as that in Ghent created shortly after the Great Famine of 1315–17. Finally, a reliance on grain imports was yet another crucial strategy in ensuring the steady supply of provisions to the urban population. Around 1300, the shipment of grain from East Germany, Poland and Baltic lands to England was a commonplace. In 1317, amidst the Great Famine, Edward II extended special privileges to grain merchants from Sicily, Spain and Genoa, all areas unaffected by the famine. The most important grain trade hubs were Boston, Hull, Lynn and Ipswich.[19]

Seigniorial autarky in the age of commercialisation

In other words, despite a series of potential hazards, there is no doubt that the widespread presence of local markets, both in towns and their rural hinterland, the commercial activities of cornmongers, the proliferation of credit, a sophisticated network of grain storages and the international grain trade all contributed significantly to the successful provisioning of urban communities in the late medieval period. Naturally, one would expect these communities, whether family households or religious congregations, to rely heavily on local markets. And it is precisely here where one comes upon one of the most intriguing and somewhat incomprehensible enigmas relating to the economic history of the late Middle Ages. Notwithstanding the highly developed networks of commercial crop supply, very few, if any, major urban conventual households (cathedrals, monasteries, colleges) relied entirely upon the local market to provision themselves on a daily, weekly and yearly basis. Instead, they chose to depend, for the most part, on their directly managed demesnes, which produced and dispatched considerable amounts of grain every year. For instance, in the era of direct demesne management, Norwich Cathedral Priory demesnes dispatched about 50 and 75 per cent of their annual wheat and malted barley, while about 80 per cent of all grain supplied to the priory on an annual basis derived from

---

17. Ibid., p. 100 and C. Briggs, *Credit and village society in fourteenth-century England* (Oxford, 2009), pp. 37–9, 47–51 and 61–2.
18. Campbell *et al.*, *A medieval capital*, pp. 102–3; J. Claridge and J. Langdon, 'Storage in medieval England: the evidence from purveyance accounts', *EcHR*, forthcoming; the early view version is available at http://www.blackwellpublishing.com/journal.asp?ref=0013-0117.
19. N. Hybel, 'The grain trade in northern Europe before 1350', *EcHR*, 55 (2002), pp. 219–47.

the demesnes.[20] Similarly, between 1300 and 1380 only some 25 per cent of all Canterbury Cathedral Priory's grain came from the market,[21] and comparable figures are found at Durham Cathedral Priory.[22] Neither Peterborough Abbey nor St Paul's Cathedral in London spent anything on grain purchases around 1300.[23] The only major conventual house to have relied on the market was Westminster Abbey: between c.1300 and 1380 some 65 per cent of its grain supply came from purchases.[24] But the case of Westminster Abbey was an exception rather than the rule, and was attributable to its physical situation in the single most commercialised centre of the country. In the majority of cases conventual households tended to rely heavily on direct supply by their own agricultural producers, rather than on local markets.

Norwich Cathedral Priory, the subject of the present study, was by no means an exception. It was not until the late fourteenth century that these communities diverted their energy from demesne production and augmented the share of annual market purchases to meet the provisioning requirements of their houses. But even when the demesnes were leased out and the era of direct demesne management was long over, these houses still largely depended on annual fixed food farms (grain rents), paid by the farmers of their demesnes in lieu of cash rents. What accounts for that? Is it possible that local urban markets, despite their sophisticated nature, were still insufficient to satisfy the daily dietary needs of the brethren? Were these markets, in reality, not as sophisticated and developed as they seem at first sight? Were these religious institutions themselves not commercialised enough to integrate into the network of urban markets? Or was it more profitable and more efficient to rely on the direct supply of grain?

In order to appreciate this economic enigma better, it is essential to consider the wider economic structures of late medieval seigniorialism in England. In essence, the period between c.1200 and 1450 can be characterised as a gradual shift from a farming-based economy to a directly managed economy and back. In other words, in the course of the first half of the thirteenth century, after a prolonged period of demesne leasing to better-off tenants, lords reverted to the direct exploitation of their demesnes. The chronology differed from estate to estate: thus, Winchester bishopric had its estates back in hand by 1207; the Abbey of St Benet at Holm in Norfolk managed its demesnes from the 1230s; Ramsey Abbey estates were exploited directly from at least the 1240s; the earliest accounts of Norwich Cathedral Priory's manors go back to the mid-1250s; and by the 1260s and 1270s Westminster Abbey, Canterbury Cathedral and Durham Cathedral priories took their demesnes back in hand (although Durham was still leasing out several of its demesnes). Meanwhile, the lay lords were catching up with their religious counterparts, so that by 1300 the vast majority of demesnes throughout the country were managed directly by their lords.

---

20. P. Slavin, 'Feeding the brethren: grain provisioning of Norwich Cathedral Priory, c.1280–1370', PhD thesis (University of Toronto, 2008), pp. 119, 122 and 232.
21. Canterbury Cathedral Priory Archives, DCc/Granger 1–76 and Bartoner 1–60.
22. Durham Cathedral Priory Archives, Granator Rolls.
23. Campbell et al., A medieval capital, p. 204.
24. Ibid., p. 204, and Westminster Abbey Muniments, Granger's accounts, WAM 19155–19217.

Exceptional regions were the 'Celtic Fringe' (a belt stretching from the South West through the Welsh Marches and Wales to the North West) and the North East, where manorialism was at its weakest. The era of the direct cultivation of the demesne lasted until the late fourteenth century: between c.1380 and 1420 there was a gradual return to the leasing policy. With very few notable exceptions, especially in the south, by 1500 direct demesne management no longer existed.

The concepts of a rent-based economy and direct management have been classified by some German scholars, working on the early modern East German economy, as *Grundherrschaft* (cash- or lease-based seigniorial economy) and *Gutsherrschaft* (kind- or demesne-based seigniorial economy).[25] Both terms can be applied to the study of late medieval England and, as such, they will be used throughout the book. The issue of the shift from *Grundherrschaft* to *Gutsherrschaft* and back has occasioned some debate among scholars working on the late medieval English economy. It has been contended that gradual inflation between c.1180 and 1220 (or, perhaps, more specifically, between 1200 and 1206) made demesne leasing no longer profitable, whereas relying on direct production and partial marketing of the demesne produce would increase lords' real income.[26] As far as the post-Black Death return to the *Grundherrschaft* is concerned, there are largely two explanations. One, 'Ricardian' or demographic in its nature, contends that the altered labour-to-land ratio brought about by the mortality, on the one hand, and the fall in real production costs and relative prices of grain, on the other, prompted the lords to lease out their demesnes.[27] Most recently, however, John Munro offered a complementary and compelling monetary-fiscal model, arguing that the adverse combination of the fall in prices in both the agrarian and pastoral sectors of the economy (which, however, did not occur until c.1376), wage-stickiness and royal taxation and intervention in the wool trade dramatically increased the real costs of production of the lords and thus lowered their real income.[28] As we shall see later, the case of Norwich Cathedral Priory's demesne management and food provisioning seem to fully confirm the validity of Munro's model.

It also seems that Munro's model can equally explain the earlier shift from *Grundherrschaft* to *Gutsherrschaft* in the course of the first half of the thirteenth century. The very essence of *Gutsherrschaft* was that the lords were directly involved in agrarian and pastoral production, reaping the gains or bearing the losses (both financial and natural) of this production. In addition, they exercised their seigniorial power over their dependent peasants. This form of capital management was perfectly suited for the thirteenth and fourteenth centuries, characterised as they were by, on the one hand, a gradual rise and sudden and unpredictable soars in commodity prices (such as the

---

25. For instance, see W.W. Hagen, 'How mighty the junkers? Peasant rents and seigniorial profits in sixteenth-century Brandenburg', *P&P*, 108 (August 1985), pp. 80–116.
26. P.D.A. Harvey, 'The English inflation of 1180–1220', *P&P*, 61 (1973), pp. 3–30; P. Latimer, 'The English inflation of 1180–1220 reconsidered', *P&P*, 171 (2011), pp. 3–29.
27. A.R. Bridbury, 'The Black Death', *EcHR*, 26 (1973), pp. 557–92.
28. J.H.A. Munro, 'From *Gutsherrschaft* to *Grundherrschaft*: demographic, monetary and political-fiscal factors', in M. Bailey and S. Rigby (eds), *Town and countryside in the age of the Black Death: essays in honour of John Hatcher* (Turnhout, 2011).

inflations of 1200–06, 1257–8, 1294–6, 1315–17, 1347–53, 1370–71, 1391 and 1401–2) and, on the other, unchanging or falling (and hence, low) real wages of labourers. When grain and livestock prices collapsed once more in the late 1370s, the option of *Gutsherrschaft* was no longer attractive, as John Munro has contended. This issue will be addressed in a much more detailed fashion later in this book.

The present study endeavours to address these issues by considering the managerial and provisioning policies of one particular estate, that of Norwich Cathedral Priory. This was a house of a Benedictine community of some 60 monks and a further permanent staff of some 240 people (workers and lay brethren) in the pre-Black Death period. By the time of the dissolution of the priory in 1538, there were 22 brethren and probably less than a further 100 servants and workers. As we shall see later, Norwich Cathedral Priory was one of the wealthiest lords in East Anglia. Like the majority of other landed lords, Norwich Cathedral Priory exercised direct management of its demesnes both before and after the Black Death and, although several demesnes were leased out between the 1360s and 1380s, the era of direct demesne management continued until 1431, when the last of its manors, Sedgeford, was farmed out. Paradoxically enough, however, the end of the demesne exploitation era did not mean the end of direct supply of manorial grain. Although the demesnes were farmed out to better-off tenants, the priory community was not yet ready to break away from its traditional and seemingly outdated form of grain provisioning. The leased manors were roughly divided into two categories: 14 'cash-paying manors' and 6 'grain-rendering farms'. As a part of leasing contracts, the farmers of the 'grain-rendering' manors were obliged to provide the priory with fixed amounts of grain, normally in lieu of cash-rent payments.

Chapter 2

Norwich Cathedral Priory: population, food requirements and provisioning channels

The priory population, 1096–1538

Before delving into the analysis of grain supply channels, however, it is essential to consider the nature and size of the Norwich Cathedral Priory population in the period under study. The demographic history of this house goes back to its foundation in 1096, when there were 60 monks, as the late thirteenth-century *Registrum Primum* of the cathedral reports.[1] Since then and down to the Black Death this seems to have been, more or less, a constant number. This fact is verified by Bishop Goldwell's visitation of the priory in 1492, in which he stated that 'the Lord Andrew Ryngland said that the number of the brethren has not been filled up, since there are ought to be sixty brethren, but there are present just thirty eight.'[2] In any event, there is not a single pre-fourteenth-century source to shed any further light on the monastic population between 1096 and the late thirteenth century. The early master of the cellar's rolls, which contain the allocations of bread and ale to different groups of priory inhabitants, provide an indirect indication as to the size of the priory's monastic and non-monastic populations. As far as the number of the brethren is concerned, the bread and ale accounts hint that there were about 60 of them in the late thirteenth century. This corroborates the 1308 visitation of the priory by Bishop John Salmon, who mentioned in his injunctions that there were 60 brethren or more (*sexaginta uel amplius eo*).[3] On the very eve of the Black Death, in 1348–9, there were 67 monks, as the communar's roll reveals.[4] The bread accounts reveal that the number of loaves distributed among the brethren remained more or less static over the period between 1281 and 1343, which may mean that the monastic population remained largely unchanged between the 1308 visitation and the 1348–9 roll. The Black Death did not spare the monks' lives, of course: during the plague years we find dozens of rolls compiled by several different hands,[5] this frequent change of handwriting implying that the officials were dying. The post-plague statistics on the monastic population of the cathedral come from the accounts of St

---

1. The relevant part is printed in H.W. Saunders (ed.), *The first register of Norwich Cathedral Priory*, Norfolk Record Society 11 (Norwich, 1939), p. 30. I have used the original manuscript NRO, DCN 40/1.
2. 'Dompnus Andreas Ryngland dicit quod numerus confratrum non perimpletur quia deberent esse LX confratres et sunt in praesenti nisi xxxuiij'. A. Jessopp (ed.), *Visitations of the diocese of Norwich, 1492–1532*, Royal Historical Society, Camden 2nd Series 43 (London, 1888), p. 73. This passage is quoted in H.W. Saunders, *An introduction to the rolls of Norwich Cathedral Priory* (Norwich, 1930), p. 160.
3. NRO, DCN 92/1.
4. NRO, DCN 1/12/7.
5. This fact was noted in Saunders, *Introduction*, p. 186.

Leonard's Priory, itself a dependent cell of Norwich Cathedral Priory.[6] There were just 40 monks in 1353–4, which suggests that at least 40 per cent of the brethren had died during the pestilence.[7] Although the pestilence returned several times in the course of the late fourteenth and fifteenth centuries, it seems that most of its recurrent attacks spared the priory. The post-Black Death decades show a slow but sure recovery, and in 1368–9 there were 53 brethren.[8] Between then and 1464 there were always between 45 and 55 monks. Between 1464 and 1466, the number of the brethren fell from 46 to 36 as a result of a recurrent outbreak of the plague. Between 1466 and 1478 there was a pronounced recovery in which the figures rose back to 46, but numbers started falling once more from 1478 onwards, and especially after 1485, the year of an outbreak of sweating disease, when number fell from 40 to 35. It was not until 1504, however, that the real decline was felt. Between then and 1535 there were between 30 and 35 monks. When the priory was dissolved in 1538, there were just 22 brethren.[9]

The demographic history of the Norwich monks reflects larger population trends in late medieval England, both within and without the world of the cloister. Thus, in Westminster Abbey at least half of the monks died during the troubled years of 1348–9, as the Westminster accounts reveal.[10] Meaux Abbey (Yorkshire) had 49 monks in 1348, but lost as many as 32 in 1349.[11] Peterborough Abbey shows similar mortality figures, with only 30 out of 64 monks surviving the plague.[12] Certainly, the Black Death did not discriminate between various classes and the conservative estimate suggests that about 40 per cent of the populations of both England and Wales died in the course of these disastrous years. The recurrent outbreak of the plague in 1463–6 was witnessed both in monasteries and in the wider world.[13] Finally, the sweating disease of 1485 was a disaster on a national scale.[14]

---

6. St Leonards' accounts are deposited at the Norfolk Record Office, and their shelfmark is NRO, DCN 2/3.
7. NRO, DCN 2/3/2.
8. NRO, DCN 2/3/6.
9. Saunders, *Introduction*, p. 161. On late medieval monastic population in England, see B. Harvey, *Living and dying in England, 1100–1540: the monastic experience* (Oxford, 1993), pp. 112–45, and B. Harvey and J. Oeppen, 'Patterns of morbidity in late medieval England: a sample from Westminster Abbey', *EcHR*, 54/2 (2001), pp. 215–39 (on Westminster); J. Hatcher, 'Mortality in the fifteenth century: some new evidence', *EcHR*, 39 (1986), pp. 19–38 (on Canterbury Priory); J. Hatcher, A.J. Piper and D. Stone, 'Monastic mortality: Durham Priory, 1395–1529', *EcHR*, 59/4 (2006), pp. 667–87.
10. B. Harvey, *Westminster Abbey and its estates in the Middle Ages* (Oxford, 1977), p. 144. For a comprehensive description of the Westminster accounts, consult B. Harvey, *The obedientiaries of Westminster Abbey and their financial records, c.1275–1540* (Woodbridge, 2002).
11. G.G. Coulton, *Five centuries of religion*, vol. III (Cambridge, 1936), p. 555.
12. Ibid., p. 555.
13. P. Nightingale, 'Some new evidence of crises and trends of mortality in late medieval England, *P&P*, 187/1 (2005), pp. 48–9; Harvey and Oeppen, 'Patterns of morbidity', p. 236; J. Hatcher *et al.*, 'Monastic mortality: Durham Priory, 1395–1529', *EcHR*, 59/4 (2006), pp. 677–8.
14. R.S. Gottfried, 'Population, plague and the sweating sickness: demographic movements in late-fifteenth century England', *Journal of British Studies*, 17/1 (1977), pp. 12–37.

It appears that the numbers and the population trend of the Norwich brethren were comparable to those of other cathedrals and monasteries of the same period. For instance, the size of Canterbury's monastic community fluctuated between 60 and 70 persons in the years 1300–48; subsequently there were 44 brethren in 1376, 61 in 1381 and 80 in 1391.[15] Between 1395 and 1505 their number fluctuated between 75 and 95,[16] including 25 obedientiaries.[17] By the end of the thirteenth century Westminster Abbey housed around 50 monks, a number which remained largely unchanged between 1375 and 1529.[18] At Glastonbury Abbey there were 59 monks, in addition to 20 lay brethren, 19 corrodians and 60 servants, in 1323.[19] The monks of Durham Priory amounted to 90 in 1274, 85 in 1283, 81 in 1343 and 73 in 1345; there was then, more or less, a constant number of 70 between 1406 and 1494.[20] Ely Cathedral was populated by 70 monks in the thirteenth century, although by 1345 their numbers had fallen to 49 and in 1349 to 28; in 1352–3 there were 35 brethren.[21] There were over 60 brethren at St Swithun's Priory, Winchester, in 1325, and between the end of the fourteenth century and its dissolution this priory consistently housed around 45 monks.[22] The decline of Rochester's community was even more pronounced: there were 35 monks in 1317 and 1333, 23 between 1385 and 1416 and as few as 16 in 1540.[23] The monastic communities of Abingdon, Bury St Edmunds and Peterborough all contained about 80 persons around 1300.[24] Finally, Battle Abbey, a smaller monastic house, had some 60 monks in the thirteenth century and around 30 monks in the last decades of the fourteenth century.[25]

Although the *de jure* head of Norwich Cathedral Priory was the bishop of Norwich, the *de facto* one was the prior. The bishop had his own, separate, residence within the cathedral close, but in reality he was hardly ever present there, spending a considerable amount of time on various perambulations, both within and without his diocese. The prior, on the other hand, was constantly available to his monks for help and advice. The monastic community itself can be roughly divided into two main groups: ordinary monks and the obedientiaries, who held special offices and duties.

---

15. B. Dobson, 'The Monks of Canterbury in the later Middle Ages, 1220–1540', in P. Collinson, N. Ramsay and M. Sparks (eds), *A History of Canterbury Cathedral* (Oxford, 1995), p. 117.
16. J. Hatcher, 'Mortality in the fifteenth century: some new evidence', EcHR, 39 (1986), p. 23.
17. R.A.L. Smith, *Canterbury Cathedral Priory* (Cambridge, 1943), pp. 36–51, esp. 49.
18. Harvey and Oeppen, 'Patterns of morbidity', p. 221; Harvey, *Living and dying*, p. 73.
19. M. Ecclestone, 'Dairy production on the Glastonbury Abbey demesnes, 1258–1334', MA thesis (University of Bristol, 1996), p. 25.
20. R.B. Dobson, *Durham Priory, 1400–1450* (Cambridge, 1973), pp. 52–5; Hatcher *et al.*, 'Monastic mortality', p. 670.
21. Coulton, *Five centuries*, p. 558.
22. J. Greatrex, 'St. Swithun's Priory in the later Middle Ages', in J. Crook (ed.), *Winchester Cathedral: nine hundred years* (Chichester, 1993), pp. 144–5.
23. A. Oakley, 'Rochester Priory, 1185–1540', in N. Yates and P.A. Welsby (eds), *Faith and fabric: a history of Rochester Cathedral, 604–1994* (Woodbridge, 1996), p. 52.
24. Coulton, *Five centuries*, p. 558.
25. Ibid.; E. Searle (ed.), *The cellarers' rolls of Battle Abbey, 1275–1513*, Sussex Record Society 65 (Lewes, 1967), p. 15.

Norwich Cathedral Priory had 12 obedientiaries. Arguably, the most important was the master of the cellar (*magister cellarii*). He had the largest number of duties, including the provisioning of grain, fuel, raw materials and wool. He was also in charge of building and repairing buildings, as well as commissioning manuscripts.[26] The next most important official was the cellarer (*cellerarius*), who, as his title suggests, was responsible for providing the brethren with food other than grains. He was also in charge of the bakery and brewery, as well as the larder.[27] The sacrist (*sacrista*) looked after ecclesiastical matters such as the liturgy, the cemetery and the altars and shrines of the saints – the most famous and venerated of which was St William of Norwich, a boy allegedly killed by Jews in 1144. He also looked after the tower clock, first mentioned in 1291.[28] The chamberlain (*camerarius*) was responsible mainly for monastic garments, as well as the priory mill.[29] The almoner (*elemosinarius*) was burdened with various charitable activities, including the distribution of alms and food among the poor of the town. The office of almoner had its own granary, in which the grain for distribution-in-alms was stored.[30] As we shall see later, this grain came from both the local market and the manors appropriated to the office of the almoner. The hosteler (*hostilarius*) was attached to the guest hall and looked after visitors. Perhaps the most peculiar duty of this obedientiary was cleaning the latrines of faeces with lime.[31] The monastic orchard was run by the gardener (*gardinarius*).[32] The infirmerer (*infirmarius*) looked after sick brethren and provided them with remedies, dry fruit and spices.[33] The precentor (*precentorius*) shared some liturgical duties with the sacrist, but his main responsibilities were to train the boys' choir and to arrange festive processions. He was also the keeper of the priory seal.[34] The pitancer (*pitancerius*) and communar (*communarius*), appearing on the same account, were responsible mainly for building materials and stones, as well as for supervising masons and carpenters.[35] And finally, the refectorer (*refectorarius*), contrary to what his name suggests, supervised the general maintenance of the buildings, and their furniture and utensils.[36]

Obviously, the monks were not the only inhabitants of the priory. Three more groups should be noted: labourers receiving their annual stipend, servants (*famuli*) and occasional guests. H. Saunders suggested that there were about 270 mouths to be

---

26. On his duties, consult Saunders, *Introduction*, pp. 76–91.
27. Saunders, *Introduction*, pp. 92–101.
28. Ibid., pp. 102–13.
29. Ibid., pp. 114–20.
30. Ibid., pp. 121–7.
31. Ibid., pp. 128–9.
32. Ibid., pp. 130–31. His accounts have now been published by C. Noble (ed.), *Farming and gardening in late medieval Norfolk*, Norfolk Record Society 61 (Norwich, 1997).
33. Saunders, *Introduction*, pp. 132–3.
34. Ibid., pp. 134–6.
35. Ibid., pp. 137–41. Their accounts have been partially (up to 1329–30) transcribed and printed in E. Ferrie and A.B. Whittingham (eds), *Communar rolls of Norwich Cathedral Priory*, Norfolk Record Society 41 (Norwich, 1974).
36. Saunders, *Introduction*, pp. 142–4.

fed each day: 50 monks, 150 workers, 20 *famuli* and 50 visitors.[37] This estimation might be too conservative, since it ignores some labourers mentioned in the rolls. He also failed to distinguish between 'domestic workers' and 'manual workers'. The first category means persons performing tasks not involving physical labour, while, as its name suggests, the second category included various occupations based on manual work. And, most importantly, Saunders did not utilise one source of major importance (which was perhaps unknown to him). The document in question is a *c.*1300 list of annual recipients of candles distributed by the sacrist. The list constitutes a part of the sacrist's register – that is, a cartulary containing a vast bulk of earlier charters pertaining to the manors appropriated to this obedientiary[38] – and is vitally important for reconstructing the size of the priory's labourer population. The document suggests that there were approximately 200 regular workers around 1300, to whom we should add about ten additional workers hired on a contractual basis. These were mostly building-related labourers, whose names and stipends appear in the communar and pitancer's rolls. This total of about 210 workers was by no means a constant figure and its fluctuation is reflected in the detailed distribution of bread and ale among various residents of the priory, which were recorded on the dorse of the master of the cellar accounts until 1343.

The second group was the local *famuli*, monastic servants living within the precinct. In effect, these were lay brethren, a resident group found in most Cistercian establishments and select Benedictine houses, including Canterbury Cathedral Priory and Westminster Abbey.[39] Saunders suggested the figure of 20 for this group.[40] This estimation is probably not too far from reality, especially between the 1260s and the 1280s, when the *famuli* received slightly less than one-third of what the brethren did. Unfortunately, the number of *famuli* was not specified in the obedientiary accounts and we therefore have to estimate it using the bread and ale accounts as an indirect source. As the latter indicate, the total number of the servants varied from decade to decade and it seems that their number stood at between 25 and 30 between *c.*1300 and 1350.

The remaining inmates were occasional guests and day-labourers: that is, transient visitors. The pre-Black Death accounts indicate that about 50 visitors visited the priory each year. Among these were manorial carters, local nobles and their messengers, minstrels and jugglers (*hystriones*) hired for Christmas and Pentecostal plays, as well as young brethren studying theology at Oxford.[41] These temporary guests never remained at the priory for a long time, however, and hence it would be problematic to include them among the constant priory inmates. Certainly, if ten visitors remained at the priory for two months, for instance, they cannot be counted as ten persons living at the priory in a given year. A better solution would be to estimate their number on the

---

37. Ibid., pp. 89–91, 162–3.
38. NRO, DCN 40/11, fols 42r–44v.
39. Harvey, *Living and dying*, pp. 18–21.
40. Saunders, *Introduction*, pp. 162.
41. On Norwich scholars sent to Oxford, see N.P. Tanner, *The church in late medieval Norwich* (Toronto, 1984), pp. 31–2.

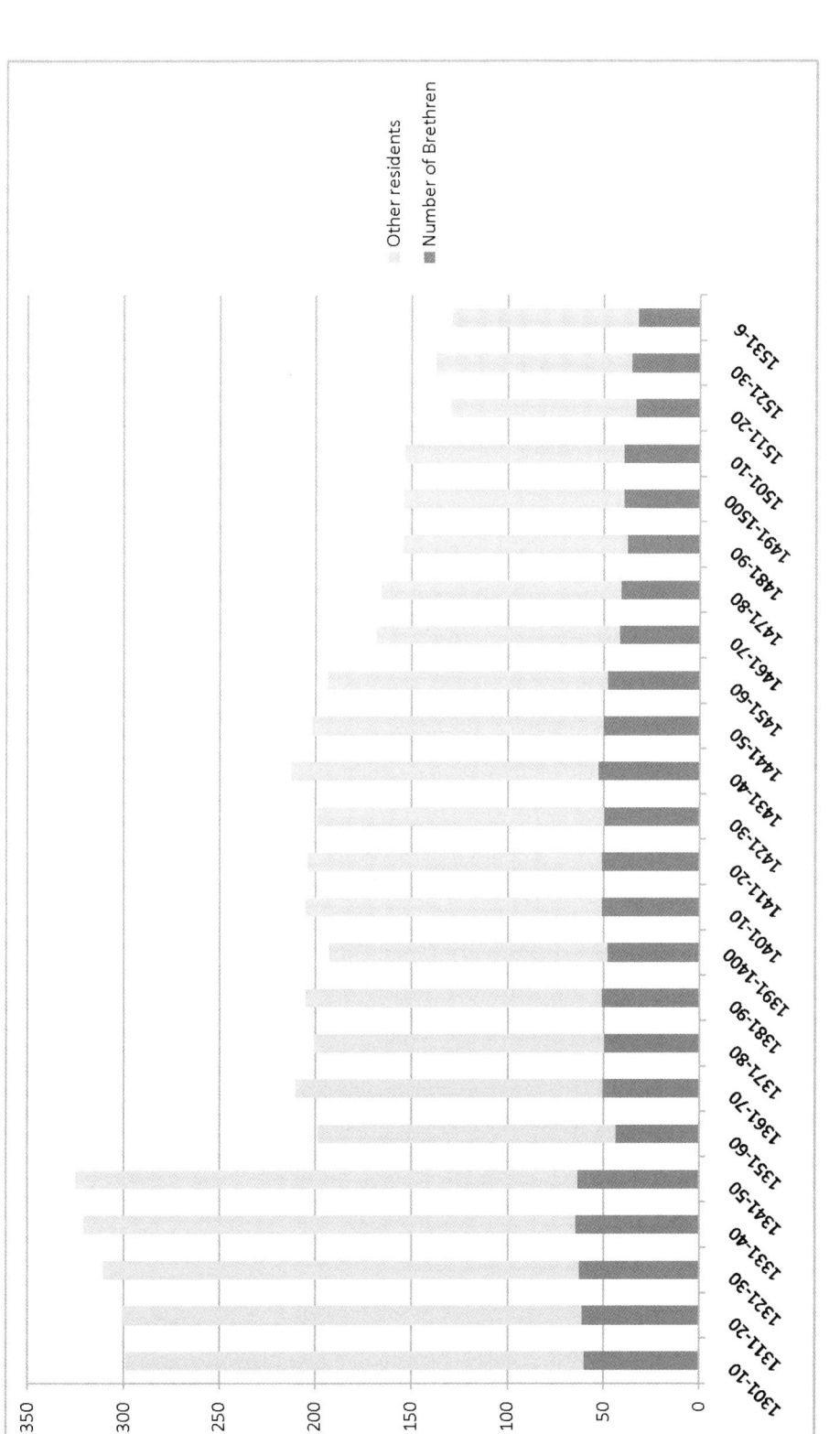

Figure 2.1 Estimated population of Norwich Cathedral Priory, 1301–1536. *Source:* NRO, DCN 1/1–13, 2/3/2–10 and 92/1 (1,333 rolls in total).

basis of the relative length of their stay. Normally, the lengths of their visits could vary anywhere between several days and several months. Allowing a generous period of 1.5 months per person, we arrive at the estimation that about six visitors were staying at the priory on a daily basis.

The demographic fluctuation within each group can be inferred from the varying numbers of loaves distributed among the inmates (see Chapter 7). Unfortunately, between 1343 and 1495 the master of the cellar rolls do not contain the bread and ale accounts. As a result, the task of estimating the non-monastic (and, hence, overall) population of the priory becomes virtually impossible. Nevertheless, an approximate number of the non-monastic residents can be inferred from various references in all the surviving obedientiary accounts, studied together. A very crude reconstruction is shown in Figure 2.1. In 1495 the number of lay inhabitants was about 111, while by 1510 the number seems to have fallen to some 100 people. This number remained more or less stable until the dissolution of the priory in 1538.

The estimations above, with all their obvious shortcomings, suggest that Norwich Cathedral Priory was a house to a large number of residents. Its population size is well comparable with that of other large conventual houses. Thus, around 1400, Westminster Abbey, a much more grandiose establishment than that at Norwich, housed only 50 brethren and 100 labourers, in addition to an uncertain number of lay brethren.[42] The average ratio of lay residents to nuns in fifteenth-century nunneries in the diocese of Norwich varied between 0.25 and 4.4, with an average 2.10 lay residents to one nun: a somewhat smaller figure than in Norwich Cathedral Priory, where the average ratio stood at about 4:1 and 3:1 in the pre-Black Death and post-pestilence periods, respectively.[43] It should be noted, however, that Norwich Cathedral Priory was much more than just a monastic house: it was the main ecclesiastical establishment of the entire county of Norfolk and the seat of the bishop. Its precinct embraced a large area containing, apart from the cloister and the cathedral, numerous buildings, orchards, gardens, meadows and a canal (Figure 2.2). But it was also a major centre of economic activities, a sort of pre-modern corporation overseeing and managing vast natural and financial resources. To sustain such an establishment would require a large workforce. This was certainly the situation in various monastic and canonical establishments through England. Thus, even a smaller house such as Bolton Priory, which had fewer than 20 canons and lay brethren, housed around 200 persons.[44]

In other words, the priory's population accounted for about 2 per cent of the total population of Norwich. Such a large community would undoubtedly have large provisioning requirements, whose satisfaction would be a challenge on an everyday basis. Before discussing the channels used and strategies undertaken by the priory authorities and their many agents and officials, let us consider the annual grain requirements of the house.

---

42. Harvey, *Living and dying*, pp. 18, 73, 164–5.
43. M. Oliva, *The convent and the community in late medieval England* (Woodbridge, 1998), pp. 125–9.
44. I. Kershaw, *Bolton Priory: the economy of a northern monastery, 1286–1325* (Oxford, 1973), p. 132. This estimation is based on the quantities of bread and ale consumed there – a methodology utilised later in the present book.

The grain requirements of Norwich Cathedral Priory

In his now classical monograph on living standards in late medieval England, Christopher Dyer has estimated that an average late medieval English male peasant would have consumed about 2900 kilocalories (kcal) on a daily basis.[45] This estimation can perhaps be used to calculate the nutritional requirements of the priory workers and the *famuli*, but not the monks. As part of the upper reaches of society, the brethren adopted some aspects of aristocratic lifestyle, particularly diet. The daily calorific intake of an aristocratic family would have been much higher than that of a peasant one, and it would include a good deal of animal protein, a high fat and low fibre content and a meagre intake of vitamins A and C.[46] A fifteenth-century Provencal nobleman and his household members may have consumed as many as 4580 kcal daily each.[47] In her extensive and innovative study of everyday life at Westminster Abbey, Barbara Harvey has shown that the average daily food and drink placed before a monk would have contained an energy value of approximately 6210 kcal. Harvey contended, however, that the monks would have consumed only about 60 per cent of the offered food, making their daily intake about 3730 kcal.[48] More recently, monastic archaeologist Philippa Patrick argued, on the basis of skeletal analysis of about 300 skeletons from London monasteries, that in reality the monks probably consumed much more than has been commonly assumed. She suggests about 6000 kcal per regular day and about 4500 kcal per fasting day. As a result of this over-eating, the monks frequently suffered from osteoarthritis (a disease representing the failure of the moving joints of the body).[49] Still, much remains to be done, in the fields of both palaeopathology and economic history, in order to determine whose estimation is the more secure. As far as the Norwich brethren are concerned, each of them was allowed one loaf of 'monks' bread' (*panis monachorum*), rendering approximately 2550 kcal each, as well as one gallon of finer ale, each yielding about 1280 kcal, on a daily basis.[50] While it is obvious that the brethren

---

45. C. Dyer, *Standards of living in the later Middle Ages: social change in England, c.1200–1520* (Cambridge, 1989), p. 134. This estimation is accepted by Campbell et al., *A medieval capital*, p. 32.
46. Dyer, *Standards of living*, p. 64.
47. F. Stouff, *Ravitaillement et alimentation en Provence aux XIVe et XVe siècles* (Paris, 1970), p. 46.
48. Harvey, *Living and dying*, pp. 34–71, esp. 69–70.
49. P. Patrick, 'Creaking in the cloisters: observations on prevalence and distribution of osteoarthritis in monks from medieval London', in G. Helmig, B. Scholkmann and M. Untermann (eds), *Centre, region, periphery: medieval Europe, Basel 2002* (Basel, 2002), pp. 89–93; P. Patrick, 'An archaeology of overindulgence', *Archaeological Review from Cambridge* 20/2 (2005), pp. 98–117; P. Patrick, '"Greed, gluttony and intemperance"? Testing the stereotype of the "obese medieval monk"', PhD thesis (University College London, 2005). On the archaeology of osteoarthritis, see J. Rogers, 'The palaeopathology of joint disease', in M. Cox and S. Mays (eds), *Human osteology and archaeology and forensic science* (London, 2000), pp. 163–82. On the connection between overeating, obesity and osteoarthritis, see T.D. Spector, 'The fat on the joint: osteoarthritis and obesity', *Journal of Rheumatology*, 17 (1990), pp. 357–65. For other archaeological findings on monastic obesity and osteoarthritis, see T. Waldron, 'DISH at Merton Priory: evidence for a "new" occupational disease?' *British Medical Journal*, 291 (1985), pp. 1762–3; J. Rogers and T. Waldron, 'DISH and the monastic way of life', *International Journal of Osteoarchaeology*, 11 (2001), pp. 357–65.
50. See below, Chapter 7.

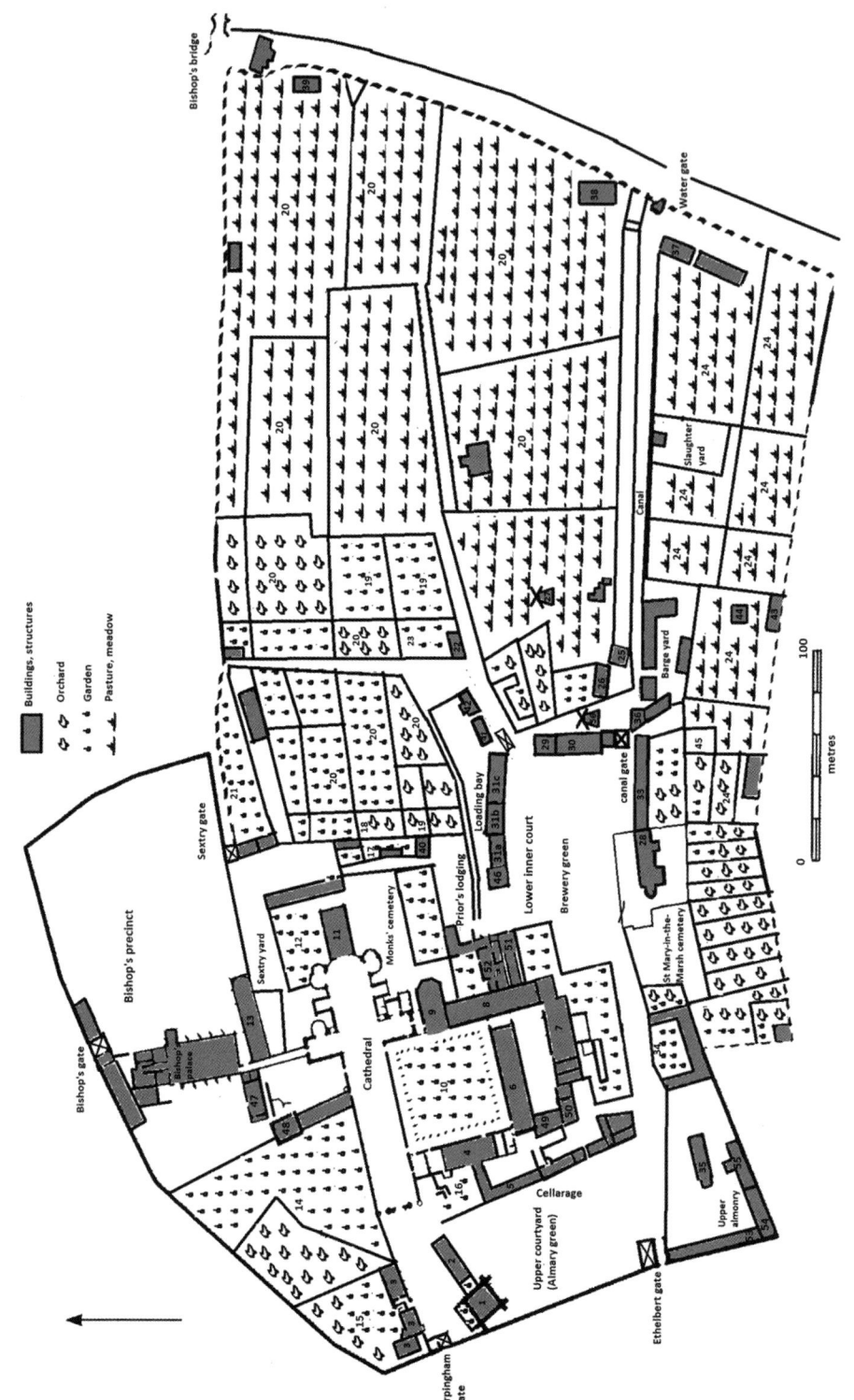

1 Clocher
2 Workshops
3 Carnary College
4 Hostry
5 Cellars
6 Refectory
7 Infirmary
8 Dormitory
9 Chapter House
10 Cloister
11 St Mary's Chapel (Cathedral)
12 St Mary's Garden
13 St Mary's Chapel (Bishop's)
14 Preaching yard
15 Carnary garden
16 Hostiller's garden
17 Loadhouse, glasshouse
18 Vineyard
19 Prior's gardens (?)
20 Gardener's territory
21 St Helen's garden
22 Chamberlain's office
23 Chamberlain's garden
24 Cellarer's meadows and pastures
25 Boathouse
26 Quay
27 Wind-mill
28 St Mary-in-the-Marsh Church
29 Bakery
30 Brewery
31 The Great Granary: (a) wheat; (b) oat(?); (c) malt
32 Bishop's lodgings
33 Stables
34 Lower Almonry
35 St Ethelbert Church
36 Barn
37 Granary and hay grange
38 Curing house
39 Fish house
40 Lead house
41 Wardroper's office
42 Gardiner's chequer
43 Smithy and forge
44 Dovehouse
45 Swannery
46 Steward's house
47 Bishop's hall
48 De Losinga's tower
49 Kitchen
50 Meat kitchen
51 Monks' latrine
52 Prior's hall
53 Almoner's hall, stables and cookhouse
54 Almoner's granary
55 Almoner's office
56 Horse-mill

Figure 2.2 Norwich Cathedral Priory precinct (drawing by the author).
Sources: NRO, DCN 1/1/–12; A.B. Whittingham, 'The development of the close since the Reformation', in G.A. Metters (ed.), *The parliamentary survey of dean and chapter properties in and around Norwich in 1649*, Norfolk Record Society 51 (Norwich, 1985), p. 114; C. Noble, 'Aspects of life at Norwich Cathedral Priory in the late medieval period', PhD thesis (University of East Anglia, 2001), p. 128; R. Gilchrist, *Norwich Cathedral close: the evolution of the English cathedral landscape* (Woodbridge, 2005), *passim*.

did not consume their daily rations in their entirety, there is no doubt that the portions placed before them were of heroic proportions. As we shall see later, the monks may have consumed only about half of the calories available in their daily meals. If this estimate is accurate, then it appears that, each day, an average Norwich monk may have consumed about 1915 kcal deriving from grain-based products, while the total value of grain-based products placed before him may have been around 3830 kcal.

For the lay residents of the priory, a different calorific multiplier altogether is required. Grain-based products were the most important part of the diet of late medieval commoners and it was from these foods that the majority of calories in such people's diets derived. It has been estimated that grain contributed about 70 per cent of total calories consumed in London *c.*1300 and we may use this figure as a guideline in calculating the calorific requirements of the non-monastic residents of the priory.[51] After the Black Death, and in particular after the 1370s, when grain prices collapsed and real wages rose, the share of grain-based products within the workers' diet fell by about 20 per cent. Using an approximate figure of 1915 kcal per monk and 2030 and 1740 kcal per labourer/servant (that is, 70 and 60 per cent of 2900 kcal *c.*1300 and *c.*1400), we may estimate that around 1300 the population of the priory consumed about 219 million kcal of grain annually (42 million were consumed by the brethren and 177 million by the lay residents). A century later these figures should have fallen as a result of the population decline and improvements in the diet of commoners. It may be suggested, therefore, that *c.*1400 the overall figures stood at about 134 million kcal of grain a year (about 36 million of which would be consumed by the brethren and 98 million by the servants and workers). Finally, around 1500, the figures may have fallen further, to about 100 million kcal of grain (28 million for the monks and 72 million for the remaining population).

Humans, however, were not the only residents of the cathedral precincts. In addition, the priory housed an uncertain number of horses, kept and looked after at local stables. For the most part these were fine riding horses (*palefridi*), known by proper names; there were also a number of mill-horses.[52] Although the accounts do not specify their numbers, the size of the horse population can be estimated from the quantities of fodder consumed by it in the course of a fiscal year. Between 1263 and 1430 some 250 quarters of oats and oat bran were consumed by local horses, in addition to occasional allowances of legumes and loaves of a cruder kind of bread (*panis militis*) (discussed below). Translating these figures into their calorific equivalent renders around 160 million kcal a year. Allowing a generous estimate of 20,000 kcal a day per palfrey, we arrive at about 22 beasts. However, it is likely that the actual number of horses was somewhat higher: as some later accounts specify, the horses were also stall-fed with grass.[53] It is evident, however, that the priory horses were treated much better than their manorial counterparts, as will be shown later. Until

---

51. Campbell *et al.*, *A medieval capital*, pp. 33–4. Note, however, that in the countryside local workers derived about 80 per cent of their diet from grain-based products. See C. Dyer, 'Changes in diet in the late Middle Ages: the case of harvest workers', *AHR*, 36 (1988), p. 26.
52. Thus, we find several rolls mentioning the names of these horses, such as Diggard, Grisel, Bai and Lanteyn. This fact is discussed in Saunders, *Introduction*, p. 79.
53. NRO, DCN 1/1/94–108.

Table 2.1
Grain supply of Norwich Cathedral Priory, 1261–1536.

	In quarters				As percentage			
	Market	Manors	Other	Total	Market	Manors	Other	Total
1261–70	454.5	2068.9	436.9	2960.3	15.4%	69.9%	14.8%	100.0%
1271–80	468.6	1773.9	332.8	2575.3	18.2%	68.9%	12.9%	100.0%
1281–90	586.9	2329.2	290.2	3206.3	18.3%	72.6%	9.1%	100.0%
1291–1300	701.7	2250.1	561.2	3513.0	20.0%	64.1%	16.0%	100.0%
1301–10	662.7	2260.2	314.1	3237.0	20.5%	69.8%	9.7%	100.0%
1311–20	664.4	2046.3	314.9	3025.6	22.0%	67.6%	10.4%	100.0%
1321–30	704.4	1848.7	93.8	2646.9	26.6%	69.8%	3.5%	100.0%
1331–40	468.5	1703.7	603.6	2775.8	16.9%	61.4%	21.7%	100.0%
1341–50	430.8	1766.8	492.3	2689.9	16.0%	65.7%	18.3%	100.0%
1351–60	185.4	886.0	347.3	1418.7	13.1%	62.5%	24.5%	100.0%
1361–70	238.5	923.6	325.6	1487.7	16.0%	62.1%	21.9%	100.0%
1371–80	427.5	941.8	310.4	1679.7	25.5%	56.1%	18.5%	100.0%
1381–90	568.6	613.3	289.9	1471.8	38.6%	41.7%	19.7%	100.0%
1391–1400	465.5	596.7	269.2	1331.4	35.0%	44.8%	20.2%	100.0%
1401–10	337.3	833.7	250.6	1421.6	23.7%	58.6%	17.6%	100.0%
1411–20	392.3	736.4	233.0	1361.7	28.8%	54.1%	17.1%	100.0%
1421–30	349.3	710.3	212.9	1272.5	27.4%	55.8%	16.7%	100.0%
1431–40	407.1	660.3	208.7	1276.1	31.9%	51.7%	16.4%	100.0%
1441–50	347.6	703.1	188.8	1239.5	28.0%	56.7%	15.2%	100.0%
1451–60	509.0	716.0	178.9	1403.9	36.3%	51.0%	12.7%	100.0%
1461–70	269.0	808.3	155.1	1232.4	21.8%	65.6%	12.6%	100.0%
1471–80	706.8	829.0	132.8	1668.6	42.4%	49.7%	8.0%	100.0%
1481–90	645.0	798.0	116.2	1559.2	41.4%	51.2%	7.5%	100.0%
1491–1500	411.0	800.9	92.6	1304.5	31.5%	61.4%	7.1%	100.0%
1501–10	544.0	802.0	108.9	1454.9	37.4%	55.1%	7.5%	100.0%
1511–20	706.0	733.0	235.1	1674.1	42.2%	43.8%	14.0%	100.0%
1521–30	587.3	409.0	75.4	1071.7	54.8%	38.2%	7.0%	100.0%
1531–6	350.3	409.0	49.1	808.4	43.3%	50.6%	6.1%	100.0%
1261–1350	571.4	2005.3	382.2	2958.9	19.3%	67.8%	12.9%	100.0%
1351–1430	370.6	780.2	279.9	1430.6	26.0%	54.5%	19.5%	100.0%
1431–1536	496.7	697.2	141.9	1335.8	37.2%	52.3%	10.5%	100.0%

Source: NRO, DCN 1/1/1–110.
Note: Manors = demesnes, tithes and grain farms until 1431; from 1431, grain farms only.

the 1430s the palfreys were given mostly oats and oat bran. From the 1430s onwards, however, the priory authorities cut down the oat allowances drastically, allocating larger quantities of grass, found in abundance on the Cellarer's Meadows (in the south-eastern corner of the priory precinct), adjacent to the stables. In the 1490s, during the construction of the 'Great Stable', presumably on the site of the Cellarer's Meadows, much hay and straw was purchased to compensate for temporary losses of grassland. Between 1454 and 1536 the overall quantities of oats and oat bran distributed among horses fell from around 155 to 15 quarters a year, with the shortfall made up of grass-based fodder. This, however, implied not only the declining feeding standards of horses, but also their declining numbers, which went hand in hand with the shrinking numbers of brethren and priory staff. By the time of the priory's dissolution in 1538, it had probably no more than ten horses in the local stables.

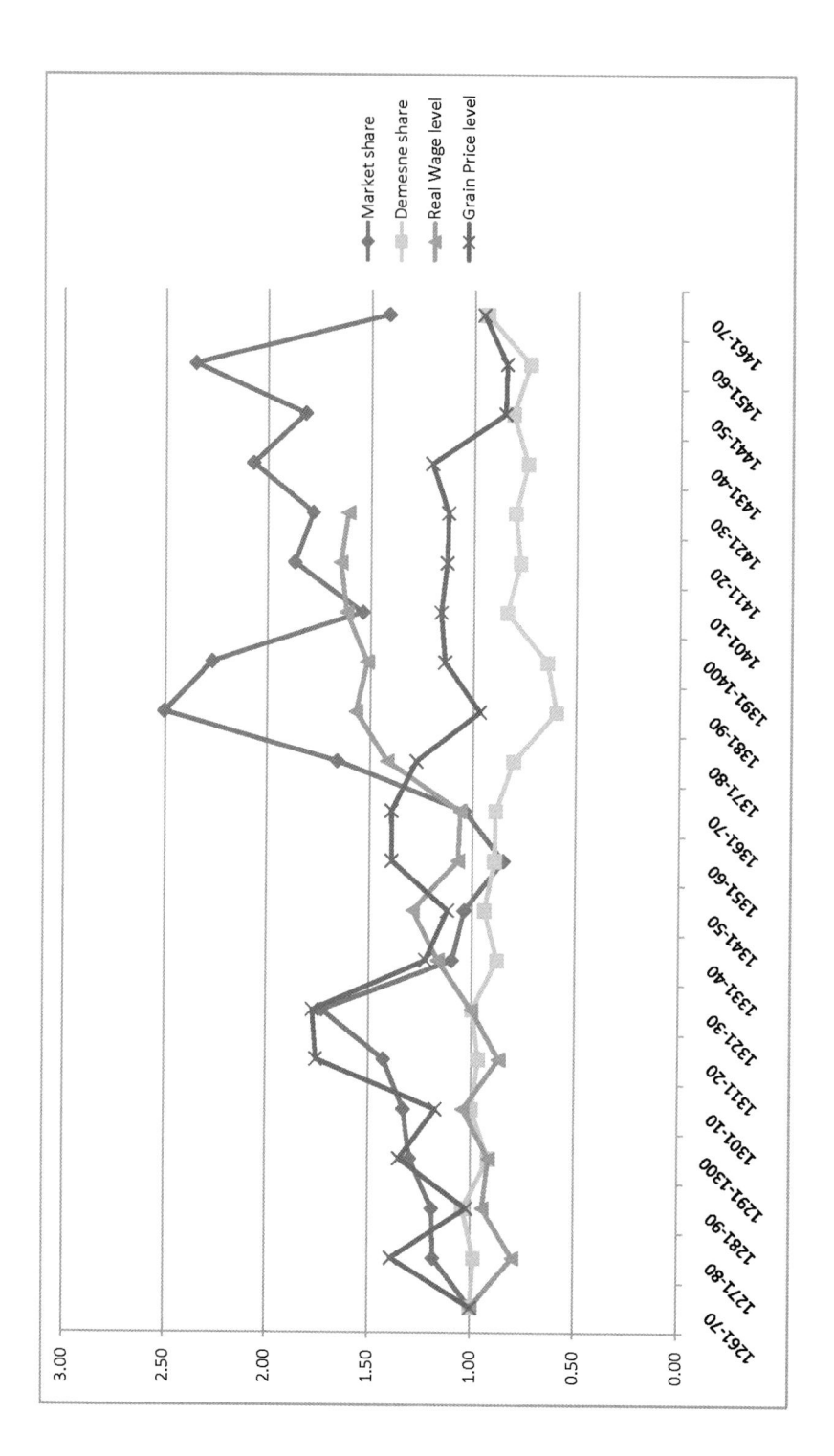

Figure 2.3 Market and demesne shares of grain supply, real wages and grain prices, 1261–1460 (indexed on 1261–70).
Sources: NRO, DCN 1/1–12 (Norwich and Norfolk grain prices); J.H. Munro, John Munro's revisions of the Phelps Brown and Hopkins 'basket of consumables' commodity price series and craftsmen's wage series, 1264–1700 and John Munro's revised tabulations of David Farmer's series of English 'national' agrarian wages, both http://www.economics.utoronto.ca/munro5/ResearchData.html (accessed 11 October 2011).

Table 2.2
Grain-supply balance at select conventual houses, 1285–1528 (in quarters).

House	Years	Period	Purchased	Manors	Total supply	Purchased as % of total supply	Manors as % of total supply
Canterbury Cathedral	1311–46	A	404.8	1550.4	2282.7	17.7%	67.9%
Canterbury Cathedral	1354–6	B	800.6	823.3	1750.7	45.7%	47.0%
Canterbury Cathedral	1374–99	C	1070.9	0.0	1658.8	64.6%	0.0%
Westminster Abbey	1348–9	A	1501.9	182.0	2454.6	61.2%	7.4%
Westminster Abbey	1356–74	B	229.4	115.2	710.9	31.9%	18.2%
Westminster Abbey	1377–1407	C	435.7	345.1	1202.5	34.9%	26.9%
St Paul's Cathedral	1285–6	A	0.0	1575.0	1575.0	0.0%	100.0%
Durham Cathedral	1295–1347	A	492.3	3131.2	3841.9	13.4%	81.1%
Durham Cathedral	1376–1402	B	504.0	1852.6	2356.6	20.6%	79.4%
Peterborough Abbey	1309–10	A	102.9	4266.4	4528.8	94.2%	2.3%
Peterborough Abbey	1387–8	B	625.0	2164.0	2991.3	72.3%	20.9%
Glastonbury Abbey	1362–3	B	97.4	2379.9	3001.3	3.2%	79.3%
Hereford Cathedral	1294–1343	A	26.8	879.5	906.7	3.0%	97.0%
Hereford Cathedral	1401–1473	C	1.8	491.4	496.0	0.4%	99.1%
Ely Cathedral Priory	1307–1346	A	0.0	1918.3	2306.0	0.0%	83.2%
Ely Cathedral Priory	1356–1397	B	11.2	1384.4	2192.6	0.5%	63.1%
Ely Cathedral Priory	1399–1528	C	779.3	75.3	1684.7	46.3%	4.5%
Ramsey Abbey	1422–4	C	1230.8	1069.4	2494.8	48.8%	43.1%
Bolton Priory	1311–25	A	184.6	2161.1	2416.6	7.6%	89.4%
Average		A	339.2	1958.0	2539.0	24.6%	66.0%
		B	377.9	1453.2	2167.2	29.0%	51.3%
		C	703.7	396.3	1507.4	39.0%	34.7%

Sources: Canterbury Cathedral Archives, Granger 4–37, 70–76, 89–95, Bartoner 4–34, 52–66; Westminster Abbey Muniments WAM 19155–19217; W.H. Hale (ed.), *Domesday of St. Paul's of the Year MCCXII*, Camden Society Old Series 69 (London, 1858), pp. xlviii–li; Durham Cathedral Archives, granator accounts 1296–1401; Northamptonshire Record Office, Fitzwilliam 2389 and PDC AR/I/9; Longleet House, MS 10643; Hereford Cathedral Archives, R630–R637c; Cambridge University Library, EDC EDC 1/F/4/1–53; British Library, Add. Roll 34714 and I.M. Kershaw and D.M. Smith (eds), *The Bolton Priory compotus, 1286–1325*, The Yorkshire Archaeological Society 154 (1999–2000) (Woodbridge, 2000).

Note: A = pre-Black Death period; B = late *Gutsherrschaft* period (between the Black Death and leasing out of the demesnes); C = *Grundherrschaft* period.

Getting grain: sources and resources

Recruiting such mammoth amounts of grain to satisfy the requirements of the humans and horses was by no means a straightforward task, especially during the troublesome fourteenth century, which saw a series of environmental and socio-economic crises. Over the entire period we may discern three main channels of grain supply: the manors (which included both demesne grains and tithes deriving from appropriated churches); the market (both in and outside Norwich); and food farms, consisting of cereals, paid by the farmers of the leased demesnes or their parts. The overall picture is shown in Table 2.1.

Manorial grain, consisting of demesne harvests, tithes and food farms, provided the single most important channel through which food was provisioned to the Norwich brethren and their dependents. As Table 2.1 indicates, there were some visible changes over the period. Between the 1260s and the 1370s manorial grain accounted for 60 to 70 per cent of all the supply to the priory. Markets contributed a much smaller share (between 15 and 25 per cent of the total supply). The remainder came mostly as carryovers from the previous years, as well as occasional gifts and contributions. The importance of carryovers will be discussed in greater detail later in this study. The situation changed from the late 1370s, however, when the markets' share grew significantly, representing 39 and 35 per cent of the total supply in the 1380s and 1390s respectively. This undoubtedly reflects the beginning of the decline of direct demesne management, when the priory authorities leased out several demesnes because of rising costs of production and declining food prices: processes which resulted, inevitably, in falling real income for lords and rising real wages for agricultural labourers. This meant that the proportion of grain obtained from markets had to be increased; however, when the prices rose once more in the first years of the 1400s and the leased demesnes were taken back in hand the extent of the priory's grain transactions at local markets diminished accordingly. As we have seen, the manors continued to be the single most dominant channel of grain supply after the end of the *Gutsherrschaft* period, when the brethren continued receiving annual grain supply from the leased manors in the form of food farms, although during the 1470s the markets' share of the priory's grain supply suddenly doubled from 21 to 42 per cent. The balance shifted in favour of the manor once again in the 1490s, when the share of the grain deriving from the markets fell to 31 per cent. During the last three decades of the priory's life, nearly or slightly over half of all the priory's grain came from the markets.

    In other words, despite the fact that over the entire period less and less manorial grain ended up in the priory granary, the brethren were, in fact, never capable of entrusting the provision of their community entirely to the markets. With the exception of the 1520s, more than half of the cereal supply came from the manors, whether as harvests or food farms.

    In order to appreciate the changes in the supply balance, it is necessary to consider several variables dictating the annual grain supply policies of the priory authorities. The monetary variable is connected to the behaviour of grain market prices and the real wages of agricultural workers. As Figure 2.3 shows, there seems to have been an inverse relationship between grain price levels and the share of grain purchased at market, on the one hand, and the wages of agricultural workers and the share of demesne grain, on the other, at least between the 1320s and the 1430s. In other words, the combination of relatively low real wages and high market prices prompted the priory authorities to increase the quantities of grain shipped from the demesne to the Norwich headquarters. This was especially true after *c.*1376, when grain prices collapsed while real wages of agricultural workers rose a great deal; it was also then that the priory authorities decided to lease out several of their demesnes in the hope of profiting from the new economic reality. It is hardly surprising, then, that it was precisely in that decade that the supply balance started shifting more and more towards the market. Between 1370 and 1390 the share of the priory's grain supplied from markets rose from 16 to 39 per cent. Once prices began to rise once more in the 1390s the priory took the leased demesnes back in hand and augmented the proportion of demesne grain consumed by the brethren. Real wages, however, did not fall; instead, they continued rising notwithstanding the high prices, which prevailed until *c.*1445. This, in turn, prompted the lords to abolish the *Gutsherrschaft* management altogether, but to make sure, at the same time, that the grain supply could still partially be obtained from non-market sources: namely from food farms.

The grain supply of Norwich Cathedral Priory in a wider context

Were these patterns of grain supply extraordinary? A comparative look at other late medieval households may provide an answer. To that end, numerous accounts from demesnes belonging to contemporary religious houses have been consulted. For the purpose of the present exercise, Table 2.2 divides the available evidence into three main periods: the pre-Black Death period, the late *Gutsherrschaft* period and the *Grundherrschaft* era. Since the timing of the shift from *Gutsherrschaft* to *Grundherrschaft* differed from estate to estate and from demesne to demesne, exact years have been specified for each house. Roughly speaking, two converging tendencies can be identified here. One was an increase in reliance on markets after the Black Death, and chiefly with the end of direct demesne management in the late fourteenth and early fifteenth centuries. Thus, at Canterbury Cathedral Priory the share of purchased grain rose from 18 to 46 and 65 per cent across the three periods. Similarly, there were hardly any purchases of grain at Ely Cathedral Priory before the farming of its demesnes *c.*1398, but after that date almost half of all grain supply came from purchases. And at Peterborough Abbey purchases represented only about 2 per cent of the total grain supply in the early fourteenth century; but at the turn of that century the figure stood at about 21 per cent. At Durham Cathedral Priory the share of purchases rose from 13 to 21 per cent between the pre-Black Death and post-1350 periods. In most cases, the remainder came from either food farms paid by the lessees of the demesnes or from grain carried over from previous years and stored at local granaries. Thus, in the course of the fifteenth century the Ely monks were consuming only about half of the available supply, carrying over the other half to the next year.

The second tendency was contrary to the first, and involved either the reduction of the relative rates of purchases or their stabilisation at the same level. Thus, Westminster Abbey authorities cut the proportion of their grain purchases from about 61 to 32 per cent of the total cereal supply after the Black Death. At Hereford Cathedral, crop purchases were virtually unknown to the local canons during both the *Grundherrschaft* and *Gutscherrschaft* eras. Similarly, the brethren of Glastonbury Abbey acquired very little cereals through purchases in the 1360s. Both Westminster Abbey and Hereford Cathedral relied strongly on food farms to secure their daily bread supply. Glastonbury Abbey, on the other hand, was still extracting its grain provision from its directly managed demesnes. It should be noted that Glastonbury Abbey was one of the most conservative landed lords in England, which managed its demesnes directly all the way to the 1490s, so it is hardly surprising that it chose to rely on its manors as the most important source of its food supply. Westminster Abbey was located at the heart of the single most commercialised centre in the country, a situation which allowed its brethren to be closely involved in local markets. Hereford Cathedral, on the other hand, was located in a relatively backward region, which was very weakly commercialised. Its most important market centre, Leominster, was significant mostly as a wool producer and distributor, but not as a grain hub. Therefore, it was undoubtedly convenient for the Hereford canons to rely on food farms from their demesnes rather than go to pains to search for cereals at local, relatively underdeveloped markets.

There is no doubt that the supply patterns of Norwich Cathedral Priory fit into the first model. In the pre-Black Death period its reliance on purchases was on a modest scale, comparable with that of conventual houses such as Canterbury and Durham cathedral priories. While the proportions of purchases rose after the pestilence, the priory authorities were not yet ready to increase their levels significantly. The new reality of the *Grundherrschaft* era, however, turned purchases into a significant channel of food supply.

Why two channels? Economic instability, risk aversion and diversified portfolios

Although monetary factors and market forces played an important role in the economy of late medieval England, the endogenous factors were not the only economic protagonists. It is impossible to study and appreciate various long- and short-term economic processes without considering the impact of the exogenous aspect: that is, nature.[54] No matter how developed and sophisticated the grain market was, its efficiency would, ultimately, depend on various vagaries of nature. Most of all, the degree of success and failure of harvests, and hence food availability, depended largely on annual weather fluctuations. On the estates of Norwich Cathedral Priory, just as anywhere else in England, crop yields tended to vary a great deal not only from year to year, but also between different places within the same year. Thus, in 1273 barley yields, measured in ratios between reaped and sown amounts, varied between 2.1 and 4.6 across ten demesnes. Similarly, in 1303 wheat yields were anywhere between 2.0 and 9.1 across 14 demesnes. Overall, between 1273 and 1350, the coefficient of variation for annual yields across the demesnes was 0.28 for wheat, 0.24 for rye and barley and 0.33 for oats. Similarly, the yields varied not only geographically but also chronologically. For instance, at Plumstead wheat yields stood at 8.0 and 3.5 in 1305 and 1306 respectively. At Taverham, barley yields were miserably low, standing at 1.37 in 1307 and rising to 3.13 in the following year. Many more examples can be added here, without mentioning famine years, when the gap in yields between two years tended to be especially apparent. Between 1273 and 1350 the coefficient of variation within the same demesnes was 0.25 for wheat, 0.32 for rye, 0.22 for barley and 0.31 for oats. Normally, yields of 20 per cent or less below the average level would occur approximately once in three years, while about 8 per cent of all wheat harvests could be qualified as disastrous (with yields below 60 per cent of the average level). Barley, on the other hand, was a more tolerant crop than wheat, and yields of less than 20 per cent of the average levels are observed approximately once in four years, while true harvest failures account for about 6 per cent of all harvests.[55]

In other words, nature tended to be highly treacherous, and both producers and consumers stood completely helpless against its vagaries. The pronounced variations in crop yields meant not only the changing fortunes of different manors but also oscillations on local grain markets. After all, all merchandise came from the fields and

---

54. On the importance of nature as a mover of the late medieval economy, see B.M.S. Campbell, 'Nature as historical protagonist: environment and society in pre-industrial England' (the 2008 Tawney Memorial Lecture), *EcHR*, 63/2 (2010), pp. 281–314.

55. These figures are calculated from Bruce Campbell's database of crop yields. See B.M.S. Campbell, Three centuries of English crops yields, 1211–1491, available: http://www.cropyields.ac.uk (accessed 11 October 2011).

a large number of harvest failures across places within a single area could have a devastating impact upon the grain market, and chiefly upon its wheat sector. This unstable reality made the quotidian task of grain provisioning all the more challenging. It seems that the priory authorities may have been aware of those potential dangers and did their best to avoid them. One way to minimise the risk of running into difficulties of recruiting sufficient amounts of grain to satisfy the dietary needs of the priory community was to rely on more than one channel of grain supply: thus, if one channel of grain supply failed or performed badly, the other one could take up the slack. In other words, if the demesnes failed, the markets could come to the rescue, and the other way around. It was precisely because of that fact that the brethren were so keen on preserving both channels of food provisioning, despite the complete retreat from direct management in 1431. In effect, this dual strategy can be regarded as a rational measure of security against crop failures, by diversifying the portfolio of food supply.

Perhaps the term 'diversified portfolio' appears somewhat anachronistic when dealing with late medieval food security, but its idea and implications were certainly mirrored in the economic behaviour of the Norwich Cathedral Priory authorities. The application of this concept to late medieval (and, indeed, pre-industrial) economies was first made by Donald McCloskey in his study of the survival of open-field systems in northern Europe. Here, he contended that the practice of this system reflects the tendency of peasant communities to minimise potential risks of harvest failures and famines by diversification of the access of each peasant's household to as many strips of land as possible, which mirrors diversification of assets in an investment portfolio.[56] McCloskey was then followed by a number of economists, who expanded or amended her views.[57] Although the arguments of McCloskey and other economists suffer from some methodological shortcomings (mostly because of their heavy reliance on econometric analysis and anachronistic economic models, rather than historical material), the idea itself could, perhaps, be taken forth and applied to other topics of late medieval economic history. The case of grain provisioning of large conventual houses could potentially be one such topic.

---

56. D. McCloskey, 'The persistence of English common fields', in W.N. Parker and E.L. Jones (eds), *European peasants and their markets: essays in agrarian economic history* (Princeton, NJ, 1975), pp. 93–120.

57. Thus, C.T. Bekar and C.G. Reed, 'Open fields, risk and land divisibility', *Explorations in Economic History*, 40/3 (2003), pp. 308–25.

Chapter 3

Norwich Cathedral Priory's grain market, 1260–1538

Geographic extent of the priory grain market

Despite the fact that the importance of the market was second to that of the directly managed demesnes, it is nevertheless appropriate to discuss its structure and dynamics first. As we have seen, around 1300 Norfolk was undoubtedly one of the most commercialised regions in England. In addition to 283 markets and fairs, there were a large number of 'informal' markets in the form of demesnes and farms trading in grain and other agricultural produce. In many instances, late medieval grain buyers preferred to rely on these informal avenues, rather than on public markets.[1] This was mainly because farmers and demesne managers usually offered a 5 per cent discount, known as *avantagium mercatoris*.[2] Norwich Cathedral Priory was no exception here. In the course of the entire period under study its authorities always preferred, as much as was possible, to purchase their grain at the farm gate rather than at local public markets. Moreover, during the *Gutsherrschaft* era, the priory's manorial officials, in virtually all cases, sold the annual crop surplus with the merchant's discount at the demesne gate. In other words, the priory authorities depended a good deal on 'informal markets', outside the Norwich marketplace. Although references to *avantagium mercatoris* are ubiquitous in the annual accounts of the priory, the data on the geography of grain purchases are quite patchy.

Our information about the structure and dynamics of the priory's grain trade comes from the master of the cellar accounts. Unfortunately, and with the exception of ten rolls running between 1279 and 1298, most pre-1382 accounts did not specify the locations of grain purchases.[3] There are occasional references to the provenance of purchased grain between c.1353 and 1380, but these are too patchy to be subjected to statistical analyses. From 1382 onwards, however, the annual accounts provide very detailed descriptions of the locations of purchases and, in most cases, the names of merchants or institutions which supplied the brethren with grain. Despite the scarcity of evidence from the pre-Black Death era, a comparison between the accounts of 1279–98 and those post-1383 sheds much light on the structure of grain markets before and after the pestilence.

As Figures 3.1 and 3.2 show, the brethren relied on a variety of grain-trading *loci*, with the geography of grain purchases differing between the two periods. In the pre-Black Death era, as exemplified by the accounts from 1279–98, the brethren relied

---

1. R.H. Britnell, 'The marketing of grain in England, 1250–1350', available: http://www.dur.ac.uk/r.h.britnell/articles/Grainframe.htm (accessed 11 October 2011).
2. On this practice, consult R.H. Britnell, '*Avantagium Mercatoris*: a custom in medieval English trade', *Nottingham Medieval Studies*, 24 (1980), pp. 37–50.
3. NRO, DCN 1/1/4–12.

Norwich Cathedral Priory's grain market, 1260–1538

- Market or demesne/farm
- △ Norwich Priory demesne
- ✠ Ecclesiastical source

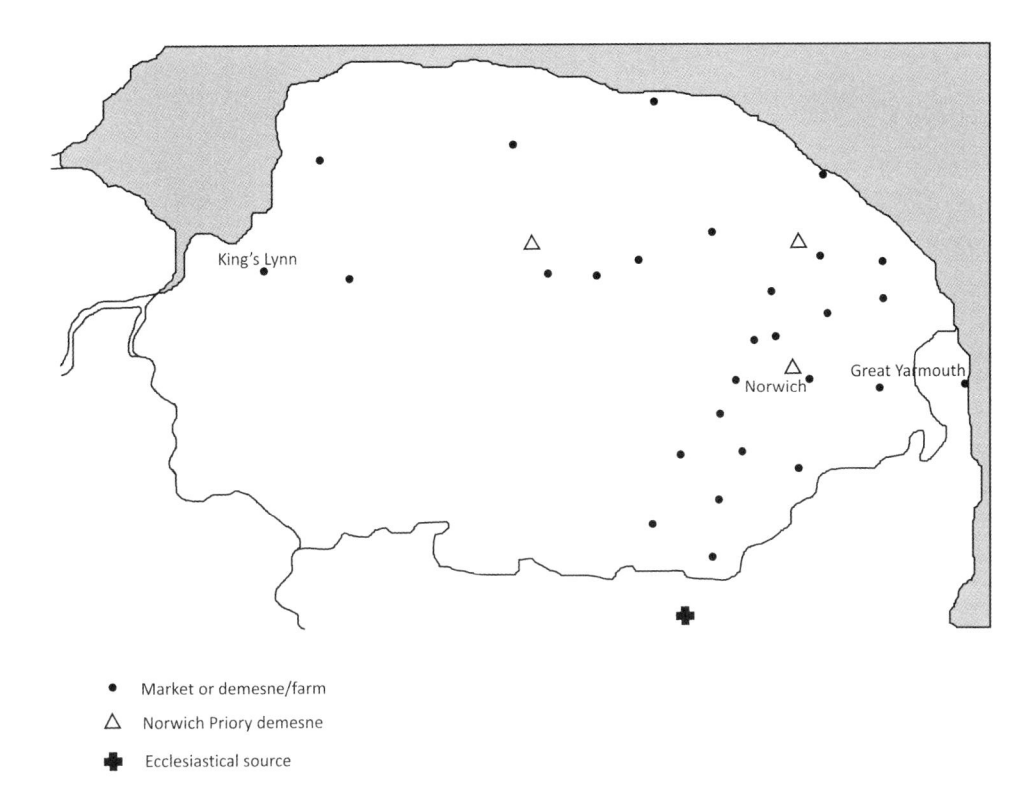

Figure 3.1 Grain market of Norwich Cathedral Priory, 1279–98. *Source*: NRO, DCN 1/1/4–12.

on quite a large area of local grain hubs extending from Hoxne, Suffolk (23.8 miles to the south of the priory), to Weybourne Hall (29.5 miles to the north of the priory), and from King's Lynn (43.6 miles to the west of the priory) to Great Yarmouth (20 miles to the east of the priory). The total grain hinterland of Norwich Priory was about 1800 square miles, with the average distance to a hub from the priory 14.5 miles. The majority of the grain hubs were situated in the eastern part of Norfolk and, somewhat surprisingly, not in the immediate hinterland of Norwich. At the same time, about 37 per cent of all grain was purchased in or around Norwich (Table 3.1). This is not to overestimate, however, the importance of the Norwich grain market (*forum frumenti*), whose share accounted for only 6 per cent of all purchases. In reality, most grain purchased in Norwich was, in fact, in the form of 'door-to-door' deliveries provided by local grain producers and merchants. In all other cases, the grain was purchased at local markets and farms. The vast majority of the grain hubs contributed no more than about 5 per cent each to the total supply. The only exception was Bromholm (19.8 miles to the north of the priory), which contributed about 13 per cent to the total. It is plausible that this multitude of grain-supplying hubs reflects overpopulation and pressure on land in late medieval Norfolk. Before the Black Death, Norfolk was the most densely settled county in England; around 1330, there were 137 taxpayers, in contrast with the national average of 55 taxpayers, per ten square

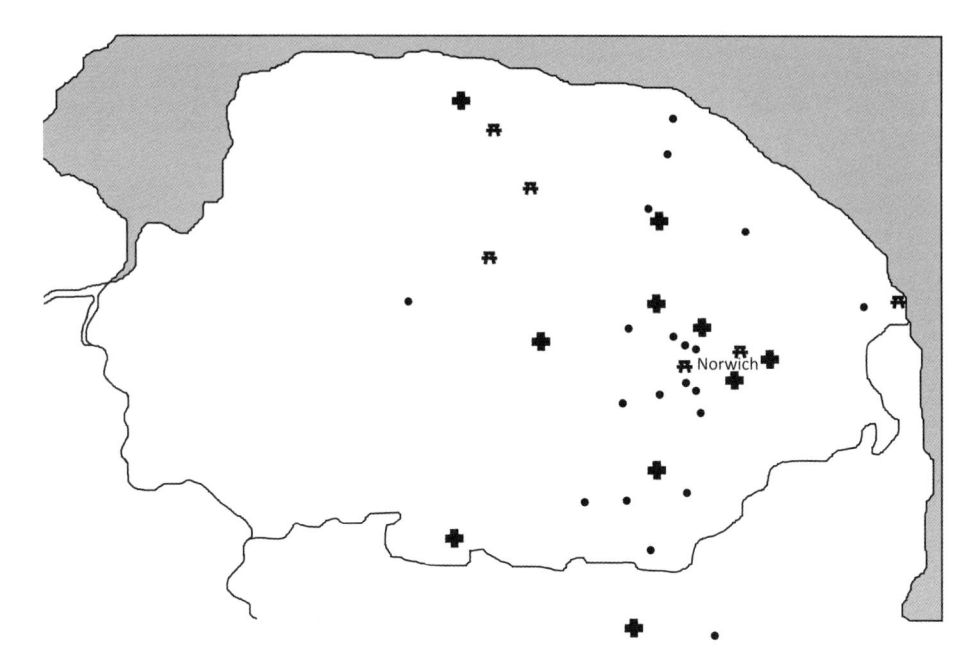

- • Market or demesne/farm
- ✠ Ecclesiastical source
- ⊞ Ecclesiastical source and/or leased demesne of Norwich Priory

Figure 3.2 Grain market of Norwich Cathedral Priory, 1382–1538. *Source*: NRO, DCN 1/1/59–110.

miles.[4] Overpopulation may have made grain surpluses rare and small, and possibly for that reason the brethren were compelled to rely on many small-scale purchases from numerous farms and markets.

The grain hinterland in the post-Black Death era was quite different. Many more hubs were now situated in the immediate vicinity of the priory (Figure 3.2). Its longitudinal axis now extended all the way from Wighton in the north (30.1 miles from the priory) to Hoxne, Suffolk, in the south (23.8 miles from the priory), while its latitudinal axis spread out from Kempstone in the west (31.6 miles from the priory) to Hemsby in the east (21.3 miles from the priory). The total area of the grain hinterland was nearly identical to that in 1279–98 (about 1716 square miles), with 13 miles as the average distance to a hub from the priory. It should be noted, however, that about 80 per cent of all the purchased grain came from places less than 2.5 miles from the town (Table 3.1). Norwich alone contributed about 67 per cent of all the purchased grain, with the vast majority of this grain coming, again, not from the local marketplace but from local merchants supplying the grain directly to the cathedral precinct. Thus,

---

4. B.M.S. Campbell and K. Bartley, *England on the eve of the Black Death: an atlas of lay lordship and wealth, 1300–1349* (Manchester, 2006), pp. 330–31.

Table 3.1
The extent of Norwich Cathedral Priory's grain market, 1279–98 and 1382–1538.

Distance from Norwich Cathedral Priory (miles)	1279–98 Quarters	As % of total	1382–1538 Quarters	As % of total
< 5	254.6	36.9%	503.7	80.4%
5–15	215.8	31.2%	29.4	4.7%
15–25	185.8	26.9%	84.2	13.4%
>25	34.8	5.0%	9.1	1.5%
Total	691.0	100.0%	626.4	100.0%

Source: NRO, DCN 1/1/4–12 and 59–110.

between 1383 and 1536, only about 3 per cent of all purchased grain came from the Norwich marketplace (Table 3.2). The more distant farms, on the other hand, contributed still smaller shares of grain to the priory's granary (only some 1.45 cent of all grain was purchased on farms situated at a distance of 25–30 miles from Norwich). It seems that the post-1350 geography of the priory's grain market reflects the wider socio-economic context of the post-pestilence reality. With pressure on land relieved and personal and economic freedom increased, local peasants were now able to participate in local grain trade more actively, while their production surpluses became more readily available for purchase and consumption. This may explain why the priory authorities managed to purchase the bulk of the required grain without travelling far from their residence.

The grain trade: reputation and trust

Why did most grain purchases come from outside of Norwich marketplace? A close reading and analysis of available evidence indicates that there were two main reasons for this. First, it should be noted that the *forum frumenti* of Norwich was of a rather modest size, occupying approximately 20,900 square feet.[5] It is certain that its stalls could not have satisfied the dietary requirements of the priory community, which, at the peak of its population in the early fourteenth century, required some 3000 quarters of grain, or more, on an annual basis. These figures were undoubtedly well beyond the supplying capacities of Norwich marketplace. But a far more important factor was the vendors themselves. These can be divided into three distinctive groups: (1) local merchants; (2) manorial tenants and, later, farmers; (3) local churchmen and ecclesiastical institutions. About 64 per cent of the identified suppliers were local merchants, living and working in Norwich or in its immediate vicinity. As prosopographic evidence suggests, many of these were people of high socio-economic and (local) political standing. For instance, among the grain suppliers of the priory in the 1530s were John Brend Sr and John Brend Jr, evidently a father and a son, who belonged to a wealthy and influential family of East Anglian gentry which also

---

5. On late medieval Norwich marketplaces, see P. Dunn, 'Trade', in C. Rawcliffe and R. Wilson (eds), *Medieval Norwich* (London, 2004), pp. 231–2. The calculations derive from p. 232.

Table 3.2
Sources of purchased grain supply, 1383–1536.

Years	Norwich market	Lay merchant	Bailiff, farmers	Ecclesiastical source	Tithes vending	Total
1383–7	12.26%	79.02%	8.72%	0.00%	0.00%	100.00%
1413–20	14.52%	50.15%	30.79%	4.55%	0.00%	100.00%
1421–30	0.00%	73.07%	21.20%	5.73%	0.00%	100.00%
1431–40	0.05%	26.42%	29.33%	44.20%	0.00%	100.00%
1441–50	0.00%	77.12%	0.67%	22.21%	0.00%	100.00%
1453–5	0.00%	57.72%	17.21%	25.07%	0.00%	100.00%
1493–6	1.18%	75.20%	10.12%	13.50%	0.00%	100.00%
1501–2	0.92%	91.70%	0.00%	7.37%	0.00%	100.00%
1531–6	0.00%	47.30%	26.13%	0.00%	26.57%	100.00%
Average	3.21%	64.19%	16.02%	13.63%	2.95%	100.00%

Source: NRO, DCN 1/1/64–110.

gave England a dynasty of famous bell makers.[6] In 1531, 5 quarters of maslin (a wheat and rye mixture) and 30 quarters of malted barley were purchased from Thomas Brewe, 'citizen and alderman of Norwich'. Again, aside from his high administrative rank, this person also belonged to the knightly and powerful family of the Brewes.[7] Many more examples could be cited here.

Over the entire period, manorial tenants and farmers accounted for about 16 per cent of all known vendors, although the figures varied from decade to decade, as Table 3.2 suggests. In some cases, they supplied the priory with relatively large quantities of grain. Thus, we witness the priory authorities purchasing 30 quarters of malt from North Elmham and 80 quarters of oats from Hindringham in 1279–80, 10 quarters of malt from Plumstead in 1282–3 and a further 33 quarters of wheat from North Elmham and Gateley in 1283–4.[8] This indicates that the priory tenants, despite many customary burdens, could still actively participate in local market trade, and appears to contradict some widespread assumptions regarding the excessive exploitation of late medieval English peasants by their lords, who did not allow the former to market their surplus and, thus, impeded economic development during the late Middle Ages.[9] After the end of the *Gutsherrschaft* era the priory continued relying

---

6. The members of the Brende family, with their economic activities, appear in various contemporary documents. See, for instance, J.J. Muskett and C.H.E. White, 'Church goods in Suffolk', *East Anglian*, New Series, 1 (1885–6), p. 25.

7. For instance, the substantial personal wealth of Sir Thomas Brewe, knight (to be distinguished from Thomas Brewe the merchant and alderman), is attested in his will from 10 July 1479 (NRO, PRCC, Register Goldwell 7/12 (Norwich Consistory Court Probate Records, 1472–99), fol. 242r).

8. NRO, DCN 1/1/5–7.

9. For example, R. Brenner, 'Agrarian class structure and economic development in pre-industrial Europe', *P&P*, 70 (1976), pp. 30–74, reprinted in T.H. Aston and C.H.E. Philpin (eds), *The Brenner debate: agrarian class structure and economic development in pre-industrial Europe* (Cambridge, 1985), pp. 10–63.

on the manorial peasants, some of whom now became farmers of its demesnes. Thus, in 1413 (18 years before the lease of the last demesne), the farmers of North Elmham sold 120 quarters of wheat and 90 quarters of malted barley to the priory, which, collectively, represented about 31 per cent of all grain purchased in that year.[10]

Local churchmen can be divided into two main groups. The first consisted of rural rectors and vicars, whose annual income derived from the sales of grains received as tithes from their parishioners. In some cases, these grain vendors were, in fact, parish priests from the vills where the priory's manors were situated. Thus, in 1413, the brethren acquired 23 quarters of wheat from the rector of Hindringham,[11] while in 1446 the vicar of Plumstead sold the priory 31.5 quarters of wheat.[12] In other words, the purchased grain still derived, albeit indirectly, from the priory's tenants or farmers. In other instances the cereals were bought from parishes not associated with the priory, all nevertheless located in Norfolk. These included Beeston, Blofield, Bridgham, Horsford, Postwick, Tasburgh, Tuddenham and Wighton. The second group of ecclesiastics was made up of heads and officials of several religious institutions. For instance, in 1423 Geoffrey de Norwich, prior of Hoxne, supplied the brethren with 9.25 quarters of wheat for £39;[13] and, in 1446, 5 quarters of wheat were acquired from Hugh Acton, master of the Great Hospital of Norwich.[14]

Strikingly, there were several instances when the master of the cellar, the official responsible for the grain supply, purchased cereals from other monastic officials within the priory. Thus, in 1446 Robert Breckenham, the cellarer of the priory, sold 31.5 quarters of wheat to John Lynne, the master of the cellar.[15] In 1438 Lynne's predecessor, John Elington, bought 9 quarters of wheat and 15.5 quarters of oats from Thomas Cambridge, the almoner.[16] In the same year, 3 quarters of wheat and 2.5 quarters of malted barley were acquired from John Elingham, the sacrist.[17] Again, Norwich Cathedral Priory was by no means an exception here. For instance, in the first quarter of the fourteenth century, the canons of Bolton Priory tended to rely not only on local religious institutions and clergymen but also on their own priory's officials when it came to grain purchases. Thus, in 1298–9, they purchased 10 quarters of oats from the priory cellarer.[18]

While the sources do not reveal if the reliance on this very specific network of grain suppliers was a deliberate and conscientious policy of the priory authorities, it is likely that these choices may have been rewarding. In effect, the three groups, despite their different socio-economic standings and backgrounds, had one thing in common: they can all be

---

10. NRO, DCN 1/1/71.
11. NRO, DCN 1/1/71.
12. NRO, DCN 1/1/87.
13. NRO, DCN 1/1/76.
14. NRO, DCN 1/1/87.
15. NRO, DCN 1/1/87.
16. NRO, DCN 1/1/82.
17. NRO, DCN 1/1/82.
18. Kershaw and Smith, *Bolton Priory compotus*, pp. 205–7, 221–5, 239–43, 260–62, 280–83 and passim.

classified as 'trust-groups' as far as their supply of grain to the priory community is concerned. To be more precise, here we are dealing with a 'particularised trust', extended to persons with particular attributes and affiliations, and to be distinguished from a 'generalised' trust applying to strangers.[19] Each of these groups possessed distinctive attributes that conveyed trustworthiness in the eyes of the priory authorities. The grain merchants of Norwich, in addition to being grain merchants, also carried social reputation and prestige deriving from their administrative positions (such as alderman, in the case of Thomas Brewe) and blood ties to local gentry and knightly families. Social reputation, whether individual or collective, added a great deal to the trustworthiness of traders in the pre-modern era, when protective and enforcing institutions such as merchant courts were still relatively under-developed compared with their modern equivalents.[20] The respected social status of these grain merchants would probably have minimised the potential moral hazards related to commercial transactions.

Similarly, the manorial tenants and farmers represented another 'trust-group'. Firstly, the dependence between the tenants and the priory was bilateral. For the manorial peasants, the priory was not only their lord but also a trade partner who was willing to purchase the surplus of their produce. For the priory, the tenants were not only rent-payers and demesne cultivators but also grain suppliers. Secondly, the priory authorities were personally acquainted with the manorial bailiffs, who were responsible for carrying out the grain sales. Similarly, they certainly knew who the farmers of the newly leased demesnes were. Thirdly, and perhaps most importantly, both the peasants and the priory were theoretically protected by the legal system of the manorial and royal courts, which could adjudicate in the case of disputes related to grain sale transactions. The priory's personal acquaintance with the vendors, the mutual dependence between the parties and the existence of judicial mechanisms all seem to have contributed to the establishment of mutual trust between the priory and the tenants/farmers, which, in turn, may have played a decisive role in minimising the risk of fraudulent transactions. It should be noted that the Norwich brethren were by no means the sole example of a late medieval lord purchasing agricultural produce from his tenants. For instance, when Ely Cathedral Priory farmed out its demesnes c.1398, most of the grain purchases were made from their farmers. Interestingly, the Ely brethren were now purchasing the same amounts of grain from the tenants that they used to receive from them in the *Gutsherrschaft* era.[21] Similarly, between 1286 and 1325 the canons of Bolton Priory acquired a certain percentage of their annual grain supply from their own tenants.[22]

Just as the tenants depended upon the priory socially and economically, so did the Norfolk clergymen depend upon it spiritually and politically. Both the rural rectors and vicars and the heads of religious institutions of the diocese of Norwich were subject to

---

19. On the importance of a 'particularised' form of trust between merchants in pre-industrial Europe, see S. Ogilvie, *Institutions and European trade: merchant guilds, 1000–1800* (Cambridge, 2011), pp. 427–32.
20. On the significance of social status and reputation in pre-1800 trade, see F. Trivellato, *The familiarity of strangers: the Sephardic diaspora, Livorno and cross-cultural trade in the early modern period* (New Haven, CT, 2009), pp. 164–5, 274–5.
21. Cambridge University Library, EDC 1/F/4/20–53.
22. Kershaw and Smith, *Bolton Priory compotus*, pp. 205–7, 221–5, 239–43, 260–62, 280–83 and passim.

the spiritual authority of the diocese's overseer, the bishop of Norwich. The latter also was *de jure* head of Norwich Cathedral Priory, and a judicial authority in all matters involving churchmen from his diocese. The subordination of these clergymen to the episcopal authority and the legal protection and security that the bishop could provide to the brethren would have been important factors minimising all possible moral hazards related to grain purchases. In addition to this subordination, however, local religious houses such as the Great Hospital of St Giles and Hoxne Priory shared many common features and concerns with Norwich Cathedral Priory. Hoxne and Norwich Cathedral Priory were both Benedictine establishments. The Great Hospital and the priory were charitable institutions, caring for urban paupers. All three houses can be regarded as conventual establishments, with a permanent community of inmates. One of the common concerns of these houses was food provisioning for their communities.

It is most certain, however, that the particularised trust was especially central and crucial when grain transactions took place between different members of the priory community. The priory community was a closed society, fostering multiplex relationships among its brethren. In other words, the brethren were linked not only as the members of one Benedictine community but through a whole series of common social ties, concerns and interests. To a large degree, their multiplex relationships were similar to those of late medieval guild members, as most recently studied by Sheilagh Ogilvie. It was through these relationships that guild members acquired a strong trust in each other.[23] The same can undoubtedly apply to late medieval conventual communities, of which Norwich Cathedral Priory is only one example.

Can we, then, speculate that all these factors may have been yet another factor in increasing the mutual trust between grain suppliers and the priory and, thus, diminishing the potential risks connected with grain trade? One thing is obvious. In the case of all three 'trust-groups', Norwich Cathedral Priory was able to extend its 'particularised' form of trust not only because of the high social status and reputation of Norwich grain merchants, the personal acquaintance with demesne farmers and the vocational proximity to other religious houses, but also because of mutual dependence between the priory community and these 'trust-groups'. The dependence was both social and economic. Norwich grain merchants were people of high social standing and, as such, no doubt preferred to deal with customers of an equal status. Demesne farmers could expect to remain on good terms with their landlords by supplying them grain produce. Finally, the religious houses of Norfolk and northern Suffolk undoubtedly needed the support of the most powerful figure in the region, the bishop of Norwich, and the most influential institution, Norwich Cathedral. It was this mutual dependence that fostered and strengthened that particularised trust so essential for the successful and smooth trade in grain.

Quantities of purchased grain

It would be impossible to appreciate the extent of the grain market of Norwich Cathedral Priory without looking at the actual quantities of grain that it purchased. As Table 3.3 indicates, the figures fluctuated from decade to decade and differed across

---

23. Ogilvie, *Institutions and European trade*, pp. 6–13 and 428.

Table 3.3
Annual grain purchases (in quarters), 1261–1536.

	Purchased wheat	As % of total wheat supply	Purchased malt and fresh barley	As % of total malt and barley supply	Purchased oats and oat bran	As % of total oats and bran supply	Purchased maslin and rye	All grain purchased	As % of total grain supply
1261–70	214.5	22.15%	40.0	2.26%	200.0	98.04%	0.00	454.5	15.4%
1271–80	160.3	22.03%	88.7	5.53%	219.7	90.04%	0.00	468.6	18.2%
1281–90	233.7	25.70%	50.8	2.59%	302.4	89.43%	0.00	586.9	18.3%
1291–1300	150.7	17.85%	142.9	6.82%	408.2	71.26%	0.00	701.7	20.0%
1301–10	256.9	32.52%	57.0	2.79%	348.8	86.11%	0.00	662.7	20.5%
1311–20	195.5	26.12%	165.8	8.65%	303.1	84.35%	0.00	664.4	22.0%
1321–30	235.4	30.58%	215.0	13.25%	254.0	100.00%	0.00	704.4	26.6%
1331–40	146.7	22.20%	121.2	6.57%	199.9	74.48%	0.63	468.5	16.9%
1341–50	118.1	16.83%	72.7	4.48%	239.8	65.51%	0.25	430.8	16.0%
1351–60	58.7	16.08%	20.3	2.16%	106.4	95.63%	0.00	185.4	13.1%
1361–70	40.6	9.39%	34.6	3.89%	163.3	98.90%	0.00	238.5	16.0%
1371–80	112.1	25.44%	52.2	5.38%	259.0	98.04%	3.20	426.5	25.4%
1381–90	95.6	26.53%	129.7	16.95%	325.1	98.99%	16.50	566.9	38.6%
1391–1400	145.5	37.11%	0.0	0.00%	320.0	99.62%	0.00	465.5	35.0%
1401–10	82.6	24.76%	0.0	0.00%	252.7	99.49%	2.00	337.3	23.7%
1411–20	104.8	29.19%	92.2	11.45%	192.4	98.82%	3.00	392.3	28.8%
1421–30	143.2	28.41%	158.6	22.02%	45.0	98.15%	2.50	349.3	27.4%
1431–40	244.5	81.42%	116.1	12.87%	29.1	67.94%	12.45	402.1	31.6%
1441–50	209.2	79.11%	42.5	4.98%	67.3	85.16%	28.56	347.6	28.0%
1451–60	249.9	82.04%	90.0	10.04%	146.4	88.17%	22.63	509.0	36.3%
1461–70	175.3	69.70%	0.0	0.00%	87.8	82.38%	6.00	269.0	21.8%
1471–80	235.3	75.66%	427.3	33.42%	44.3	75.42%	0.00	706.8	42.4%
1481–90	321.0	81.03%	180.8	18.39%	57.0	78.40%	86.25	645.0	41.4%
1491–1500	183.4	71.11%	182.8	18.86%	18.8	64.84%	25.94	411.0	31.5%
1501–10	280.0	73.76%	230.0	22.27%	19.0	63.76%	15.00	544.0	36.9%
1511–20	145.1	78.18%	447.8	33.75%	19.5	61.90%	93.63	706.0	42.2%
1521–30	166.0	93.95%	339.4	42.18%	12.4	89.22%	69.50	587.3	54.8%
1531–6	195.3	88.35%	109.7	20.39%	15.6	91.21%	29.69	350.3	43.3%
1261–1350	190.2	24.0%	106.0	5.9%	275.1	84.4%	0.1	571.4	19.3%
1351–1430	97.9	24.6%	61.0	7.7%	208.0	98.5%	3.4	370.2	26.0%
1431–1536	216.0	79.3%	205.0	20.4%	48.8	78.0%	37.7	507.6	37.9%

Source: NRO, DCN 1/1/1–110.

the three main periods (the pre-Black Death era, the waning of the demesne period and the *Grundherrschaft* years of 1431–1536). In the pre-1350 decades, the priory purchased anywhere between 455 and 704 quarters of grain a year, with an annual average of 567 quarters (190 quarters of wheat, 102 quarters of malt and 275 quarters of oats). Over that period, the purchases accounted for about 24 per cent of all wheat, 6 per cent of all malt and barley, and 84 per cent of all oats and oat bran, the disparities in the figures for different grains reflecting the overall balance of grain supply of the priory. While most malted barley and much of the wheat was supplied directly from the demesnes, virtually no oats and oat bran, fed to horses, came from the manors, as we shall see later. On average, the purchases represented some 19 per cent of the total grain supply of the priory. Between 1350 and 1430 the average figure stood at 370 quarters a year, including 98 quarters of wheat, 61 quarters of malt and 208 quarters of oats, as well as meagre amounts of rye and maslin. Undoubtedly, these decreased figures reflect the demographic reality of the post-pestilence era, which saw a pronounced fall in the priory population and, consequently, a decline of its grain requirements in absolute terms. In relative terms, grain purchases now accounted for about 26 per cent of the total crop supply of the priory. As regards oats, virtually all the supply (98.5 per cent) derived from the purchases. The figures for wheat and malt remained largely unchanged from the previous period. In the course of the third period, between 1431 and 1536, average annual grain purchases rose to about 507 quarters a year, consisting of about 216 quarters of wheat, 205 quarters of malt and 84 quarters of oats, in addition to 37 quarters of maslin. The share of purchases of wheat rose from 27 to 79 per cent of the total supply, while the figures for malt rose from 7 to 20 per cent of the total supply. These changes mirror the post-1431 economic reality, when the demesnes were farmed out and the importance of the market rose. This was especially true as regards wheat: it should be kept in mind that the vast majority of food farms received from the leased demesnes came in the form of malt, rather than wheat. Hence, it is not surprising that the figures for malt did not rise as much as those for wheat. Overall, about 39 per cent of the priory's entire grain supply came from purchases in the *Grundherrschaft* era.

Although these general trends reflect long-term processes within the priory's economy, the figures, naturally, varied not only from decade to decade but also from year to year. Both monetary and environmental factors, often inter-connected, stood behind those fluctuations. As we have seen in the previous chapter, it is likely that the quantities of grain purchased were, in many cases, determined by the price levels and there is indeed a good degree of negative correlation between prices and amounts of purchased grain. For instance, in 1273, when a quarter of wheat was selling for 7s 2d, only 25.5 quarters of wheat were purchased. Yet, seven years later, when the wheat price fell to 5s 10½d a quarter, as many as 372.25 quarters of wheat were acquired from various vendors.[24] However, this inverse relation should not be taken as a given. In years of dearth and famine, when the demesnes were unable to dispatch the planned amounts of grain, the priory authorities had no choice but to increase the numbers of grain purchases that they made. Thus, between 1315 and 1321 the amounts of grain purchased, especially malt, were unprecedentedly high, clearly

---

24. NRO, DCN 1/1/2 and 5.

Table 3.4
Frequency of crop purchases by Norwich Cathedral Priory, 1271–1536.

	Wheat	Malt	Oats	Other grains	Total	Purchased quarters per transaction
1271–80	11.0	4.0	9.5	1.0	25.5	18.4
1281–90	16.3	3.3	8.7	0.5	28.8	20.4
1291–1300	3.8	10.5	7.3	0.5	22.0	31.9
1351–60	3.0	5.3	2.0	1.0	11.3	16.5
1361–70	1.5	5.6	1.0	3.0	11.1	21.5
1371–80	4.7	4.7	1.0	2.0	12.3	34.6
1381–90	4.7	3.8	1.0	2.0	11.5	49.3
1391–1400	2.3	4.3	1.0	1.0	8.6	54.2
1401–10	2.3	4.1	1.0	1.0	8.4	40.0
1411–20	6.2	4.3	1.5	1.0	13.0	30.1
1421–30	3.4	3.9	2.0	1.0	10.3	34.0
1431–40	11.8	4.2	5.3	1.3	22.7	17.7
1441–50	9.2	3.6	6.0	2.5	21.3	16.3
1451–60	17.0	3.1	11.5	4.0	35.6	14.3
1461–70	6.0	3.7	1.0	1.0	11.7	22.9
1491–1500	5.7	2.8	3.0	2.3	13.8	29.8
1501–10	4.0	3.2	1.0	1.0	9.2	59.3
1511–20	14.0	4.0	1.0	5.0	24.0	29.4
1521–30	14.0	5.1	1.0	5.0	25.1	23.4
1531–6	14.0	3.9	1.0	5.0	23.9	14.6
1271–1300	10.4	5.9	8.5	0.7	25.4	23.6
1351–1430	3.5	4.5	1.3	1.5	10.8	35.0
1431–1536	10.6	3.7	3.4	3.0	20.8	25.3

Source: NRO, DCN 1/1/1–110.

indicating difficulties in obtaining sufficient quantities directly from the demesnes during the famine years of 1315–17 as well as the disastrous harvest of 1321. In the 1350s the figures were exceptionally low. Thus, between 1353 and 1357 they stood at 143 quarters a year, compared with 630 quarters in 1347. Interestingly enough, the 1353–7 figures were lower than in 1352 (261 quarters), which shows that the priory authorities must have had serious problems in securing grain from the demesnes during the Black Death years.[25] In 1417, the priory purchased 577 quarters of various grains. Three years later, only 110 quarters were purchased (50 quarters of wheat and 60 quarters of malted barley).[26] Many more examples can be cited.

Frequency and seasonality of transactions

How often did transactions take place? Surprisingly, the question of frequency of grain sales and purchases in late medieval England has not yet been adequately studied, notwithstanding the abundance of data, especially within the manorial sector. In the case

25. NRO, DCN 1/1/42–45.
26. NRO, DCN 1/1/73–74.

of Norwich Cathedral Priory, the detailed information about the transaction frequencies is found in the master of the cellar accounts from the 1270s through to the 1290s, and in virtually all the post-Black Death rolls with the exception of the 1470s and 1480s. The earliest surviving master of the cellar account (1263–4) does not specify the frequency of purchases.[27] The decennial distribution of transaction frequencies is shown in Table 3.4.

As Table 3.4 indicates, in the late thirteenth century replenishing the total stock of the granary would require about 13 annual transactions, each involving over 24 quarters of grain. These figures differed across decades and grain types. Thus, wheat was purchased more often than any other grain (around 10 transactions a year); oats were purchased around 8.5 times a year; while annual transactions of malted barley stood at about 6. It is unclear if these figures reflect only those three decades, or if they reveal the general trends in the pre-Black Death period. Between c.1350 and 1430, the overall numbers of transactions did not change a great deal. On the other hand, the quantities of grain acquired at each transaction rose to 35 quarters. This, undoubtedly, mirrors the post-Black Death land–population ratio, which allowed the rural producers to market larger portions of their agricultural produce. In other words, more grain could be now purchased from a single vendor. The real change, however, came with the end of the *Gutsherrschaft* economy. First, the overall number of annual transactions rose from about 11 to 21 a year. The number of annual transactions of wheat rose particularly, with 11 transactions a year on average. The figures were particularly high in the 1450s (on average, 17 annual transactions) and between the 1510s and 1536 (on average, 14 annual transactions). The figures for oats rose from 1 to about 3 transactions a year. Conversely, the number of transactions involving malt remained fairly static.

What accounts for these changes in transaction frequencies after 1431? First and foremost, the new patterns of grain acquisition, with the end of direct management are one factor. Although the bulk of the priory's grain was still arriving from the manors in the form of grain rents paid by local farmers, the vast majority of these food farms came in the form of malted barley, while wheat was sent in meagre quantities, ranging from 10 to 30 quarters a year. This fact forced the priory authorities to increase the levels of wheat purchases to meet the annual bread requirements of their community. As we have already seen, the amounts of wheat purchased from various sources did indeed increase in the post-1430 decades.

Changes in storage costs could be yet another possible factor. As we shall see below, after the Black Death, and especially after c.1376, there was a pronounced rise in storage costs per unit of grain. One way to minimise these costs was to switch to smaller-scale and more frequent transactions, meaning that smaller volumes of grain would be stored in a granary over the entire year. In other words, storing smaller amounts of grain for shorter periods of time was less costly than storing large volumes over longer periods.

What was the seasonality of grain purchases? Unfortunately, very few accounts provide any information on this subject. In fact, in the-pre Black Death era, there is only one roll (the 1279–80 roll of the master of the cellar) which specifies precise dates of purchases. Its contents, however, do not allow us to make any generalisations regarding seasonal patterns of sales, prices and consumption. All we can learn from this roll is the state of affairs in that given year. The account reveals that there were four

---

27. NRO, DCN 1/1/1.

major purchase seasons: around St Luke's Day (18 October), around the Feast of Epiphany (6 January), Easter Day (21 April 1280) and St James' Day (25 July).[28] Wheat prices were at their lowest around Easter (7½d per bushel = 5s per quarter), while they seem to have reached their annual peak in late July (10d per bushel = 7s per quarter). The prices were almost identical in October 1279 and January 1280 (around 8½d per bushel = 5s 9d per quarter). These prices seem to be practically identical to those in London in the same year.[29] It is rather surprising that the Easter prices were actually lower than those in October, since the general rule is that wheat prices rose from November, peaked between March and July and fell again afterwards.[30] But, as noted above, a single roll does not necessarily reflect trends. It should be noted that the number of purchasing seasons specified in the roll is not to be equated with the number of transactions, which was, as we have seen, considerably higher than four. It is apparent that each major purchase season included several grain transactions.

Apart from that single roll, there are no more such detailed accounts. The next best thing are two late fourteenth-century accounts (1379–80 and 1382–3) which distinguish between the amounts of grain purchased in the beginning of the accounting year (that is, around Michaelmas), and those acquired at 'various times of year'.[31] Although these two documents are too patchy to allow any definitive conclusions to be drawn, they can still be quite revealing. In 1380, 14 per cent of wheat was purchased shortly after Michaelmas, while three years later as much as around 42 per cent of wheat was purchased at that time. In other words, these two accounts reveal that the seasonality of purchases was by no means constant and that the quantities of cereals purchased in the same seasons in different years could vary greatly.

Were these transaction frequencies extraordinary when compared to other collegial households? To answer this question is by no means easy. Notwithstanding the abundant surviving material, very few monastic grain accounts specify the frequency of transactions. In most cases the accounts tend to be succinct and summary, recording only the overall expenditure and total number of quarters purchased. As we have seen, most pre-Black Death accounts of the master of the cellar did not specify the number of transactions either, and this practice of omitting the particulars was a general rule. Nevertheless, there are several accounts that provide comparative data. Thus, between 1299 and 1325, the canons of Bolton Priory were purchasing grain about 11 times a year, acquiring, on average, about 20 quarters per transaction.[32] In 1295, the canons of Hereford Cathedral purchased 35 quarters of wheat in 5 transactions (that is, 7 quarters per transaction).[33] In other words, Norwich Cathedral Priory was purchasing their grain supply with a greater frequency than Bolton Priory and Hereford Cathedral. This, however, does not mean that the former was exceptional: the silence of other conventual accounts

---

28. NRO, DCN 1/1/13 (1297–8 roll).
29. Campbell *et al.*, *A medieval capital*, p. 200.
30. Ibid., pp. 96–7.
31. NRO, DCN 1/1/57 and 59.
32. Calculated from Kershaw and Smith, *Bolton Priory compotus*.
33. Hereford Cathedral Archives, R631.

does not mean the purchases were not occurring with the same frequency there. Moreover, both Bolton Priory and Hereford Cathedral had fewer mouths to feed and, therefore, are only to be expected to have purchased less grain over fewer transactions.

Norwich grain prices, 1264–1536: between endogenous factors and exogenous shocks

No discussion of markets or market behaviour is complete without the analysis of prices. In the previous sections we have seen that the provisioning patterns were, often, dictated and shaped by the fluctuation of grain prices at a local level. To study the behaviour of Norwich grain prices a long chronological series has been created based on all the surviving obedientiary rolls (1185 in total), running between 1264 and 1536. Because of the vast nature of these accounts there are very few chronological gaps, which, nevertheless, had to be filled up by extrapolating price data from other Norfolk accounts, mostly demesne ones, and adjusting them, whenever needed, to the movement of 'national prices'. The complete picture is represented in Table 3.5 (in quinquennial means).

In some cases the prices remained more or less stable over a dozen years, while in other cases they fluctuated a great deal from year to year. Although the causes behind the long- and short-term fluctuations, deflations and inflations cannot be satisfactorily explained, they should, nevertheless, be sought in exogenous shocks and endogenous factors.[34] Thus, the high prices of 1294–5 were undoubtedly brought about, at least partially, by the Gascon War with France (1294–1303). The military campaigns as well as the defensive coinage debasement by Philip IV of France (1285–1314) in 1295 resulted in a massive outflux of English currency and the increased circulation of bad coins in England.[35] The exceedingly high prices of 1315–17 and then of 1322–3 were caused by the disastrous weather of 1314–16 and 1321 and the subsequent harvest failures.[36] It should be noted that, in sharp contrast with some other regions, the prices in Norwich and elsewhere in Norfolk stood high until 1328 inclusive. This could reflect a series of local failed harvests in 1323 and

---

34. The 'monetarist' approach to the study of price and wage behaviour in late medieval Europe is masterfully conveyed in J.H.A. Munro, 'Wage stickiness, monetary changes, and real incomes in late medieval England and the Low Countries, 1300–1500: did money matter?', *Research in Economic History*, 21 (2002), pp. 185–287. The 'environmentalist' approach is advanced by Campbell in his 'Nature as historical protagonist', pp. 281–314, esp. 284–9.

35. M. Prestwich, 'Edward I's monetary policies and their consequences', *EcHR*, 22 (1969), pp. 409–12.

36. I. Kershaw, 'The great famine and agrarian crisis in England, 1315–1322', *P&P*, 59 (1973), pp. 3–50; W.C. Jordan, *The great famine: northern Europe in the early fourteenth century* (Princeton, NJ, 1996), pp. 43–60.

37. On the Norwich Cathedral Priory demesnes, low yields were recorded in 1323 at Martham (29 per cent below average) and in 1323 at Gnatindon (21 per cent below average), Hindringham (21 per cent below average) (26 per cent below average) and Taverham (24 per cent below average). Calculated from Campbell's *Three centuries* database (http://www.cropyields.ac.uk). On the climate of East Anglia in that period, consult H.E. Hallam, 'The climate of eastern England, 1250–1350', *AHR*, 32 (1984), pp. 124–32; M. Bailey, '*Per Impetum Maris*: natural disaster and economic decline in eastern England, 1275–1350', in B.M.S. Campbell (ed.), *Before the Black Death: studies in the 'crisis' of the early fourteenth century* (Manchester, 1991), pp. 184–208.

Table 3.5
Crop prices in Norwich, 1264–1536 (in shillings per quarter).

	Wheat	Maslin	Rye	Peas	Oats	Oat bran	Barley	Malt	Composite index	Norwich wheat as % of Oxfordshire-Cambridgeshire wheat	Norwich malt as % of Oxfordshire-Cambridgeshire malt
1264–1270	4.77	4.12	3.47	2.92	2.14	1.22	3.82	4.06	1.02	1.09	1.20
1271–5	7.18	5.84	4.50	3.58	2.81	1.60	4.20	5.69	1.37	1.13	1.19
1276–80	6.64	5.20	3.76	3.44	2.40	1.33	3.98	4.99	1.23	1.29	1.18
1281–5	6.16	4.94	3.71	3.90	1.85	1.05	3.52	4.29	1.15	1.06	0.79
1286–90	4.66	3.69	2.73	2.68	1.60	0.91	3.22	2.93	0.87	1.17	0.81
1291–5	7.54	6.54	5.55	5.28	2.15	1.20	5.20	5.46	1.52	1.10	0.96
1296–1300	5.58	4.81	4.05	4.07	2.28	1.15	4.37	5.25	1.23	1.01	1.05
1301–5	5.42	4.19	2.97	3.06	1.90	1.11	3.85	3.92	1.02	1.10	0.93
1306–10	6.50	5.52	4.53	4.74	2.42	1.65	4.73	4.86	1.35	1.16	1.02
1311–5	6.09	5.01	3.92	3.88	3.02	1.37	4.45	5.16	1.27	1.04	1.14
1316–20	10.07	8.06	6.05	7.81	4.80	1.63	7.08	9.63	2.16	1.04	1.12
1321–5	11.32	8.59	5.86	5.93	2.93	1.66	5.42	6.87	1.90	1.34	1.12
1326–30	7.03	5.61	4.20	4.73	2.19	1.01	4.05	6.07	1.37	1.43	1.33
1331–5	6.51	5.60	4.70	5.06	2.15	1.07	4.63	5.06	1.36	1.21	0.99
1336–40	5.25	4.14	3.02	3.08	2.10	0.87	3.26	4.79	1.04	1.15	1.37
1341–5	4.14	3.55	2.96	2.66	1.73	0.82	3.06	3.94	0.89	1.01	1.11
1346–50	7.36	5.47	3.58	3.67	2.25	1.17	3.48	4.31	1.22	1.36	1.00
1351–5	8.43	6.31	4.19	5.12	3.62	1.51	4.66	6.06	1.55	1.17	1.02
1356–60	5.64	4.66	3.67	3.06	2.54	1.31	3.75	4.45	1.12	0.93	0.88
1361–5	5.53	4.85	4.17	4.00	3.36	1.61	4.01	5.39	1.27	0.79	0.76
1366–70	7.93	7.78	7.64	4.88	3.27	1.66	4.97	5.75	1.71	0.99	1.00
1371–5	7.45	5.78	4.10	3.16	2.96	1.69	3.86	4.68	1.29	0.96	1.04
1376–80	5.69	4.46	3.24	3.21	2.12	1.21	3.05	4.67	1.07	1.17	1.14
1381–5	5.22	4.73	4.24	2.79	2.10	1.20	3.02	3.94	1.05	0.95	0.89
1386–90	4.18	3.85	3.52	2.39	1.96	1.12	2.21	3.74	0.88	0.97	0.96
1391–5	5.67	4.29	2.92	2.49	2.21	1.26	2.99	4.23	1.00	1.14	0.95
1396–1400	5.91	4.97	4.03	4.24	2.53	1.44	3.72	4.29	1.20	1.08	0.94
1401–5	6.44	4.44	2.44	2.67	2.42	1.38	2.97	4.44	1.04	1.05	0.91

	Wheat	Maslin	Rye	Peas	Oats	Oat bran	Barley	Malt	Composite index	Norwich wheat as % of Oxfordshire-Cambridgeshire wheat	Norwich malt as % of Oxfordshire-Cambridgeshire malt
1406–10	5.81	4.87	3.92	3.96	2.79	1.59	3.01	3.74	1.14	1.07	0.87
1411–5	4.47	4.02	3.56	5.52	2.08	1.19	2.83	3.73	1.06	0.97	0.87
1416–20	6.84	5.88	4.93	4.62	2.62	1.49	3.20	4.90	1.33	1.09	1.07
1421–5	6.19	4.68	3.17	4.08	2.27	1.30	2.97	3.69	1.09	1.25	0.87
1426–30	5.90	4.72	3.54	4.92	2.08	1.18	2.93	4.06	1.14	1.05	0.88
1431–5	5.14	4.43	3.73	5.40	1.85	1.06	2.80	3.56	1.09	0.89	0.82
1436–40	7.69	6.12	4.54	4.05	2.06	1.18	4.00	4.82	1.35	0.92	0.90
1441–5	3.86	3.26	2.67	3.65	1.82	1.04	2.13	3.65	0.85	0.97	1.22
1446–50	3.98	3.90	3.81	3.35	1.65	0.94	2.27	3.52	0.91	0.70	1.02
1451–5	4.24	4.39	4.54	3.27	1.58	0.90	2.20	3.27	0.95	0.77	0.87
1456–60	4.41	3.89	3.37	3.71	1.55	0.88	2.34	2.97	0.90	0.81	0.91
1461–5	4.01	3.97	3.93	4.64	2.00	1.14	2.63	3.73	1.01	0.78	0.98
1466–70	5.35	4.69	4.03	3.65	1.86	1.06	2.83	3.75	1.06	0.97	1.05
1471–5	4.71	4.50	4.29	4.38	2.00	1.14	3.07	3.98	1.09	0.97	1.11
1476–80	6.09	4.93	3.77	5.11	1.58	0.90	2.59	3.04	1.10	1.01	1.02
1481–5	6.73	6.27	5.80	6.93	2.47	1.41	5.57	4.52	1.55	0.91	0.88
1486–90	6.07	5.56	5.05	4.06	1.36	0.77	2.01	2.61	1.08	1.13	0.82
1491–5	5.08	4.42	3.76	4.88	1.48	0.84	2.08	2.60	0.98	1.05	0.73
1496–1500	6.71	5.57	4.43	4.80	1.63	0.93	1.96	3.05	1.14	1.33	0.93
1501–5	6.46	5.91	5.36	5.02	1.88	1.08	4.25	3.30	1.29	0.97	0.87
1506–10	4.61	4.83	5.06	5.03	2.14	1.22	3.43	3.03	1.11	1.02	0.93
1511–5	7.16	5.79	4.41	7.10	2.39	1.37	4.09	3.34	1.34	1.18	1.00
1516–20	9.76	6.83	3.90	5.99	2.00	1.14	3.98	4.64	1.50	1.54	1.07
1521–5	9.37	7.85	6.32	4.64	1.82	1.04	4.50	4.37	1.57	1.35	0.88
1526–30	8.36	8.41	8.46	8.25	2.34	1.33	5.20	5.80	1.89	1.00	0.93
1531–6	7.52	9.45	11.38	7.42	2.53	1.44	3.89	4.18	1.87	0.91	0.72

Sources: NRO, DCN 1/1–12 (1185 rolls); J.H. Munro, John Munro's revisions of the Phelps Brown and Hopkins 'basket of consumables' commodity price series and craftsmen's wage series, 1264–1700, http://www.economics.utoronto.ca/munro5/ResearchData.html (please note that Phelps Brown and Hopkins' price series derives mostly from the counties of Oxfordshire and Cambridgeshire.

Notes: In 'Composite index' column, the prices are indexed on 1451–75.

1324 brought about by wet autumns and winters.[37] On the other hand, there was a serious problem of clipped and counterfeit money circulating all over the country in the early 1320s which was not resolved until 1324.[38] The low prices of 1333–46 may have been created by the combination of favourable weather, which was responsible for a dozen consecutive good harvest years (with the exception of the dry summer of 1339), and a relative scarcity of specie, reflected in mining statistics. Between 1332 and 1345 crop yields were about 27 per cent above the average.[39] On the other hand, between 1332 and 1342 annual mint outputs amounted to about £1643: an abysmally low figure compared with that of previous years, especially before 1322. Thus, between 1306 and 1310, as much as £125,836 a year was minted. These five years, however, were rather exceptional, and the annual figures stood at £33,493 and £22,760 in 1311–15 and 1316–20 respectively.[40]

In 1347 wheat prices suddenly soared almost twofold compared with the previous year. This rise may have stemmed from three factors. First, there was the full-scale military campaign against France, culminating with the battle of Crécy (26 August 1346).[41] Second, there was a sudden inauguration of gold minting in 1344, which increased the annual minting output from £14,753 to £79,955 and decreased the bi-metallic (silver:gold) ratio in England from about 17.0:1.0 to 11.5:1.0.[42] As a rule, there is a strong correlation between the levels of coinage output and those of commodity prices. Finally, the harvest of 1345 was mediocre, at the very best.[43]

Paradoxically, the prices were exceedingly high during the disastrous years of 1350–53, notwithstanding the fact that England lost at least 40 per cent of its population. This contradicts the Ricardian logic emphasising the inverse relationship between population growth and price levels. First, the high prices of the pestilence years may reflect the scarcity of working hands to cultivate the soil and, consequently, reduced harvests. Second, they may also have been caused by three back-to-back harvest failures of 1349–51, which stemmed not only from the widespread mortality and lack of a workforce, but also from the cold and wet weather of those years.[44] It is possible that both factors contributed to the high prices. In 1354 prices collapsed once more and they remained around 1296–1305 levels until 1369; in 1370–71, they

---

38. M. Mate, 'High prices in early fourteenth century England: causes and consequences', *EcHR*, 28 (1975), p. 13.
39. Calculated from Campbell's *Three centuries* database (http://www.cropyields.ac.uk).
40. Calculated from J.H.A. Munro, *John Munro's database of coinage output in England* (http://www.economics.utoronto.ca/munro5/MoneyCoinage.htm) (accessed 11 October 2011).
41. On the connection between warfare and price movement during the Hundred Years War, consult J.H.A. Munro, 'The "New institutional economics" and the changing fortunes of fairs in medieval and early modern Europe: the textile trades, warfare and transaction costs', *Vierteljahrschrift für Sozial- und Wirtschaftgeschichte*, 88/1 (2001), pp. 1–47.
42. P. Spufford, *Money and its use in medieval Europe* (Cambridge, 1988), p. 272.
43. Nationally, the 1346 harvest was 17 per cent below average. Calculated from Campbell's *Three centuries* database (http://www.cropyields.ac.uk).
44. As Campbell most recently contended. See Campbell, 'Four famines and a pestilence', p. 34; B.M.S. Campbell, 'Agriculture in Kent in the High Middle Ages', in S. Sweetinburgh (ed.), *Later medieval Kent, 1220–1540* (Woodbridge, 2010), p. 45.

soared again to their 1350–53 level. This may have been caused by the disastrous harvests of 1369 and 1370, when harvests on some of the priory demesnes were between 40 and 60 per cent below average.[45] Although prices fell once more in 1372, it was not until 1376, the year of the 'Good Parliament', that they drastically collapsed. It can hardly be a coincidence that the beginning of the deflation went hand-in-hand with a drastic decline in the volume of minted coinage. The overall output fell from an annual average of £35,810 in 1371–5 to £11,519 in 1376–80 and £8200 in 1381–5.[46] In other words, it was not until c.1376 that the post-Black Death deflation became definitive and prolonged.[47]

The deflation which ensued in 1376 cannot be solely attributed to decreased coinage output, however. With the exception of 1390, crop yields were exceptionally high in all years between 1376 and 1399, both in Norfolk and elsewhere in the country; over this period they were 13 per cent higher than average. It should not be surprising that the failed harvest of 1390 resulted in high grain prices in 1391, while the excessively high yields of 1391, on the other hand, caused prices to collapse once more a year later. Similarly, the relatively high prices of 1401–02 may have been created by the bad harvests of 1400–01,[48] while the low yields of 1416 may well have driven up the grain prices in the following year.[49] Apart from these three years, however, prices did not oscillate until the late 1430s. The terrible harvests of 1437–8, resulting from a short-term climatic anomaly, inflated prices once more.[50] Just like the short-term inflations of 1315–17 and 1350–53, the high prices of 1438–40 stress the

---

45. Thus, the wheat yields at Eaton, Melton, Plumstead and Sedgeford were 60, 58, 60 and 52 per cent below average in 1369. The yields fared better in the following year, but, then again, the wheat yield at Plumstead was some 45 per cent below average. Calculated from Campbell's *Three centuries* database (http://www.cropyields.ac.uk).

46. Calculated from Munro's *John Munro's database of coinage output* (http://www.economics.utoronto.ca/munro5/MoneyCoinage.htm).

47. A more detailed and most important study on the post-Plague prices and wages is J.H.A. Munro, 'Before and after the Black Death: money, prices and wages in fourteenth-century England', in T. Dahlerup and P. Ingesman (eds), *New approaches to the history of late medieval and early modern Europe: selected proceedings of two international conferences at the Royal Danish Academy of Sciences and Letters in Copenhagen in 1997 and 1999*, Historisk-filosofiske Meddelelser, no. 104 (Copenhagen, 2009), pp. 335–64.

48. At Hindringham, Martham and Sedgeford, the crop yields were approximately 45 per cent below average in 1400. The information about the harvest of 1401 can be extracted from only one surviving account, that of Sedgeford, which, nevertheless, indicates that the yields were only 68 per cent the average level. On the national level, the crop yields stood at 63 per cent of their national level. Calculated from Campbell's *Three centuries* database (http://www.cropyields.ac.uk).

49. The Norfolk yields were about 30 per cent below average in that year. Nationally, the yields were about 61 per cent of their normal level. Calculated from Campbell's *Three centuries* database (http://www.cropyields.ac.uk).

50. The years of 1436–9 were exceedingly cold in Europe. It is unclear what stood behind this short-term climatic anomaly, but, as Campbell has recently advanced, the eruption of Mount Fuji may have been a contributing factor. See Campbell, 'Four famines and a pestilence', pp. 30 and 46. National crop yields were about 51 and 39 per cent below average in 1437 and 1438, respectively, as calculated from Campbell's *Three centuries* database (http://www.cropyields.ac.uk).

profound impact of climatic anomalies on the economy. It should be noted that monetary factors did not seem to have contributed anything to this inflation: between 1437 and 1440 only £9369 was minted per year, compared to £47,922 per year between 1431 and 1435.[51] Minting output was badly depressed until the debasement of Edward IV (1461–83) in 1464–5 because of both failed military campaigns in France towards the end of the Hundred Years War and a chronic scarcity of precious metals across northern and western Europe known as the 'Bullion Famine'.[52] Moreover, between the 1440s and the 1460s Norwich experienced a harsh political and economic crisis which resulted in a serious slump in trade and fall in rental income.[53] This strongly correlates with the low grain prices between 1441 and 1469. Interestingly enough, however, the debasement of 1464–5 did not drive up prices, which, with some minor exceptions, exhibited long-term stability until c.1513 – that is, until the beginning of the 'Price Revolution'. It seems that all those short-term inflations should be viewed against the environmental shocks of the period. Thus, the elevated prices of 1478–9 and 1482–3 may well have something to do with the harvest failures of 1476–8 and 1481–2. The oscillations of the early sixteenth century, on the other hand, cannot be divorced from the contemporary monetary policies of Henry VIII (1507–49), in particular the two debasements of 1526. Although these are overshadowed by the Great Henrican Debasement of 1542–53, they are still clearly reflected in the increased minting output and, consequently, risen prices of 1528–9.[54]

A close analysis of grain price movements reveals that the two approaches – the 'monetarist' and the 'environmentalist' – do not contradict, but, on the contrary, complement each other, for it is impossible to appreciate both the short- and long-term trends in price oscillations without considering these two sides of the coin. Thus, in 1315–17, 1350–53 and 1438–40 nature was fully responsible for elevating prices, while in 1294–5, 1347 and 1528–9 we should blame institutional and monetary factors for driving prices up. In some cases, it is likely that nature and institutions collaborated in controlling price behaviour. Perhaps the best example is the period of low prices 1333–46, which saw a dozen years of good harvests while also experiencing an enormous slump in minting output.

Market integration?

To what degree did the situation in Norwich reflect that elsewhere in the country? As Table 3.5 shows, although Norwich and 'Oxfordshire-Cambridgeshire' prices marched in generally the same direction, they exhibited some visible differences nevertheless. With some exceptions, wheat and malt prices were markedly higher in Norwich than

---

51. Calculated from Munro's *John Munro's database of coinage output* (http://www.economics.utoronto.ca/munro5/MoneyCoinage.htm).
52. The situation is analysed by Munro ('Wage stickiness').
53. A. King, 'The merchant class and borough finances in late medieval Norwich', DPhil thesis (University of Oxford, 1989), p. 394.
54. For a full-scale study of the Henrican debasements, see J.H.A. Munro, 'The coinages and monetary policies of Henry VIII (r. 1509–1547): contrasts between defensive and aggressive debasements', University of Toronto Working Paper no. 417 (MUNRO: no. 40), November 2010.

elsewhere in the country in the pre-Black Death period. From 1356 onwards, however, Norwich prices varied a great deal, falling short of, matching and exceeding the 'Oxfordshire-Cambridgeshire' level. Thus, in the periods of 1356–65, 1431–40, 1451–60, 1481–5 and 1531–6 both wheat and malt prices in Norwich fell behind those elsewhere in the country; and between 1446 and 1465 wheat was selling considerably cheaper in Norwich than elsewhere. It should be kept in mind, however, that different crops did not march hand-in-hand with each other. For instance, in the periods of 1406–10 and 1421–5, Norwich malt prices were below the 'Oxfordshire-Cambridgeshire' level (0.87:1.00), while the wheat ones exceeded it (1.25:1.00). Between 1441 and 1445, on the other hand, Norwich malt prices stood well above the 'Oxfordshire-Cambridgeshire' average (1.22:1.00), while its wheat was slightly less expensive than in other regions. This divergence between the two grains was especially apparent between 1486 and 1536, when wheat prices were relatively high while those of malt were, in most cases, below the 'Oxfordshire-Cambridgeshire' level.

This brings us to the question of market integration. According to some evidence, late medieval and early modern grain markets in England and elsewhere in Europe achieved a good degree of integration, measured, *inter alia*, in price levels in different market regions and commercial involvement between different geographic areas. Cases for market integration have been made for the Low Countries, Sicily, Germany, and, of course, England, where price data is particularly abundant.[55] While these studies indeed provide a great deal of evidence in defence of market integration in various parts of Europe, it should not be taken for granted as a universal and ubiquitous phenomenon, as the case of Norwich's prices shows. What were the reasons for these price differences between Norwich and other regions? Are they connected to institutional inefficiency, which could not provide commercial security and thus decrease transaction costs in order to encourage market integration? Or, perhaps, were transportation costs too high to promote market integration? Contemporary evidence from Norwich proves otherwise. In the late medieval period Norwich was one of the most important commercial centres in England, and maintained strong commercial links not only with its rural hinterland and other major commercial towns, including London, Winchester and Newcastle, but

---

55. Consider, for instance, various studies on the subject in J.A. Galloway (ed.), *Trade, urban hinterlands and market integration c.1300–1600*, Centre for Metropolitan History, Working Papers Series, No. 3 (London, 2000); Britnell, *Britain and Ireland*, pp. 130–33; M. Aloisio, 'A test case for regional market integration? The grain trade between Malta and Sicily in the late Middle Ages', in L. Armstrong, I. Elbl and M.M. Elbl (eds), *Money, markets and trade in late medieval Europe: essays in honour of John H.A. Munro* (Leiden, 2007), pp. 297–309; D. Nicholas, 'Commercial credit and central place function in thirteenth-century Ypres', in L. Armstrong, I. Elbl and M.M. Elbl (eds), *Money, markets and trade in late medieval Europe: essays in honour of John H.A. Munro* (Leiden, 2007), pp. 310–48; R.W. Unger, 'Thresholds for market integration in the Low Countries and England in the fifteenth century', in L. Armstrong, I. Elbl and M.M. Elbl (eds), *Money, markets and trade in late medieval Europe: essays in honour of John H.A. Munro* (Leiden, 2007), pp. 349–81. More recent contributions include V.N. Bateman, 'The Evolution of markets in early modern Europe, 1350–1800: a study of wheat prices', *EcHR*, 64 (2011), pp. 447–71, and J. Dijkman, *Shaping medieval markets: the organization of commodity markets in Holland, c.1200–c.1450* (Leiden, 2011).

also with overseas merchants, mostly from Hanseatic ports but also from the Low Countries.[56] Furthermore, and in most cases, the municipal authorities, headed by four bailiffs and from 1404 onwards by a mayor and two sheriffs, themselves came from the mercantile class. Some fifteenth-century mayors were elected from among prominent long-distance merchants, who, as such, must have had a strong interest in promoting trade and offering protection to merchants.[57] But, although Norwich had all the required preconditions for an integrated market, its price levels were not, in many cases, uniform with those in other places.

Perhaps an answer is to be sought in the local context of Norwich and its hinterland. After all, each town and region experienced different periods in different ways. Thus, although on the national level demographic growth was, for the most part, halted after the Great Famine of 1315–17/22, there is compelling evidence that Norfolk continued to experience population growth all the way up to the Black Death.[58] Could this partially explain the fact that post-famine prices in Norfolk remained high until 1328, in contrast with the situation in other parts of England? Also, unlike some other urban centres, Norwich does not seem to have experienced 'urban decay' in the course of the fifteenth century. On the contrary, its authorities managed to cope with the post-Black Death reality remarkably well and, as a result, its social and economic life continued to be vibrant. This is not to say, however, that the town knew no crises in the post-Black Death era. Thus, in 1443 John Gladman, a wealthy merchant, led a popular revolt against the priory which, although nobody was injured, had harsh consequences for Norwich: its liberties were seized, its citizens were fined 3000 marks and it was placed under royal rule. Although the *status quo ante* was restored in 1447, the city's economy was depressed for at least 15 years.[59] This, in turn, may explain why Norwich grain prices were lower than elsewhere in the country between *c*.1446 and 1465.

The gaps in price levels cannot, however, be explained solely by the urban context. After all, crops were produced on country fields, and because of that fact it is essential to consider the unique rural milieu of the Norwich hinterland. As we shall see in the following chapter, *c*.1300 Norfolk was one of the most progressive and productive agricultural regions in England. It practised one of the most intensive agricultural regimes in the country, allocating large proportions of its arable to barley and

---

56. B. Ayers, 'Archaeological evidence for trade in Norwich from the 12th to the 17th centuries', in M. Gläser (ed.), *Lübecker Kolloquium zur Stadtarchäologie im Hanseraum, II: Der Handel* (Lübeck, 1999), pp. 25–35; P. Nightingale, 'Norwich, London, and the regional integration of Norfolk's economy in the first half of the fourteenth century', in J.A. Galloway (ed.), *Trade, urban hinterlands and market integration c.1300–1600*, Centre for Metropolitan History, Working Papers Series, No. 3 (London, 2000), pp. 83–101; Dunn, 'Trade'. It should be noted, however, that after the Black Death the national commercial importance of Norwich was lost to Yarmouth, a toll-free port (Dunn, 'Trade', p. 228).

57. Dunn, 'Trade', p. 227.

58. B.M.S. Campbell, 'Population pressure, inheritance and the land market in a fourteenth century peasant community', in R.M. Smith (ed.), *Land, kinship and life-cycle* (Cambridge, 1984), pp. 87–134.

59. King, 'The merchant class', p. 394.

60. B.M.S. Campbell, 'Commercial dairy production on medieval English demesnes: the case of Norfolk', *Anthropozoologica*, 16 (1992), pp. 107–18.

specialising in malt production and commercial dairy farming.[60] Norfolk malt was renowned for its fine quality, and it was because of this that its relative price was higher than elsewhere in England, at least in the pre-Black Death period.[61] Also, as manorial accounts indicate, Norwich demesnes succeeded in attaining higher wheat yields than many other parts of the country, thanks to both institutional arrangements and favourable environmental conditions.[62] This, in turn, may well explain why wheat prices in Norwich stood above the 'Oxfordshire-Cambridgeshire' level. In order to appreciate the peculiarity of Norwich market developments better, it is necessary to divert from urban trade and focus on countryside production, as exemplified by the landed estates of Norwich Cathedral Priory in the *Gutsherrschaft* era.

---

61. See Chapter 4.
62. B.M.S. Campbell, 'Agricultural progress in medieval England: some evidence from eastern Norfolk', *EcHR*, 36 (1983), pp. 26–46; B.M.S. Campbell, 'Arable productivity in medieval England: some evidence from Norfolk', *JEH*, 43 (1983), pp. 379–404; B.M.S. Campbell, *English seigniorial agriculture 1250–1450* (Cambridge, 2000), pp. 317–22.

Chapter 4

Grain production on Norwich Cathedral Priory demesnes

The era of direct management

By 1300 Norwich Cathedral Priory was one of the wealthiest landlords in East Anglia in general and Norfolk in particular. It possessed 20 demesnes shared between several monastic officials, all but one located in Norfolk (one demesne, Denham, was situated in northern Suffolk).[1] Around 1300, the total size of its arable holdings approached 3000 acres and its annual income was around £1500 (see Figure 4.1). The size of its landed possessions and income is commensurate with those of the Abbey of Bury St Edmunds, a fellow great East Anglian lord located in the neighbouring county of Suffolk. The landed estates of most other Norfolk lords, both religious and lay, were considerably smaller, in many cases including just one or a few manors.[2] At the same time, however, Norwich Cathedral Priory was exceeded in wealth by another major East Anglian lord, the bishop of Ely, who at around the same time held some 50 demesnes spread across Norfolk, Suffolk, Cambridgeshire, Huntingdonshire, Hertfordshire and Essex, which yielded between £3000 and £3500 a year.[3] Most other religious magnates, however, were less wealthy than the bishop of Ely. Also in eastern England, Ramsey Abbey and Peterborough Cathedral Priory had between 20 and 25 demesnes each.[4] In the West Midlands, Worcester Cathedral Priory and the bishop of Worcester had 25 manors each.[5] In Hampshire and Wiltshire, Winchester Cathedral Priory was endowed with some 22 manors.[6] Elsewhere in the country, a few magnates were considerably wealthier then these. Thus, Westminster Abbey, patronised by the royal family, possessed over 50 demesnes scattered all over the country and yielding about £1700 a year.[7] Canterbury Cathedral Priory, headed by the most influential religious figure in the country, the Archbishop of Canterbury, held slightly over 60 manors, mostly in Kent, adding some £2500 to its yearly income.[8] Only

---

1. R. Virgoe, 'The estates of Norwich Cathedral Priory', in I. Atherton, E.C. Fernie and C. Harper-Bill (eds), *Norwich Cathedral: church, city and diocese, 1096–1996* (London, 1996), pp. 339–59.

2. On the lordship of Norfolk manors, see Campbell, *English seigniorial agriculture*, pp. 453–66 (Appendix 2).

3. E. Miller, *The abbey and bishopric of Ely: the social history of an ecclesiastical estate from the tenth century to the early fourteenth century* (Cambridge, 1951), pp. 77–81.

4. J.A. Raftis, *The estates of Ramsey Abbey: a study in economic growth and organization* (Toronto, 1957), p. 20; K. Biddick, *The other economy: pastoral husbandry on a medieval estate* (Berkeley, CA, 1989).

5. C. Dyer, *Lords and peasants in a changing society* (Cambridge, 1980), p. 8; Worcester Cathedral Archives, C529–869.

6. J. Hare, 'The bishop and prior: demesne agriculture in medieval Hampshire', *AHR*, 54/1 (2006), pp. 187–212.

7. Harvey, *Westminster Abbey*, pp. 335–64.

8. F.R.H DuBoulay, *The lordship of Canterbury: an essay on medieval society* (London, 1966).

Grain production on Norwich Cathedral Priory demesnes

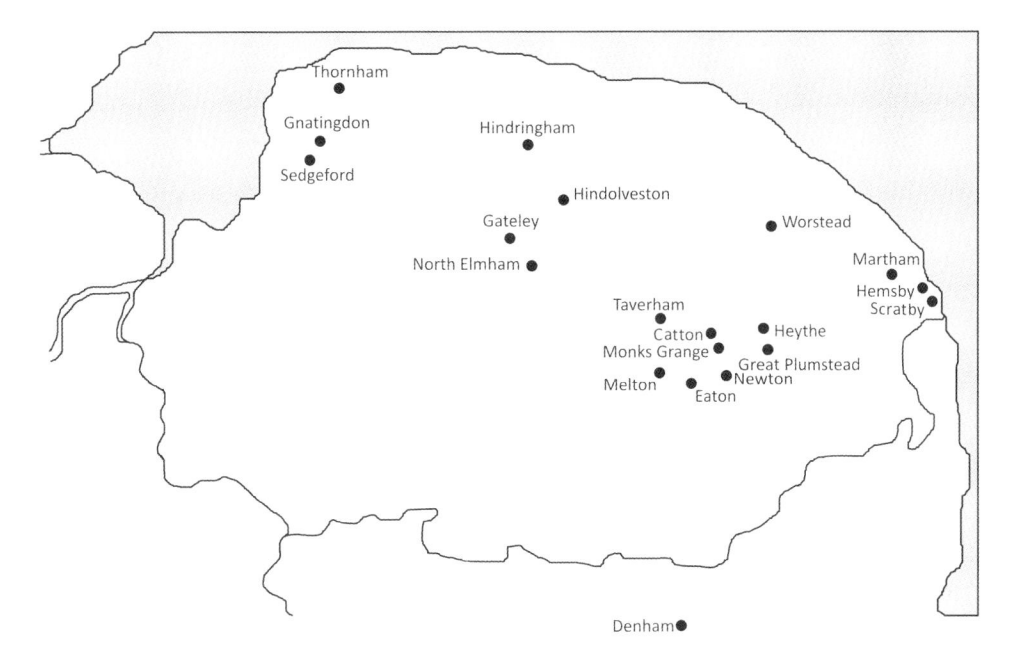

Figure 4.1 Landed estates of Norwich Cathedral Priory in the early fourteenth century.

a few magnates were wealthier than these. Glastonbury Abbey, associated with the legendary King Arthur and the Holy Grail, owned around 40 demesnes in the southern counties around the same time.[9] The bishop of Winchester had 57 manors, mostly in Hampshire, earning him about £3000 a year.[10] None, however, could trump the estates of the Knights Templar, which consisted of at least 103 directly managed demesnes on the eve of their suppression in 1308–10.[11] But even this gargantuan estate pales before the manorial empires of Guy Beauchamps, earl of Warwick, and Gilbert de Clare, earl of Gloucester and Hertford, each endowed with over 150 manors.[12]

The manors of Norwich Cathedral Priory were unevenly scattered throughout the county (Figure 4.1). Nine demesnes were concentrated in the immediate hinterland of Norwich, within a radius of around five miles. Two of these demesnes, Monks Granges and Heythe (the latter created around 1330) were, in effect, home farms. These manors were situated on the crossroad of four regions: central Norfolk, south Norfolk, north-eastern Norfolk and Broadland. The hinterland of Norwich is diverse in geology and soil types, which range from light to medium loams, through clays to chalky soils

---

9. I.J.E. Keil, 'Estates of Glastonbury Abbey in the later Middle Ages', PhD thesis (University of Bristol, 1964).
10. B.M.S. Campbell, 'A unique estate and a unique source: the Winchester Pipe Rolls in perspective', in R.H. Britnell (ed.), *The Winchester Pipe Rolls and medieval English society* (Woodbridge, 2003), pp. 21–43.
11. TNA, E 358/18–20.
12. Campbell and Bartley, *Eve of the Black Death*, pp. 69–71.

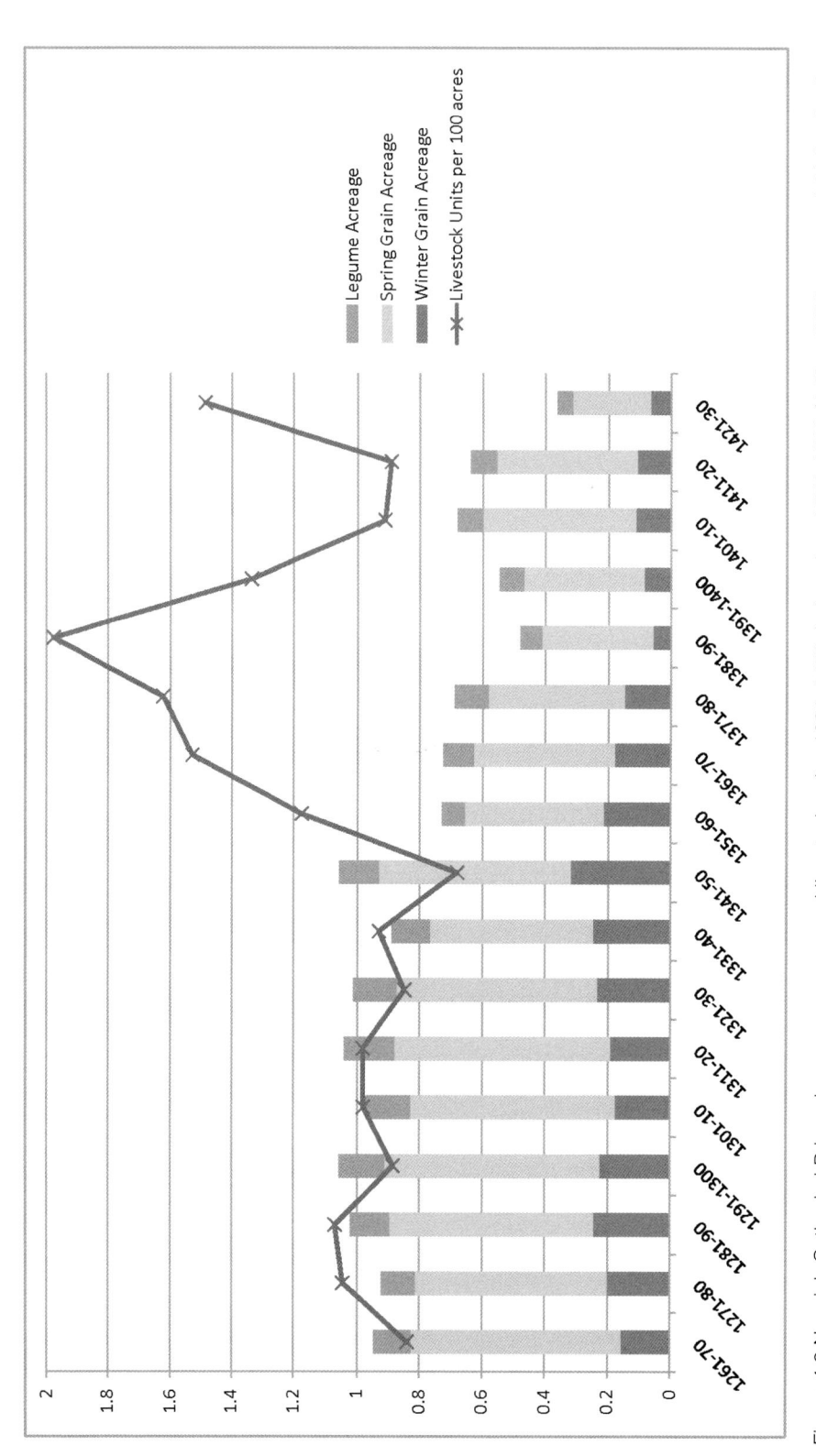

Figure 4.2 Norwich Cathedral Priory demesne acreage and livestock units, 1261–1430, indexed on 1271–1300 (1.00 = 2722 acres and 31.9 animal units per 100 acres).
Source: Manorial accounts database.

and patches of acid sands. On the eastern coast, there were three productive demesnes, Martham, Scratby and Hemsby, all located in Flegg district, characterised by particularly fertile and easily worked medium loamy and clayey soils, and lying close to Great Yarmouth. The manor of Worstead was located on deep loams in the north-east of the county. In central Norfolk three further demesnes, Gateley, Hindolveston and North Elmham, were on boulder-clay soils and situated in relative isolation from any major town. Finally, four further demesnes were situated in north-west Norfolk. Three of these, Thornham, Sedgeford and Gnatingdon (the two latter were amalgamated into one settlement sometime before 1281, although they were still considered two separate demesnes, and later farms, until at least the sixteenth century) were located on light chalky soils very close to the sea, while Hindringham was further inland, on heavy boulder-clay soils. With the exception of Hindringham and Hindolveston, no demesne was elevated higher than 200 feet (61m) above sea level; moreover, the coastal manors of Martham and Hemsby, as well as the majority of Norwich's immediate hinterland, were located at an altitude of between 3 and 12 feet (0.9–3.7m). Outside Norfolk, the Norwich brethren were endowed with the manor of Denham, situated on the clayey soils of the Eye district in north Suffolk.

The aggregate size of the demesne of the Norwich brethren varied from decade to decade, depending on the size of sown acreage and the number of the demesnes in hand. Although leases were not a commonplace before the Black Death, the priory authorities farmed out three demesnes (Hindolveston, Hindringham and Thornham) in the 1330s, when grain prices (temporarily) collapsed, only to take them back in the following decade, when prices soared once more. Around the same time, Denham was no longer managed directly and it is possible that it was leased out as early as the 1320s. Shortly after the pestilence, however, the brethren leased out four demesnes in addition to Denham: Catton, Hindolveston (which, nevertheless, was taken back in hand in the 1360s), Thornham and North Elmham. In the course of the 1380s and 1390s Eaton, Melton, Monks Granges, Plumstead and Taverham followed. This leasing policy was reversed in the two first decades of the fifteenth century, when most demesnes were taken back in hand. The temporary revival of direct management, however, was short-lived; in the course of the 1420s the demesnes were set at farm again and in 1431 Sedgeford, the last manor to be directly exploited, was leased out too. The era of *Gutsherrschaft* on the demesnes of Norwich Cathedral Priory was over.

As Figure 4.2 indicates, total livestock numbers began to fall, slowly but surely, from the 1280s. This decline can be explained by both exogenous and institutional factors. First, the Great Cattle Pestilence of 1319–20 killed about 62 per cent of English and Welsh bovids.[13] Unlike those in many other parts in England, the managers of Norwich

---

13. T.P. Newfield, 'A cattle panzootic in early fourteenth-century Europe', *AHR*, 57 (2009), pp. 155–190; P. Slavin, 'The fifth rider of the apocalypse: the great cattle plague in England and Wales and its economic consequences, 1319–1350', in S. Cavaciocchi (ed.), *Le interazioni fra economia e ambiente biologico nell'Europa preindustriale, secc. XIII–XVIII. Proceedings of the 41st Study-Week of the Fondazione Istituto Internazionale di Storia Economica 'F. Datini'* (Firenze, 2010), pp. 165–79; P. Slavin, 'The great bovine pestilence and its economic and environmental consequences in England and Wales, 1318–50', *EcHR*, forthcoming; the early view version is available at: http://onlinelibrary.wiley.com/journal/10.1111/(ISSN)1468–0289/earlyview.

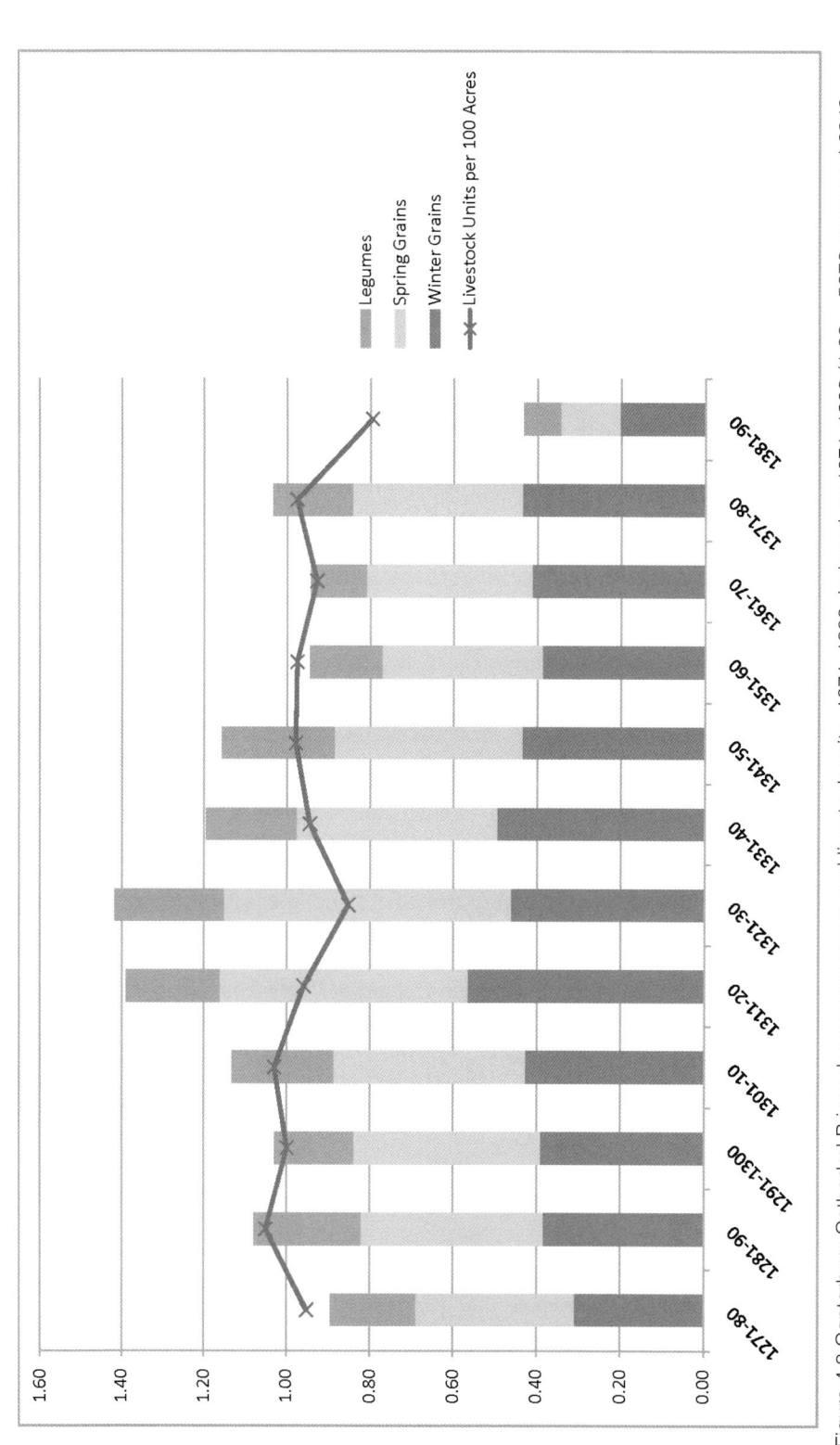

Figure 4.3 Canterbury Cathedral Priory demesne acreage and livestock units, 1271–1390, indexed on 1271–1300 (1.00 = 5276 acres and 2948 livestock units).
Source: Manorial accounts database.

Cathedral Priory's estates seem to have taken a deliberate decision not to restock to the pre-1319 numbers of oxen, which were replaced with horses (it would require about 1.33–1.5 oxen to perform the same work as one horse).[14] Moreover, from *c.*1310 and chiefly after the bovine murrain, there was a growing tendency to lease out dairy cows (with their annual issue) to local tenants.[15] The situation changed in the immediate aftermath of the Black Death, when the relative numbers of livestock rose to unprecedented levels, undoubtedly reflecting the shift from arable husbandry to pastoralism after the plague. This, however, was a temporary resurgence and between 1400 and 1420 livestock density started declining once more, as the priory authorities augmented the arable share of their husbandry. However, during the 1420s, the last decade of direct management, the figures of livestock density rose again, corresponding with the shrinkage of the arable sector. It should be noted, however, that the pastoral sector was secondary in importance in the *Grundherrschaft* economy of Norwich Cathedral Priory, as it was in that of Norfolk and East Anglia in general. This region practised one of the most intensive agricultural regimes in the country, strongly relying on arable and allocating a large proportion of its acreage to spring grains.[16] Indeed, over the decades, this disproportion between winter and spring grains was the distinctive feature of Norfolk agriculture, as exemplified by the demesnes of Norwich Cathedral Priory. Over the entire period under study, between 60 and 70 per cent of all arable was sown with spring crops. Barley was the predominant crop here, occupying around 80 per cent of the spring acreage.

In terms of its chronology and fluctuations in its structure, the *Grundherrschaft* economy of Norwich Cathedral Priory differed in many ways from that of other late medieval lords. First, the Norwich brethren tended to keep their demesnes in hand somewhat longer than their other counterparts. Although the majority of the demesnes was permanently leased out within two or three decades of the Black Death, the era of direct management was not over until 1431. For comparison, between *c.*1380 and 1405 most of the demesnes of Canterbury Cathedral Priory, Westminster Abbey, Bury St Edmunds Abbey, Worcester Cathedral Priory, the bishopric of Worcester and Durham Cathedral Priory were farmed out on a permanent basis.[17] Second, the differences were not only chronological, but also structural. As Figure 4.3 demonstrates, on Canterbury Cathedral Priory demesnes the winter and spring acreages were similar in extent and distribution. Moreover, the decline within Canterbury's arable sector began *before* the Black Death, from the third decade of the fourteenth century onwards. Interestingly enough, the pestilence itself did not decrease the total acreage under arable as

---

14. J. Langdon, *Horses, oxen and technological innovation: the use of draught animals in English farming from 1066 to 1500* (Cambridge, 1986), pp. 159–64.
15. P. Slavin, 'Between death and survival: Norfolk cattle, *c.*1280–1370', *Fons Luminis*, 1 (2008), pp. 53–7.
16. Campbell, *English Seigniorial agriculture*, pp. 172–83; Campbell and Bartley, *Eve of the Black Death*, pp. 209–30.
17. Harvey, *Westminster Abbey*, p. 268; F.R.H. DuBoulay, 'Who were farming the English demesnes at the end of the Middle Ages?' *EHR*, 17/3 (1965), pp. 445–6; Dyer, *Lords and peasants*, p. 147; R.A. Lomas, 'The Priory of Durham and its demesnes in the fourteenth and fifteenth centuries', *EHR*, 31/3 (1978), p. 345.

Table 4.1
Arable composition of English demesnes, c.1300:
Norfolk, eastern England, northern England and national.

	Wheat	Rye/maslin	Legumes	Oats/dredge
Norwich Cathedral	10.61%	12.91%	14.58%	13.50%
Norfolk	12.26%	11.99%	13.58%	14.80%
Lincolnshire	36.38%	10.89%	12.38%	23.44%
Suffolk	26.41%	16.27%	11.97%	31.67%
Cambridgeshire	27.66%	11.90%	8.80%	36.87%
Northern	14.16%	10.83%	2.00%	72.12%
National	30.00%	7.37%	12.00%	34.00%

Source: Manorial accounts database.
Note: Northern counties include Cumberland, Durham, Lancashire, Northumberland and Yorkshire. Unfortunately, no Westmorland account survives from that period.

drastically as it did on Norwich Cathedral demesnes. While the latter experienced a steady fall in its arable acreage in the post-Black Death decades, there is good evidence that there was a recovery in the size of crop acreage on the demesnes of Canterbury Cathedral Priory. In the 1370s the total arable acreage at Canterbury was slightly larger than it was in the 1290s, the peak of the direct management period. The main change, however, came in the 1380s, when most demesnes were leased out, never to be recovered. The pastoral sector, too, exhibits different behaviour from Norwich's, remaining more or less stable between the 1270s and the 1370s (in terms of stocking density, measured in animal units per 100 acres). The only exception was the 1320s, when Canterbury estates suffered heavy losses during the bovine mortality.[18] Numbers of animals fell once more in the 1380s, marking the end of the *Gutsherrschaft* economy on Canterbury Cathedral Priory demesnes.

The comparison of these two *Gutsherrschaft* economies indicates pronounced regional differences in agricultural regimes between different parts of England. Does the arable structure of Norfolk, however, characterised by a strong bias towards barley growing, reflect the wider regional context of eastern England? In order to appreciate the composition of the arable acreage on Norwich Cathedral Priory's estates, it is instructive to compare it with both regional and national trends in agriculture. Table 4.1, based on over 3600 manorial accounts, provides both a regional and a national sample of arable structures around the year 1300. As the table indicates, the arable structure of Norwich Cathedral Priory estates reflects, virtually exactly, the situation elsewhere in Norfolk. What is truly remarkable, however, is that the situation was different once we leave Norfolk and go to the adjacent counties: Lincolnshire, Suffolk and Cambridgeshire. Despite having many geographic and ecological features in common with Norfolk (such as the Fens, coastal settlements, the Wash, the predominance of clayey soil and lowland relief), these counties' agrarian structures were altogether different. Lincolnshire was much more orientated towards wheat production, while barley did not exceed 17 per

---

18. Campbell, 'Agriculture in Kent', pp. 48–9; Slavin, 'The great bovine pestilence'.

Barley	Winter grains	Spring grains	Demesne arable (average acreage)	No. of accounts examined
48.40%	23.52%	61.90%	188.2	142
47.30%	24.26%	62.09%	192.6	269
16.90%	47.27%	40.34%	148.7	48
13.68%	42.68%	45.35%	212.6	95
14.76%	39.56%	51.63%	225.8	45
0.88%	24.99%	73.01%	188.1	80
16.63%	37.37%	50.63%	206.4	1618

cent of its acreage around 1300. The proportion of barley was even smaller in Suffolk and Cambridgeshire (around 15 per cent), while oats occupied around one-third of all the arable acreage at around the same time. In the northern counties, just as in Norfolk, there was a pronounced biased towards spring-sown crops: almost three-quarters of all arable was sown with spring oats (to be distinguished from winter oats, found on a very small number of demesnes in England and Wales). In fact, an oat monoculture was widespread on some northern demesnes, as well as in Derbyshire and Shropshire.[19] This was also the situation on some De Lacy demesnes in Lancashire, as well as on several Cumbrian estates of Isabella de Fortibus.[20] Barley, on the other hand, was virtually unknown in the north, and legumes too were rarely grown in those regions. South of the Humber the proportions of winter and spring grains were more equal, but even here exceptions were not unheard of. For instance, on one Kentish estate of Canterbury Cathedral Priory (Stone-cum-Ebony), as much as 85 per cent of its total arable acreage (some 130 acres) was allocated to oats.[21] On the national level, oats clearly exceeded barley, while rye was a much less widespread grain than wheat.

Norfolk's figure for barley of 47 per cent is only an average one and the share of this crop varied from place to place across the county. Thus, at Worstead (the manor of St Benet on Holm, rather than that of Norwich Cathedral Priory), Eaton, Heigham-by-Norwich and Catton between 70 and 80 per cent of all arable was sown with barley. At Earsham and Gateley, on the other hand, barley occupied no more than 10–15 per cent. But these two manors were exceptions, and the majority of Norfolk demesnes were indeed clearly barley-orientated. Outside Norfolk, there were very few demesnes

---

19. I.S.W. Blanchard, 'Economic change in Derbyshire in the late Middle Ages', PhD thesis (London School of Economics, 1967), pp. 28–9.
20. TNA, SC 6/824/1–15; SC 6/1094/11; Durham Cathedral Archives, Lytham accounts; P.A. Lyons (ed.), *Two compoti of the Lancashire and Cheshire manors of Henry de Lacy, Earl of Lincoln*, Chetham Society 122 (Manchester, 1884).
21. Canterbury Cathedral Archives, DCc/Ebony/1–32.

that could match these figures in terms of barley specialisation. Thus, at Highclere and Prior's Barton (both Hampshire), Enford (Wiltshire), Westonzoyland (Somerset) and Dunningsworth and Westley (both Suffolk) barley occupied slightly more than a half of all arable around 1300: truly impressive proportions for non-Norfolk demesnes.[22] It is important to distinguish between winter sown- and spring-sown barley, the former being far less common than the latter. In effect, there is no difference between the two crops (*Hordeum vulgare* L.), except that winter-sown barley is much less advantageous because of its intolerance to cold (and therefore it is planted much less as a sinter crop). It is not surprising, then, that no more than some 1.5 per cent of all arable was sown with winter barley (in contrast with some 17 per cent dedicated to spring barley) at the national level.[23] With the exception of two demesnes, West Walton and Wiggenhall, it was the spring variety of barley that was grown in Norfolk.[24]

What accounts for this unusual structure of arable husbandry in Norfolk? Why did its lords and their demesne managers chose to allocate such large proportions of their land to barley? And, most intriguingly, how can we explain specialisation in barley as an all-Norfolk phenomenon? In other words, why we do not find the same bias in the neighbouring counties of Suffolk, Cambridgeshire and Lincolnshire, despite common environmental features, as we have seen? Several explanations can be offered. First, we may consider the demographic factor. Norfolk was the most densely settled county in England in the first half of the fourteenth century, with approximately 137 taxpayers per ten square miles around 1330.[25] Population pressure inevitably leads to poverty and, consequently, falling living standards. In many cases, as our accounts indicate, barley was baked into bread the price of which was cheaper (and the content of which was, in accordance, coarser) than that of bread made of wheat or maslin. With less *per capita* capital in hand, Norfolk's inhabitants could afford only a cheaper and coarser option for their daily bread, and the expansion of the barley acreage would have catered for this scenario ideally. However, Norfolk was not the only well-populated county. Even if not to the same degree, Oxfordshire, Rutland, Huntingdonshire and Bedfordshire were relatively densely populated as well (with 114, 105, 98 and 91 taxpayers respectively per ten square miles),[26] and there is no evidence that there was widespread consumption of barley bread in those counties.

Perhaps the unique structure of Norfolk's arable husbandry was shaped instead by the very distinctive quality of this county's malt. As Bruce Campbell has shown, it is likely that Norfolk malt was renowned for its exceptional quality because its relative price was higher than elsewhere in England (in the pre-Black Death period one bushel of malted barley was worth about 94 per cent of one bushel of wheat in Norfolk and about 110 per cent of one bushel of malted barley on a national level). This fact made

---

22. Hampshire Record Office, HantsRO, 11M59/B1/50–75; HantRO, Winchester Cathedral Accounts, Composite Rolls for 1280, 1282, 1283, 1299, 1307, 1308, 1309, 1311, 1312, 1314, 1315, 1316, 1318 and 1324.
23. Calculated from the MAME (manorial accounts) database (see Bibliography).
24. NRO, Hare 4021/210x2 and NRO, DCN 61/62.
25. Campbell and Bartley, *Eve of the Black Death*, pp. 330–31.
26. Ibid.

malted barley a highly commercialised grain in this county, while its abundance and fine quality guaranteed a steady demand for it both inside and outside Norfolk.[27] It is most likely that the surplus was destined to be consumed outside Norfolk.

However, one should also consider the environmental factors which may have accounted for the predominance of barley in Norfolk. It should be born in mind that East Anglia in general, and Norfolk in particular, is the driest region in England, with extensive areas of freely draining soils. Barley is far more draught-tolerant than wheat and, therefore, would be much more suited to the local climate and environmental conditions of Norfolk.

In addition to the explanations advanced above, we may also consider regional cultural customs and preferences as an additional factor in Norfolk's arable structure. That Norfolk and Norfolkians had distinctive dietary customs and traditions is reflected in an anonymous thirteenth-century satirical poem *Descriptio Northfolchie*, which mocked the agricultural and culinary practices of the local population.[28] In other words, it is possible that the unique composition of Norfolk arable agriculture, allocating a large proportion of its available arable land to barley, is in fact related to local customs going much further back than the late Middle Ages.

Regional and chronological trends in crop geography

Naturally, agricultural trends on Norwich Cathedral Priory estates varied not only from demesne to demesne but also from decade to decade and year to year. Table 4.1 captures the general situation around one benchmark period in order to provide a wider geographic context for those trends. In order to appreciate the complexity and dynamics of the picture, however, it is necessary to consider each demesne individually, across the entire time period (Table 4.2). Chronologically speaking, there was a piecemeal expansion of the winter wheat acreage at the expense of rye, the only other grain commonly sown as a winter crop. Thus, at Eaton, between the 1260s and 1350s, the wheat share grew from zero to over 20 per cent of all the winter acreage. Similarly, Newton-by-Norwich increased its wheat share from 10 to some 70 per cent between the 1260s and the 1360s. At Gnatingdon and Sedgeford, two adjacent demesnes, wheat occupied between a quarter and one-third of all winter fields in the pre-Black Death period, but in the early fifteenth century it occupied about three-quarters of the winter acreage. There is no doubt that this reflects the new socio-economic and environmental reality of the post-pestilence era. The dramatic change in the land–labour ratio brought about by the plague, which killed some 40 per cent of England's population, led, especially after *c.*1376, to a collapse in grain prices and a

---

27. B.M.S. Campbell, 'Matching supply to demand: crop production and disposal by English demesnes in the century of the Black Death', *JEH*, 57/4 (1997), p. 836; Campbell, *English seigniorial agriculture*, p. 223.

28. A.G. Rigg, '"Descriptio Northfolchie": a critical edition', in A. Bihrer and E. Stein (eds), *Nova de Veteribus: Mittel- und neulateinische Studien für Paul G. Schmidt* (Munich and Leipzig, 2004), pp. 577–94. I am grateful to the editor for his reference to medieval depictions of Norfolk, as well as for some valuable suggestions. The social image of the Norfolchians is discussed further in Slavin, 'Feeding the brethren', pp. 16–19.

Table 4.2
Crop specialisation on Norwich Cathedral Priory demesnes, 1261–1430.

Wheat as percentage of all winter grains

	a	b	c	d	e	f	g	h	i	j	k	l	m	n	o
1261–70	100%	0%	90%	34%	56%	86%	71%	34%	0%	10%	33%	52%	36%	21%	74%
1271–80	100%	0%	98%	34%	77%	95%	72%	61%	0%	11%	37%	46%	35%	18%	79%
1281–90	100%	0%	83%	23%	81%	91%	100%	84%	0%	38%	21%	60%	28%	12%	54%
1291–1300	100%	10%	90%	31%	88%	85%	81%	77%	0%	20%	37%	53%	31%	4%	49%
1301–10	93%	0%	95%	26%	97%	100%	83%	93%	0%	32%	24%	69%	25%	0%	53%
1311–20	100%	18%	95%	25%	98%	100%	85%	91%	0%	43%	33%	49%	26%	0%	80%
1321–30		3%	98%	27%	98%	98%	100%	94%	6%	51%	43%	48%	30%	2%	72%
1331–40		0%	85%	27%	100%			92%	3%	55%	36%	53%	35%	5%	
1341–50		16%	100%	24%				84%	0%	60%	43%	69%	30%	4%	47%
1351–60		23%		36%		100%	100%	100%		64%	100%	74%	36%	18%	87%
1361–70		18%		57%		100%	100%	100%		69%		100%	57%	36%	
1371–80		19%		56%		100%	100%	100%				75%	58%	29%	
1381–90				45%			100%	100%				53%	59%	28%	
1391–1400				59%		100%	100%	100%				46%	68%	27%	
1401–10				72%		100%	100%	100%				42%	75%	26%	
1411–20				74%		100%	100%	100%				52%	85%	24%	
1421–30				71%			100%	100%				70%	70%	15%	

Barley as percentage of all spring grains

	a	b	c	d	e	f	g	h	i	j	k	l	m	n	o
1261–70	84%	89%	38%	65%	91%	65%	75%	80%	81%	93%	89%	90%	69%	85%	93%
1271–80	84%	96%	29%	67%	92%	66%	80%	93%	87%	93%	84%	91%	68%	87%	91%
1281–90	81%	94%	32%	62%	92%	69%	76%	93%	79%	97%	98%	87%	70%	82%	96%
1291–1300	82%	93%	41%	67%	92%	64%	79%	92%	78%	99%	89%	86%	72%	82%	91%
1301–10	85%	91%	50%	68%	94%	66%	79%	95%	89%	97%	100%	88%	73%	87%	90%
1311–20	83%	86%	49%	72%	95%	66%	79%	96%	85%	95%	85%	90%	72%	87%	90%
1321–30		89%	51%	74%	95%	69%	80%	96%	91%	92%	88%	86%	73%	87%	88%
1331–40		93%	44%	75%	95%			96%	89%	92%	89%	84%	78%	77%	
1341–50		98%	55%	76%		64%	70%	89%		91%	92%	83%	76%	81%	85%
1351–60		85%		87%		72%	72%	86%		90%	78%	82%	84%	89%	91%

	a	b	c	d	e	f	g	h	i	j	k	l	m	n	o
1361–70		87%		81%		68%	73%	88%		90%		75%	86%	86%	
1371–80		86%		83%			75%	88%				75%	86%	86%	
1381–90		85%		82%			77%	87%				71%	86%	85%	
1391–1400				86%		65%	75%	87%				76%	87%	83%	
1401–10				88%		64%	72%	88%				78%	87%	82%	
1411–20				88%		65%	74%	90%				81%	90%	80%	
1421–30				87%			74%	89%				76%	86%	77%	

Legumes as percentage of all crops sown

	a	b	c	d	e	f	g	h	i	j	k	l	m	n	o
1261–70	24%	7%	20%	10%	14%	10%	13%	22%	11%	8%	7%	15%	11%	5%	25%
1271–80	25%	5%	16%	11%	14%	18%	11%	23%	3%	9%	12%	9%	11%	7%	19%
1281–90	31%	6%	19%	11%	16%	17%	16%	11%	9%	7%	7%	11%	13%	5%	22%
1291–1300	24%	7%	12%	12%	16%	19%	14%	17%	9%	10%	9%	14%	14%	6%	22%
1301–10	26%	10%	15%	12%	18%	23%	14%	18%	9%	10%	7%	14%	12%	7%	20%
1311–20	26%	6%	14%	13%	20%	23%	15%	19%	8%	12%	9%	11%	13%	7%	21%
1321–30		4%	13%	12%	22%	20%	10%	21%	9%	14%	9%	11%	11%	7%	19%
1331–40		3%	7%	14%	22%			20%	9%	13%	9%	11%	16%	5%	
1341–50		6%	19%	13%		15%	14%	10%		13%	11%	14%	12%	7%	18%
1355–60		5%		8%		20%	13%	12%		13%	3%	14%	8%	7%	13%
1361–70		2%		16%		14%	11%	18%		13%		18%	15%	8%	
1371–80		2%		14%			16%					20%	18%	8%	
1381–90				14%			13%					18%	17%	8%	
1391–1400				15%		15%	12%					18%	14%	8%	
1401–10				13%		15%	12%					17%	10%	8%	
1411–20				12%		17%	12%					19%	12%	8%	
1421–30				13%			12%					21%	11%	5%	

Source: Manorial accounts database.

Notes: a = Denham; b = Eaton; c = Gateley; d = Gnatingdon; e = Hemsby; f = Hindolveston; g = Hindringham; h = Martham; i = Monks Granges; j = Newton-by-Norwich; k = North Elmham; l = Plumstead; m = Sedgeford; n = Taverham, o = Thornham. Those demesnes that did not participate in the direct provisioning of the priory (Catton, Melton, Scratby and Worstead) were not included in the sample. In addition, the home-farm of Heythe, which seems to have been a temporary creation functioning between c.1330 and 1370, and for which only two accounts survive, has not been included in the sample.

rise in real wages, and thus to an evident rise in the living standards of the common populace. This allowed them to switch to finer and relatively more expensive consumables, and it seems that wheat bread came to gradually replace coarser kinds of bread all over the country.[29] This, naturally, increased demand for wheat and wheat loaves, which prompted many lords, including the Norwich brethren, to augment the relative share of this grain.

The fluctuations of spring-sown crops were much less drastic. In most cases, barley occupied a disproportionally large share of the spring grain acreage. The only exception was Gateley, which allocated far larger proportions of arable for oats than barley. But, even here, the figures for barley rose from about 29 to 55 per cent between the 1270s and 1340s. Similarly, barley was expanding at the expense of oats in Gnatingdon and Sedgeford, climbing to the figure of about 90 per cent at the end of direct management period. The only demesne exhibiting a contrary trend was Plumstead, where the figures for barley actually fell (from some 90 to 75 per cent over the entire period). Otherwise, the oat–barley ratio tended to remain more or less stable throughout the entire period. Similarly, the legume acreage did not show much oscillation over time.

Although one can follow common chronological trends in demesne agriculture, the geographic differences were much more pronounced, with the structure of arable acreage varying from demesne to demesne. Thus, some demesnes were biased more towards rye- or maslin-growing, rather than wheat cultivation. For instance, before the 1340s Eaton grew no wheat. Similarly, wheat cultivation was largely unknown at Monks Granges. Conversely, very little rye was grown at Hindolveston. Oats occupied about one-third of the entire arable acreage at Gateley, but generally accounted for less than 5 per cent at Hembsy, Martham, Newton and Thornham. Legumes, too, exhibit a pronounced degree of variation between manors. Thus, they occupied around one-quarter of all arable at Denham and Thornham, while Eaton, Monks Granges, North Elmham and Taverham devoted less than 10 per cent of their cultivable land to legumes.

What, then, accounts for these regional differences? What determined what was grown? There has been some scholarly debate regarding the different factors that influenced crop cultivation choices in late medieval England. In their collaborative study of London's hinterland around 1300, Bruce Campbell and his colleagues have argued that the geography of crops was largely dictated and impacted by market-determined economic rent and, consequently, transportation costs.[30] Campbell and his colleagues were influenced by Johann-Heinrich Von Thünen's vision of cities' rural hinterlands, as expressed in his *Isolated State* (*Der isolierte Staat*, 1826). Von Thünen concluded that the types of goods produced on different rural settlements are dictated by their distance from urban markets and by transport costs.[31] 'The crop that produces the greater economic rent per unit area will occupy sites nearest the town; the crop

---

29. D. Stone, 'The consumption of field crops in late medieval England', in C.M. Woolgar, D. Serjeantson and T. Waldron (eds), *Food in medieval England: diet and nutrition* (Oxford, 2006), pp. 22–5.
30. Campbell *et al.*, *A medieval capital*, pp. 128–9.
31. J.H. von Thünen, *Der isolierte Staat in Beziehung auf Landwirtschaft und Nationalökonomie* (Berlin, 1910). The English translation is J.H. von Thünen, tr. Carla M. Wartenberg, *Isolated state: an English edition of Der isolierte Staat* (Oxford, 1966).

that yields a lower economic rent will be located on lands at greater distances.'[32] He divided the hinterland area into six different sub-zones. Zone 1 is a narrow area of 'free [cash] cropping' (*Freie Wirtschaft*) specialising in perishable products such as fruits, hay, fodder grains, straw and milk.[33] Zone 2, the 'forestry' (*Forstwirtschaft*), is devoted to woodlands supplying the town with fuel and wood materials. Such materials are bulky and hence it is more profitable to have them as close to the town as possible, in order to keep the transportation costs as low as possible.[34] Grain production begins with Zone 3, or the 'crop alteration zone' (*Fruchtwechselwirtschaft*). This zone is characterised by the most fertile soils of the entire region, on which fallows were reduced, legumes cultivated and livestock managed to the maximum extent.[35] Zone 4, the 'improved system' (*Koppelwirschaft*), lies on lands inferior to those of Zone 3, and is marked by the alternation of land between arable and pasture and the combination of grain and diary production. According to Von Thünen, the zone ends 24.7 miles (39.75km) from the town.[36] Beyond Zone 4 lies Zone 5, the 'three-field system' (*Dreifelderwirtschaft*), with the most extensive grain production, dedicated to arable and pasture and free of fodder cultivation. This zone stretches from 24.7 (39.75km) to 31.5 miles (50.69km) from the town.[37] The first five zones constitute about 40 per cent of the total hinterland and they are the ones supplying the town; the remaining 60 per cent are formed by Zone 6, which is devoted mostly to livestock management and wool production (*Viehzucht*). The grain grown here is not intended to supply the town, because the distance between the two areas is too great to make this economic.[38]

Von Thünen himself understood that this is rather an unrealistic model, possible only in ideal geographical and geological conditions. However, studies of the London provisioning zone have shown that he was not too far from the mark. Wheat, the most expensive grain per unit volume and unit value and the least expensive in terms of transportation costs, was indeed grown in particularly large proportions far from London, while oats, the bulkiest grain commanding the lowest price and therefore the highest transportation costs were the specialism of the manors lying within reasonable proximity to the city.[39]

More recently, the relevance of the Von Thünen model in late medieval agriculture was challenged by Harry Kitsikopoulos. For him, it was household consumption requirements within the seigniorial sector that determined the choice, and

---

32. As summarised by D. Grigg, *The dynamics of agricultural change: the historical experience* (London, 1982), p. 136.
33. Von Thünen, *Der isolierte Staat*, pp. 16–17=Von Thünen, *Isolated state*, pp. 9–11.
34. Ibid., pp. 129–45=pp. 106–23.
35. Ibid., pp. 161–3=pp. 140–41.
36. Ibid., p. 163=p. 142.
37. Ibid., p. 163=p. 143.
38. Ibid., pp. 167–78=pp. 149–58.
39. Campbell *et al.*, *A medieval capital*, pp. 141–3, 175–6.
40. H. Kitsikopoulos, 'Urban demand and agrarian productivity in pre-plague England: reassessing the relevancy of Von Thunen's Model', *Agricultural History*, 77/3 (2003), pp. 482–522.

Table 4.3
Exogenous and endogenous determinants of crop geography on
Norwich Cathedral Priory estates, c.1300.

Independent variables	Wheat proportion	Rye/maslin proportion	Barley proportion	Oats /dredge proportion	Legume proportion
a. Exogenous					
Wheat proportion	1.000				
Rye/maslin proportion	-0.865	1.000			
Barley proportion	-0.673	0.496	1.000		
Oats/dredge proportion	0.246	-0.223	-0.770	1.000	
Legume proportion	0.571	-0.707	-0.567	0.163	1.000
Sown acreage	-0.242	0.015	-0.034	0.400	-0.025
Livestock units per 100 acres	0.356	-0.305	0.093	-0.099	-0.229
Land value	0.340	-0.528	0.247	-0.461	0.469
Loamy soil	0.020	-0.168	0.416	-0.377	-0.119
Clayey soil	0.479	-0.236	-0.478	0.128	0.288
Sandy soil	-0.424	0.521	0.225	-0.117	-0.350
Chalky soil	-0.267	0.066	-0.112	0.411	0.084
Altitude (metres)	0.544	-0.420	-0.747	0.583	0.414
Distance to river	-0.154	-0.126	-0.150	0.423	0.242
b. Endogenous					
Distance to Norwich (in miles)	0.222	-0.392	-0.415	0.500	0.403
Distance to closest large town	0.519	-0.552	-0.590	0.479	0.491
Distance to closest market	0.153	-0.085	-0.603	0.640	0.240
Market or fair	0.147	-0.242	0.353	-0.449	-0.018
Wheat marketed	-0.288	0.219	0.003	0.127	0.004
Rye marketed	0.344	-0.164	0.183	-0.202	-0.218
Barley marketed	0.381	-0.277	-0.152	0.012	0.061
Oats marketed	0.036	-0.011	-0.086	0.174	-0.098
Legumes marketed	0.129	-0.170	0.288	-0.522	0.131
Wheat sent to Norwich	0.263	-0.184	0.072	-0.250	0.008
Malt sent to Norwich	-0.335	0.299	0.366	-0.297	-0.212

Sources: Manorial accounts database; British Library, MS Stowe 936 and Add. MS 57973; the altitude data has been obtained from the *Google Earth* programme (accessed, at various points, between 2009 and 2011); soil data has been obtained from the Cranfield University-based *Soilscapes* website (http://www.landis.org.uk/soilscapes/; accessed 12 October 2011) and H.C. Darby, *The Domesday geography of eastern England* (Cambridge, 1971); the market and fair data has been obtained from the Institute of Historical research-based website *Gazetteer of markets and fairs in England and Wales to 1516* (http://www.history.ac.uk/cmh/gaz/gazweb1.html; accessed 12 October 2011).

Notes: Grain proportion = a relative share of each grain within the total arable acreage; sown acreage = total acreage under crop; livestock units per 100 acres = stocking density of livestock units (that is, raw numbers of animals converted into their unit equivalent, according to their relative value and contribution to the economy) per 100 sown acres; land value = financial value of each acre of sown land; altitude = height above sea level; distance to river = distance of a demesne from the closest navigable river; distance to Norwich/closest town/market = distance between a demesne and the specified destinations; market or fair = presence of a market or fair within a vill where a demesne was located; grain marketed = the proportion of the AGCR sold; grain sent to Norwich = the proportion of the AGCR sent to the priory.

consequently the geography, of crop growing.[40] In his likening of late medieval manorial estates to modern firms, he contended, in a somewhat generalising manner, that all strata of late-medieval producers could, in theory, choose between answering their consumption requirements and maximising the profits from their landed holdings, while the lords have always preferred to go with the first option.[41]

Crop geography determinants: environment, markets and consumption

Which of the two models fits the case of Norwich Cathedral Priory's estates? Can we apply either of these models to the situation in late medieval Norfolk? One thing that the two approaches have in common is their emphasis on institutional – endogenous – factors. While there is no doubt that institutions have a strong impact on economic choices, preferences, behaviour and development, one cannot disregard the exogenous side of the coin. And indeed, in recent years, there has been a growing awareness of the crucial role of nature as a 'historical protagonist'.[42] Perhaps one way to see what factors, endogenous and exogenous, shaped the geography and choice of crop specialisation is to juxtapose each crop's share on every manor (as dependent variable) against a series of independent variables, and see if there is any clear correlation between them (Table 4.3).

Table 4.3 is divided into two groups of independent variables. Let us consider the exogenous ones first. To begin with, the degree of wheat bias had a profound impact on the allocation of rye and legume acreage. Wheat was the least tolerant crop and it is not surprising, then, that as such it affected other crops more than any other grain. Invariably there was a strong negative correlation between the share of wheat and that of rye. The manors with comparatively large wheat acreages had either very small rye fields or did not cultivate this grain at all. Also, because of its capricious nature, wheat dictated a heavier reliance on legumes as an important fertilising agent. Therefore, the demesnes with comparatively large wheat acreages would also allocate a relatively large proportion of their arable to legumes. This was the case in Denham, Gateley, Hindolveston and Martham demesnes, each of which allocated between 15 and 25 per cent of their acreage to legumes. On the other hand, rye-orientated manors, including Catton, Eaton, Monks Granges, Newton-by-Norwich, North Elmham and Taverham, allocated less than 10 per cent of their total acreage to legumes.

In addition, we should consider the total size of the sown arable acreage as another possible factor shaping the geography of crop cultivation. In particular, there seems to have been a good degree of correlation between the total size of the arable area and a concentration on oat cultivation. The larger the acreage tended to be, the larger the proportions of oats that were sown. This is hardly surprising: oats were a crop of secondary importance when compared with barley, and only larger demesnes could

---

41. H. Kitsikopoulos, 'Manorial estates as business firms: the relevance of economic rent in determining crop choices in London's hinterland, *c.*1300', *AHR*, 56 (2008), pp. 142–66.

42. As coined by Bruce Campbell in the title of the Tawney Memorial Lecture, delivered at the annual meeting of the Economic History Society, University of Nottingham, 30 March 2008, subsequently published, in an altered version (Campbell, 'Nature as historical protagonist').

Bread and Ale for the Brethren

afford the luxury of allocating larger shares of their arable to the cultivation of this grain. Livestock density, measured in livestock 'units' per 100 acres, had a degree of impact on crop geography, too. The wheat-orientated demesnes also tended to have highest densities of livestock, while the rye-biased manors tended to stock fewer animals. This is not surprising, since one would expect to find high livestock densities on those demesnes allocating large acreages to fodder crops, and, as we have seen, there was a strong correlation between wheat and legume acreage.

Soil types were yet another crucial factor in determining the geography of crops. Since each crop has a different degree of 'tolerance' to various ecological factors, it is obvious that only certain types of soil would suit certain crops. Loam, considered to be the 'best' soil (in the proportions, approximately, 40 per cent sand, 40 per cent silt and 20 per cent clay), suits virtually all kinds of crop-cultivation. Clays, although heavy and impermeable, contain a relatively high level of vital nutrients and hence can also be regarded as good soil, although it is hard to work. Chalky soils tend to dry out and block the uptake by plants of some vital chemical elements, such as iron and manganese. The poorest type of soil, however, is sand. Sandy soils, composed of particles of weathered stones, are freely draining and often acid, and they are prone to both over-drying and the leaching of their nutrients.[43] It is hardly surprising, then, that the geography of soils was instrumental in shaping the geography of crops. Thus, loamy soils could equally accommodate wheat, barley and legumes; while rye and oats, the two most tolerant crops, were usually reserved for inferior types of soil. Wheat-orientated demesnes were also found on clayey soils, while chalky and sandy soils provided the most unfavourable conditions for wheat-growing, as the negative correlation between the three variables show. Rye, the cheaper and much more tolerant substitute to wheat, was grown chiefly on sandy soils, particularly in the immediate hinterland of Norwich. Demesnes with large proportions of oats, the most tolerant crop of them all, were, unsurprisingly, found on chalky soils. In theory, barley could be grown on any soil. However, three manors, Denham, Gateley and Hindolveston, which allocated relatively small amounts of land to barley, were all located on clayey soils. Similarly, there is no clear correlation between legumes and the types of soil, with the exception of the sandy soils: Eaton and Taverham, both located on this type of soil, devoted small proportions of their arable to legumes. The impact of type and quality of soil can be summarised as follows: the less tolerant the crop was, the better the soils that the crop was likely to have been found on.

The quality of the soil and its connection to the geography of crops are also reflected in the financial values of arable and pasturage on each manor. There seems to be a clear correlation between higher values and the tendency to allocate larger proportions of land to wheat and legumes. This indicates that soils providing good conditions for wheat-growing were especially prized, while legumes contributed a great deal to a further improvement of their qualities. Furthermore, the extent of legume cultivation reflects the degree of cropping intensity. Thus, the manor of Thornham, albeit located on comparatively poor soil (light chalk), was valued at 18s an acre in the pre-Black

---

43. The information on UK soil types and their attributes can be found on the Soilscapes: soils dataset covering England and Wales website, Cranfield University-based project, http://www.landis.org.uk/soilscapes/ (last accessed 26 October 2011).

Death period, which is comparatively higher than other demesnes. Before the Black Death as much as around 20 per cent of its arable land was devoted to peas. A closer look into rotations at Thornham reveals that this demesne practised a long fallow, or 'ley', system of rotation, whereby land was cropped for 3–4 years and then put down to ley (fallow with grasses grown) for another 3–4 years. The same practice was employed at Bircham, not far from Thornham.[44] Martham and Hemsby, the two most highly valued demesnes (at 36d per acre) similarly devoted close to 20 per cent of their arable to peas cultivation, and had little fallow.

Another exogenous factor to be considered here is altitude. It should be borne in mind, however, that Norfolk is a flat county, rarely exceeding 300 feet (91m) above sea level. Therefore, the differences in elevation between the manors were not profound and the correlation coefficient between the two variables may not necessarily be reflective of this inverse relationship between altitude and crop specialisation in the case of Norfolk. Nevertheless, it is clear that some demesnes with relatively large shares of wheat and oats tended to be situated at a higher altitude than those focusing on rye and barley production. Thus, Denham, Gateley, Gnatingdon, Hindolveston and Hindringham, all situated over 150 feet (46m) above sea level, devoted comparatively large proportions – well above the county average – of their acreage to wheat and/or oats. On the other hand, rye-orientated manors, including Eaton, Newton and Taverham, were located between 10 and 50 feet (3–15m) above sea level.

Distance to or from rivers could be another factor in shaping the geography of crop cultivation. Navigable rivers were used by late medieval grain producers and traders to ship their merchandise to local markets because, in general, river transportation was both faster and cheaper than that by road.[45] The impact of proximity to rivers seems to be particularly significant in the case of oats. This crop was relatively cheap and bulky and as such, was, in most cases, destined for domestic consumption by tenants and animals, rather than to be sold on markets or sent to the Norwich headquarters. Around 1300, only two demesnes, Gateley and Hindolveston, both allocating higher than average proportions of their acreage to oats, marketed relatively large amounts of oat produce (between 20 and 30 per cent of their annual oat revenue). Unsurprisingly, these manors were both located close to rivers.

There can be little doubt, therefore, that exogenous factors played an important role in shaping regional variations in crop specialisation on the priory demesnes. One cannot ignore the endogenous factors, however. Physical distance between the demesnes and other points of distribution, namely local markets, whether rural or urban, seems to have had at least a partial impact on crop geography. As far as winter crops are concerned, the wheat-orientated manors such as Denham, Gateley, Hemsby, Hindolveston, Hindringham and Worstead were located farther away from Norwich, while those located within its immediate hinterland, including Catton, Eaton, Monks Granges, Newton-by-Norwich and Taverham, tended to concentrate on rye. Similarly, wheat-focused demesnes tended to be situated remotely from two other large towns, Great Yarmouth and King's Lynn. Rye was the most commercialised crop,

---

44. TNA, SC 6/930/1–33.
45. Campbell *et al.*, *A medieval capital*, pp. 193–8; J. Landers, *The field and the forge: population, production, and power in the pre-industrial West* (Oxford, 2003), p. 73.

destined to be sold, as a cheaper and coarser alternative to wheat, to the poor townsfolk. It was only natural, then, for the suburban demesnes to concentrate on rye, all the more so given that their acid and sandy soils were well suited to this crop. In the case of the spring crops, those manors that were more distant from markets devoted larger shares of their acreage to oats than did the demesnes near Norwich and other market centres, which allocated comparatively large proportions of their spring acreage to barley. In addition, the presence of markets or fairs on the demesnes had a similar effect on crop specialisation. The barley-orientated demesnes tended to have 'formal' markets or fairs, while the oat-focused ones did not have any trading hubs. This correlation between crop specialisation and physical proximity to markets, however, should not be taken at face value. As we shall discuss below, there is no evidence that manorial officials sold the demesne produce on local markets in that period. Instead, the bulk of crops were sold at the demesne gates to itinerant merchants. Hence, in the case of the suburban demesnes it was profitable to specialise in rye not because of their proximity to Norwich market, but rather because of their proximity to Norwich grain merchants, who would undoubtedly find the prospects of purchasing crops nearby attractive. Similarly, the proximity of oat-orientated manors to rivers made the transportation of marketed grain more convenient not for the demesne bailiffs but rather for local merchants.

Commercialisation, as measured in the proportion of the harvested grain that was disposed of by being sold, is another factor to be considered. Here, the impact of commercialisation is hardly felt within any crop sector, with a very low correlation between the degree of crop specialisation and the proportion of the harvests that was marketed. This does not mean, however, that around 1300 the Norwich Cathedral Priory estate was under-commercialised when compared with some other regions. As we shall see later in this chapter, in that period the priory's demesne officials marketed large quantities of rye and legumes.

Finally, the extent of the consumption needs of the Norwich brethren is yet another factor that must be taken into consideration here. Since it was mostly wheat and malted barley that were dispatched from the manors to the priory, we shall consider only these two grains. In both cases, the correlation between crop specialisation and the proportions of the harvested grain sent to the Norwich headquarters was not high enough to allow any generalisations to be made, but in some cases the connection is undeniable. Thus, Hemsby, Hindolveston and Martham, all relatively large demesnes sending considerable proportions of their annual crop production to Norwich, were among the most wheat-orientated manors within the estate. Likewise, Eaton, North Elmham and Taverham, which dedicated over 60 per cent of their arable to barley, shipped almost all of their malted barley to the Norwich headquarters. Denham and Gateley, on the other hand, both relatively small demesnes which allocated, respectively, only 40 and 24 per cent of their acreage to barley, neither malted nor sent this grain to the priory at all.

Having dealt with both the exogenous and endogenous factors as likely determinants of the geography of crop cultivation, what conclusions can we reach? First, the environment seems to have been a very decisive factor in shaping geographic patterns of crop specialisation. Soil type and quality, as well as altitude, could determine what crops were grown on each demesne. As far as institutional factors are concerned, Von Thünen's idealistic economic rent and market proximity model seems to be partially applicable to the Norwich Cathedral Priory estates. On the

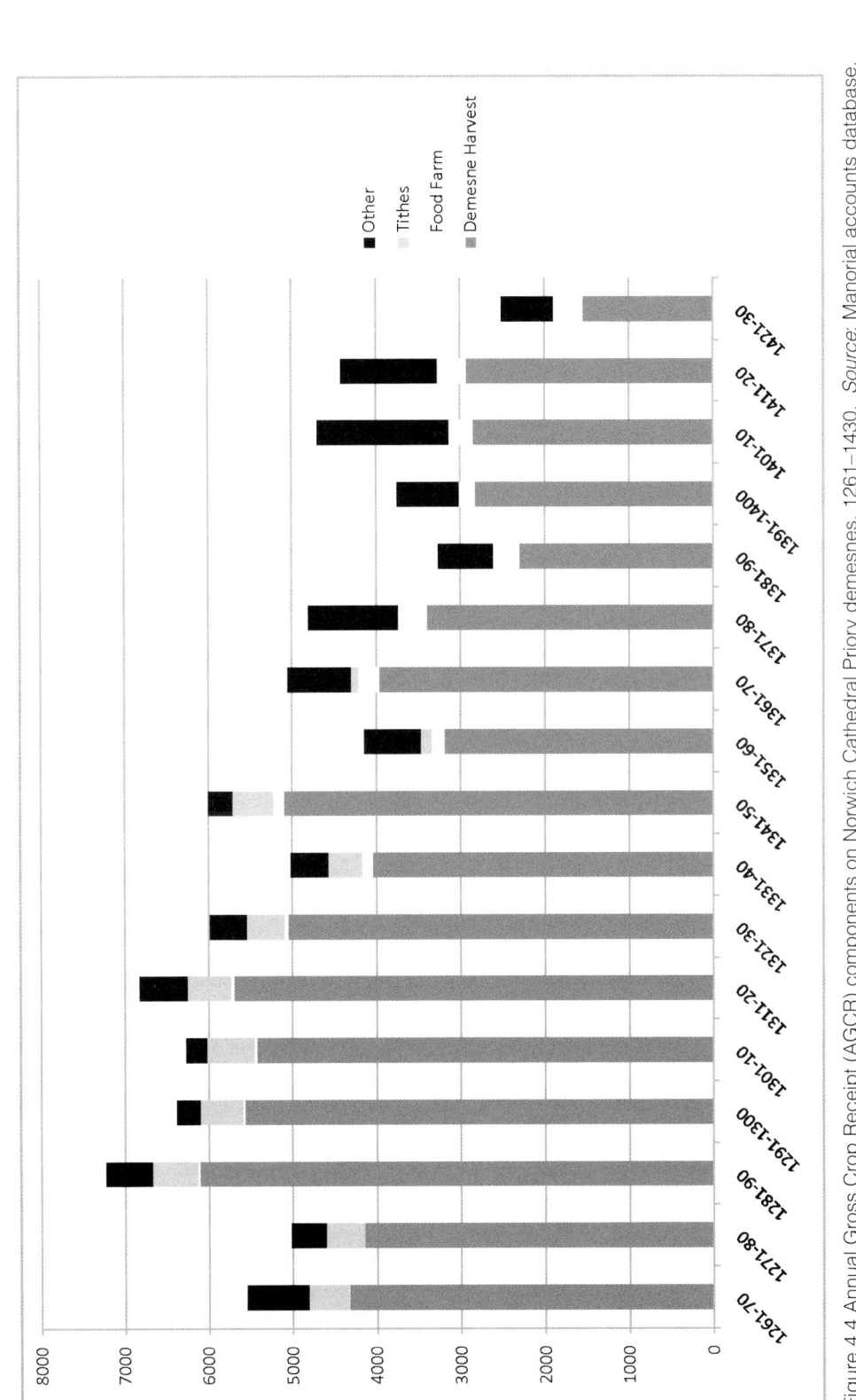

Figure 4.4 Annual Gross Crop Receipt (AGCR) components on Norwich Cathedral Priory demesnes, 1261–1430. *Source*: Manorial accounts database. *Note*: All figures are given in quarters.

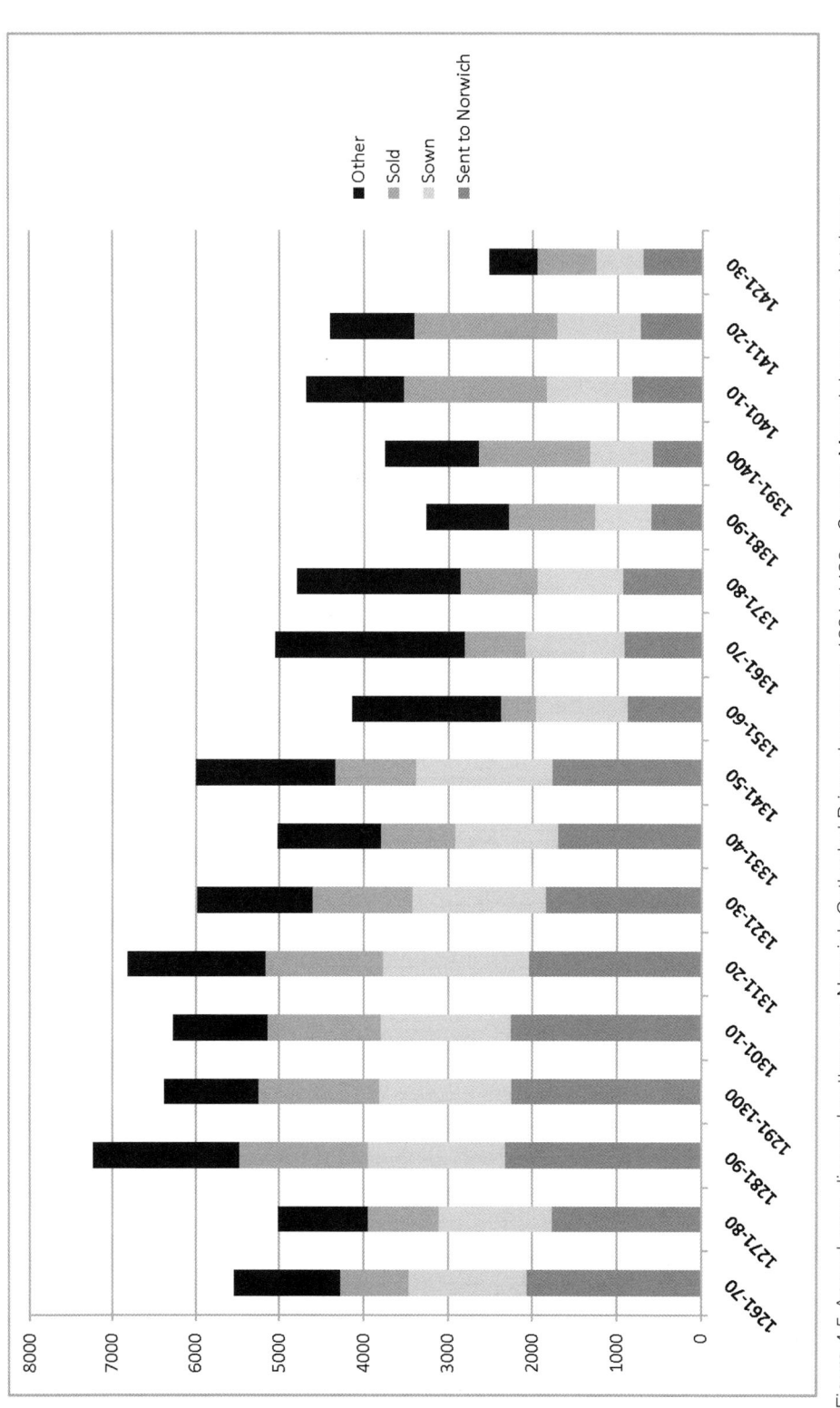

Figure 4.5 Annual crop disposal patterns on Norwich Cathedral Priory demesnes, 1261–1430. *Source:* Manorial accounts database.
Note: All figures are given in quarters.

one hand, the wheat-growing manors tended to be situated at some distance from the priory, while rye-orientated ones were concentrated around the town, which correlates with Von Thünen's prediction of the 'ideal hinterland'. On the other hand, however, barley-orientated manors were found relatively close to Norwich, while larger proportions of oats were cultivated on more distant demesnes, which contradicts the Von Thünen model. Finally, in some cases there was a correlation between crop specialisation and the relative share of the grain produced by the demesne and sent to Norwich for the direct provisioning of the brethren. This indicates that the autarkic consumption needs of the Cathedral household could have been another possible factor in shaping the spatial patterns of crop-growing. To appreciate the geography of crop cultivation better, however, it is necessary to look at the extent of annual grain and legume receipts.

Annual crop disposal: chronological and regional patterns

Each demesne account carefully distinguished between several components, or forms, in which the annual crop produced was received and disposed of (Figures 4.4 and 4.5). The single most significant component of the annual gross crop receipt (hereafter, AGCR) was annual harvest issues from fields, which accounted for about 84 per cent of the total AGCR before the Black Death and about 70 per cent in the post-pestilence era. By the end of the *Gutsherrschaft* era, it accounted for about 62 per cent of the AGCR. Tithes were collected from churches appropriated to the priory and they contributed a further 8 per cent to the total AGCR before *c.*1350, although the figures varied considerably across demesnes. Thus, some parish churches situated in the manors were not appropriated to the priory and, because of that, did not pay grain tithes. At North Elmham, tithes accounted for as much as 45 per cent of the AGCR.[46] After the Black Death, the priory authorities commonly leased out or sold crop tithes to various people, so that by 1365 no tithes were received directly from parishioners.[47] The third important component was grain rents, or food farms, rendered by tenants in grain in exchange for leased parcels of land or the right to use demesne mills. Indeed, the accounts distinguish between 'land farms' (*firme terre*) and 'mill farms' (*firme molendini*).[48] These farms did not represent more than about 1 per cent of the AGCR before the Black Death. After the pestilence, however, and especially in the 1360s, the figures rose until they accounted for about 7 per cent of the AGCR. The rest of the AGCR came from grain carryovers remaining in barns from previous years, whose importance is addressed in Chapter 6, as well as gifts received from other manors and occasional purchases.

The outgoing part of the granary accounts contains information about the

---

46. See Slavin, 'Feeding the brethren', pp. 107–9.
47. B. Dodds, *Peasants and production in the medieval north-east: the evidence from tithes, 1270–1536* (Woodbridge, 2007), pp. 162–71; R.N. Swanson, 'A universal levy: tithes and economic agency', in B. Dodds and R.H. Britnell (eds), *Agriculture and rural society after the Black Death: common themes and regional variances* (Hatfield, 2008), pp. 104–12.
48. On mill leasing, see J. Langdon, *Mills in the medieval economy: England, 1300–1540* (Oxford, 2004), pp. 185–218.

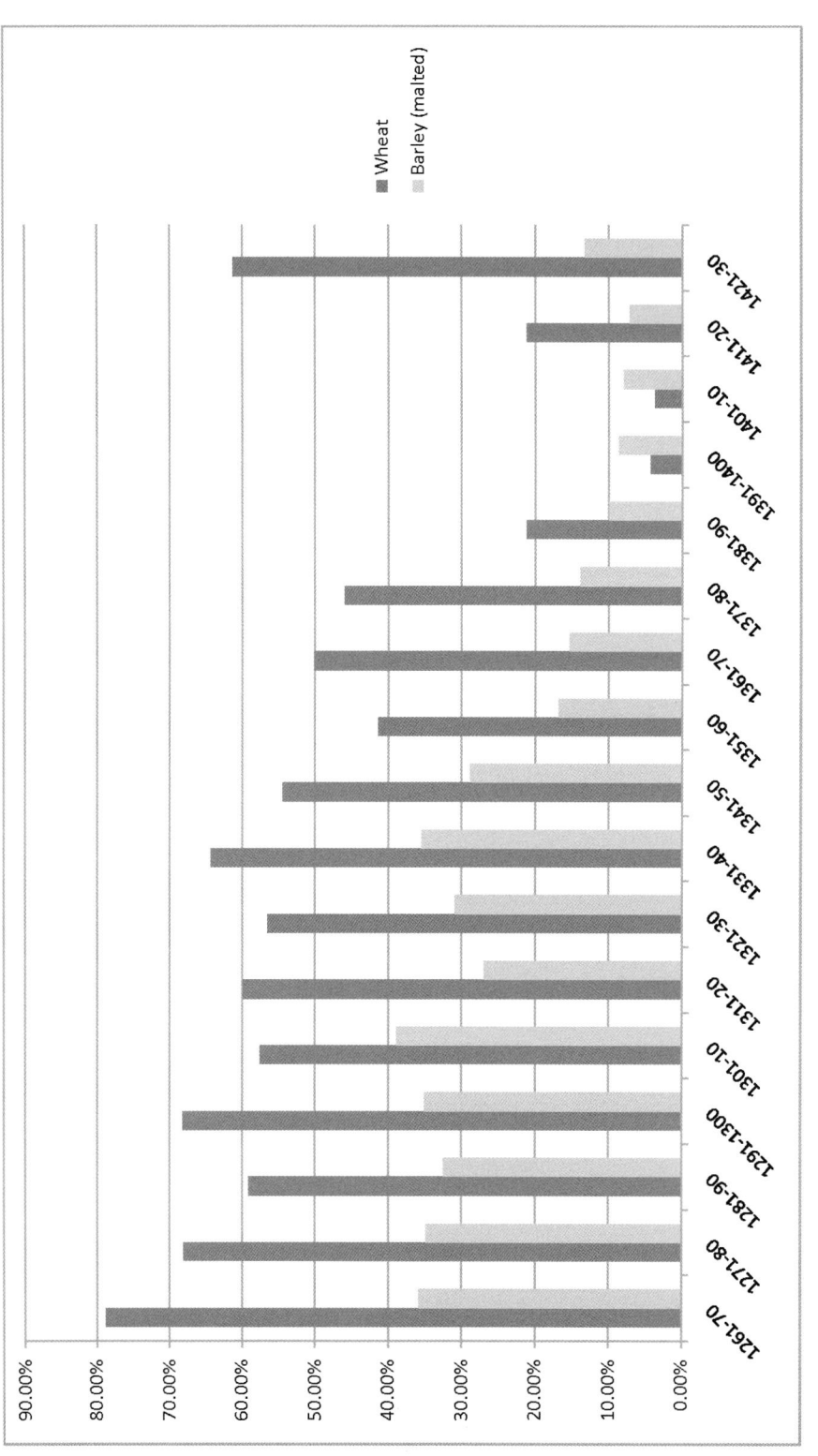

Figure 4.6 Proportions of raw wheat and malted barley sent to Norwich, as percentage of Annual Gross Crop Receipt (AGCR) of wheat and barley, 1261–1430. *Source*: Manorial accounts database.

dispatching of grain to Norwich, sales, storing, seeding, alms and gift-giving, grain allowance to harvest workers and demesne animals, and the conversion of barley into malt. Although it shows a perhaps somewhat oversimplified picture, Figure 4.5 divides the outgoing grain into four main categories: seeding, provisioning the priory, selling and 'other (more minor) expenses'. Almost invariably, between 20 and 25 per cent of the AGCR was spent on seeding and this figure did not fluctuate much over the period. There were, naturally, some notable exceptions, reflecting attempts to improve harvests. Thus, at Gateley, in 1272, 1288 and 1332 the reeves invested 62, 81 and 87 per cent of the wheat AGCR in seeding. It should be borne in mind, however, that Gateley, despite its situation on relatively rich clay soils, attained notoriously low wheat yields when compared with other Norfolk demesnes.[49] This fact may have prompted its demesne managers to allocate disproportionally high amounts of the AGCR to seeding in these years. On the other hand, there were some instances when seeding accounted for only a meagre percentage of outgoings. This was especially true in cases of demesnes where tithes formed a relatively large proportion of the AGCR. In North Elmham, which derived about 45 per cent of its AGCR from grain tithes paid by local parishioners, seeding accounted for only 4 per cent of the total AGCR outgoing over the entire period.

It was the other three outgoing sectors that underwent significant alterations between the 1270s and the 1430s, with the Black Death serving as a clear boundary of change. Let us consider annual grain shipment to Norwich first. Before the 1350s, about 33 per cent of all the AGCR was dispatched to Norwich, for the brethren's provisioning. After the pestilence, however, the figure fell considerably, amounting to about 18 per cent of all the AGCR between the 1350s and the 1410s. There was a brief recovery in the 1420s, when the figures rose to 27 per cent, but this was short-lived and by 1431 none of the demesnes were administered directly by the priory's officials. These are, however, average figures, and the actual extent of direct provisioning varied across demesnes and types of crop. While most demesnes dispatched rather generous amounts of wheat and malted barley, hardly any rye, oats or legumes were ever shipped to the priory (Figure 4.6).[50] As far as wheat is concerned, 63 per cent of the AGCR was sent to the brethren in the pre-Black Death period. Shortly after the pestilence, the figures fell to 41 per cent. During the 1380s there was a further decline, to 21 per cent, while in the 1390s and 1400s only some 4 per cent of all wheat receipt was sent to Norwich. Surprisingly, and notwithstanding the nearing end of the *Gutsherrschaft* economy, the relative proportion of wheat produced destined to be dispatched to Norwich increased in the 1410s and especially the 1420s, when its levels matched the pre-1350 ones. Barley exhibited very similar behaviour. Before the Black Death, the demesnes sent about 33 per cent of their AGCR, in malted form, to Norwich. In the immediate aftermath of the plague, the figures fell to 17 per cent and continued falling into the 1410s, reaching their lowest level at 7 per cent, only to

---

49. Between the 1270s and the 1330s the wheat yields averaged 3.69:1.00, compared to 4.10:1.00 for all of Norfolk. Campbell, *English seigniorial agriculture*, pp. 309–47; Campbell, *Three centuries* (http://www.cropyields.ac.uk).

50. With some minor exceptions: thus, in the 1330s and 1340s, meagre amounts of rye, maslin, peas and oats came occasionally from the demesnes. NRO, DCN 1/1/31–40.

slightly climb again in the 1420s to about 13 per cent. These figures varied not only across decades but also across demesnes. Thus, Catton, Melton and Worstead did not dispatch any grain at all. Gnatingdon sent only 20 and 7 per cent of its wheat and barley AGCR, respectively. Hemsby, the most productive demesne, on the other hand, dispatched no less than 82 and 58 per cent its wheat and malted barley receipt, respectively, in the pre-1350 period.

Over the entire period, about 36 per cent of all barley was converted into malt, mostly to be sent to Norwich. Before the Black Death, the lion's share of all malted barley (about 92 per cent) was dispatched to Norwich. The main change came during the 1360s, when the figure fell to 45 per cent and then fluctuated between 30 and 53 per cent between that decade and the end of the direct demesne management era. Barley malting was purely a rural enterprise in our context, taking place invariably on the demesnes before the product was sent to the Norwich headquarters. As Judith Bennett has shown, the ale-brewing industry was well developed in the English countryside around that time.[51] At the same time, however, ale-production was also carried out at a brewery within the cathedral precincts. Several factors may account for this division between rural malting and urban brewing. First, we should consider transportation costs. Malting increases the volume of barley by 14 per cent and lowers its density, reducing its weight by 25 per cent.[52] As Bruce Campbell and his colleagues have estimated, a bushel of malted barley weighing 34.5lb (15.7kg) (25 per cent less than a bushel of raw barley) would have produced about 50 pints (28.41 litres) of strong or 95.61 pints (54.33 litres) of weak ale. In other words, dispatching barley in its malted form was obviously the most convenient option for the priory authorities in saving on transportation costs, since one bushel/quarter of malted barley was 25 per cent lighter than that of raw barley, and anywhere between 45 and 71 per cent of its brewed weight. Another important factor to be considered here was the existence of the priory's brewery, which had professionally trained and highly qualified staff and produced more than one type of ale, as we shall see later. The ale drunk by the brethren was undoubtedly of a finer quality than the rather coarse ale produced on the manors for local consumption.

As might be expected, the patterns of annual crop sales fluctuated in accordance with dispatching trends. Before the Black Death, no more than 19 per cent of the AGCR was sold. Afterwards the proportion of sold crops increased, reaching a peak in the years 1390–1420, when about 35 per cent of the AGCR was sold. The two most commercialised grains were rye and maslin, cheaper and coarser alternatives to wheat which were demanded in large quantities by the poor, whether rural or urban. It is no wonder, then, that most rye-orientated demesnes were concentrated around Norwich. In both the pre- and post-Black Death decades, sales of rye accounted for about 45 per cent of its AGCR. The highest degree of rye commercialisation was achieved at North Elmham. Between the 1260s and the 1340s this demesne sold around 76 per cent of its AGCR of rye, investing the remainder in seeding. The degree of commercialisation of wheat and barley was less significant. Until *c.*1370, annual

---

51. J.M. Bennett, *Ale, beer and brewsters in England: women's work in a changing world, 1300–1600* (Oxford, 1996), pp. 45–50.
52. Campbell *et al.*, *A medieval capital*, p. 34, note 59.

sales accounted for 14 per cent of all wheat and 17 per cent of all barley receipts. After the 1370s, the figures rose to 30 per cent for wheat and 32 per cent for barley, undoubtedly reflecting the increasing demand for finer grains that went hand-in-hand with the rise in living standards of the commoners in the post-Black Death period, and especially in the late 1370s. Rye and maslin were followed by legumes, which achieved commercialisation rates nearly as high as the former in the pre-1350 period. On average, 41 per cent of the annual legume receipt was sold before the plague. Like rye and maslin, legumes were an important part of the diet of local peasants. Their functional versatility (legumes could be baked as pottage, used as fodder and utilised as a fertilising agent) and comparatively cheap price gave them a significant commercial advantage over other crops in the Black Death period. During the 1350s, however, the demand for legumes seemingly decreased and, consequently, sale levels fell to 15 per cent of AGCR expenditure, remaining low for the remaining period, averaging 23 per cent of AGCR outgoings. Again, this has to do with the gradually improving living standards in the post-pestilence period, when more and more peasants could afford finer types of food than legume pottage.

Who purchased the crops? As we have seen, Norfolk was blessed with an exceptionally sophisticated network of local markets and fairs, while the pre-Black Death population growth of Norwich, Great Yarmouth and King's Lynn contributed greatly to the commercialisation of this county. Did the priory authorities and their demesne managers utilise that convenient commercial reality by selling their crops at local markets and shipping them into urban centres to be sold there? Unfortunately, the manorial accounts of Norwich Cathedral Priory do not specify where and by whom the crops were purchased. On the other hand, virtually omnipresent references to sales 'in merchant's advantage' (*in avantagio mercatoris*) suggest that, in most cases, grain was sold at the demesne gate, rather than local markets and fairs.[53]

As regards 'other' outgoings (see Figure 4.5), these, as a rule, meant the retaining of the crop on the demesne for various purposes. In most cases, this share of crops was distributed during the year as food allowances among *famuli* and as fodder for draught animals. Between c.1260 and 1290 about 32 per cent of legumes and oats were given to horses and, occasionally, to oxen. From c.1290 onwards, however, the demesne officials cut down the overall share of fodder crops to be distributed among draught animals. From that point until c.1400, draught animal fodder (mostly for horses), accounted for about 20 per cent of all AGCR expenditure, while more oats and legumes were sold at market. On the eve of the demise of direct management, the figure for the share of crops used as fodder stood at about 10 per cent of all the AGCR. In some cases, small amounts of grain and legumes were given to non-working – usually weakened – animals. Thus, at Sedgeford, local demesne managers were allocating, annually, between 10 and 40 quarters of rye to sheep, whose numbers fluctuated between 900 and 1800 heads before the Black Death.[54] Some accounts

---

53. Britnell, '*Avantagium Mercatoris*'.
54. For instance, 1313–14, 1333–4 and 1380–81. For the Sedgeford sheep flocks and wool industry, see N. Morimoto, *The sheep farming of Norwich Cathedral Priory in the 13th and 14th centuries*, Discussion Paper No. 2, Institute of Industrial Sciences, Nagoya Gakuin University (Seto City, 1977).

Table 4.4
Annual Gross Crop Receipt (AGCR) disposal, c.1300 and c.1400: Norwich Cathedral Priory and other collegial houses.

	Demesnes sampled	Harvest as % of AGCR	Total acquisition	Sent to headquarters	Sown	Sold	Other
c.1300 (±10 years)							
Norwich Cathedral Priory	16	86.6%	6320.4	31.6%	25.1%	22.1%	21.1%
Winchester Cathedral Priory	21	87.0%	8698.5	14.7%	26.8%	22.1%	36.4%
Bury St Edmunds Abbey	8	94.7%	3347.9	4.4%	34.0%	18.3%	60.4%
Glastonbury Abbey	32	81.6%	7098.2	33.4%	25.3%	10.1%	31.3%
Ramsey Abbey	16	77.4%	8064.9	28.5%	25.2%	2.7%	43.6%
Peterborough Abbey	21	80.6%	9649.9	31.6%	24.8%	4.6%	39.0%
Crowland Abbey	3	43.0%	1595.4	26.1%	16.6%	8.5%	48.8%
Bolton Priory	9	93.9%	3172.5	34.1%	18.6%	1.0%	46.3%
Canterbury Cathedral Priory	30	82.0%	11243.5	10.0%	23.0%	33.1%	33.9%
Westminster Abbey	38	84.0%	13371.7	18.2%	24.0%	16.0%	41.8%
Merton College	6	84.4%	1523.3	0.0%	16.3%	38.1%	45.6%
Sampled demesnes	200						
Weighted average		83.2%		26.4%	23.2%	12.1%	38.6%
c.1400 (± 20 years)							
Norwich Cathedral Priory	5	69.6%	2153.3	5.9%	21.1%	35.0%	38.0%
Winchester Cathedral Priory	12	88.1%	3751.1	21.9%	28.5%	10.9%	38.7%
Bury St Edmunds Abbey	11	75.7%	4467.4	9.7%	24.0%	23.5%	42.8%
Glastonbury Abbey	8	85.5%	1086.0	33.0%	25.4%	9.7%	31.9%
Ramsey Abbey	14	78.0%	5082.8	24.6%	24.5%	9.5%	41.4%
Peterborough Abbey	4	79.2%	1796.4	17.1%	33.5%	6.8%	42.6%
Canterbury Cathedral Priory	21	87.1%	4965.9	8.3%	38.97%	19.1%	33.6%
Westminster Abbey	21	87.3%	4121.8	9.2%	30.47%	26.3%	34.1%
Merton College	6	65.0%	1554.6	0.1%	24.59%	32.5%	42.7%
Sampled demesnes	102						
Weighted average		80.2%		18.0%	26.7%	14.8%	39.3%

Source: Manorial accounts database.
Note: The figures appearing under the heading 'Total acquisition' are given in quarters.

reveal that non-working animals were usually given inferior or corrupt grains. Thus, on the same demesne in 1371, two bushels of 'bad (wheat) chaff worth nothing' (*debile corallum nullius valoris*) were used to sustain piglets, capons and hens.[55]

Crop disposal in a wider context

It is impossible, nonetheless, to appreciate the nature and patterns of annual crop harvest disposals on the manors of Norwich Cathedral Priory without placing them in a wider context. One obvious means of doing so is to compare the situation on Norwich Cathedral Priory's manors with that on demesnes belonging to other conventual institutions. To that end, complementary data from 184 demesnes *c.*1300 and 97 demesnes *c.*1400, all belonging to ten conventual houses whose estates were located in different parts of the country, were analysed (Table 4.4). The estates of Winchester Cathedral Priory were divided between Hampshire and Wiltshire. The demesnes of Bury St Edmunds Abbey were situated in Suffolk. The manors of Glastonbury Abbey were located in the southern counties of Wiltshire, Hampshire, Devon, Dorset and Somerset. Ramsey Abbey and Peterborough Abbey controlled a network of demesnes in the East Midlands. Crowland Abbey possessed several manors in Cambridgeshire. Bolton Priory, situated in the Yorkshire Dales, drew upon several home farms located in its immediate vicinity. The vast majority of Canterbury Cathedral Priory's manors were found in Kent, although some were located elsewhere (Sussex, Surrey, Essex, Middlesex, Suffolk and Norfolk). The enormous estate of Westminster Abbey was scattered throughout numerous counties, from Sussex in the south to Rutland in the north, from Essex in the east to Worcestershire in the west. Finally, the far more modest estate of Merton College was divided, for the most part, between Oxfordshire, Buckinghamshire and Surrey.

As Table 4.4 indicates, the disposal patterns were different from estate to estate and these differences reflect the institutional arrangements and preferences of each individual community. Around 1300, with the exception of Crowland Abbey, all estates drew heavily on their harvests as the main component of the AGCR, while tithes, gifts and occasional purchases represented only insignificant portions of it. Crowland Abbey demesnes, on the other hand, relied strongly on tithes and receipts from elsewhere. A century later, however, the situation was somewhat different. While on some estates, such as Winchester Cathedral Priory, Glastonbury Abbey, Canterbury Cathedral Priory and Westminster Abbey, harvests still represented by far the largest part of their AGCR, the manors of Norwich Cathedral Priory, Bury St Edmunds Abbey and Merton College came to rely more on grain rents paid by local farmers. These rents became a prominent feature of the post-Black Death seigniorial economy, reflecting the gradual shift from *Gutsherrschaft* to *Grundherrschaft*; but in the case of Norwich Cathedral Priory they are attested long before the end of its direct demesne management, as shown below.

Outgoing patterns varied across estates too, despite some apparent similarities. Thus, *c.*1300 the demesnes of Norwich Cathedral Priory, Glastonbury Abbey, Ramsey Abbey, Peterborough Abbey, Crowland Abbey and Bolton Priory dispatched between

---

55. NRO, DCN 60/35/39.

Table 4.5

Demesne grain production costs and grain value on Norwich market, 1261–1430.

	Quarters harvested (including tithes)	Total expenditure (in £ sterling)	Nominal production costs per one quarter (in shillings)	Real production costs per one quarter (in shillings)	Weighted market value per quarter (in shillings)	Real production costs as % of market value	Real wages of agrarian workers, indexed on 1451–75
1261–70	5540.2	429.1	1.55	1.83	3.55	0.52	49.3
1271–80	5014.4	422.4	1.68	1.53	4.23	0.36	39.3
1281–90	7231.1	595.6	1.65	1.77	3.44	0.51	46.6
1291–1300	6378.3	640.1	2.01	1.68	4.69	0.36	45.1
1301–10	6270.4	597.9	1.91	1.88	4.18	0.45	51.3
1311–20	6821.4	582.7	1.71	1.15	5.83	0.20	42.8
1321–30	5981.0	534.7	1.79	1.41	5.27	0.27	49.4
1331–40	5016.1	458.6	1.83	1.93	4.04	0.48	57.5
1341–50	6000.0	464.5	1.55	1.77	3.51	0.50	63.6
1351–60	4141.9	371.4	1.79	1.50	4.61	0.33	52.8
1361–70	5052.7	565.9	2.24	1.64	4.83	0.34	52.3
1371–80	4800.1	586.9	2.45	2.31	3.82	0.60	69.9
1381–90	3264.1	809.3	4.96	5.55	2.84	1.95	77.4
1391–1400	3753.6	634.4	3.38	3.47	3.59	0.96	74.8
1401–10	4691.7	664.8	2.83	2.67	3.47	0.77	79.7
1411–20	4410.6	706.6	3.20	3.27	3.67	0.89	81.1
1421–30	2513.9	649.2	5.16	5.35	3.57	1.50	79.4
Pre-1350 decades	6028.1	525.1	1.74	1.66	4.31	0.41	49.4
Post-1350 decades	4078.6	623.6	3.25	3.22	3.80	0.92	70.9

Sources: Manorial accounts database; NRO, DCN 1/1/1–110; J.H. Munro, John Munro's revised tabulations of David Farmer's series of English 'national' agrarian wages, http://www.economics.utoronto.ca/munro5/ResearchData.html (accessed 11 October 2011).
Notes: Real production costs are nominal production costs deflated by the price index. The real wages are those of threshers, winnowers, reapers and binders.

a quarter and one-third of their AGCR to their headquarters. On the other hand, the demesnes of Winchester Cathedral Priory, Canterbury Cathedral Priory and Westminster Abbey sent much smaller shares of their AGCR to their urban households. Manors of Bury St Edmunds Abbey shipped hardly any grain to their headquarters, while Merton College did not rely on direct provisioning at all. Around 1400, perhaps somewhat surprisingly, the patterns of direct provisioning were still, more or less, the same on most estates. Only the demesnes of Norwich Cathedral Priory and Peterborough Abbey cut down the relative share of grain shipment to their headquarters.

Partially at least, these differences in figures relating to direct provisioning of the houses can be explained by variations in the degree of commercialisation of the estates. Thus, Canterbury Cathedral Priory and Merton College sold, respectively, 33 per cent and 38 of their AGCR *c.*1300. Other houses sold much less than that: Glastonbury Abbey, Peterborough Abbey and Crowland Abbey sold between 5 and 10 per cent of their AGCR on local markets, and Ramsey Abbey and Bolton Priory tended to market only meagre shares of their AGCR. Around 1400, however, we witness a pronounced rise in the commercialisation of some demesnes. The manors of Norwich Cathedral Priory, Ramsey Abbey and Westminster Abbey all increased their shares of annual grain sales. Conversely and quite paradoxically, however, both Winchester Cathedral Priory and Canterbury Cathedral Priory diminished their relative proportions of crop sales.

How, then, can we rank the demesnes of Norwich Cathedral Priory against other estates? There is no doubt that between 1300 and 1400 they underwent a significant degree of commercialisation. Around 1300 they tended to devote more crops to the direct provisioning of their lord than most other conventual estates did. Yet, at the same time, it does not mean that they were less commercialised than other demesnes: they allocated almost a quarter of their AGCR to marketing, a far larger figure than most other estates in the country around the same time. A century later Norwich Cathedral Priory seems to have become one of the most commercialised conventual estates, selling around 35 per cent of its AGCR on local markets. This development stands in sharp contrast to the demesnes of Winchester Cathedral Priory, Glastonbury Abbey and Canterbury Cathedral Priory, which all either decreased their relative shares of marketed grain or showed no signs of commercial growth.

Production costs

How expensive was it to produce the annual harvest? This is an essential question, whose answer can contribute a great deal to our understanding of the decline of the *Gutsherrschaft* economy on the one hand and the feeding patterns of late medieval conventual communities on the other. Production costs can be measured in two ways: absolute figures, namely the sums of cash spent on producing an annual crop harvest, which included expenditure on arable labour (manuring, ploughing, seeding, supervising, weeding, harvesting) as well as on draught animals (mostly plough-horses) and agricultural tools; and relative terms, namely the production costs of one unit of grain or, better yet, one unit of grain *compared* with the market price of the same unit.

As Table 4.5 shows, before the Black Death the demesne managers spent, collectively, about £525 a year, while the real production cost per unit stood at 1s 8d per one quarter of crop, namely about 41 per cent of the market value of the same

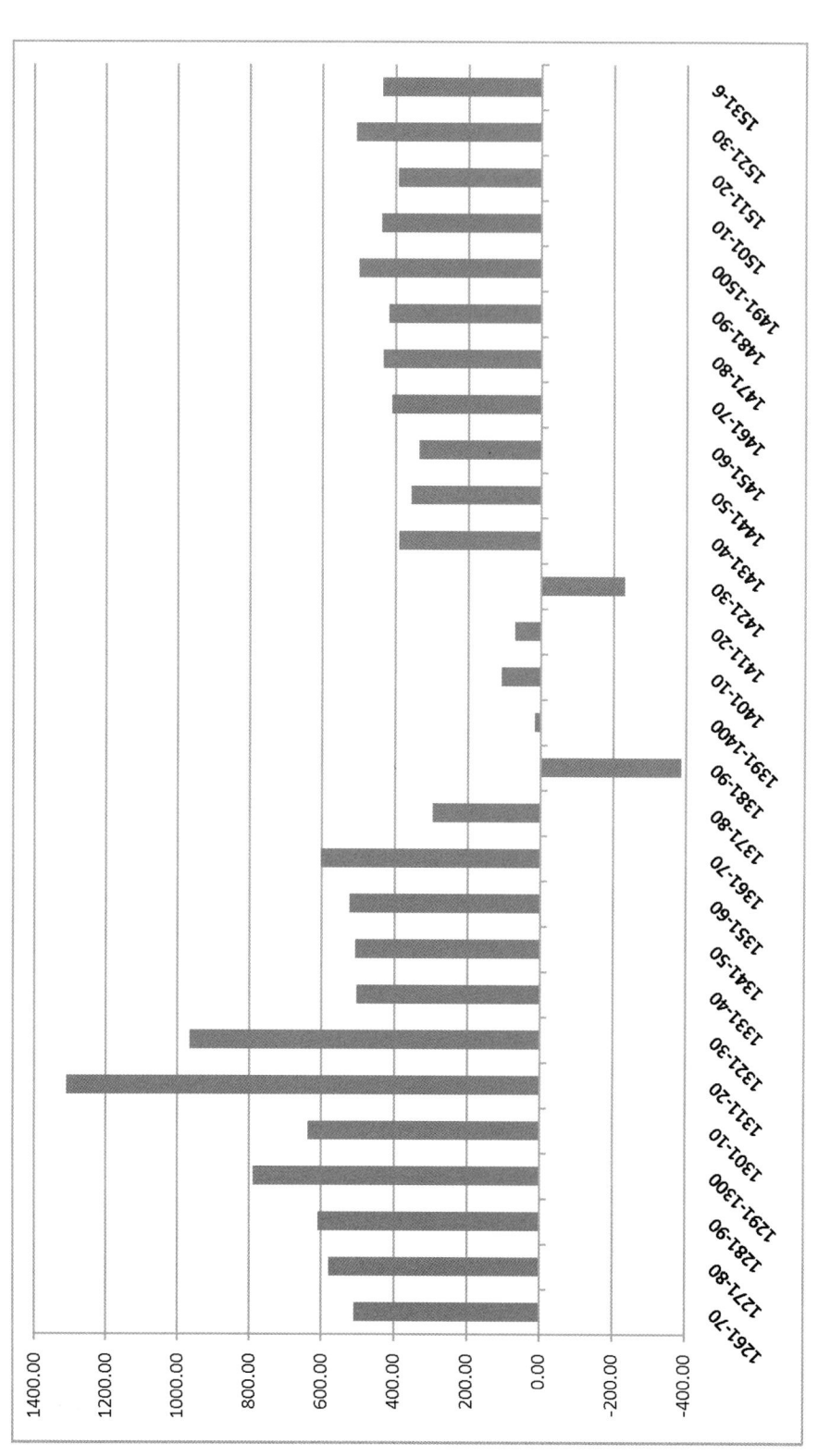

Figure 4.7 Net annual profit from the arable sector of Norwich Cathedral Priory, 1261–1536 (in £ sterling).
Sources: Manorial accounts database; NRO, DCN 1/1/1–110.

crop. This favourable situation reflects the monetary reality of the pre-pestilence period. As the table shows, while crop prices tended to rise rather than fall the real wages of agricultural workers (*famuli*) were depressed until *c*.1376. This meant that the costs of agricultural works (as well as transportation and storage costs, as we shall see later) were relatively low. This combination was most certainly adverse to the *famuli*, but highly profitable for the lords, and there is little doubt that it was a good reason to rely more on demesne production, rather than on local markets, for the provisioning of their households. Moreover, it was probably why the lords were so keen on keeping their demesnes in hand, rather than farming them out. The advantage of direct demesne management became especially apparent during the agrarian crisis of 1314/15–17/22, which saw three back-to-back harvest failures before 1320 (crop yields were 40 per cent below average in 1315, 60 per cent below average in 1316 and about 10 per cent below average in 1317) as well as an additional disastrous harvest in 1321 (about 33 per cent below average). While market prices soared drastically, the nominal wages of agricultural workers were depressed until 1322. With the exception of another disastrous famine year of 1597, the years of the Great Famine, and especially 1316–17, mark the single lowest point in the history of real wages of English workers before the Industrial Revolution.[56]

However, things changed quite drastically in the aftermath of the Black Death, when total production costs, in absolute figures, rose to about £624 a year. This is notwithstanding the fact that the volume of grain produced fell because of both demesne leases and the shrinkage of the remaining demesnes. In other words, the real production costs per unit of grain rose considerably after 1350, amounting at their height to about 92 per cent of the market value of the crops. The unit costs of production soared especially after the collapse of agricultural production prices in 1376, which marked the beginning of a period of a prolonged inflation and sharply rising real wages of workers, both agricultural and otherwise. During the 1380s the production costs of demesne grain, both nominal and real, rose to an unprecedented level because of the adverse combination of sharply falling prices and rising real wages. Although production costs fell in the 1390s, they still remained near the levels of the market value of crops. When production costs rose above market prices in the 1420s because of falling grain prices and rising wages, it was no longer profitable to rely on the demesne grain, in particular, and to manage the demesnes directly, in general. Although, as we have seen, after 1376 grain purchases were playing an increasingly important role in provisioning the priory, the latter was not yet ready to entirely entrust the grain provisioning of their household to the market. Instead, grain farms came to replace the demesne crop receipts.

The shift from *Gutsherrschaft* to *Grundherrschaft* solved not only the problem of rising production costs but also that of steeply declining net profits within the arable sector. As Figure 4.7 indicates, before the 1370s the directly managed demesnes were a highly profitable form of investment which yielded most promising returns. The annual net profit (financial value of harvested crops *minus* annual costs of production) varied anywhere between £500 and £1300. The changing post-Black Death reality altered this picture altogether. Between the 1360s and 1380s net profits fell from £602

---

56. Campbell, 'Four famines and a pestilence', p. 39.

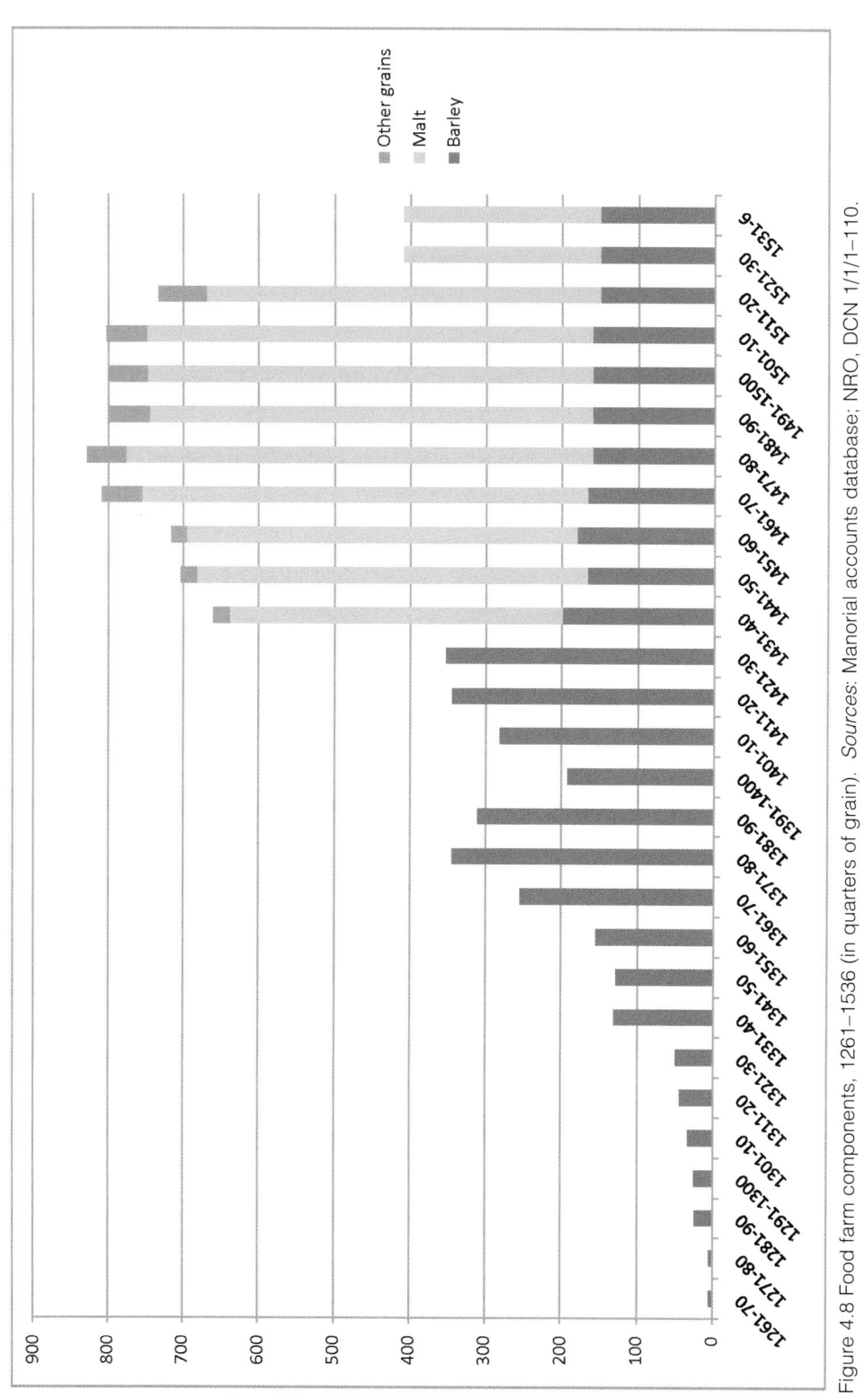

Figure 4.8 Food farm components, 1261–1536 (in quarters of grain). *Sources:* Manorial accounts database; NRO, DCN 1/1/1–110.

to the deficit of -£386 a year. Even when production costs temporarily fell in the 1390s, net profit was far below its pre-1370s levels. During the 1420s, when prices fell and production costs rose, net profit fell well below zero. There can be little doubt that the priory authorities, just as many other landed lords, may have realised that the *Gutsherrschaft* form of land management was too archaic and inefficient to justify its continuation. It was in this context that the markets, both formal and informal, and food farms came to play an increasingly important role in provisioning conventual households in late medieval England.

Food farms

Although the real signs of a piecemeal decline of the demesne did not begin until after the Black Death, small-scale leases of demesne field parcels commenced long before that. In most cases, the tenants paid the priory with barley, rather than cash. Thus, at Thornham between 1263 and 1298 tenants rented several acres of demesne fields for the fixed sum of five quarters of barley.[57] And at Monks Granges between 1287 and 1328 several acres of barley fields were leased to one Ives de Possewyck for the fixed sum of seven quarters of barley. After Ives' death around 1330, the lease was continued under his heirs for the same sum.[58] However, the importance of pre-Black Death grain farms should not be overstated: the land- and mill-farms represented, collectively, about 1 per cent of the AGCR. The main change came in the 1350s and especially in the 1360s, when an increasing number of barley field parcels were farmed out to local tenants (Figure 4.8). The latter were obliged to pay rent in grain, rather than in cash. This, perhaps, was a more favourable option for the lords, given the fact that grain prices tended to rise until 1376. In the course of the 1360s about 700 acres of barley fields were leased out in return for the annual payment of about 250 quarters of barley (with an average rate of about 2.5 bushels of grain per acre). The rent figures fell in the course of the 1380s and 1390s, when several demesnes were completely leased out for cash, but recovered in the 1400s, when the same demesnes were, temporarily, taken back in hand. In the 1420s, shortly before the demesnes were leased out for good, the brethren were receiving about 350 quarters of barley from the farmers on an annual basis.

Once the last demesne, Sedgeford, was leased out in 1431, however, the priory authorities decided to alter some leasing contracts and convert five of their former demesnes – Hemsby, Martham, Newton, Plumstead and Taverham – to grain rents from cash rents. Another leased demesne, North Elmham, commutated from cash to kind payments about 30 years later. The demesnes were leased out for several years, usually five or seven. The fact that the levels of grain farms changed from decade to decade indicates that the priory authorities tended to change the terms of leasing contracts by increasing the sums of grain due to be delivered annually. Between 1431 and 1480 the figures rose, collectively, from 660 to 829 quarters of grain a year. It should be borne in mind, however, that the figures were fixed for the duration of a leasing contract. The overall figures remained fairly constant for three decades, amounting to around 800

---

57. NRO, DCN 60/37/1–8.
58. NRO, DCN 60/26/7–25.

Bread and Ale for the Brethren

quarters a year. In the course of the 1510s, however, they collapsed to 733 quarters, while a decade later they fell further to slightly over 400 quarters a year. This was due to the fact that three leased demesnes, North Elmham, Plumstead and Newton, ceased to provide the brethren with grain farms, having switched back exclusively to cash rents. This undoubtedly reflects the decreased demand for grain because of the shrinking population of the priory in the early sixteenth century.

The main difference between food farms before and after 1431 is the fact that before that date they were collected individually from each farmer, while after that date they were rendered collectively from each leased demesne. The pre-1431 accounts provide some important insights into the conditions of grain rents, which could vary from farmer to farmer. Thus, according to the 1373 account from Gnatingdon, the duration of each individual leasing contract varied from four to seven years, while one farmer, Walter Edol, was leased half an acre for his lifetime (*ad terminum vite sue*). Similarly, the amounts of grain rendered and the land units leased differed from household to household. Thus, Thomas de Wodehous of Hindolveston was renting 14 acres of a barley field for just 2.5 quarters a year in the late 1360s.[59] At Hindringham, in the late 1370s, Roger Say and Henry Permonett were cooperatively renting 28 acres for 10.5 quarters a year. In the same place and around the same time, Alan Pynch was leasing just one perch of land for the annual rent of one quarter a year.[60] In some instances, several scattered parcels were leased out to the same individual. In the vast majority of the cases the lessees were male, although some isolated instances of the leasing of parcels to women, including widows, occur in the accounts. Thus, in 1364 at Martham three rods of a barley field were leased to the widow of William Caison.[61] Examples of sub-leasing are not unheard of. For instance, in 1377 Bryce Lucy of Hindringham was subleasing 2.75 acres to another tenant, Roger Say, also of Hindringham.[62] In some exceptional cases, barley parcels were leased out alongside pasture. Thus, in the late 1370s, John Casyn of Hindringham was rendering annually three bushels of barley for three rods of barley field with an unspecified amount of pasture. The subject of post-Black Death land fragmentation through leasing and sub-leasing is yet to be studied in detail.

As Figure 4.8 indicates, both before and after Black Death, the vast majority of food farms were associated with barley. Before 1431, no other grain but fresh barley was rendered, while, after that date, malted barley accounted for about 70 per cent of all food farms. Receiving barley in malted form was undoubtedly profitable for the priory, because it helped to save on brewing costs. The remainder was made up of fresh barley (about 25 per cent) and small amounts of wheat, maslin, rye and oats, collectively constituting the final 5 per cent of the total. Likewise, each leased demesne contributed a different share of the total. Thus, Hemsby, the single most productive demesne, contributed about 30 per cent of the total grain farms. Newton and Martham, likewise, contributed almost a quarter each. The share of North Elmham, Plumstead and Taverham, on the other hand, accounted for about 8 per cent each.

---

59. NRO, Lest/IC/19; DCN 60/18/42.
60. NRO, DCN 60/20/31.
61. NRO, NNAS 6894 20 D1.
62. NRO, DCN 60/20/31.

Conclusions

A detailed analysis of crop harvesting and disposal on the Norwich Cathedral Priory demesnes is most revealing. Aside from the unique structure of both the production and the disposal patterns practised by the priory demesnes, the analysis reveals much wider economic issues and phenomena with much potential for future research. One such topic is the relative commercial conservativism of the Norwich Cathedral Priory authorities, which should not be equated with economic insufficiency. Its pronounced tendency to distance itself from the market, either as a vendor or a buyer, and to rely, instead, on its directly managed demesnes, proved to be an efficient and rational economic strategy for the priory in the pre-Black Death period. In this era of environmental shocks, low real wages, fluctuating prices and, therefore, unstable markets it was only natural for the Norwich brethren to keep their demesnes in hand and exploit them as much as they could. After the Black Death, but chiefly from 1376 onwards, the situation was altogether different: production costs went up considerably, making the *Gutsherrschaft* economy no longer profitable. At the same time, however, the priory was not yet ready to switch entirely to the market to secure its daily bread. The obvious compromise was to retain the direct supply of grain from the demesnes without their direct management. This was made possible with the introduction of the annual food farms from six of the leased demesnes.

Another major issue deriving from the analysis of the demesne accounts is the tension between ecology and institutions as the determinants of crop-growing. As we have seen, in many instances environmental factors such as soil type and altitude seem to have played a paramount role in shaping the geography of crop cultivation. On the other hand, endogenous factors such as the distance from a town or the degree of commercialisation were also important. In other words, we cannot stick to a single model, such as that proposed by Von Thünen, to explain this phenomenon. As we saw in the previous chapter, nature and institutions seem often to have been two sides of the same coin and, as such, should not be studied in isolation from each other.

The unique structure of demesne agriculture in Norfolk is yet another intriguing topic. A strong focus on the spring crops, chiefly barley, was the predominant feature of Norfolk agriculture. Despite many common topographic and environmental features shared with the neighbouring counties of Suffolk, Cambridgeshire and Lincolnshire, Norfolk hardly resembled any of these in terms of the trends in crop-growing. What accounted for that? Were these unique trends dictated by some local market and demographic conditions peculiar only to Norfolk? Or was it a matter of regional cultural identity, in which the malting industry played a significant role? These and other questions are yet to be studied in detail and there is no doubt that such studies will bear most fruitful yields.

Chapter 5

Shipping the produce: transportation requirements, strategies and costs

Grain transportation: sources and resources

As we have seen in the previous chapter, the demesne harvest did not remain in the demesne barns. Much of it was sent to Norwich, to be processed and consumed by the monastic community and their servants and guests. In other words, the crops, mostly wheat and (malted) barley, were loaded on carts and taken to the town. In order to ensure regular deliveries of grain to their Norwich headquarters, the priory authorities relied on two main channels: their right to extract carting services from some of their manorial tenants and the services of hired manorial carters, almost invariably *famuli*, employed at the harvest period. Unfortunately, our information about the actual process of grain shipping is very limited, because the accounts did not, as a rule, record specific details of this process. To partially reconstruct the picture, we have to rely not only on the demesne accounts but also on the so-called *Stowe Survey*, or customary extent of the priory's manors, compiled at various stages between 1275 and 1292. The demesne accounts provide a great deal of information about demesne horses, manorial carters – whether those hired during or outside the harvest time – and the maintenance costs of carts and horses. In particular, the accounts are vital for establishing the numbers of carters and the terms of their employment. The *Stowe Survey*, on the other hand, records in considerable detail various dues of the manorial tenants, which, in some cases, included carting duties. In addition to these two sources, a large number of the central monastic accounts, chiefly the rolls of the master of the cellar, are used. These rolls abound in data about Priory carters and boatmen, which, although seem to have been rarely employed for transporting the grain from the demesne to the priory, are, nevertheless, important for our analysis and the discussion.

During the entire period under study, Norwich Cathedral Priory had sufficient means and resources to ensure the steady transportation of its grain supply, whether dispatched directly from the demesnes or bought from various Norfolk markets. First and foremost, the priory had a substantial number of horses on its demesnes which functioned as both ploughing and carting animals. In most, if not all, cases the terms *equi* and *stotti* were interchangeable in the accounts. In addition to the demesne stots, there were also a number of carting horses in the priory's own stables. Horses, however, would be useless without carters, who fell into three main groups: those who owed customary carrying dues to the priory in return for their holdings; those who were hired for the purpose, usually local *famuli*, both during and outside harvest; and the permanent and stipendiary staff of two priory carters. Although the vast majority of the demesne grain seems to have been transported on carts during or shortly after the harvest season, the priory authorities also used an additional mean of transportation: the boat. The priory is known to have possessed a substantial boat, constructed in 1320–21 and stationed on the Yare, in addition to a couple of 'small boats', two 'galleys' and the 'Marsh boat', which serviced the Broads. In addition, the demesnes of Eaton, Newton, Plumstead and Taverham are known to have possessed, in various periods, at least one boat each,[1] while, in addition to the priory boatmen, one boatman usually appears among other stipendiary *famuli* at Plumstead and Newton. Just as in the case of the carters, the priory had a permanent staff of two stipendiary boatmen. The regular staff of the priory boatmen and carters became important towards the end of the direct management era, and especially after 1431, when the brethren had no choice but to rely on both carters and boatmen to transport the grain from the leased demesnes, where the lessees paid the rent in both cash and kind.

Demesne horses

Before turning to the humans, however, let us first deal with the main source of carting labour: the horse. Although, as John Langdon has shown, most manorial accounts tend to clearly distinguish between 'carting' and 'plough' horses (the latter also known as affers or stots), the Norwich Cathedral Priory demesne rolls did not, for the most part, differentiate between the two.[2] As the language of these accounts suggests, the terms *equi* (cart horses) and *stotti* (plough or draught horses) are invariably interchangeable. For example, the Sedgeford roll from 1300–1301 states that 17.50 quarters of oats were given *in prebendum ii equorum manerii* (as fodder to two manorial *equi*), while the livestock account on the same roll does not list a single *equus*, referring to the horses as *stotti* instead.[3] Many such examples could be added here.[4] In other words, our sources reveal quite clearly that the manorial horses tended to function as both plough and carting horses.[5]

Table 5.1 indicates that although the overall figures fell, reflecting a piecemeal retreat from direct management, relative numbers of horses (that is, the average number of horses per demesne) did not decline much over the entire period. Nor did they fluctuate much. Interestingly enough, this stands in contrast with the situation elsewhere in England, in particular in the 1320s, when many lords and their demesne officials tended to augment horse numbers to compensate for mass losses of oxen in the Great Cattle Pandemic of 1319–20.[6] In Norfolk, however, there was no need to replace oxen with horses, since it had been a pronouncedly horse-orientated county decades before the panzootic.[7]

As far as feed is concerned, there were three main components: grass (whether fresh or dried as hay), grain straw, and crops (mostly oats, but also legumes and occasionally spring legume–oats mixtures). Naturally, the conversion of these

---

1. The sole reference to the Eaton boat is found in the 1320–21 master of the cellar roll (NRO, DCN 1/1/28). The only reference to Taverham's is entered into the 1315–16 account of the same official (NRO, DCN 1/1/25). Neither of the two manors is known to have had a boatman.
2. J. Langdon, 'The economics of horses and oxen in medieval England', *AHR*, 30 (1982), p. 33.
3. NRO, Lest/IB/16.
4. NRO, DCN 60/33/14, 20, 22; NRO, DCN 60/14/11a, 12; NRO, DCN 60/20/15.
5. Langdon indeed mentioned that 'there was some overlapping in function'. See Langdon, 'The economics of horses and oxen', p. 33.
6. Langdon, *Horses, oxen*, pp. 164–70; Slavin, 'The great bovine pestilence'.
7. Campbell, *English seigniorial agriculture*, pp. 129–31.

Table 5.1
Annual fodder requirements on the manors of Norwich Cathedral Priory, 1261–1430.

	Total numbers of demesne horses	Horses per demesne	Grass (total allocation, in tonnes)	Straw (total allocation, in tonnes)	Crop (total allocation, in tonnes)	All fodder (allocation, in tonnes)	Fodder per horse (in tonnes)	Grass (calorific contribution)	Straw (calorific contribution)	Oat and oat bran (calorific contribution)	Peas (calorific contribution)	Other crops (calorific contribution)	Total calorific contribution
1261–70	139.2	8.2	234.7	123.4	38.1	396.3	2.8	56.4%	24.4%	19.0%	0.3%	0.0%	100.0%
1271–80	142.9	8.4	271.0	111.7	30.6	413.3	2.9	63.4%	21.5%	15.1%	0.0%	0.0%	100.0%
1281–90	162.3	9.5	247.6	161.1	50.1	458.8	2.8	51.0%	27.3%	21.3%	0.4%	0.0%	100.0%
1291–1300	138.6	8.2	225.8	142.1	34.7	402.6	2.9	54.5%	28.2%	16.0%	1.3%	0.0%	100.0%
1301–10	147.8	8.7	267.5	139.7	30.2	437.4	3.0	60.5%	26.0%	10.2%	3.2%	0.0%	100.0%
1311–20	146.0	8.6	257.3	152.0	28.2	437.5	3.0	58.9%	28.6%	8.5%	4.0%	0.0%	100.0%
1321–30	138.5	8.7	267.5	133.3	19.0	419.8	3.0	64.6%	26.5%	6.6%	2.4%	0.0%	100.0%
1331–40	109.6	8.4	198.1	111.8	20.0	329.8	3.0	60.4%	28.0%	6.9%	4.6%	0.0%	100.0%
1341–50	126.8	7.9	230.5	133.7	20.4	384.6	3.0	60.8%	29.0%	6.2%	4.0%	0.0%	100.0%
1351–60	104.0	6.9	219.2	92.3	8.3	319.7	3.1	70.5%	24.4%	3.5%	1.6%	0.0%	100.0%
1361–70	102.3	8.5	174.6	112.6	19.7	306.8	3.0	57.1%	30.3%	9.5%	3.2%	0.0%	100.0%
1371–80	114.2	9.5	226.9	107.0	14.0	347.8	3.0	66.4%	25.8%	4.6%	1.9%	1.3%	100.0%
1381–90	82.2	8.2	164.2	72.7	11.6	248.5	3.0	66.8%	24.3%	4.2%	1.5%	3.2%	100.0%
1391–1400	82.4	7.5	166.4	83.6	6.1	256.1	3.1	67.5%	27.9%	1.6%	0.4%	2.7%	100.0%
1401–10	101.6	7.8	192.0	104.5	13.9	310.5	3.1	63.2%	28.3%	2.9%	1.4%	4.1%	100.0%
1411–20	99.9	8.3	199.4	98.3	10.0	307.7	3.1	66.7%	27.1%	2.7%	1.9%	1.5%	100.0%
1421–30	91.0	7.6	203.0	56.0	12.4	271.5	3.0	74.6%	16.9%	4.0%	2.5%	2.0%	100.0%
Average, 1261–1350	139.1	8.5	244.4	134.3	30.1	408.9	2.9	58.9%	26.6%	12.2%	2.3%	0.0%	100.0%
Average, 1351–1430	97.2	8.1	193.2	90.9	12.0	296.1	3.0	66.6%	25.6%	4.1%	1.8%	1.9%	100.0%

Source: Manorial accounts database.

Notes: Calculations derived from the assumption that a late medieval non-war-horse was about 20 per cent smaller in size than modern ones and as such, would require approximately 14,600 kcal on a daily basis. The quantities of non-grain fodder (that is, hay and grass deriving from both pasturage and hay), unspecified in the accounts, as well as its calorific equivalent, is reckoned using the following guidelines: in around 1300, straw contributed about 26 per cent to the total calorific intake of horses. Since straw, as a by-product of cereal production, was sensitive to the proportions of land under crop, the decennial change in relative calorific contribution of straw was reckoned in accordance with the decennial change in the total amounts of harvested crops. The remainder of the calories came from grassland (pasturage and hay). The calories are then converted into their approximate weight equivalents (in tonnes).

elements into their weight and calorific equivalents should be taken with caution, but they should not be too greatly removed from reality.

As the table reveals, there were some significant changes in the composition of horse fodder over the entire period. First, the pre-Black Death period is marked by a gradual increase of the relative (per capita) contribution of grass at the expense of oats. After the Black Death, however, the demesne managers tended to allocate even larger proportions of grass-based fodder for horse consumption. Second, after the pestilence we witness some new crops joining oats as fodder. These were *pulmentum* (legume–oats mixture), which to a large degree came to replace peas, and occasionally rye, normally given to sustain ailing animals. Between the 1350s and the 1400s an estimated calorific share of fodder based on crops and legumes fell from about 10 to some 5 per cent. These shifts undoubtedly reflect larger socio-economic and ecological trends. Demographic growth and congestion prior to the pre-Black Death would have prompted the demesne managers to cut down the proportion of oats in horse fodder in favour of using them to feed manorial *famuli*, a decision which would have necessitated the augmenting of the horses' diet with grass-based fodder. This strategy seems to be especially crucial within the Norfolk context: as we have noted earlier, this was the single most congested county in the first half of the fourteenth century.[8] Indeed, the account rolls demonstrate that the bailiffs allocated larger and larger amounts of oats, in both relative and absolute terms, to manorial employees. After the Black Death we may trace a relative switch from arable-orientated husbandry to a more pastoral form of agriculture. This change gained ground especially after *c.*1376, when there was a pronounced crossvergence between falling crop prices and rising real wages. It was no longer attractive to the lords to engage in labour-intense forms of agriculture commanding low prices and high unit costs. In many cases, these changes prompted the lords and their demesne officials to cut back the arable proportion of the demesne and increase its pasturage part, which was associated with more extensive types of husbandry, especially sheep rearing. These changes are reflected in the increased proportions of grass-and straw-based fodder, and the reduced shares of oats and legumes fed to horses.

The 'Great Boat' (*magna navis*)

In addition to horses and carting equipment, the priory possessed a number of boats, each serving a different purpose. Throughout the entire period under study, these included the 'great' and the 'small' boat (*magna* and *parva navis/batella*); two barges; and the 'Marsh' boat, servicing the Broads. There is no doubt that the single most substantial vessel here was the 'Great Boat'. Although the old *magna batella* was in existence since at least the 1260s, in 1320–21 a new boat was constructed using 219 wooden planks, thousands of nails and a large number of other buildings materials. The overall cost of its construction was £12 18s 6d. Although the accounts do not specify dimensions, a reference to the 219 wooden planks used in its construction may hint that this boat could have been up to 5m in length, some 2m in width and some 1.5m in breadth, if, as archaeological evidence of late medieval English ships

---

8. Campbell and Bartley, *Eve of the Black Death*, pp. 330–31.

suggests, each plank measured approximately 1m in length and 0.35m in breadth.[9] As some later master of the cellar accounts indicate, this boat could carry 200 quarters of malt on three trips. This implies a capacity of about 18 tons, equivalent to either 45 quarters of wheat or 66 quarters of malted barley. These figures are comparable with those of some other late medieval English cargo ships.[10]

There is no evidence that the great ship was used for carrying the demesne grain before the 1390s. From that time onwards, however, it was used, as indicated above, to carry about 200 quarters of malt from Hemsby to the priory headquarters each year. After the demesnes were leased and the priory shifted from *Gutsherrschaft* to *Grundherrschaft*, the boat continued to function as a transporter of food farms of malt rendered by the Hemsby farmers. It is also possible that the boat was carrying grain from neighbouring Martham. Some post-1390 master of the cellar rolls specify that the malt was carted from Hemsby (and possibly Martham) to the nearby port of Great Yarmouth, where it was picked by the priory boatmen and shipped directly to the priory granary. Shipping the manorial grain, however, was far from the only function of the great boat. Its large carrying capacity was successfully exploited to ship large freights of fuel, stone, iron, lumber and building materials, as indicated in many master of the cellar accounts.

Transporting services: customary dues

A crucially important role in maintaining horses and transporting grain from the demesnes to Norwich was played by manorial tenants. As far as carting services are concerned, we have to distinguish here between customary tenants owing carrying dues from their holdings through custom, and manorial carters hired alongside with other *famuli* in the harvest time. In other words, the Norwich Cathedral Priory authorities used their seigniorial rights to extract services owed by peasants and relied on hired work in order to effect the delivery of demesne grain to the cathedral precinct. Although in some cases the customary tenants with carrying duties and hired carters could be the same people, each group is to be treated separately. Let us begin with the customary tenants. It should be remembered that carting services were, in many cases, a part of manorial obligations in late medieval England.[11] Along with their obligation to cart grain to the priory, tenants also functioned as transporters of rural products to the market. These included not only grains and legumes, but also dairy products, poultry, game, fish, wood, stone and building materials. Who were these carrying tenants?

Our sources shed some light on the social and economic status of these tenants. It should be noted, however, that most peasants were exempt from carting and only a

---

9. S. McGrail, *Ancient boats in north-west Europe: the archaeology of water transport to AD 1500* (London, 1987), p. 127; D.M. Goodburn, 'Reused medieval ship planks from Westminster, England, possibly derived from a vessel built in the cog style', *International Journal of Nautical Archaeology*, 26/1 (1997), pp. 26–38.
10. McGrail, *Ancient boats*, p. 200.
11. D.L. Farmer, 'Marketing the produce of the countryside, 1200–1500', in E. Miller (ed.), *The Agrarian History of England and Wales, vol. III 1348–1500* (Cambridge, 1991), pp. 347–58.

small minority of tenants had such duties. It is unclear why these peasants were obliged to cart for the priory, but it is likely that this was a customary obligation going back to the early days of the priory, and possibly even further back. The manor of Eaton was an exceptional case, in which every tenant was obliged to perform the carting service, albeit on a relatively limited scale.[12] Our main source of information is the *Stowe Survey*, an extent of the Norwich Cathedral Priory estates compiled at various points between c.1275 and 1292. This document lists the tenants' names and also describes their holdings, customary dues and services. Thanks to this detailed survey, we can learn not only about the extent of the carting obligations of each tenant but also about his social and economic status on the eve of the fourteenth century.

The carting service, or arriage (*averagium* or *arregium*), was known in two main forms: as an individual obligation of a tenant, or as a collective burden of the entire manor. Far the most common form was the former; as noted above, only Eaton had to perform arriage collectively (see below). There are no distinctive socio-economic features which served as criteria for the carrying service; both poor and well-to-do peasants performed arriage. For instance, Nicholas *clericus*, a tenant from Eaton, held as much as 28 acres of arable, 3 acres of meadow, 4.25 acres of heath and 4 acres of marsh, had goods assessed at 6s 9½d and had to pay an annual customary payment (*ad auxilium*) of 12½d.[13] Nicholas was certainly a very prosperous tenant by any standard. On the other hand, his neighbour Benedict le Leche had no more than a cottage valued at 9½d and was unable to pay any customary payment at all.[14] An average carrier in Eaton held 8.50 acres of arable, had possessions valued at 2s and paid a customary payment of 5½d.[15] An average carrying tenant in Hindringham in the 1280s held 9.76 acres of land, had goods assessed at 2s 3d and paid around 8d as an annual customary due.[16] Yet both tenants were obliged to cart. In Hindringham, out of 113 surviving tenant names, 48 (that is, around 42 per cent) had to perform arriage.[17] Hindolveston, on the other hand, had only one family performing carrying duties (out of 128).[18] The tenants of Monks Granges, Newton, North Elmham, Plumstead, Sedgeford and Taverham were exempt from arriage and the situation was unclear in Denham, Gnatingdon, Gateley and Thornham.

The situation at Martham was far more complicated. Its extremely detailed survey provides a unique insight into the chronological dynamics of the carrying services, as it depicts the state of affairs both c.1200 and in 1292. Around 1200, only seven households (out of the total 108) were responsible for carting. Because of demographic growth in the course of the thirteenth century, its population grew more

---

12. 'Et omnes homines prioris de Etone cariabunt uj minas frumenti a Sechford usque Norwycum'. *Terrarium Prioratus* (British Library, MS Stowe 936), fol. 26r.
13. Ibid., fol. 23v.
14. Ibid., fol. 25v.
15. Calculated from 30 holdings in Eaton. Ibid., fols 23r–25v.
16. Ibid., fols 23r–25v.
17. Calculated from around 100 holdings in Hindringham. Ibid., fols 2r–8r.; British Library, MS Add. 57973, fols 1r–1v.
18. *Terrarium Prioratus*, fol. 10r.

than threefold (there were 345 households by 1292) and its holdings were divided and subdivided further. As a result, we find as many as 45 households performing the carrying tasks in 1292.[19] Needless to say, the holdings of these 45 carrying tenants were much smaller than those of their seven colleagues *c.*1200: on average, the latter possessed about 0.75 acres of arable land, while the former held about 5 acres each. Typical of this plot subdivision was the land of Thomas Knight. Around 1200, this peasant held 12 acres, while almost a century later his parcel was divided among 11 tenants.[20] Hence, roughly speaking, the carriers of Martham were the poorest tenants. It is hardly surprising that the 45 tenants had to carry the same customary amount of grain, malt, poultry and hay as their predecessors: after all, it was the population that had grown, not the land. We shall return to the amounts and conditions later.

As is stated above, tenants with carrying duties did not form any distinctive social group, since, along with these duties, they were burdened with multiple tasks – just as were most other peasants. For instance, Richard Raremere of Hindringham, in addition to his carrying duties, also had to plough and manure land, sow and reap crops, look after and render chickens and eggs, thresh and weed grass, stack grain sheaves (*cornbote*) and malt barley.[21] A certain Thomas of Hindringham, in addition to his carrying duties, was required to perform numerous other tasks, including serving as the bailiff (*prepositus*) of the same manor.[22] The tenants occupying the land once belonging to Agnes Keneman in Martham had a choice of either carrying hens to Norwich or driving swine there.[23] There are countless similar examples of tenants performing numerous agricultural and administrative tasks other than the carting service.

Perhaps the most striking thing is that the carrying obligations did not distinguish between men, women, laymen or clerks. In other words, they were imposed on holdings, rather than on individuals. There are several examples of carting dues extracted from women. For example, Alicia Lambert of Hindringham, who held four acres of arable land assessed at 1s 4d, had to cart one load (*lod*, probably equal to one full carriage) of grain to the town each year.[24] Isabelle Pondermakere of Eaton, possibly a widow, who had two acres of land valued at just 5d, was subjected to the arriage duties just as were her fellow-inhabitants.[25] Clerks with carting duties are mentioned in the survey, too. One of them was Nicholas *clericus* of Eaton, whose wealth has already been described above. Another was one William *capellanus*, who held 2.5 acres of arable in Martham *c.*1200 and whose plot was settled by four families in 1292. William's obligation was to carry the dominical hay down to the manor's bridge.[26] It is unclear if the clerics themselves performed the carrying duties. One

---

19. *Terrarium Prioratus*, fols 37r–115v.
20. Ibid., fols 39v–40v.
21. Ibid., fol. 2r.
22. Ibid., fol. 5r.
23. Ibid., fols 53r–53v.
24. Ibid., fol. 3v.
25. Ibid., fol. 25r.
26. Ibid., fols 69r–69v.

possibility is that these churchmen actually held their plots, along with their customary duties, from the priory. This, however, does not mean that the physical task of carting was actually performed by women or priests: it is important to differentiate between the duty and its execution, and these women and clerks might have relied on somebody else to fulfil these obligations, perhaps a male relative, friend or wage-earner. Certainly, Nicholas *clericus* of Eaton was wealthy enough to afford to hire some layman to perform the carting task. It would be unjustified, however, to reach any definite *argumentum ex silentio*.

Now let us turn to the conditions of the carrying obligations. These varied both from family to family and from place to place. Eight families of Hindringham, holding between 0.22 and 4 acres each, had to carry hens to Norwich.[27] Nineteen other households were obligated to cart between one and two *lods* (presumably, full carts),[28] although, unfortunately, the survey does not specify what these *lods* consisted of. Several peasants of Hindringham were obliged to carry a coomb (half a quarter) of wheat or malt to Norwich.[29] One tenant, Richard Raremere, had to cart as much as 28 coombs a year.[30] Clearly, he was an exception, rather than the rule. In Hindolveston there was only one family with carting duties. Its members – William, son of Ralf; his half-brother John, son of Simon; and their common mother, Agnes – had 'to cart, with their companions, demesne grain and malt to Norwich, until all of it will be carted completely'.[31] In other words, they were burdened with carting the manor's entire supply of wheat and malt to the priory. In contrast, and as noted above, the peasants of Eaton were responsible collectively for the carrying of their share of grain and malt, so that the entire village community carted their demesne production.[32]

Some tenants were required to carry goods from manors other than their own. For example, the tenants of Eaton were also obliged to carry 6 *mine* (18 quarters) of wheat to Norwich and 21 carriages of peat (used as fuel) from Gidingheythe.[33] Similarly, some villagers of Hindringham had also to cart grain to Hindolveston, a neighbouring manor.[34]

Not every household charged with carting had to perform its duty each year. For example, two tenants of Martham were obliged to cart every other year, while three of their fellow-villagers had to carry every third year.[35] The most common carting time was Pentecost, which is hardly surprising. This feast falls between 10 May and 13 June, exactly when the wheat prices were at their highest.[36] It was certainly profitable

---

27. Ibid., fols 2r–8r.; British Library, MS Add. 57973, fols 1r–1v.
28. *Terrarium Prioratus*, fols 2r–8r.
29. Ibid., fols 2r–8r.; British Library, MS Add. 57973, fols 1r–1v.
30. *Terrarium Prioratus*, fol. 2r.
31. Ibid., fol. 10r.
32. Ibid., fol. 26r.
33. Ibid., fols 25v–26r.
34. Ibid., fols 2r–8r.
35. Ibid., fols 53r–53v and 69r–69v.
36. Campbell *et al.*, *A medieval capital*, pp. 199–202.
37. *Terrarium Prioratus*, fol. 3r.

for the priory authorities. Only one tenant was obliged to carry malt in August, while another was requested to transport two carriages of grain in the autumn.[37] At that time of year grain prices were still comparatively high, especially for barley and ale.

The carrying tenants did not perform their task entirely for free. Most were paid *ad cibum*, namely in food, which was served at the guest hall of the priory (*in aula hospitum*) once the product was delivered. The extent of *ad cibum* varied from case to case. For instance, some peasants from Martham would normally receive a gallon of ale and a loaf of bread.[38] Richard Line of Hindringham was offered a loaf of bread and a piece of cheese.[39] Line's colleagues from Hindolveston were rewarded with bread and ale at the guest hall.[40] The carrying tenants of Eaton going to Sedgeford in order to transport its grain and ale to the town were served a supper (*cena*) there; upon their arrival at Norwich they received food and drink (*cibum et potum*) at the guest hall.[41] For carrying 21 carriages of peat (used as fuel) from Gidingheythe, or 9 carts of hay from Eaton to the priory, each carrier enjoyed two meals (*duo repastus*).[42]

Transporting services: harvest *famuli*

Manorial tenants owing carting dues formed only a tiny minority of all the available carting power, however. A much more significant role in the carting of grain from the field to the monks' table was played by local *famuli*, hired around the harvest time for a period usually lasting for about five weeks, from early August until early–mid September. We are very fortunate to possess very detailed information about this group of carters, whose numbers and terms of employment were carefully recorded in the 'costs of harvest' section of the demesne accounts.

Harvest time was arguably the single busiest period in the agricultural year of the demesne. It was then that manorial authorities and officials had to take care of some particularly urgent tasks, including reaping the grain grown on both the winter and spring fields, storing it in local barns and carting it to markets or their lords' headquarters. In addition, some matured animals were driven to be sold at local markets or fairs. In most cases, local servile or customary dues were insufficient to perform all the harvest tasks and demesne lords had to rely also on additional hired work, provided first and foremost by local *famuli* or, roughly defined, the team of permanent labourers on medieval demesnes.[43] Here, carters represented an indispensable and integral part of a *famuli* team, alongside a bailiff, reeve, cook (usually also serving as bakers and brewers), clerk, tithe collector and a number of messors and reapers. The language and terminology of the demesne are generally

---

38. Ibid., fol. 39v.
39. Ibid., fol. 3r.
40. Ibid., fol. 10r.
41. Ibid., fol. 26r.
42. Ibid., fol. 26r.
43. On *famuli*, see M.M. Postan, *The famulus: the estate labourer in the XIIth and XIIIth Centuries* (Cambridge, 1954) and especially, D.L. Farmer, 'The *Famuli* in the later Middle Ages', in R.H. Britnell and J. Hatcher (eds), *Progress and problems in medieval England: essays in honour of Edwards Miller* (Cambridge, 1996), pp. 207–36.

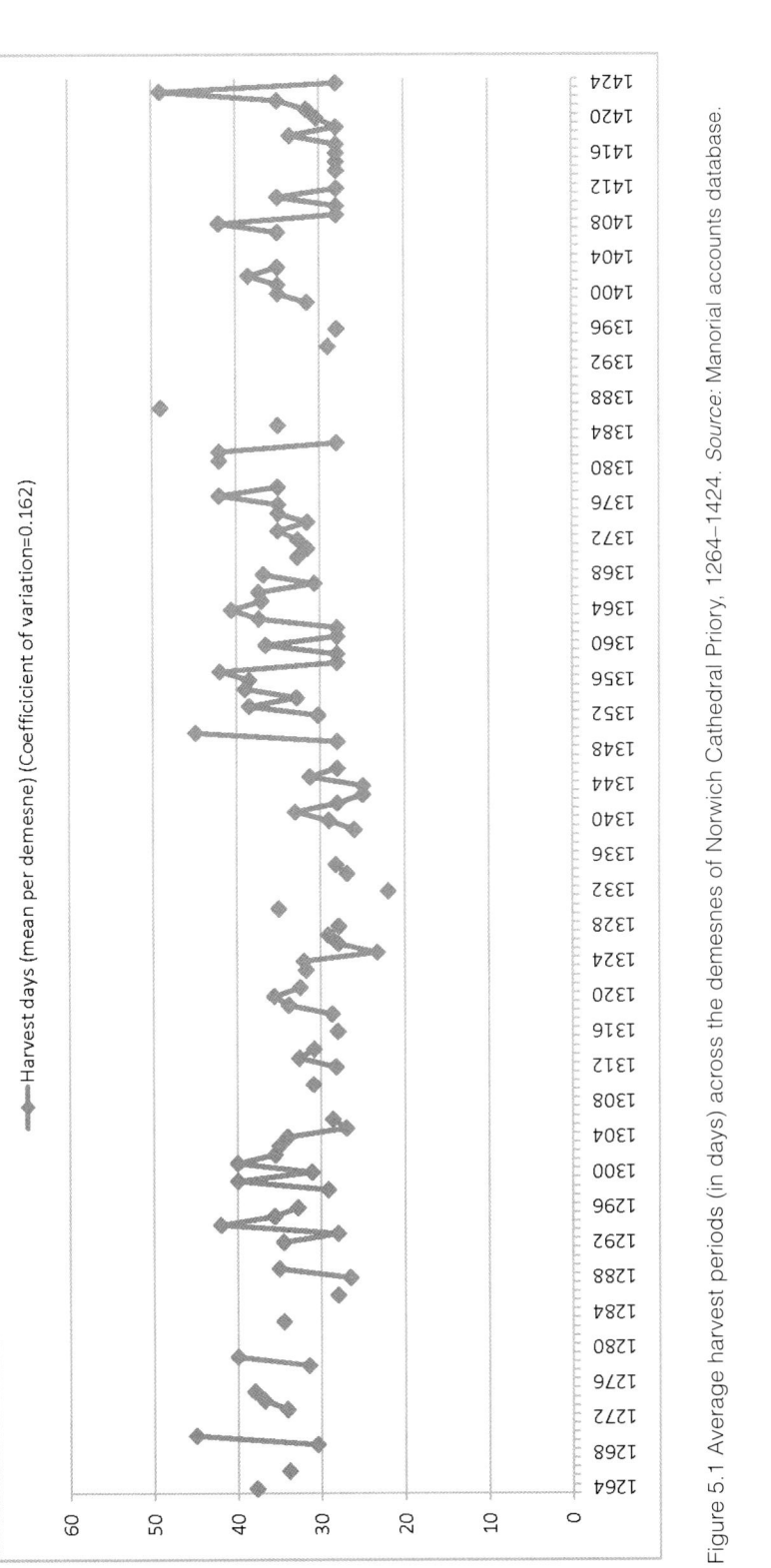

Figure 5.1 Average harvest periods (in days) across the demesnes of Norwich Cathedral Priory, 1264–1424. *Source:* Manorial accounts database.

straightforward, and in the vast majority of cases the carters are referred to as *carrectarii*. Some accounts, however, are less helpful in their description of the carters, and simply refer to them as *famuli*, despite the fact that the proper occupation of other workers are given.[44] Thus, the 1325 account from Gateley distinguishes the 'head-carter' (*magister famulus*), while the other carter is merely called *socius eius* (his associate).[45] Interestingly, the *magister famulus* was paid 4s while his assistant was given 2s 6d during the harvest period. This, undoubtedly, means that there was a clear hierarchy within the carting workforce that was similar to power structures within other working occupations around that time. The 1356 accounts from Martham referred to carters as *famuli carrectarii*.[46] Furthermore, two Gateley accounts used, quite puzzlingly, the term *fugatores carruce* (namely, plough-drivers), in describing its carters.[47] It is unclear whether this is a clerical error, or whether, in Gateley, the functions of *carrectarii* and *fugatores carruce* overlapped.

One possible reason for describing the manorial carters as *famuli carrectarii* was to distinguish them from priory carters, occasionally hired as reinforcement. Thus, in 1314 at Monks Granges, two priory carters (*carrectarii Prioratus*) were used in addition to the permanent staff of four carters.[48] Similarly, in 1383, at Plumstead, two 'conventual carters' (*carrectarii cenobiales*), in addition to four manorial *carrectarii*, were recruited.[49] Reliance on priory carters became particularly widespread in the post-Black Death era, when the priory authorities had to cope with the problem of labour scarcity. Fortunately, Norwich Cathedral Priory had a permanent staff of, usually, two carters. In addition, there were some instances when carters from other demesnes came to the rescue. Thus, in 1360 and 1372 the carters of Plumstead were assisted by their colleagues from Monks Granges.[50]

What were the terms of the employment of the manorial carters? First and foremost, they were hired for the entire period of harvest. Naturally, the duration of harvest varied from year to year and from demesne to demesne, depending on both local weather conditions and the available working force (Figure 5.1).[51] As a result, agricultural wages paid to carters and other harvest *famuli*, whether in kind or cash, tended to oscillate a great deal from year to year. As David Farmer has shown, 'of all the agricultural wages, the most susceptible to short-term changes were the payments given to harvesters'.[52] Sudden and unexpected vagaries of nature could alter the

---

44. Thus, the accounts of Gateley tend to use *carectarius* and *famulus* as synonyms.
45. NRO, DCN 60/13/22.
46. NRO, NNAS 5892 20 D1.
47. NRO, DCN 60/13/25 and NRO, DCN 62/2.
48. NRO, DCN 60/26/15.
49. NRO, DCN 60/29/36.
50. NRO, DCN 60/29/30 and 33.
51. On the duration and seasonal variations of harvest on Norwich Cathedral Priory demesnes, see K. Pribyl and C. Pfister, 'The beginning of the grain harvest in Norfolk as a proxy for mean April–July temperatures, c.1270 AD–1430 AD', *Geophysical Research Abstracts*, 11 (2009), p. 784.
52. D. Farmer, 'Prices and wages', in H.E. Hallam (ed.), *The Agrarian History of England and Wales, vol. II 1042–1350* (Cambridge, 1988), pp. 766–7.

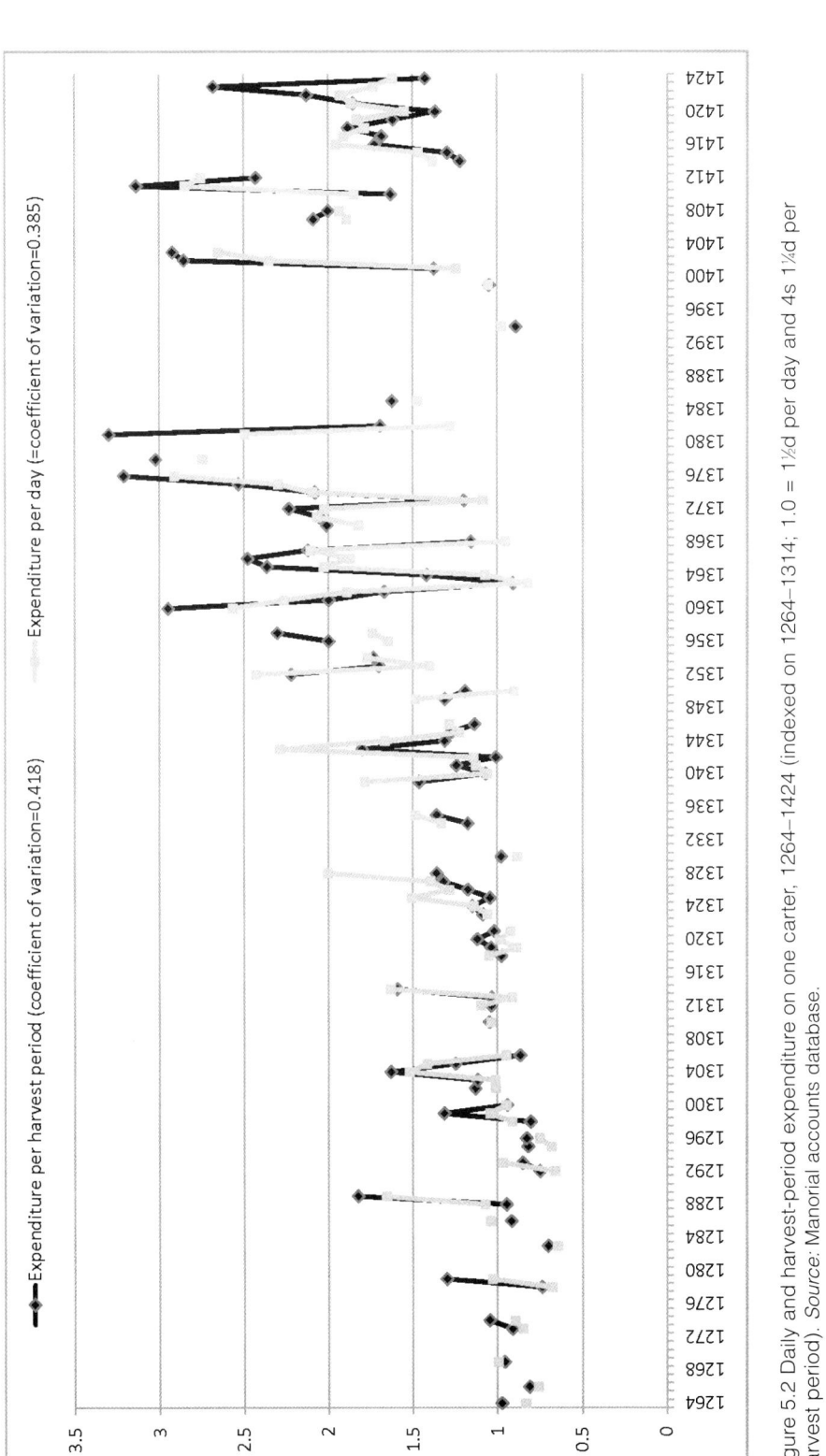

Figure 5.2 Daily and harvest-period expenditure on one carter, 1264–1424 (indexed on 1264–1314; 1.0 = 1½d per day and 4s 1½d per harvest period). *Source*: Manorial accounts database.

Bread and Ale for the Brethren

levels of daily wages paid to harvest workers, carters among them, quite drastically. For instance, the length of the 1385 harvest at Sedgeford was 35 days, while the harvest of 1387 lasted for the exceptionally long period of seven weeks. During the harvest of 1385, each of the six carters was receiving about 3½d a day (10s 6d per harvest), while in 1387 daily wages rose to about 6¼d (that is, nearly 19s over the harvest period) per carter.[53] It is unclear what commanded this difference. Naturally, neither the priory authorities and their officials nor the hired carters and other *famuli* could have predicted weather patterns or the length of harvests, and this uncertainty seems to have been a major difficulty for both employers and employed. What is clear, however, is that varying levels of urgency in getting crops out of the field (where they may have been exposed to rain or excessive drought) might explain the variation in costs from year to year.

As Figure 5.2 clearly indicates, there were indeed some considerable yearly fluctuations in nominal daily wages (whether in cash or kind) of carters. Before 1350, particularly costly years were 1289, 1304, 1305, 1314, 1325, 1327, 1328, 1339, 1343, 1344 and, as expected, 1349. After the Black Death, years with exceedingly high wages were 1352, 1360, 1361, 1365, 1367, 1374, 1375, 1378, 1381, 1402, 1403, 1411 and 1412. Back-to-back years with great fluctuations in wages include 1288 and 1289 (1½d and 2½d a day, respectively), 1303 and 1304 (1½d and 2½d a day, respectively), 1305 and 1306 (2¼d and 1½d a day, respectively), 1313 and 1314 (1½d and 2½d a day, respectively), 1339 and 1340 (2¾d and 1¾d a day, respectively) and 1342 and 1343 (1¾d and 3½d). In the post-Black Death era these fluctuations became even more pronounced. Thus, in 1352 daily wages were 3¾d per carter, while a year later they stood at 2¼d. Between 1362 and 1363, they fell from 3d to 1¼d. Generally speaking, the value of coefficient of variation for carters' wages over the entire period is close to 40 per cent (0.396 in the pre-Black Death period and 0.358 in the post-1350 era). As expected, the nominal daily wages of manorial carters went up after the Black Death, reflecting wider monetary trends in the new reality. Over a period of 80 years after the pestilence, average wages per carter stood at approximately 2¾d a day, as compared with some 1¾d a day in the pre-1350 period. At the same time, however, the difference between *absolute* expenditure (as measured in cash spent on one carter during the entire harvest period) and *relative* expenditure (as measured in cash spent on one carter per work-day) seems to have never been too wide, as Figure 5.2 indicates.

Does the behaviour of carters' wages resemble that of other workers' wages? The answer is yes and no. It certainly resembles the behaviour of other *harvesters'* wages. As evidence from other late medieval estates shows, daily wages indeed oscillated not only from year to year but also within the same season. Thus, on the Oxfordshire demesne of Holywell, belonging to Merton College, day wages rose from 1½d to 2½d during the summer of 1309.[54] Similarly, the wages of other agricultural labourers,

---

53. NRO, Lest/IB/41 and 42.
54. Farmer, 'Prices and wages', p. 767.
55. David Farmer's series of English 'National' Agrarian Wages Database, edited and revised by J.H.A. Munro: John Munro's revised tabulations of David Farmer's series of English 'national' agrarian wages, available: http://www.economics.utoronto.ca/munro5/ResearchData.html (accessed 11 October 2011).

Shipping the produce: transportation requirements, strategies and costs

including threshers, winnowers, reapers, thatchers and salters, oscillated a great deal from year to year, both before and after the Black Death.[55] On the other hand, non-agricultural wages tended to remain unchanged for much longer periods of time. Thus, the nominal wages of one mason stood at 3d a day for the entire period from 1359 until 1407; in 1407 masons' wages rose to 4d and remained at that level until 1545.[56]

We should keep in mind, however, that the wages cited above are merely average figures. In fact, expenditure varied from demesne to demesne. For instance, between 1264 and 1349 demesne officials could expect to spend, per harvest season, about 3s 6d on one carter in Hindringham and Martham, about 4s in Hindolveston, about 4s 3d in Gnatingdon, about 5s 6d in Gateley, nearly 6s in Denham, slightly over 7s in Eaton, as much as 8s 6d in Newton and an overwhelming 12s 5d in Monks Granges. Naturally, these figures rose after the Black Death. These differences in wages are especially striking given the fact that the length of harvests would not vary much across the demesnes in the same year. Moreover, there was no legal difference in status between different *famuli*: all the peasants living on the manors of Norwich Cathedral Priory were customary tenants. What is certain, however, is that Norwich Cathedral Priory was not an isolated case in this period. As David Farmer has shown, with the exception of the bishopric of Winchester no other late medieval lord managed to successfully fix the stipends paid to their *famuli*. Thus, the annual stipends of one *famulus* varied between 6s and 13s across several demesnes of the bishopric of Worcester, and on the estate of Bury St Edmunds Abbey wages differed from manor to manor.[57] The reasons behind these differences in wages are yet to be studied in detail.

The structure and composition of carters' wages is yet another aspect to be considered here. With the exception of the manor of Gateley, the *famuli*-carters were paid in kind, rather than in cash, in the pre-Black Death period.[58] After the pestilence, however, two tendencies can be discerned. First, on some manors the carters secured payments in cash in addition to grain wages. Such was the situation at Plumstead, Sedgeford and Taverham. At Sedgeford, between 1361 and 1410, the kind and cash components of the carters' wages occupied in general an equal proportion. In the 1370s the cash component accounted for about 65 per cent of the total stipend. The cash share fell in the first decade of the fifteenth century, when it accounted for about 38 per cent of a carter's wages.[59] The relative shift from kind to cash payments undoubtedly reflects the ability of the carters and other *famuli* to negotiate better terms of employment. This was undoubtedly much to the employers' disadvantage, who would obviously have preferred to pay in kind, especially in a period of falling grain

---

56. J.H.A. Munro, John Munro's revisions of the Phelps Brown and Hopkins 'basket of consumables' commodity price series and craftsmen's wage series, 1264–1700, http://www.economics.utoronto.ca/munro5/ResearchData.html (accessed 11 October 2011).
57. Farmer, 'The *Famuli*', pp. 231–2.
58. Between c.1306 and the Black Death, Gateley had carters, one 'head-carter' and his companion, with the former being paid between 3s and 4s per harvest time, and the latter being paid 2s 6d per the same period. See NRO, DCN 60/13/13–26A. Unfortunately, no post-Black Death accounts survive for this demesne.
59. NRO, Lest/IB/25–57.

prices. This seems to have been especially crucial from the 1370s onwards, when, after some three decades, grain prices collapsed and a prolonged period of price deflation and high real wages ensued. The second post-plague change was partial commutation of customary carting dues into harvest carrying services. In other words, an increasing number of carters preferred to commute their customary duties into cash payments for carting service during harvest. This is hardly surprising in the context of the post-Black Death reality, when more and more lords were willing to let their tenants commute their customary duties into cash payments. This commutation process would earn the tenants more time and energy to invest in their own husbandry, while the lords would enjoy an additional source of cash income. This scenario was particularly suited to both parties in the light of the deflation that had ensued since the late 1370s, and which, effectively, marked the beginning of the end of the *Gutsherrschaft* era.[60]

Although in the vast majority of cases carters were employed for the entire duration of harvest, there were some instances when additional carters were hired, for shorter periods of time. For instance, at Sedgeford 20 additional carters were hired for just one day in 1372 and two auxiliary carters were hired for one week in 1402.[61] The 1265 account roll from North Elmham is particularly striking because it provides a unique glimpse into methods of payment to the short-term employed carters. According to that account, in addition to 15 harvesters, including 6 carters, there were *alii carrectarii mutuati et conducti* ('other carters, employed in credit and hired [presumably, for cash]').[62] This passage suggests that, at least in some isolated cases, auxiliary carters were not paid in ready cash or kind, but were hired on credit. Interestingly, short-term employments were normally more costly than those lasting for the entire period of harvesting. The two 'irregular' Sedgeford carters hired in 1402 were paid 5s 3d each for just one week of services, in contrast with the six permanent carters each paid 7s for the duration of harvest, lasting 42 days.[63] At Worstead, in 1357 each of the two additional carters hired for four days was paid the stipend of 2s 1½d (6¾d per diem), while its four regular carters, employed for 30 days of harvest, were paid 10s 5d each (4d per diem).[64] This gap between the wages of regular and short-term employed carters can perhaps be explained by the fact that the irregular carters were expected to provide their own horses, carts and other equipment. As a rule, every two carters came with one cart. At Sedgeford in 1372, 20 irregular carters came with 10 carts. In 1378, 60 men were carting grain with 30 carts on the same demesne. In 1381, 10 additional carters were hired with 5 carts.[65] Each cart was pulled by two or three horses. Thus, at North Elmham in 1306, two horses hauled one cart that was hired together with its driver.[66] On the other hand,

---

60. On commutation of services, consult J.A. Raftis, 'The structure of commutation in a fourteenth-century village', in T.A. Sandquist and M.R. Powicke (eds), *Essays in medieval history presented to Bertie Wilkinson* (Toronto, 1969), pp. 282–300.
61. NRO, Lest/IB/32 and 51.
62. NRO, DCN 60/10/3.
63. NRO, Lest/IB/51.
64. NRO, DCN 60/39/21.
65. NRO, Lest/IB/32, 35 and 37.
66. NRO, DCN 60/10/11.

Shipping the produce: transportation requirements, strategies and costs

Table 5.2
Total numbers of harvest *famuli* and carters, and annual expenditure on them.

	All famuli	Carters	Carters as % of all famuli	Total expenditure on all famuli (in £ sterling)	Total expenditure on all carters (in £ sterling)
1261–70	278.5	85.0	30.5%	62.2	19.0
1271–80	319.7	90.2	28.2%	68.1	19.2
1281–90	348.8	103.5	29.7%	74.2	22.0
1291–1300	343.5	102.4	29.8%	76.3	22.8
1301–10	337.7	99.7	29.5%	86.2	25.4
1311–20	358.1	100.2	28.0%	100.4	28.1
1321–30	344.7	92.0	26.7%	120.1	32.1
1331–40	292.3	70.1	24.0%	94.6	22.7
1341–50	363.0	84.8	23.4%	125.8	29.4
1351–60	222.5	57.5	25.8%	114.0	29.4
1361–70	235.3	62.0	26.3%	118.0	31.1
1371–80	244.2	54.0	22.1%	105.8	23.4
1381–90	225.3	57.0	25.3%	91.1	23.1
1391–1400	193.0	50.3	26.1%	81.3	21.2
1401–10	257.3	61.5	23.9%	105.3	25.2
1411–20	254.1	62.4	24.6%	98.0	24.1
1421–30	260.0	62.0	23.8%	98.9	23.6
Pre-1350	331.8	92.0	27.7%	89.7	24.5
Post-1350	236.5	58.3	24.8%	101.6	25.1

Source: Manorial accounts database.

at Worstead, three horses pulled one cart in 1358.[67] It is likely that, in most cases, a single cart was pulled by three rather than two horses: contemporary evidence, such as an illustration from the Luttrell Psalter which depicts a harvest wagon hauled by three horses,[68] suggests that grain carts were pulled usually by three or four horses in this period.[69]

In some cases, demesne officials rented carting equipment and individual horses without carters. This was particularly the case in North Elmham, whose accounts have abundant references to this practice. Between 1265 and 1321 its officials rented, each year, a number of carts (ranging from one to four). The rented carts were specified in the accounts as *carrecte conducte/locate* (hired/leased carts). The rental price changed from year to year, fluctuating from 2s to 6s apiece for the entire harvest season. It is unclear what accounted for these differences in prices, as there is no positive correlation between the prices and length of harvests. The harvest of 1320 lasted 40 days, during which the demesne officials spent 2s 10d on renting one cart. The harvest of 1321, on the other hand, continued for 36 days, in the course of which

---

67. NRO, DCN 60/39/21.
68. J. Backhouse, *Medieval rural life in the Luttrell Psalter* (Toronto, 2000), p. 24, Plate 13.
69. Campbell *et al.*, *A medieval capital*, pp. 58–9; J. Masschaele, 'Transport costs in medieval England', *EcHR*, 46 (1993), p. 268.

the officials paid 6s for one rented cart.[70] It is possible that the vast differences in lease prices was due to the varying quality and capacity of each individual cart.

Finally, let us consider the actual numbers of manorial carters in both absolute and relative terms. As shown in Table 5.2, before the Black Death there were, on average, slightly fewer than 100 carters employed on all the demesnes in a single year. This figure represented about 27 per cent of all the employed *famuli*. After the pestilence, the overall number of carters fell in conjunction with the physical shrinkage of the demesne and, accordingly, with the decline of the required labour force. The total average number now fell to about 58 for the entire estate, which accounted for some 24 per cent of all harvest labour. As would be expected, the total expenditure on all the harvesters in general and the carters in particular rose a great deal, in *relative terms*. The overall number of the carters and the levels of expenditure on them will serve as guidelines in the reconstruction of carting logistics and the estimation of priory officials' cost savings in the next section.

Were these figures unique in comparison with other religious estates around that time? In his important study on late medieval *famuli*, David Farmer provides a detailed breakdown of various occupations of manorial labourers on a number of estates. A comparison between the situation on the Norwich Cathedral Priory demesnes and that on other manors reveals that the differences were indeed profound (Table 5.3). Thus, before 1350, there were, on average, about 23 permanent *famuli*, including 5 carters, on every Norwich Cathedral Priory demesne. On other lords' demesnes, the overall numbers of manorial *famuli* and the relative share of carters among them seem to have been much lower. Thus, on the demesnes of the bishopric of Winchester, Glastonbury Abbey, Canterbury Cathedral Priory and Battle Abbey hardly any carters were employed by manorial officials. This striking contrast suggests that, compared with other religious lords, Norwich Cathedral Priory relied much more on hired labour than on mandatory services. Two possible explanations for this contrast can be offered here. First, it is possible that Norwich Cathedral Priory appreciated the advantages of hired labour, in terms of its efficiency and reliability, over customary services. After all, securing a good harvest and reliable grain delivery were constant challenges for all manorial lords and the difference between coerced labour and a hired workforce could mean a great deal. It is certainly the case that Norwich Cathedral Priory was a more successful producer than many other major religious lords in that period, not least because of its institutional arrangements.[71] The second possible explanation could be that the social make-up of Norfolk, a county with a very high proportion of free peasantry whose origin goes back to Viking times, could have influenced and shaped local customs and traditions.[72] With the exception of all Eaton peasants and individual families in Hindringham, Hindolveston and Martham, Norwich Cathedral Priory's tenants were, as the analysis of the *Stowe Survey* suggests, exempt from mandatory carting of the lord's grain, apparently as a result of protection afforded by

---

70. NRO, DCN 60/10/17–18.
71. Campbell, 'Agricultural progress' and 'Arable productivity'.
72. B.M.S. Campbell, 'The agrarian problem in the early fourteenth century', *P&P*, 188 (2005), pp. 3–70; B. Dodwell, 'The free peasantry of East Anglia in Domesday', *Norfolk Archaeology*, 27 (1941), pp. 145–57.

Table 5.3
Carters and *famuli* on Norwich Cathedral Priory demesnes and other religious estates, c.1340 and c.1380.

c.1340 Estate	Sampled demesnes	All famuli	Carters	Carters as % of all famuli	Famuli per demesne	Carters per demesne
Norwich Cathedral Priory	16	363.0	84.8	23.4%	22.7	5.3
Winchester bishopric	48	579	39.5	6.8%	12.1	0.8
Glastonbury Abbey	8	80.5	5	6.2%	10.1	0.6
Canterbury Cathedral Priory	11	84.5	8.5	10.1%	7.7	0.8
Bury St Edmunds Abbey	4	33	4	12.1%	8.3	1.0
Westminster Abbey	19	164	23.5	14.3%	8.6	1.2
Battle Abbey	5	55.5	2.5	4.5%	11.1	0.5
Merton College	4	26.5	5	18.9%	6.6	1.3
Worcester Cathedral	4	33.5	5	14.9%	8.4	1.3
Durham Cathedral	6	65.5	10	15.3%	10.9	1.7
Ramsey Abbey	5	38	7	18.4%	7.6	1.4
Weighted average				11.72%	11.72	1.50

c.1380 Estate	Sampled demesnes	All famuli	Carters	Carters as % of all famuli	Famuli per demesne	Carters per demesne
Norwich Cathedral Priory	11	225.3	57.0	25.3%	20.5	5.2
Winchester bishopric	48	512.5	44.5	8.7%	10.7	0.9
Glastonbury Abbey	8	56.5	2	3.5%	7.1	0.3
Canterbury Cathedral Priory	11	82.5	7.5	9.1%	7.5	0.7
Bury St Edmunds Abbey	4	32	5	15.6%	8.0	1.3
Westminster Abbey	19	113.5	14	12.3%	6.0	0.7
Battle Abbey	5	48.5	1	2.1%	9.7	0.2
Merton College	4	12	1.5	12.5%	3.0	0.4
Worcester Cathedral	4	24.5	2	8.2%	6.1	0.5
Durham Cathedral	6	44	5	11.4%	7.3	0.8
Ramsey Abbey	5	30	6	20.0%	6.0	1.2
Weighted average				11.05%	9.45	1.16

Source: Manorial accounts database.

local custom. At the same time, however, one should keep in mind that despite a relatively high proportion of free tenants, rents and services in kind were recorded with a higher frequency in Norfolk than in most other parts of England, at least on lay manors, which have been studied in great detail by Bruce Campbell.[73] On the other hand, reliance on services does not necessarily negate reliance on hired labour. Indeed, the two could peacefully co-exist side by side.

---

73. Campbell, 'Agrarian problem'; Campbell and Bartley, *Eve of the Black Death*, p. 254.

Transporting services: stipendiary *famuli*

Although it is likely that much grain-carting to Norwich could have been completed in the course of the harvest period, there is no doubt that, in some cases, additional time and resources were required to accomplish this task. This is especially true if a demesne was situated a considerable distance from Norwich and if it had to supply the priory with exceptionally large quantities of grain. For instance, if only demesne horses were employed in the harvest season, then the *famuli* of Hemsby would have managed to cart only about half of the grain from that manor destined to be consumed by the brethren. Although there is little doubt that the peasants' stots were used from time to time, as we shall see later, the length of harvests was, in some cases, too short to allow the carters to perform their task entirely. Because of that, a small number of demesne carting *famuli* were employed, usually for short periods, outside harvest time. These carters appear in the *stipendia* section of the accounts, alongside other stipendiary *famuli* hired on different terms and for different purposes throughout the year. The total number of these *famuli* varied from place to place, depending, as a rule, on the size of each demesne. Thus, in the 1270s and 1280s there were as many as 18 *famuli* at Hemsby, the largest and most productive demesne.[74] On the small demesne of Gateley, on the other hand, the number fluctuated from one to two *famuli* before *c.*1300. On average, there were seven stipendiary *famuli* on each demesne, generally including one reeve, several plough-drivers, one dairymaid, one cowherd and one carter. Newton and Plumstead also had one boatman each, but it is unclear if grain shipping was one of the functions of these boatmen. Interestingly enough, several accounts hint that in some cases plough-drivers and carters were, in fact, the same people.[75] Although there was, normally, one stipendiary carter per demesne, some places hired two and occasionally three carters in some years.[76] Some demesnes, including Denham, Gateley and Taverham, on the other hand, did not have stipendiary carters at all. It is plausible that, in many cases, some stipendiary and harvest carters were, in fact, the same people.

The terms and length of stipendiary carters' employment varied from year to year. In most cases they were hired for several terms (usually two or three), running several months each. For instance, at Thornham one carter was hired for the winter and Lent terms in 1277–8. Yet, in 1351–2, his successor was hired for three terms (the Invention of the Cross, the Purification and the summer terms).[77] After the Black Death there was an increasing tendency to shift from seasonal (*ad x terminos*) to annual employment (*per annum integrum*). Thus, around 1369 the carters (and other *famuli*) of Plumstead switched from a three-term employment to a full-year employment. 'Seasonal' or 'full-year' employment does not, however, mean that the carters were working each day, judging by their stipends. At Sedgeford, a carter received around 7½d in the winter and Lent terms, which indicates that the total number of working days was no more

---

74. Although in the 1290s the number fell to 12 *famuli*.
75. Thus, in several instances, one person was serving as both *carrectarius* and *tenens/tentor/fugator caruce*. For example, NRO, DCN 60/37/11 (Thornham, 1309–10), NRO, DCN 60/39/9 and 15 (Worstead, 1327–8 and 1349–50).
76. The number of carters ranged from two to three at Gnatingdon and Newton-by-Norwich.
77. NRO, DCN 60/37/4 and 21.

than six or seven (allowing around 1¼d as a daily wage of an agricultural worker).[78] In other words, 'Lent term' should by no means be identified with a work period lasting about six weeks. The same thing can be said about the 'full-year term'. At Plumstead in 1369–70 one carter was receiving annual wages of about 8¾s. This sum, however, could have purchased about 37 full days of work of a carter (allowing 2¾d a day). The 'full-year' employment, therefore, did not mean about 270 days of work, but a much shorter period.[79]

Transporting services: priory carters and boatmen

At the priory itself there was permanent staff of two carters and two boatmen, each hired, jointly by the master of the cellarer and cellarer, on the full-year employment basis. Unlike the manorial sector, where different *famuli*, with the exception of dairymaids, received more or less the same salary, wages varied across the occupations of the priory employees, as Table 5.4 indicates. Thus, the annual stipend of one carter stood at around 9s 8d a year in the pre-Black Death period. During the 1350s, however, a *per capita* carter's stipend rose from 10s to over 18s 7d a year and continued to rise thereafter, peaking at 49s in the 1460s. In the following decade it fell to 30s because the cellarer was no longer hiring carters and a number of other workers and the master of the cellarer became the sole employer of these labourers. Boatmen's wages fluctuated accordingly. In the course of the fourteenth century they rose from about 7s 8d in the pre-Black Death period to over 19s 6d towards the end of the century. Between *c.*1400 and 1450 they fluctuated between 20s and 28s a year *per capita*. After *c.*1450 these wages disappear from the annual payroll and, as a result, we remain ignorant about the fate of the boatmen after that date. The wages of carters and boatmen mirror, to a large degree, those of the priory cooks, whose stipend increased considerably after the Black Death. From *c.*1420 onwards the cook was the best-paid employee within the priory. Conversely, the wages of bakers and brewers did not increase much until the 1400s.

These figures are *per capita* wages. In reality, the levels of payment could vary between two workers within the same sector. Thus, the post-1420 accounts of the master of the cellar clearly distinguish between the stipend of the 'master-carter' and his assistant (called, interchangeably, *pagus*, *socius* and *subbigator*). Normally, the former's wages were between 50 and 75 per cent higher than those of the latter. Obviously, these numbers are merely nominal wages paid by the master of the cellar, not to be confused with real wages of the same workers. Moreover, these annual wages are not necessarily to be equated with the total income of the said

---

78. G. Clark, 'The long march of history: farm wages, population, and economic growth, England, 1209–1869', *EHR*, 60/1 (2007), pp. 97–135.

79. It should also be borne in mind that, in the post-Black Death period, agricultural workers rarely needed more than 250 days of work to support their families. See R.C. Allen and J.L. Weisdorf, 'The working year of English day labourer, *c.* 1300–1830' (University of Oxford Working Paper, 2010) available: http://graduateinstitute.ch/webdav/site/international_history_politics/users/stefano_ugolini/public/papers/Weisdorf.pdf (accessed 11 October 2011).

Table 5.4
Annual wages of select priory employees paid jointly by the master of the cellar and the cellarer, 1261–1536.

	Carter	Boatman	Winnower	Cook	Keeper of the Granary	Baker	Brewer
1261–70	8.0	2.5		9.0		23.0	21.6
1271–80	9.8	3.5		9.0		24.2	22.6
1281–90	10.0	3.5		9.0		24.5	22.8
1291–1300	10.0	5.7		9.0		23.5	21.9
1301–10	9.8	10.6		9.0		23.6	23.6
1311–20	10.0	11.0		9.0		24.0	24.0
1321–30	10.0	11.0		9.0		24.0	24.0
1331–40	10.0	10.7		11.0		24.0	24.0
1341–50	10.0	10.8		11.0		24.0	23.9
1351–60	18.6	13.1		11.0	2.5	20.6	20.6
1361–70	20.0	19.7	3.1	20.0	10.0	23.1	23.1
1371–80	26.5	24.8	3.7	20.0	10.0	23.1	23.1
1381–90	35.3	14.2	5.0	30.0	10.0	26.8	25.0
1391–1400	36.7	12.5	5.0	40.0	10.0	28.4	27.6
1401–10	42.3	20.5	5.0	40.0	13.3	34.9	42.2
1411–20	46.6	28.7	5.0	50.0	18.8	37.0	50.3
1421–30	43.7	22.5	6.7	51.6	17.5	36.8	43.6
1431–40	41.4	24.0		52.0	26.7	39.2	39.2
1441–50	41.3	24.0		46.9	17.0	36.7	38.4
1451–60	41.3			59.4	20.0	33.7	33.7
1461–70	48.9			51.4	20.0	34.3	20.8
1471–80	30.0			63.0	23.0	32.5	32.5
1481–90	30.0			73.3	26.7	24.0	30.0
1491–1500	30.0			73.3	26.7	26.7	30.0
1501–10	30.0			73.3	26.7	26.7	26.7
1511–20	26.7			73.3	26.7	20.0	53.3
1521–30	25.9			73.3	26.7	20.0	53.3
1531–6	26.7			73.3	26.7	23.3	40.0
Pre-Black Death period	9.7	7.7		9.4		23.9	23.2
1351–1430	33.7	19.5	4.8	32.8	11.5	28.8	31.9
1431–1536	33.8			64.8	24.2	28.8	36.2

Source: DCN 1/1/1–110, 1/2/1–115.

employees, who may have had additional employment and income sources outside the priory. But since this assertion cannot be substantiated by textual evidence, it remains hypothesis.

As the master of the cellar rolls suggest, priory carters and boatmen were not closely involved in transporting the grain from the demesnes to the Great Granary before the end of the fourteenth century. While it is known that in some isolated cases the priory labourers assisted their manorial colleagues in this duty, it was not until the 1390s that they became an indispensable part of grain transportation. As many master of the cellar accounts indicate, before that decade the main function of the priory carters and boatmen was to transport fuel, stone, iron and building materials from various places in Norfolk. With the end of the direct management era, however, the priory authorities could no longer rely on either the customary or hired services of the manorial *famuli*, who were now displaced by the regular staff of priory boatmen and carters. For the most part, the former were now responsible for transporting grain farms from the demesnes. The first reference to the priory servants carrying large quantities of grain to the Great Granary is found in the 1390–91 account of the master of the cellar. In that year, the boatmen were paid 28s for shipping wheat and malt from Great Yarmouth to Norwich.[80] This, however, does not mean that Great Yarmouth was the point of origin: as later accounts demonstrate, the grain was brought there from the nearby demesne of Hemsby.[81] The priory boatmen were active in transporting the grain from Martham and Hemsby until at least 1484. Priory carters, on the other hand, were not involved in the process until 1437–8. Between then and c.1480 the carters received an additional payment to their annual wages for carrying the grain from the two leased manors, Plumstead and Taverham. The post-1480 accounts, however, do not indicate that the boatmen and carters were functioning in this capacity and it is unclear who was responsible for delivering the grain to the Great Granary in the course of the last decades of the priory's existence. To make things even more obscure, the boatmen disappear from the list of priory servants in the 1450s. The carters, on the other hand, remained among the servants until the end and their annual stipend in the final decades of the priory fluctuated between 26 and 30s a year.

Carting requirements and logistics

What strategies did the priory authorities undertake in order to ensure a steady supply of grain from their demesnes? How much was carted each year? The answers to these questions are vital for understanding the complex mechanisms of grain delivery in the period under study. To begin with, reconstructing transportation trends and calculating its costs are by no means easy tasks. Unlike their recording of harvesting and livestock rearing, our accounts say very little about grain transportation and those references that do exist tend to be rather indirect. For instance, most accounts specify the amount of grain shipped to Norwich (in quarters) and the number of horses found on the demesnes. In order to estimate the approximate number of carts required to transport the crops and the approximate costs of delivery we have to rely on external evidence. Nevertheless, we may, with clear reservations, attempt to reconstruct the picture.

First, it is necessary to establish the ratio between the amounts of delivered grain and the number of cartloads and horses required to ship it. It has been estimated that c.1300 a quarter of wheat weighed about 424 lb, while a quarter of malted barley would have weighted around 294 lb, given the fact that malting increases the volume and lowers the density of barley by some 25 per cent.[82] Late medieval evidence also indicates that a single cartload, pulled by two, three or occasionally four horses, could carry about 3 quarters of wheat or 4.24 quarters of malted barley.[83] On the basis of these assumptions, we arrive at the calculations shown in Table 5.5. As approximate as they may be, these estimates provide us with a rough guide as to the annual

---

80. NRO, DCN 1/1/66.
81. NRO, DCN 1/1/82.
82. Campbell et al., *A medieval capital*, p. 34, note 59 and p. 42.
83. Ibid., pp. 58–9; Masschaele, 'Transport costs', p. 268.

Table 5.5
Amounts of grain sent to Norwich Cathedral Priory, and estimated numbers of carts, horses and boat-trips required for delivery, 1261–1480.

	Grain carted (in quarters)	Grain shipped (in quarters)	Total cartloads	Total horses required	Total demesne horses available	Average return cart trips, if used only demesne horses	Boats used for shipping	Return boat trips
1261–70	2068.9	0.0	543.9	1631.8	139.2	11.7		
1271–80	1773.9	0.0	461.5	1384.4	142.9	9.7		
1281–90	2329.2	0.0	604.1	1812.2	162.3	11.2		
1291–1300	2250.2	0.0	586.9	1760.8	138.6	12.7		
1301–10	2260.2	0.0	581.1	1743.4	147.8	11.8		
1311–20	2046.3	0.0	532.6	1597.9	146.0	10.9		
1321–30	1848.7	0.0	486.3	1458.9	138.5	10.5		
1331–40	1703.7	0.0	447.5	1342.5	109.6	12.2		
1341–50	1766.8	0.0	468.7	1406.0	126.8	11.1		
1351–60	886.0	0.0	234.0	701.9	104.0	6.7		
1361–70	923.6	0.0	251.2	753.6	102.3	7.4		
1371–80	941.8	0.0	249.4	748.2	114.2	6.6		
1381–90	613.3	0.0	165.7	497.2	82.2	6.0		
1391–1400	396.7	200.0	112.9	338.8	82.4	5.8	1.0	3.0
1401–10	813.8	200.0	211.8	635.4	101.6	6.4	1.0	3.0
1411–20	536.3	200.0	146.7	440.1	99.9	5.8	1.0	3.0
1421–30	510.4	200.0	151.0	453.1	91.0	6.5	1.0	3.0
1431–40	660.3	200.0	168.3	504.9			1.0	3.0
1441–50	703.1	200.0	176.6	529.8			1.0	3.0
1451–60	716.0	200.0	180.3	541.0			1.0	3.0
1461–70	808.3	200.0	204.3	612.8			1.0	3.0
1471–80	829.0	200.0	208.8	626.3			1.0	3.0
Pre-1350 average	2005.3	0.0	523.6	1570.9	139.1	11.3		
1351–1430 average	702.7	100.0	190.3	571.0	97.2	6.4		
1431–80 average	743.4	200.0	187.7	563.0			1.0	3.0

Source: Manorial accounts database.

transportation requirements of Norwich Cathedral Priory, which appear to be impressive. In the pre-Black Death period the priory would require over 500 cartloads and some 1570 horses-trips. Ensuring such a large number of cartloads and horses-trips seems to be quite a logistical challenge, especially because the total number of demesne horses averaged around 140 in the pre-pestilence decades. The available evidence suggests, however, that there were two possible scenarios to cope with the insufficiency of demesne horse power. First, in many cases, grain was carted in several repeat trips by the same horses and carts, rather than in one expedition. This strategy is indicated in occasional entries dealing with horse fodder which specify the number of trips undertaken by stots and the quantities of oats they received. Thus, in Gnatingdon, nine horses carried 52 quarters of malt over four trips in 1305–6;[84] in

---

84. NRO, DCN 60/14/12.

1327–8, an unspecified number of horses carted 101.75 quarters of malt over six trips,[85] in 1344–5, 23 quarters of wheat were transported to North Elmham over three trips,[86] and finally, in 1362–3, 31.50 quarters of wheat were carted to Norwich over four trips.[87] In 1317–18 the villagers of North Elmham carted 47.75 quarters of wheat and 143 quarters of malt to the town in just three trips.[88] The lack of correlation between the number of trips and the actual figures of carted grain implies that each trip may have involved a different number of carts and horses. In some cases, *famuli* of certain manors were joined by their fellow-carters from other manors. Thus, the carters of Eaton carried various goods from and to Sedgeford, Hindolveston, Hindringham and North Elmham.[89] Similarly, the tenants of Hemsby assisted their fellows from Hindolveston and Sedgeford,[90] while the inhabitants of Newton and Taverham helped to carry goods from North Elmham.[91] Many more examples can be added here, all of which illustrate a degree of inter-manorial cooperation utilised by both the priory authorities and their tenants. The numbers of carting trips specified in these accounts should by no means be deciphered as the *total numbers of carting trips* undertaken by the *famuli*: after all, these are only occasional references whose main purpose was to specify not how many voyages it would take to ship the grain but the quantities of oats and peas given to horses hauling the grain. Certainly, as Table 5.5 indicated, in the pre-Black Death period it would require approximately 11 trips to cart the grain supplies to Norwich if the manorial officials relied only on the demesne horses. This number is considerably higher than the usual three or four trips specified in the accounts.

It is likely, however, that in some cases the manorial officials would turn to the second resort: *famuli*'s horses. As we have seen, in some instances the demesne officials would hire additional horses and carts, which came, undoubtedly, from the peasant sector. This was especially true in the case of the auxiliary carters employed in addition to the permanent staff of the carting *famuli*. The widespread usage of the terms 'with their own horses' (*cum equiis suis*), or 'with their own carts' (*cum carrectis suis*) implies that the auxiliary carters were expected to supply their own beasts and equipment. It is for that reason, perhaps, that they were usually paid higher daily wages than the regular *famuli*. It is also possible and quite likely that in some cases the regular *famuli*, too, had to supplement the demesne horses with their own animals to reinforce the carting capacities of each demesne. Thus, a 1251 extent of the manor of Colne in Somersham (Huntingdonshire), belonging to the bishop of Ely, specified that every cottager had to perform carting duties 'if he shall have a cart and a horse' (*si habeat carectam et equum*).[92] Unfortunately, our accounts do not state if the regular

---

85. NRO, DCN 60/14/23.
86. NRO, Lest/IC 43.
87. NRO, Lest/IC 13.
88. NRO, DCN 60/10/16.
89. NRO, DCN 60/10/9, 11a, 14, 17, 18, 19, 23 and 24.
90. NRO, DCN 60/15/5, 7 and 8.
91. NRO, DCN 60/28/4,5; NRO, DCN 60/35/17a, 18, 19.
92. British Library, MS Cotton Claudius c.XI, fols 100r and 106r. Also mentioned in Langdon, *Horses, oxen*, p. 225.

Table 5.6
Annual costs of transporting grain to Norwich Cathedral Priory, 1261–1480 (in £ sterling and as percentage).

	Carters' wages	Fodder costs	Expenditure on shoeing and cart repairs	Total carting costs	Boatmen's wages	Boat maintenance	Total shipping costs	Total transportation costs	Grain value	Transportation costs as % of shipped grain value	Transportation costs as % of all priory expenses
1261–70	18.0	6.7	14.2	38.9				38.9	379.4	10.3%	2.9%
1271–80	18.2	6.4	11.6	36.2				36.2	427.5	8.5%	2.7%
1281–90	20.9	9.4	11.4	41.7				41.7	542.2	7.7%	2.5%
1291–1300	21.6	8.2	15.8	45.6				45.6	625.6	7.3%	2.5%
1301–10	24.2	6.3	20.6	51.0				51.0	535.0	9.5%	2.7%
1311–20	26.7	8.3	22.3	57.3				57.3	707.7	8.1%	2.5%
1321–30	30.4	4.8	20.4	55.7				55.7	544.6	10.2%	2.4%
1331–40	21.6	3.9	17.5	42.9				42.9	391.6	11.0%	2.1%
1341–50	27.9	3.7	17.9	49.5				49.5	368.8	13.4%	2.6%
1351–60	28.0	2.5	15.2	45.6				45.6	257.3	17.7%	2.6%
1361–70	29.5	8.3	13.5	51.3				51.3	320.3	16.0%	2.5%
1371–80	22.2	4.2	13.2	39.6				39.6	232.7	17.0%	1.7%
1381–90	21.9	3.0	9.1	34.1				34.1	136	25.0%	1.5%
1391–1400	20.2	1.5	4.0	25.7	1.4	0.5	1.9	27.6	142	19.4%	1.7%
1401–10	23.9	3.9	7.0	34.8	0.8	0.5	1.3	36.1	205.6	17.6%	2.4%
1411–20	22.9	2.7	5.1	30.7	1.6	0.5	2.1	32.8	173.1	18.9%	1.8%
1421–30	22.4	3.2	8.8	34.5	2.3	0.5	2.8	37.3	174.7	21.3%	2.1%
1431–40	0.6	3.3	0.4	4.3	1.4	0.5	1.9	6.2	150.3	4.1%	0.4%
1441–50	1.0	3.5	0.4	4.9	1.3	0.5	1.8	6.7	110.9	6.0%	0.5%
1451–60	1.3	3.6	0.4	5.3	1.4	0.5	1.9	7.2	123.2	5.8%	0.7%
1461–70	1.0	4.0	0.5	5.5	1.4	0.5	1.9	7.4	153	4.8%	0.7%
1471–80	1.0	4.1	0.5	5.6	1.4	0.5	1.9	7.5	142.2	5.3%	0.8%
Pre-1350 decades	23.3	6.4	16.8	46.5				46.5	502.5	9.3%	2.5%
1351–1430	23.9	3.7	9.5	37.0	1.5	0.5	2.0	38.0	205.2	18.5%	2.0%
1431–80	1.0	3.7	0.4	5.1	1.4	0.5	1.9	7.0	135.9	5.2%	0.6%

Source: Manorial accounts database. *Note:* For particulars of the estimation method, see Appendix 1.

carting *famuli* were expected to provide their own horses to join the demesne ones and this scenario thus remains purely hypothetical. What is clear, however, is that there can be little doubt that transporting wheat and malt from the manors to Norwich involved a good degree of collaboration between the demesne and the peasants.

After the Black Death, the amounts of grain shipped to the Norwich brethren fell mainly because of three factors. First, the pestilence decimated the monastic population and consequently the amounts of grain consumed by the brethren fell, at least in absolute terms. Second, as we have seen, from the 1360s onwards there was an increasing tendency to lease out the demesnes. Finally, after the Black Death, the priory authorities came to rely more and more on local grain markets. Still, this did not free the demesnes from their obligation to provision the priory with grain. The average annual figures fell over the period 1351–1430 from around 2000 to 700 quarters, equivalent to just over 190 cartloads and some 570 horse-trips a year. The gap between the numbers of the demesne horses potentially available for carting and those required in order to accomplish this task became much more narrow compared with the situation in the pre-Black Death period. This meant that the demesne managers had fewer logistical concerns as far as grain shipment is concerned. Finally, the priory boatmen came into the picture from the 1390s onwards, shipping 200 quarters of malt from Hemsby. The figures did not change much in the post-1430 decades, when the era of direct management was over and the brethren were relying on the cheaper and more efficient priory carters and boatmen.

Transportation costs and savings

Now let us turn to the matter of transportation costs and savings. For our purposes, annual transportation costs can be measured as the overall payments to carters (including the wages of both permanent and auxiliary carters), *plus* occasional expenditure on rented horses and equipment, *plus* expenses on fodder, usually oats given to carting horses in relatively large quantities during harvest time, *plus* annual repairs of carts and other tools. These estimates are given in Table 5.6 and Figure 5.3. As Table 5.6 shows, although the figures varied from decade to decade, the average levels of transportation costs, in absolute terms, did not change much from the pre-Black Death period to the post-plague years, notwithstanding the decreased amounts of shipped grain. Thus, in the first decade of the fifteenth century the overall spending on grain shipment stood at below £35 a year, a figure comparable with the levels of expenditure in the 1270s. This is despite the fact that in the 1400s the total grain supply shipped to Norwich amounted to about half its 1270s equivalent by volume and value. In other words, there is a clear indication that relative transportation costs rose over the period. As Figure 5.3 reveals, the costs of transporting one quarter of crop from an average demesne to the priory rose from 1s 11d to 4s 11d between the 1290s and the 1380s. This, undoubtedly, reflects two converse monetary processes: the prolonged price deflation starting around 1376 and concurrently rising real wages. The rising real wages of the carters and the falling value of what was carted made grain transportation more and more expensive in the post-1350 decades, in both absolute and relative terms. Thus, during the 1380s the wages accounted for nearly 25 per cent of the sheer value of the shipped grain and they remained relatively high until the end of the direct demesne management period. The fact that in the 1390s the figure fell to 18 per cent does not mean that transportation became cheaper: it accounts for the fact that many

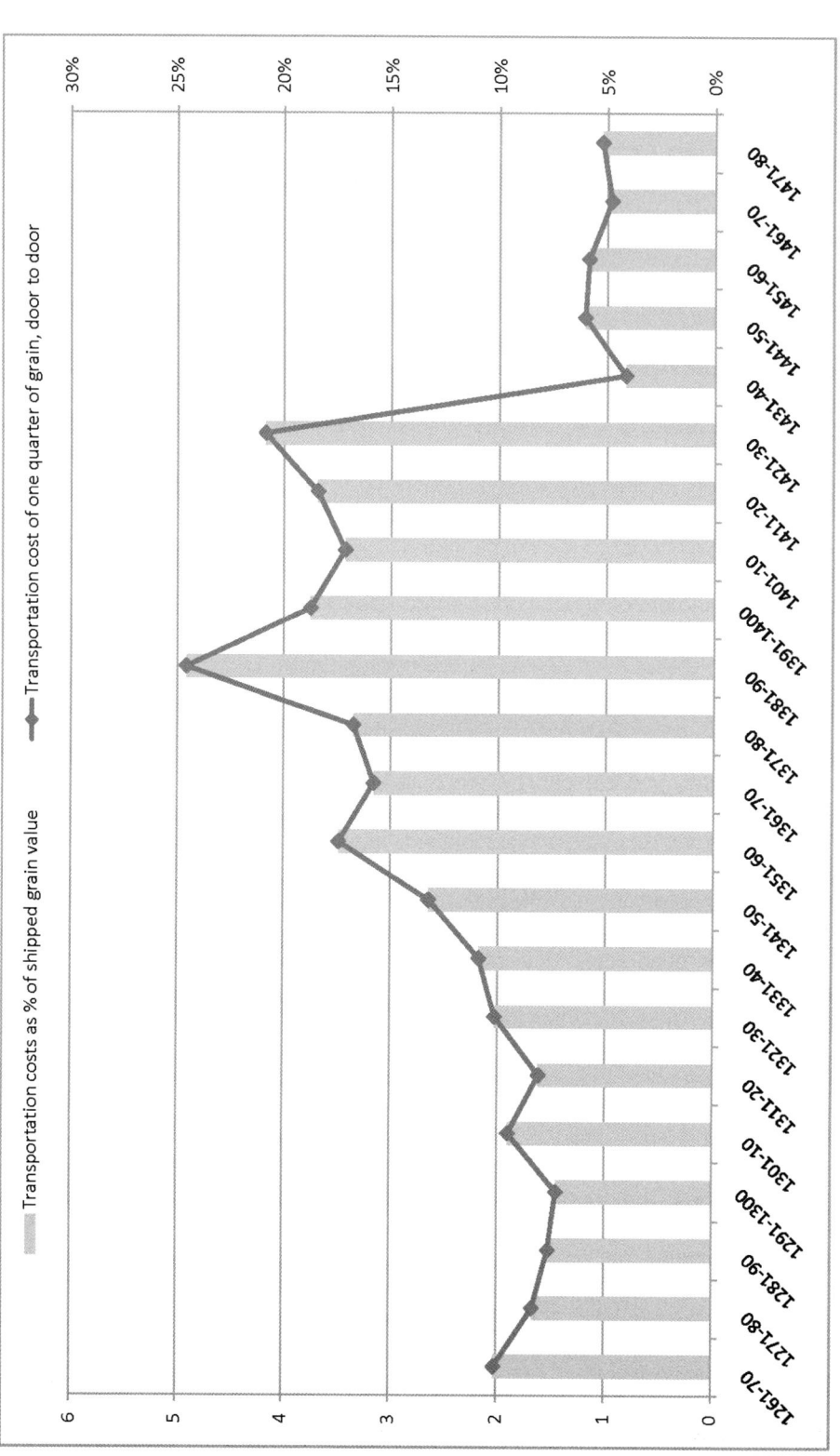

Figure 5.3 Relative transportation costs of crops from the demesnes to Norwich Cathedral Priory, 1261–1480 (door to door, in shillings per one quarter).

Shipping the produce: transportation requirements, strategies and costs

carters chose to commute their mandatory labour dues into cash payments and harvest carting services and, hence, the priory authorities spent less cash on carting the grain from the demesnes to Norwich. There can be little doubt that rising transportation costs reflected wider socio-economic changes in the post-Black Death period. The costs of the production and transportation of the demesne grain seem to have become increasingly burdensome in the eyes of the priory authorities, and the most obvious choice in adapting to the new reality was to increase the share of grain purchased at local markets at the expense of the proportion of crops shipped directly from the demesnes. This, in turn, would not be possible without sacrificing, first partially, then fully, direct management, in favour of farming out the demesnes.

One immediate profit that the shift from *Gutsherrschaft* to *Grundherrschaft* brought about was a drastic reduction in transportation costs. Within several years, the approximate transportation costs fell from about £38 to £7 a year – that is, from 18.5 to 5.2 per cent of the total value of the transported grain. The relative costs of grain transportation fell drastically, too. Thus, to transport one quarter of crop from an average demesne to the priory in the 1430s would cost just 10d, in contrast with 4s 2½d in the previous decade. These transportation costs remained between 1s and 1s 2½d per quarter between the 1440s and the 1470s. Several causes lie behind this sharp fall. First, the large carrying capacity of the *magna navis* allowed the transportation of large quantities of grain at once. As we have seen, this boat was capable of carrying no less than 200 quarters of malted barley from Hemsby to Norwich in just three return trips. In absolute terms, transporting the grain by the great boat was approximately 58 per cent cheaper than by carts.[93] Second, as some accounts indicate, the grain was carted predominantly, if not exclusively, from Plumstead and Taverham, and there is no evidence that the carters transported the grain-rents from other leased manors. It is possible that the farmers of the manors provided a free carting service as part of the lease contract, which was made up of both cash and kind components. Third, unlike in the *Gutsherrschaft* era, when the priory was fed by no fewer than 16 demesnes, only 6 manors provided the brethren with grain after 1431. Three of these manors, Newton, Plumstead and Taverham, were located close to Norwich, while Martham and Hemsby could be easily reached by the Yare. Conversely, North Elmham, which joined the five manors some thirty years after 1431, was located a considerable distance from the priory (some 17 miles). Fourth, it was considerably cheaper to maintain a boat than keep horses and the related tools and equipment. Thus, in the era of direct management each demesne spent, on average, about 20s a year on feeding horses and repairing carting equipment. The maintenance costs of the great boat were about half as much.[94] Whatever the ultimate reasons may have been, there is no doubt that the abandonment of direct cultivation allowed the priory to save a great deal on transporting their everyday bread from the manors to the granary.

Interestingly enough, the transportation costs estimated for the pre-1430 period seem to have been considerably lower than those indicated in the contemporary sheriffs' accounts in conjunction with the transporting of provisions for king's garrisons during the ongoing warfare of the late thirteenth and early fourteenth centuries. The

---

93. Thus, to cart one quarter of malted barley would cost 0.086d by boat, and about 0.190d by cart.
94. Calculated from NRO, DCN 1/1/1–79.

transportation costs specified in these sources have been studied in great detail by James Masschaele and by Bruce Campbell and his colleagues.[95] It appears that in 1295-6 the sheriff of Essex had to pay, on average, 0.35d to transport a quarter of wheat weighing 424lb for a mile, or 0.22d for a kilometre. To cart a quarter of malted barley weighting 294lb would have cost 0.23d per mile and 0.14d per kilometre.[96] Multiplying these costs by the amounts of grain shipped to Norwich *and* by the total mileage, we arrive at much higher figures than those the priory authorities spent for annual carting services. Thus, in the pre-Black Death era, the priory would have had to pay around £240 a year (that is, almost six times higher than the figures calculated from our demesne accounts) in order to transport the required amounts of demesne grain to their headquarters, had they relied on professional carting services and assuming that these carting services would have been as expensive as the sheriffs' accounts specify. How can we solve this discrepancy arising from the two sets of accounts? The sheriffs, as royal officials, relied on professional carting services rather than on a *famuli* workforce.[97] These services were seemingly more expensive, for several reasons. First, the carters were hired with their own horses, carts and other equipment. In contrast, as we have seen, the manorial officials relied, for the most part, on the demesne horses and carts, with occasional help from the tenants and additional, 'auxiliary' carters. Second, one may speculate that the carters hired by the sheriffs were highly experienced and specialised professionals, whose services were expected to be more costly than those of the *famuli*. Third, as far as the evidence of the sheriffs' accounts goes, in most cases the number of horses in a team was four and not three, as was generally the case for our manorial carters. A larger number of cart horses meant not only a larger freight capacity but also a higher speed, so vital for military logistics. Fourth, since the warfare in question was occurring, for the most part, either on the Anglo-Scottish frontier or outside England (that is, in Scotland or France), journeys were much longer than those undertaken by the manorial carters.[98] Fifth, carrying grain to provision the king's armies was a much more important task than carting grain to feed the Norwich brethren. Finally, the fact that the carters, alongside their horses and carts, were hired for short-term periods would undoubtedly make the costs of their employment more expensive than those of the manorial carters. All these factors may have made the transportation costs of royal armies' victuals considerably higher than those of the Norwich brethren's grain.

Transportation logistics: the case of Eaton carters

What were the strategies undertaken by the priory tenants in carting the annual supply of grain? Our information on this subject is rather fragmentary because the definitive evidence comes solely from the Eaton portion of the *Stowe Survey*. As we have seen,

---

95. Masschaele, 'Transport costs'; Campbell *et al.*, *A medieval capital*, pp. 193–4.
96. Campbell *et al.*, *A medieval capital*, pp. 193–4.
97. On these carters, contracted by the sheriffs, see Masschaele, 'Transport costs'; Campbell *et al.*, *A medieval capital*, p. 269.
98. This is despite the fact that, in many cases, transportation involved a combination of inland and maritime routes.

every peasant working on this demesne was obliged to perform carting services each year. The survey gives some interesting details regarding the carrying logistics, stating that 'all the Prior's men of Eaton shall carry six mines [18 quarters] of wheat from Sedgeford to Norwich. And they shall have supper for six men and fodder for six horses in Sedgeford for one night. Also, [they shall have] six sheaves of barley, or oats, in [North] Elmham [on their way] toward Norwich. And [they shall have] food and drink in the [guests'] Hall in Norwich for the men and hay for the horses.'[99]

Let us, first, consider the environmental and road conditions between each destination. There was a distance of approximately 25.50 miles (41.04km) between Sedgeford and North Elmham. As some scholars have shown, an average cart horse would make between 3.00 and 3.50 miles (4.82–5.63km) per hour.[100] If these estimations are correct, then it might have taken the Eaton carters between 7.30 and 8.50 hours to cover this distance (namely, 18 quarters of wheat), excluding occasional short stops on the way. Late medieval and early modern maps allow a detailed reconstruction of the actual itinerary.

Having arrived at Sedgeford around supper time, the Eaton carters unharnessed their horses, fed them with hay and received their evening meal. The expression *per unam noctem* implies that they spent the night at Sedgeford, having their supper and resting there. They probably commenced their next day's journey shortly before, or around, dawn, taking advantage of the cooler temperatures of the early morning. However, carting done by the light of the day was an important safeguard against the theft of carried grain. Grain thefts committed at night must have been a serious issue in late medieval England judging by the series of by-laws that forbade carting by night.[101]

Having left Sedgeford, located in north-east Norfolk, the carters would have proceeded to the south-east along a narrow lane which shortly merged into Peddar's Way, a Roman road.[102] This road, commencing by the manor of Fring, would take the carters down towards Castle Acre. On their way along Peddar's Way they would pass the manor of Great Bircham and the commons of Anmer and Harpley, which were located on the road. Before reaching Castle Acre the carters would turn from Peddar's Way near Massingham Common on to another lane. The distance between Sedgeford and Fring is two miles, and that between Fring and Massingham Common 10.50 miles (16.90km), making a total of 12.50 miles (20.12km). This means that it would take between 3.57 and 4.00 hours to reach Massingham Common from Sedgeford.

From Massingham Common the carters would take another road to the south-east down to a crossroads at Litcham. Here they would take the eastern route, passing

---

99. 'omnes homines prioris de Etone cariabunt uj minas frumenti a Sechford usque Norwycum. Et habebunt apud Sechford cenam uj hominum et cibum uj equorum per unam noctem. Item apud Elmham uersus Norwycum uj garbas ordei uel auene. Et apud Norwycum cibum et potum in aula ad homines et fenum ad equos'. *Terrarium Prioratus*, fol. 26r.

100. H. Elton, *Warfare in Roman Europe, AD 350–425* (Oxford, 1996), p. 293; Landers, *The field and the forge*, pp. 83–4.

101. W.O. Ault, *Open-field farming in medieval England: a study of village by-laws* (New York, 1972), pp. 36–7.

102. On this road, see H. Haverfield, 'Romano-British remains [in Norfolk]', in H.A. Doubleday (ed.), *A history of Norfolk*, vol. 1, The Victoria County History of England (London, 1901), pp. 302–3.

Bread and Ale for the Brethren

Table 5.7
Estimated potential transportation costs of grain, comparing the 'mixed scenario' with the inland transportation costs (in £ sterling), 1261–1430.

	a. 'Mixed transportation' costs			b. Road transportation costs	
	Cart-leg costs	Boat-leg costs	Total journey costs	Total journey costs	Mixed transportation costs as % of road transportation costs
1261–70	9.2	5.6	14.8	38.4	38.6%
1271–80	8.6	4.4	12.9	35.7	36.3%
1281–90	9.9	5.2	15.1	41.4	36.6%
1291–1300	10.9	5.4	16.3	45.4	36.0%
1301–10	12.2	5.3	17.5	50.9	34.5%
1311–20	13.7	4.4	18.2	57.3	31.7%
1321–30	13.3	4.2	17.5	55.2	31.6%
1331–40	10.2	3.6	13.9	42.6	32.5%
1341–50	11.7	3.7	15.5	48.9	31.7%
1351–60	10.8	6.3	17.1	44.9	38.1%
1361–70	12.1	7.2	19.3	50.6	38.2%
1371–80	9.4	7.4	16.8	39.0	43.0%
1381–90	8.0	5.1	13.2	33.4	39.4%
1391–1400	5.9	4.7	10.7	24.7	43.2%
1401–10	8.2	6.1	14.2	34.0	41.9%
1411–20	7.2	5.1	12.2	29.8	41.1%
1421–30	8.1	7.4	15.4	33.6	46.0%
Pre-1350 decades	11.1	4.7	15.7	46.2	34.4%
Post-1350 decades	8.7	6.2	14.9	36.2	41.4%

Source: Manorial accounts database.
Notes: For the calculations of the transportation costs, see Appendix 1.

through Litcham Common, Mileham, Stanfield and Elmham Park, to North Elmham. The distance between the two points is about 13 miles (20.92km), meaning about 3.70 to 4.33 hours of travel. By the time they arrived at North Elmham, it must have been before, or around, noon.

Having arrived at North Elmham, they would receive six sheaves of oats or barley. This is rather puzzling, since the *Stowe Survey* neither specifies whether they received the grain for human or equine consumption nor converts the sheaves into bushels. By standard measures, however, six sheaves would equal around 1.20 bushels.[103] Walter of Henley, in his influential treatise, suggested a daily intake of one sixth of a bushel

---

103. The 1332–3 *Memoranda Roll of the Exchequer* notes *lx garbas avene, quorum v faciunt buscellum, unum quarterium et dimidium* (60 sheaves of oats, of which five make a bushel, one quarter and a half) (TNA, E368, 105 m. 39d.). Although the Norfolk sheaves could well have rendered a different bushel equivalent, especially since some manors used customary measures as opposed to the standard ones used in Westminster, where the memoranda rolls were compiled, nevertheless, the 1332–3 Exchequer roll provides an approximate clue which is sufficient for our purposes.

per plough horse (around one for six horses).[104] Carting horses, however, would have required higher intakes, and so it is possible that these six sheaves were actually intended for the six carting horses of Eaton. Moreover, since the *Stowe Survey* does not mention the conversion of the oats/barley into bread/ale, we can conclude that the grain was served in its fresh, unprocessed form. The very term *garba*, appearing in this document, means a bunch or bundle of crop, bound after it was reaped.

From North Elmham the carters would continue riding the same road eastwards, through Billingford to Bawdeswell, where the road splits into two. Having taken its southbound branch, they would make their way directly to Norwich through Sparham, Attlebridge, Taverham, Drayton, Drayton Heath and Hellesdon. They would probably have entered the city through Fye Bridge Gate (*porta de Fibrigge*, from c.1550 Magdalen Gate) and take Fye Bridge Street (*Fibrigestrete*, *Fibriggegate*, from c.1700 Magdalen Street). Having crossed Fye Bridge, over the river Wensum, the carters continued along Cook Street (*vicus cocorum*, from c.1845 Wensum Street) and reached Tombland, the western entrance to the cathedral close. They entered through St Ethelbert Gate and reached their final destination, the Great Granary. The distance between the manor of North Elmham and the Great Granary is around 17.15 miles (27.60km).

Road versus river transportation: advantages and drawbacks

The case of the Eaton carters leaves one wondering why the priory authorities employed road transportation instead of relying on supposedly much cheaper and, in some cases, faster river transport. Moreover, most demesnes were either located close to rivers, or had easy access to water. Furthermore, as we have seen, the priory possessed the great boat on the Yare, constructed in 1320–21, and had a permanent staff of two boatmen employed for an annual stipend. Finally, the staff of manorial *famuli* of Newton-by-Norwich and Plumstead included one boatman between c.1300 and the Black Death.[105] In order to understand why the priory preferred to rely on road transport it is necessary to consider several factors. First, there is the difference in costs of the two types of transportation. It is important, however, to keep in mind, that a pure river transport scenario was not possible, since most demesnes were not situated directly on river banks. In other words, in virtually all cases the priory authorities would have to rely on both carters and boatmen. The potential costs of mixed river–road transportation are compared with those of road-based transport only in Table 5.7. As the table indicates, both before and after the Black Death road transport would have been a more costly option for the priory authorities. Before the pestilence, the transport of the entirety of the priory's grain supply each year would have cost about £15 14s by road and river and £46 by road. After the Black Death, the figures would have stood at around £14 18s for 'mixed' transportation and £36 for road carting. In other words, over the entire period, the mixed transportation option was about 67 per cent cheaper than the road option.

---

104. D. Oschinsky (ed.), *Walter of Henley and other treatises on estate management and accounting* (Oxford, 1971), p. 318.
105. NRO, DCN 60/28/3–5, NRO, DCN 60/29/16–25 and NRO, DCN 62/1–2.

Speed is another decisive factor to be considered here. Table 5.8 establishes approximate speed of grain transportation, measured in vehicle-hours (cart-hours and boat/cart-hours), working hours and working days, around two benchmark periods. It appears that, *c.*1300, it would have taken each demesne, on average, around 79 hours or 10.5 working days to ship the grain supply using the 'mixed' scenario. On the other hand, it would have taken some 176 hours, or 29 working days, if relying on the carting services of the *famuli* and the available demesne horses. Similarly, *c.*1400, each demesne had to spend, on average, around 86 hours or 14 working days carting the annual grain supply to Norwich. This task would have been achieved considerably faster had the priory authorities chosen to rely on the mixed scenario: it would have required approximately 34 hours (4.5 working days) to transport the grain by carts and boats.

In other words, there is no doubt that the mixed scenario would have been both cheaper and faster than the traditional carting scenario. After all, the priory had both the capital (the boat and boatmen) and resources (cash to pay the boatmen for their services) to use the more profitable option. Why, then, did they not do it? One possible hypothesis derives from the assumption that the priory authorities, like other great manorial lords of the time, regarded the service of grain transporting as part of the demesne labour, whether hired or mandatory (as in the case of the Eaton tenants). In other words, this task, alongside other manorial tasks, was reserved strictly to the tenants, and not professionally trained boatmen. After all, most male tenants must have known how to cart, but not every tenant knew how to efficiently transport vast amounts of grain by boat. But above all, it would be, perhaps, instructive to ask whether the modern economic reasoning is not somewhat anachronistic for late medieval lords and their officials. In other words, would the latter ask these questions and calculate these estimates in the same fashion as we do?

Conclusions

The issue of transportation and its logistics and costs is another important, yet understudied, aspect of the late medieval seigniorial economy. The reconstruction of its patterns appears to be frustratingly difficult, however. A meticulous analysis of all the available sources reveals that the story of grain transportation can be divided into three stages. The first stage, lasting from the beginning of direct management until the 1390s, was characterised by a reliance on the manorial carters, both hired and customary. This meant that the grain was transported by cart along roads. From *c.*1391 until the end of direct management in 1431, the priory authorities used its 'great boat' to ship malt from Hemsby and the demesne carters to carry the remainder of the grain from other demesnes. The final stage commenced with the end of the direct management era in 1431, when the brethren gave up their long-standing reliance on the manorial *famuli* and started using priory carters to cart the grain from Plumstead and Taverham. The manors of Hemsby (and possibly Martham too) were serviced by the great boat. The remainder of the grain deriving from the food farms seems to have been delivered by the farmers as part of the lease contract.

The story of grain transportation reflects wider processes and factors within the changing socio-economic milieu of late medieval England, one of which was the limitations of the seigniorial power of Norwich Cathedral Priory. Unlike some other lords, such as Glastonbury Abbey, the Norwich brethren could not secure 'free' transportation services from their tenants, simply because local customs did not

Table 5.8
Approximate speed of grain transportation by 'mixed scenario' and by carts (if relying on demesne horses only), c.1300 and c.1400.

	Mixed scenario, c.1300 Cart/boat-hours	Number of hours	Number of days	Cart transportation, c.1300 Cart-hours	Number of hours	Number of days	Mixed scenario, c.1400 Cart/boat-hours	Number of hours	Number of days	Cart transportation, c.1400 Cart-hours	Number of hours	Number of days
Denham	n/a	n/a	n/a	21.7	21.7	3.6						
Eaton	23.5	11.7	1.5	40.1	16.6	2.8	10.2	5.4	0.7	17.4	10.4	1.7
Gateley	11.1	7.2	0.9	74.7	40.8	6.8	9.4	6.7	0.9	63.2	63.2	10.5
Gnatingdon	109.8	32.2	4.4	400.4	116.2	19.4	2.0	0.6	0.1	7.4	2.6	0.4
Hemsby	1136.0	369.8	48.7	3453.3	740.0	123.3	357.9	117.0	15.4	1085.9	232.7	38.8
Hindolveston	134.1	56.4	7.4	582.2	148.0	24.7	53.4	28.0	3.8	233.1	174.9	29.1
Hindringham	270.7	73.6	9.7	818.8	141.7	23.6	170.9	60.6	8.5	518.3	259.1	43.2
Martham	498.5	162.4	22.6	1038.3	445.0	74.2	258.6	78.0	10.7	537.9	179.3	29.9
Monks Granges	n/a	n/a	n/a	20.1	3.1	0.5	n/a	n/a	n/a	9.9	1.8	0.3
Newton-by-Norwich	84.7	84.7	10.6	90.1	22.5	3.8	39.5	39.5	4.9	41.9	10.5	1.7
North Elmham	148.6	90.8	12.0	804.8	536.6	89.4	108.1	57.4	7.3	589.3	117.9	19.6
Plumstead, Great	68.9	16.1	2.3	204.0	68.0	11.3	28.1	7.0	1.0	83.3	33.3	5.6
Sedgeford	125.0	36.3	4.9	460.5	118.4	19.7	2.9	0.9	0.1	10.6	3.2	0.5
Taverham	13.7	8.0	1.1	79.2	50.9	8.5	4.7	2.9	0.4	27.0	24.0	4.0
Average	218.7	79.1	10.5	577.8	176.4	29.4	87.1	33.7	4.5	248.1	85.6	14.3

Source: Manorial accounts database.

Notes: In the case of Denham and Monks Granges, it seems, it was impossible to transport the grain using the 'mixed' scenario. Hence, only the inland carting option was taken into consideration here. Denham was long leased out by c.1400. For the particulars of the calculations, see Appendix 1.

require the latter to perform carting as customary dues. The latter seem to have been protected by the custom, which, with some notable exceptions, did not require mandatory grain carting from the demesne to the priory. Instead, the brethren had to rely, for the most part, on hired labour, deriving from manorial carters who were employed along with other harvest *famuli* in virtually unchanging numbers throughout the entire period under study. Before the Black Death, this was the most obvious solution for the priory authorities, especially given the fact that transportation costs were relatively low, especially when compared with the information contained in the sheriffs' accounts. After the pestilence, and especially after 1376, when grain prices collapsed but real wages rose, the costs of transporting grain became increasingly high. This, in turn, decreased the brethren's profit and prompted the priory authorities to start seeking more convenient alternatives. As we have seen in the previous chapters, in the post-Black Death decades, and especially from the 1370s, the brethren increased the share of purchased grain while the proportion of demesne grain dispatched to the priory shrank. At the same time, there was a slow but sure demise of demesne husbandry and a shift to food farms, which were a part of lease contract terms. The end of manorial carting and, with it, direct management was over by 1431. The shift from *famuli* to priory carters was undoubtedly profitable for the economy of the priory, because it drastically reduced the overall transportation costs of the manorial grain. Overall, it seems that transport costs, as measured by annual expenses on cart maintenance, horse fodder and the carters' wages, were considerably lower than those indicated in the sheriffs' accounts discussed above.

One puzzling question, nevertheless, remains: why did the priory authorities rely, for such a long time, on the carting services of the *famuli* rather than on the 'mixed scenario' comprised of cart transport and boat journeys performed by the priory boatmen, despite the obvious financial and logistical advantages of the latter over the former? This could perhaps have something to do with centuries-old manorial customs and practices which associated carting services with other manorial tasks, to be performed by the tenants, whether as mandatory dues or hired labour. This enigma, however, is yet to be studied in great detail, using a much larger number of demesne accounts from other lordships; if it can be resolved, it would undoubtedly shed much new light on the efficiency (or lack of such) of the late medieval English seigniorial economy.

Chapter 6

Space for grain: barns and granaries

The medieval barn and modern scholarship

Before turning to the actual grain requirements of the Norwich brethren, it would be instructive to consider another important aspect related to the process of grain delivery from the fields to the table: the space in which grain was stored, for future consumption, for sale, or for immediate processing. The question of the place and importance of storage facilities and storage economics in pre-industrial societies has long been debated by both economists and economic historians. In particular, scholars have been preoccupied with the issue of grain storage in peasant societies. In summary, the debate began with Donald McCloskey's 1976 thesis on open fields as a measure of risk aversion.[1] The response came from Stefano Fenoaltea, who contended that a better measure of risk aversion against bad weather and years of dearth was grain storage.[2] In 1990, John Komlos and Richard Landes provided a more historically accurate account of this issue, rightly criticising both McCloskey and Fenoaltea for ignoring the historical reality of late medieval Europe.[3] More recently, in one of his working papers, Gregory Clark has re-established the importance of grain storage in late medieval and early modern England, based mostly on price movements.[4] What is common to all these authors, however, is the fact that they did not consider either the actual costs of storage, as measured in rental prices and/or their ratio to the value of grain stored there, or the actual amounts of grain stored in late medieval granaries. The first shortcoming has now been rectified in a recent study of grain storage in early fourteenth-century England by Jordan Claridge and John Langdon.[5] Based on over 300 purveyance accounts between 1295 and 1349, this important study demonstrates that there was a considerable grain-storage capacity in late medieval England the functions of which included not only the preservation of crops for years of high prices but also serving as an 'intermediate station' in the milieu of commercialisation and war which characterised England in that period.

All the same, however, some essential questions related to storage and its costs, profits and efficiency are either not yet posed or remain unanswered. A close analysis

---

1. D. McCloskey, 'English open fields as behavior towards risk', *Research in Economic History*, 1 (1976), pp. 124–71.
2. S. Fenoaltea, 'Risk, transactions costs, and the organization of medieval agriculture', *Explorations in Economic History*, 13 (1976), pp. 129–51.
3. J. Komlos and R. Landes, 'Anachronistic economics: grain storage in medieval England', *EcHR*, 44 (1991), pp. 36–45.
4. G. Clark, 'Markets and economic growth: the grain market of medieval England' (University of California, Davis, working paper, 2001), available: http://www.econ.ucdavis.edu/faculty/gclark/210a/readings/market99.pdf (accessed 11 October 2011), esp. pp. 16–36.
5. Claridge and Langdon, 'Storage in medieval England'.

of various references to barns and granaries can shed much light on their place within the economy of Norwich Cathedral Priory, and contribute to the ongoing debate about the essence of storage facilities in the late medieval period. Four questions are to be posed and answered here: (1) What were the costs and, if any, profits of storing the grain? (2) Were there, as Gregory Clark contended, enough carryovers from year to year to suggest a deliberate policy in this regard? (3) If there were, did Norwich Cathedral Priory, like Pharaoh, utilise its barns and granaries to store the surpluses of good years as insurance against dearth in bad years? (4) Or were these facilities used to enable the priory authorities to speculate in grain during bad years, when prices were high?

Demesne barns: nature, layout and capacity

In the era of direct management the priory invested heavily in its demesne barns. The accounts are replete with references to the costs of maintenance of barns, which appear, as a rule, under the rubric '*custos domorum*' (costs of buildings). This rubric records, in great detail, various expenses connected to the maintenance, building and repair of different buildings within the demesne. Apart from the actual expenses, however, it also provides a great deal of information about the type of labour performed, the duration of various tasks, the number of workers hired, the types of implements and materials purchased and used and, occasionally, the physical locations of the buildings. Thanks to these references, we can reconstruct a reliable picture of how late medieval demesne barns were maintained and how they functioned.

To begin with, it is important to note that, as the accounts reveal, each demesne had several barns, each storing a different crop. Thus, there were *grangia frumenti* (wheat barns), *grangia siliginis* (rye barns, storing both rye and maslin), *grangia avene* (oat barns), *grangia ordei* (barley barns), *grangia pisarum* (pea barns, which stored all legumes, not just peas), and *domus brasei* (a malt-house). In addition, some demesnes had separate barns for hay (*grangia/domus feni*).[6] The names of the barns should not, however, be automatically identified with their contents. In some cases, for reasons of, for example, temporary congestion or repairs, barns stored several different crops. Thus, at Gnatingdon small amounts of barley carryovers were, from time to time, stored in rye and pea barns.[7] In 1317–18 at Taverham, 9.13 quarters of barley were placed in the local *domus feni*.[8] The accounts carefully distinguish between *grangie* (storages for threshed crops) and *granarie* (storages for unthreshed crops).[9] The use of the term *domus brasei* rather than *grangia/granaria brasei* may suggest that malt-houses functioned not only as storage space but also as malting facilities. In addition, the accounts distinguish between 'demesne barns' (*grangie dominice*) and 'tithe barns' (*grangie decimarum*), the latter where tithe grain was stored once estimated and separated from the remainder of the harvest. Some

---

6. For instance, at Newton-by-Norwich: NRO, DCN 60/28/4.
7. Thus, NRO, DCN 60/14/11a.
8. NRO, DCN 60/35/18.
9. Oschinsky, *Walter of Henley*, pp. 276, 290, 322, 388 and 394.

Space for grain: barns and granaries

accounts also mention 'old' and 'new barn(s)' (*vetus* and *nova grangia*). It is likely that this distinction refers to the age of the buildings. Finally, some rolls refer to the barns by their geographic situation: for instance, the 1351–2 roll from Taverham speaks about the 'eastern barn' (*grangia orientalis*).

Ubiquitous references to lumber, wooden planks, reed and other related materials, as well as to carpenters hired to repair parts of barns, suggest that the vast majority of these buildings were made of wood. On the other hand, there were several instances in which wooden parts of barns were replaced with stone. Thus, at Hindringham in 1343–4 stone walls were constructed for all the demesne barns. This project lasted one month and involved a large number of masons and other workers; the total expenditure was £7 13s 2½d.[10] Similar projects took place at Monks Granges in 1323–4 and at Taverham in 1334–5.[11] Generally speaking, timber barns were by no means an exception in late medieval England: they accounted for about 53 per cent of all barns in the southern counties. Stone barns were almost as common, while granges constructed of brick were very rare in late medieval England.[12] At the same time, however, 'stone walls' or 'stones' should not necessarily be identified with 'stone buildings'. As Christopher Dyer has shown, in the late medieval period some rural buildings were made partially of stone and partially of timber:[13] the placing of the wooden frame of the barn upon low stone 'footings' would have been a relatively cheap and efficient way of preventing rot from attacking the base of the structure.

The physical layout of the granges is yet another aspect emerging from the accounts. In many instances, different barns appear as conjoined buildings, separated one from another by walls. For instance, the 1320–21 account from Hindolveston specifies that its granary and barn were separated by a wall.[14] Occasional rolls also reveal that some barns were multi-storey buildings. Thus, at Hindringham in 1272–3 the demesne officials spent 18s on the construction of a storey (*area*).[15] This reflects the attempts of the manorial officials to utilise the full capacity of the barns. Unfortunately, we know nothing of the latter, because the accounts do not specify the measurements of the granges. The sole exception is a reference to the building of a new timber wall for the barley barn at Sedgeford in 1367–8: it measured 40 feet (12.19m) in length and 5 feet (1.52m) in height.[16] Obviously, the height of the wall is not to be equalled with the overall height of the barn, because the building had a pitched roof. On average, the ratio between the overall height and the wall height of late medieval barns was about 2.72:1.00.[17] Using this multiplier, we arrive at a height

---

10. NRO, DCN 60/20/25.
11. NRO, DCN 60/26/20 and NRO, DCN 60/35/26.
12. Calculated from N.D.K. Brady, 'The sacred barn: barn-building in southern England, 1100–1550: a study of grain storage technology and its cultural context', PhD thesis (Cornell University, 1996), Appendix 1.
13. Dyer, *Standards of living*, pp. 161–3.
14. NRO, DCN 60/18/22.
15. NRO, DCN 60/20/4.
16. NRO, Lest/IB/29.
17. Calculated from Brady, 'The sacred barn', Appendix 1.

of about 4.13m. Unfortunately, the same account does not supply the width of the barn, but this may be speculatively obtained from other evidence. On average, the ratio between the length, width and overall height of barns was about 1.00:0.35:0.30. If this assumption holds true in the case of the Sedgeford barn, it is likely that it was approximately 4.27m in width. And if this estimate is not too far removed from reality, then the barley barn of Sedgeford seems to have been rather a small facility when compared with other barns in England, which had, on average, a length of about 30m, a width of about 8.5m and a height of about 8m, rendering a volume of close to 2100 cubic metres.[18]

Demesne barns: storage costs

In virtually all cases the demesne accounts provide a very detailed breakdown of financial expenses connected to various barn works, including repairs, restoration and utensil purchases. Obviously the costs would differ not only from demesne to demesne, depending on the physical size of different barns and the work and resources required to maintain them, but also from year to year within the same demesnes. For instance, at Hindringham in 1341 the demesne officials paid just 1d for one day of work involving mounting wooden planks. Yet, two years later they spent no less than £7 14s on general repairs to all their barns, which involved over a month of work and a large number of labourers. During the 1380s demesne officials invested exceptionally large sums of money in major overhauls across virtually all the demesnes. This resulted in a considerable over-expenditure within this sector which amounted to some 230 per cent above the average levels. On average, however, each demesne could be expected to spend about 2s 6d a year on various barn maintenance works. Overall, the costs of barn maintenance and repairs across all the demesnes would have been around £1 17s 1½d and £2 9s a year in the pre- and post-Black Death period, respectively (see Table 6.1).

What were the main forms of maintenance work and how often were they performed? The single most frequent work in this conjunction was roofing (*coopertio*, *copertura*) and thatching (*arundatio*). Normally, each barn would need a roof repair every other year.[19] Fixing of ridge-pieces in wall or roof (*crestatio*) was another common task required almost as often. Other tasks, less frequently undertaken, included daubing (*daubura*) and plastering (*plastura*) of doors and walls, repairs of floors (*emendatio aree*) and padlock and key repairs and changes. This, however, is by no means an exhaustive list of all the tasks required to maintain the barns. These were basic tasks, whose main function was to protect the grain against inclement weather, vermin (mostly, mice and other rodents) and thieves. But much more was required to avoid spoilage. First, it was crucial to ensure low moisture content, to prevent mildew or unwanted germination.[20] Second, most remaining grain had to be

---

18. Calculated from ibid.
19. Calculated from the accounts with uninterrupted, or virtually uninterrupted, runs.
20. Claridge and Langdon, 'Storage in medieval England'; V. Smil, *Energy in world history* (Boulder, CO, 1994), p. 37; D.E. Briggs *et al.*, *Malting and brewing science: malt and sweet wort*, 2nd edn (Bury St Edmunds, 1981), p. 33.

Table 6.1
Annual storage costs on the demesnes of Norwich Cathedral Priory, 1261–1430.

	All grain incoming (in quarters)	Total incoming value, after spoilage (in £ sterling)	Maintenance costs (in £ sterling)	Threshing costs (in £ sterling)	Porterage costs (in £ sterling)	Total storage costs (in £ sterling)	Storage costs as % of value of stored crops	Storage costs for one unthreshed quarter of crop (in pence sterling)	Approximate storage costs for one quarter of threshed crop (in pence sterling)
1261–70	5540.2	805.0	1.0	15.8	2.0	18.8	2.3%	0.8	2.0
1271–80	5014.4	978.5	1.8	16.4	1.9	20.0	2.0%	1.0	2.4
1281–90	7231.1	1127.7	0.6	29.5	2.2	32.2	2.9%	1.1	2.6
1291–1300	6378.3	1305.3	2.3	25.0	2.4	29.7	2.3%	1.1	2.8
1301–10	6270.4	1098.5	1.8	27.1	2.7	31.6	2.9%	1.2	2.9
1311–20	6821.4	1727.1	2.4	32.6	3.0	38.1	2.2%	1.3	3.2
1321–30	5981.0	1311.3	2.3	30.0	2.9	35.2	2.7%	1.4	3.4
1331–40	5016.1	846.2	2.2	23.7	2.3	28.2	3.3%	1.4	3.4
1341–50	6000.0	939.2	2.4	32.9	2.6	37.9	4.0%	1.5	3.7
1351–60	4141.9	920.6	2.3	32.1	2.4	36.9	4.0%	2.1	4.9
1361–70	5052.7	1265.5	2.3	42.3	2.7	47.3	3.7%	2.2	5.3
1371–80	4800.1	960.1	1.1	42.2	2.1	45.5	4.7%	2.3	5.3
1381–90	3264.1	519.8	4.9	41.0	1.8	47.7	9.2%	3.5	8.1
1391–1400	3753.6	668.2	3.1	37.7	1.4	42.3	6.3%	2.7	6.3
1401–10	4691.7	933.8	2.6	46.6	1.8	51.0	5.5%	2.6	6.0
1411–20	4410.6	794.5	1.3	42.9	1.6	45.8	5.8%	2.5	5.7
1421–30	2513.9	437.6	1.9	39.6	1.8	43.3	9.9%	4.1	9.6
Pre-1350 decades	6028.1	1126.5	1.9	25.9	2.4	30.2	2.7%	1.2	2.9
Post-1350 decades	4078.6	812.5	2.5	40.6	2.0	45.0	6.1%	2.8	6.4

Source: Manorial accounts database.

threshed at some time before March, before newly hatched insects would start attacking crops in the sheaf.[21] Third, once crops were threshed and the grain moved to granaries (usually, a space adjacent to the barn), it was necessary to stir and ventilate it every two or three weeks to keep it from spoiling.[22] While nearly every account provides threshing and winnowing costs, paid to the local *famuli*, there is no information about barn supervision or stirring. Two possibilities may be offered. First, it is possible that the customary tenants were expected to watch, stir and ventilate the grain as part of their manorial dues.[23] The second possibility is that the ventilating costs were not mentioned because the vast majority of grain stored in the barns was unthreshed and therefore did not require much work in this regard. But even when grain was eventually threshed and moved from the barns to the granges, checking and stirring it every couple of weeks appear to have been easy and non-intensive tasks, commanding very low costs.

Finally, there are porterage costs to be considered. Unfortunately, the accounts reported the total transportation costs, without distinguishing between the costs of carting the grain from the field to the demesne barns and those of transporting it from the barns to the Norwich headquarters. Perhaps we may, somewhat crudely, allow some 5 per cent of the total transport costs for carting the crops from the fields to the barns, an estimate supported by the fact that the average distance between the two ends of each manor represented about 5 per cent of the average distance between each manor and the cathedral precinct.

Approximate annual storage costs, made up of several elements, are shown in Table 6.1. Maintenance expenses and threshing and winnowing costs varied from decade to decade, much depending on the level of barn repairs required and the amount of crops requiring processing, as well as the sum of the wages paid to the *famuli* involved in barn works. Porterage costs depended on the amounts of grain harvested and brought in and out each year. Overall, however, annual storage costs stood at about £30 and £45 a year before and after the pestilence respectively. These sums represent about 2.7 and 6.1 per cent of the grain's financial value both before and after the plague and amount to, per quarter of unthreshed crop, yearly storage figures of around 1.2d before and 2.8d after the Black Death.

Interestingly enough, these estimated storage costs seem to have been considerably lower than those associated with rented grain storage spaces. As Claridge and Langdon have most recently shown, using evidence mainly from purveyance accounts from the first half of the fourteenth century, the storage of a quarter of wheat would cost about 11d a year.[24] It should be remembered, however, that their study deals with threshed grain,

---

21. As described by Louis Liger in his treatise, *Le nouvelle maison rustique* (Paris, 1755), p. 581; G. Grantham, 'What's space got to do with it? Distance and agricultural productivity before the Railway Age', McGill University Working Paper (2010), available: http://ideas.repec.org/p/mcl/mclwop/2010-04.html (accessed 11 October 2011), pp. 35–6.
22. Grantham, 'What's space got to do with it?' p. 35.
23. This is not to say, however, that no barn- or granary-keepers were ever hired: thus, at Martham and Monks Granges, one *custos grangie* was employed on a regular basis before the Black Death for a meagre oblation of about 1d.
24. Claridge and Langdon, 'Storage in medieval England'.

Space for grain: barns and granaries

Table 6.2
Comparative wheat storage costs, *c.*1300 and 2010.

	Wheat price (in £ per 1000 quarters)	Storage costs (in £ per 1000 quarters per annum)	Storage costs as % of the grain value
Central storage, *c.*1300	250	45.8	18.3%
On-farm storage, *c.*1300	250	12.1	4.8%
Central storage, 2010	39615	3340.5	8.4%
On-farm storage, 2010	39615	1336.2	3.4%

Sources: Manorial accounts database;
http://www.wealdgranary.co.uk/literature/ProSeedConsultStudy.pdf;
http://www.networkgrainuk.com/documents/brochure.pdf (accessed 12 October 2011).

while the demesne barns held, for the most part, grain on the sheaf. In other words, to make a valid comparison between these two storage costs it is necessary to convert our figures, relating to unthreshed grain, into the equivalent for threshed grain. In the pre-plant-breeding era, the ratio between straw and grain in terms of their respective weights varied across crops: it stood at about 2.33:1.00 for wheat, 3.00:1.00 for rye, 4.00:1.00 for oats, 1.86:1.00 for barley and 2.50:1.00 for peas.[25] Since each crop occupied a different share in the demesne barns, we need to assign each stored crop its appropriate weight, corresponding to its share in the barns. The assignment renders 2.45:1.00 as a ratio between straw and crops and the hypothetical costs of threshed crop storage, based on the approximate conversion of unthreshed grain into its threshed equivalent, are shown in the final column of Table 6.1. As the figures indicate, for the pre-Black Death period at least, the storage costs of grain in the demesne barns were about 70 per cent cheaper than the costs appearing in the purveyance accounts. Several possible factors may account for this gap. First, just as in the case of its transportation, purveyed grain is likely to have commanded higher storage costs because of more intensive protection and supervision and, hence, higher transaction costs. Secondly, it is necessary to distinguish between *leased* and *owned* space, with the former eventually exceeding the latter in value and costs.

Were late medieval storage costs high or low when compared to today's costs? A cursory comparison, shown in Table 6.2, reveals that *c.*1300, relative costs of grain storage, as exemplified by wheat, were somewhat more costly than today. As of 2010, there are two main forms of grain storage in England: 'central storage' (vast granaries jointly rented by a number of farmers); and 'on-farm storage' (small barns owned and operated by individual farmers). About 88 per cent of all harvested grain is stored in on-farm barns, and only 12 per cent is placed in central granaries. For the purpose of the present exercise, the demesne barns correspond to the on-farm barns, while the purveyance storages can be likened to the central granaries. In both cases, unsurprisingly, the rented space appears to be more costly than the owned one in relative terms. Within the central storage sector, storage costs of wheat accounted for about 18 per cent of its financial value *c.*1300, while in 2010 the figures stood at about

---

25. I am grateful for George Grantham for this data.

Bread and Ale for the Brethren

8 per cent. As far as the on-farm storage is concerned, the difference was not as apparent: the figure stood at nearly 5 per cent c.1300 and just over 3 per cent in 2010. This insignificant difference is somewhat surprising given the fact that grain storage has undergone a series of revolutionary improvements in recent decades, such as de-humidifiers (to ensure appropriate moisture content), fans (to provide cool and dry air and to void insects), vacuum-cleaning, electronic pest-monitoring, hot air disinfestation and others. A full-scale study of the long-term movement of grain storage costs, which cannot be undertaken within the present framework, is likely to shed much light on these dynamics.

The Great Granary: layout and costs

A crucial role in storing and preserving the priory's grain was played by the Great Granary of the priory, to be distinguished from the almoner's granary, which will be discussed below. The former was located to the east of the cathedral and cloister in a square known as Brewer's Green. Its topographical location was convenient for both the brethren and carters: the buildings immediately to its east were the bakery, brewery and mills, while the monastic stables stood right in front of the granary (Figure 6.1).[26] The granary was a three-storey flint building with a lead roof and was about 35m in length, 8m in width and 7m in height,[27] giving it a potential storage capacity of 1500 cubic metres, enough to store 5340 quarters of grain.[28] Archaeological evidence proves that the granary was built on a thirteenth-century arcade no later than c.1250.[29] However, in 1316 £4 6s was spent on a new chimney and other repairs of the 'new granary' (*novum granarium*),[30] but it is possible that the 'new granary' was just one of several structures within a single compound, since, as we have seen, late medieval storage facilities consisted of several adjacent spaces. The Great Granary was not an exception: it is known to have had a separate compartment for malt, implying that each grain was stored in a separate room (Figure 6.1). Miscellaneous accounts indicate that the granary was locked with a padlock.[31] It was also decorated with a wall painting of a crown of thorns with the monograms of 'HIS' and 'Maria'.[32] In the fifteenth century the granary also served as a warehouse for the sacrist's mattresses and

---

26. It is interesting to note that nowadays there is a car park in the place of the stables.
27. I. Atherton, 'The close', in I. Atherton, E.C. Fernie and C. Harper-Bill (eds), *Norwich Cathedral: church, city and diocese, 1096–1996* (London, 1996), p. 655 (Fig. 213); B. Dodwell, 'The monastic community', in I. Atherton, E.C. Fernie and C. Harper-Bill (eds), *Norwich Cathedral: church, city and diocese, 1096–1996* (London, 1996), p. 235 (Fig. 114).
28. The calculations are based on Claridge and Langdon, 'Storage in medieval England'.
29. A.B. Whittingham, 'The monastic buildings of Norwich Cathedral', *Archaeology Journal*, 106 (1949), p. 87; C. Noble, 'Aspects of life at Norwich Cathedral Priory in the late medieval period', PhD thesis (University of East Anglia, 2001), p. 128.
30. NRO, DCN 1/1/25.
31. For instance, NRO, DCN 1/1/79.
32. A.B. Whittingham, 'The development of the close since the Reformation', in G.A. Metters (ed.), *The parliamentary survey of dean and chapter properties in and around Norwich in 1649*, Norfolk Record Society 51 (Norwich, 1985), p. 114.

Space for grain: barns and granaries

25 Boathouse
26 Quay
27 Wind-mill
28 St Mary-in-the-Marsh Church
29 Bakery
30 Brewery
31 The Great Granary: (a) wheat; (b) oat(?); (c) malt
33 Stables
36 Barn
46 Steward's house
56 Horse-mill

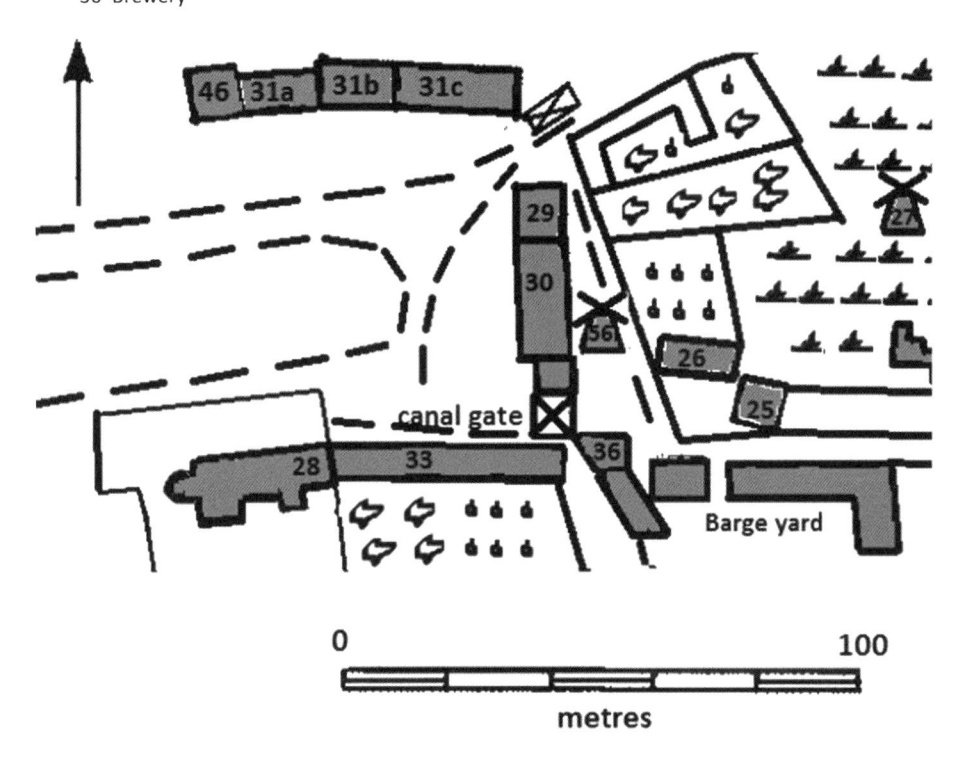

Figure 6.1 The 'provisioning compound' within the cathedral precinct.
Sources: NRO, DCN 1/1/–12; A.B. Whittingham, 'The development of the close since the Reformation', in G.A. Metters (ed.), *The parliamentary survey of dean and chapter properties in and around Norwich in 1649*, Norfolk Record Society 51 (Norwich, 1985), p. 114; C. Noble, 'Aspects of life at Norwich Cathedral Priory in the late medieval period', PhD thesis (University of East Anglia, 2001), p. 128; R. Gilchrist, *Norwich Cathedral close: the evolution of the English cathedral landscape* (Woodbridge, 2005), p. 192.

bedding.[33] After the Dissolution the site was converted into residential houses, numbers 51–55. Number 53 (Dial House), collapsed in 1904 and was rebuilt a year later.[34] It is quite possible that the original granary, which pre-dates the period of our study, was of more modest proportions and was built of timber.

---

33. Noble, 'Aspects of life', p. 128.
34. Atherton, 'The close', p. 655; R. Gilchrist, *Norwich Cathedral close: the evolution of the English cathedral landscape* (Woodbridge, 2005), pp. 191–8.

The master of the cellar was the *de jure* master of the granary, for it was he who decided how to dispose of and distribute the grain supply. But he was not the only person in charge of the granary and its resources. No less important was the part played by another monastic official, the granarer, or keeper of the granary (*granarius*). Not much is known about the nature of this office and its status, duties and responsibilities. The contemporary evidence suggests that, unlike other monastic officials, the granarer could be a layman. For instance, William Bauchun, the priory granarer in the 1290s, is known to have been a lay person, who, with his wife Magdalen, presumably resided within the cathedral precinct.[35] Perhaps most strikingly, he was a renowned and wealthy merchant of the town as well as an ardent patron of the cathedral. He is credited, among other things, with the rebuilding of a cathedral chapel that had been destroyed by enraged townsfolk during the riot of 1272. This chapel became known as Bauchun Chapel.[36] After Bauchun's departure from this office, we are virtually ignorant regarding this shadowy official. All we know is that this office was held, for over 40 years between *c.*1355 and 1398, by a Roger de Langelee, of whom nothing is known. After *c.*1398, the office was held by John Vowe.

Another interesting detail emerges from the master of the cellar rolls. These attest that, prior to 1360, the keeper of the granary did not receive a salary (*stipendium*) as other officials did. He received some modest gifts (*donaciones*) here and there, but these were rather rare instances. For example, in 1310 he received 6s 8d and in 1321 he was given 1s.[37] The situation changed after the Black Death and from 1359 the keeper of the granary received an annual stipend. The levels of the stipend rose accordingly with the wages of other priory servants; between the 1350s and the 1480s it rose from 10s to 26s a year, the latter figure then remaining unchanged until the Dissolution.[38]

What were the annual storage costs of the grain kept at the Great Granary? Unlike those of manorial barns, let alone of the centrally rented purveyance storages, the annual costs of granary maintenance were surprisingly low in the pre-Black Death decades (Table 6.3). With some exceptions, such as the building of the new granary in 1316, the granary did not require major expenditure on its maintenance. Moreover, in the pre-Black Death period, the priory did not hire a keeper of the granary on a permanent basis, thus saving on paying his wages. Before 1350, with the exception of the 1310s, the annual costs of maintenance were about 16s a year, or about 5s 3½d per 1000 stored quarters (just 0.04d per quarter). These storage costs represented only 0.1 per cent of the financial value of the stored grain. After the Black Death, costs rose considerably for several reasons. Firstly, between *c.*1356 and 1441 threshing and winnowing of purchased grains was done at the granary, which indicates that the crops were sold to the priory unthreshed, incurring additional costs. Over that period, the annual stipend of a labourer performing winnowing and threshing rose from 4s to 16s a year. After 1441, however, the winnower and his wages disappear from the records, which may indicate

---

35. B. Dodwell, 'William Bauchun and his connection with the Cathedral Priory at Norwich', *Norfolk Archaeology*, 36 (1975), p. 114; Atherton, 'The close', p. 635.
36. M. Rose, 'The vault bosses', in I. Atherton, E.C. Fernie and C. Harper-Bill (eds), *Norwich Cathedral: church, city and diocese, 1096–1996* (London, 1996), pp. 373–5.
37. NRO, DCN 1/1/21 and 28.
38. NRO, DCN 1/1/46–94.

Space for grain: barns and granaries

Table 6.3
Annual grain storage costs in the Great Granary, 1261–1536.

	All grain incomings (in quarters)	Value (in £ sterling)	Maintenance costs (in shillings)	Storage costs per 1000 quarters of grain (in shillings)	Storage costs as % of value of stored crops
1261–70	2960.3	551.6	11.0	3.7	0.09%
1271–80	2575.3	636.7	10.6	4.1	0.07%
1281–90	3206.3	565.7	15.6	4.9	0.12%
1291–1300	3513.1	809.2	15.2	4.3	0.08%
1301–10	3237.0	652.3	16.6	5.1	0.11%
1311–20	3025.6	965.1	30.5	10.1	0.14%
1321–30	2646.9	815.2	14.8	5.6	0.08%
1331–40	2775.8	603.1	13.3	4.8	0.10%
1341–50	2689.8	509.1	14.8	5.5	0.13%
1351–60	1418.7	346.4	12.6	8.9	0.16%
1361–70	1487.7	365.9	25.6	17.2	0.32%
1371–80	1679.7	352.8	27.6	16.5	0.35%
1381–90	1471.8	229.0	30.0	20.4	0.59%
1391–1400	1331.3	240.1	27.1	20.4	0.51%
1401–10	1421.6	262.4	36.4	25.6	0.62%
1411–20	1361.7	260.3	37.3	27.4	0.65%
1421–30	1272.4	265.6	46.1	36.2	0.78%
1431–40	1276.1	260.7	39.7	31.1	0.68%
1441–50	1239.5	186.9	27.0	21.8	0.65%
1451–60	1403.9	196.9	20.0	14.2	0.46%
1461–70	1232.4	202.4	20.0	16.2	0.44%
1471–80	1668.6	281.5	23.0	13.8	0.37%
1481–90	1559.2	308.1	26.7	17.1	0.39%
1491–1500	1304.5	198.4	26.7	20.4	0.60%
1501–10	1454.9	255.2	26.7	18.3	0.47%
1511–20	1674.1	347.5	26.7	15.9	0.35%
1521–30	1071.7	282.2	26.7	24.9	0.43%
1531–6	808.3	185.3	26.7	33.0	0.65%
Pre-Black Death decades	2958.9	678.7	15.8	5.3	0.10%
1351–1430	1430.6	287.0	30.4	22.6	0.52%
1431–1536	1335.8	244.4	26.3	19.6	0.48%

Source: NRO, DCN 1/1/1–108.
Notes: Since the master of the cellar rolls do not contain the granary part between 1343 and the 1490s, the figures for the missing years have been calculated from the purchase section of the master of the cellar rolls and from the manorial accounts. The levels of annual carryovers were linearly interpolated.

that from that time onwards the grain was purchased in a threshed form at local markets. Secondly, the annual stipend of the keeper of the granary rose from 17s 6d to 26s 8½d a year in the second half of the fourteenth century. Finally, and perhaps most important, the frequency of purchases and porterage increased drastically after the 1430s, chiefly within the wheat sector. Before that decade, annual wheat purchases tended to be large wholesale ones, while the average number of transactions did not exceed three a year. After the 1430s wheat was purchased at the retail level, with the number of annual wheat transactions rising to ten. This shift from wholesale to retails patterns of grain purchase had serious implications, which are discussed in the next chapter. As a rule of thumb there is a negative correlation between the frequency of retail purchases and the value of stored goods per unit. This rule is reflected well in the post-1430 costs of grain storage. Between 1431 and 1536, the priory authorities spent, on average, about 26s a year on the granary's maintenance, while the annual storage costs of 1000 quarters of grain amounted to about 20s.

The almoner's granary

Much less is known about the almoner's granary. We shall see later that, in addition to annual liveries of bread for the poor on Maundy Thursday, the almoner had his own supply of grain, deriving from both his appropriated manors and purchases, that was allocated to the needy.[39] To avoid confusion between the master of the cellar's supply and that of the almoner, an additional granary was required, known as the almoner's granary (close buildings nos 3–4). It is unclear when this granary was built, but it is first mentioned in the almoner's roll from 1339–40.[40] It is known to have been located in the south-west part of the close, just by Ethelbert Gate. Like that of the Great Granary, the location of the almoner's granary was very convenient for its purpose. It stood right between the Almonry and the almoner's house (see Figure 2.2), while its proximity to the close's entrance gave easy access to the poor begging just outside Ethelbert Gate. The almoner's granary was demolished sometime after the Dissolution and in 1701 two residential houses were built on its site by Jeremy Vynn, alderman and mayor of Norwich, and his wife Susan.[41] The granary occupied a large site, certainly no smaller than that of the Great Granary, even though it contained rather modest quantities of grain. It was served by its own keeper, about whom very little is known. In 1309–10 36s was spent on purchasing new robes for several monastic officials, the keeper of the granary included.[42] The 1328–9 and 1339–40 rolls also mention that the keeper of the granary received annual wages of 6s 8d,[43] but these were the only accounts to mention his wages. The same rolls do not mention his annual livery, or salary, though other servants' wages are noted. Can we conclude, then, that the keeper of the almoner's granary, unlike that of the Great Granary in the 1290s, was himself a monk, living within the cathedral precinct?

Barns and granaries: a tool for insurance, speculation or practical storage?

Did the barns function as a risk aversion measure against bad harvest years and high crop prices, as Fenoaltea and Clark have contended? A look into the annual patterns of crop distribution may provide a clue to this economic riddle. As we have seen in

---

39. See below, Chapter 8.
40. NRO, DCN 1/6/12.
41. Atherton, 'The close', p. 639.
42. NRO, DCN 1/1/21.
43. NRO, DCN 1/6/10 and 12.

Table 6.4
Total annual carryovers of crops stored in barns of Norwich Cathedral Priory demesnes, 1261–1430 (in quarters).

	Wheat	Rye/Maslin	Peas	Beans	Oats	Barley	Malt	Total	Grain carried over as % of all AGCR disposal
1261–70	1.5	3.3	0.1	0.0	0.5	21.9	22.2	49.4	0.89%
1271–80	1.3	0.1	0.1	0.0	2.0	7.2	32.5	43.2	0.86%
1281–90	5.8	5.9	1.0	1.3	0.3	38.4	16.5	69.3	0.96%
1291–1300	10.6	8.0	17.9	0.3	3.2	15.4	0.5	55.8	0.87%
1301–10	18.8	5.7	0.6	0.0	0.5	48.7	3.5	77.8	1.24%
1311–20	1.5	2.1	0.2	0.0	0.8	40.7	4.0	49.3	0.72%
1321–30	9.0	8.1	0.3	0.0	0.4	31.0	18.2	67.0	1.12%
1331–40	20.6	13.2	0.7	0.0	0.6	112.7	37.2	185.0	3.69%
1341–50	9.3	6.6	3.3	0.4	3.8	124.8	28.0	176.1	2.94%
1351–60	2.6	0.0	0.1	0.0	1.6	183.1	26.0	213.4	5.15%
1361–70	3.7	2.6	0.1	0.0	1.0	255.0	63.6	326.1	6.45%
1371–80	25.4	0.8	0.0	0.0	1.1	244.7	72.8	344.7	7.18%
1381–90	0.7	0.0	0.0	0.0	1.3	247.6	32.5	282.1	8.64%
1391–1400	0.0	0.0	0.0	0.0	1.3	244.6	34.0	279.8	7.46%
1401–10	29.8	0.0	0.0	0.0	1.3	312.7	34.9	378.6	8.07%
1411–20	6.8	0.0	0.0	0.0	0.0	367.0	20.9	394.6	8.95%
1421–30	16.8	0.0	0.0	0.0	0.0	287.3	10.9	314.9	12.53%
Pre-1350 decades	8.7	5.9	2.7	0.2	1.3	49.0	18.1	85.9	1.5%
post-1350 decades	10.7	0.4	0.0	0.0	0.9	267.7	36.9	316.8	8.1%

Source: Manorial accounts database.
Note: AGCR = Annual Gross Crop Receipt (see Chapter 2).

Bread and Ale for the Brethren

Table 6.5
Annual food rents and carryovers of barley on Norwich Cathedral Priory demesnes, 1261–1430 (in quarters and as percentage).

	Food rent	AGCR of barley	Carryovers	Food rent as % of AGCR disposal	Carryovers as % of AGCR disposal
1261–70	5.0	2972.9	44.1	0.2%	1.5%
1271–80	5.1	2650.5	39.7	0.2%	1.5%
1281–90	24.8	3743.8	55.0	0.7%	1.5%
1291–1300	25.5	3329.6	15.9	0.8%	0.5%
1301–10	33.3	3451.6	52.2	1.0%	1.5%
1311–20	44.1	3665.7	44.7	1.2%	1.2%
1321–30	49.8	3171.2	49.2	1.6%	1.6%
1331–40	131.2	2565.9	149.9	5.1%	5.8%
1341–50	128.3	2955.9	152.8	4.3%	5.2%
1351–60	154.6	2172.6	209.1	7.1%	9.6%
1361–70	254.2	2609.5	318.6	9.7%	12.2%
1371–80	344.8	2542.3	317.4	13.6%	12.5%
1381–90	310.7	1853.8	280.1	16.8%	15.1%
1391–1400	192.0	2024.6	278.6	9.5%	13.8%
1401–10	281.8	2557.2	347.6	11.0%	13.6%
1411–20	344.3	2411.1	387.9	14.3%	16.1%
1421–30	353.0	1361.0	298.1	25.9%	21.9%
Pre-1350 decades	49.7	3167.5	67.1	1.7%	2.2%
Post-1350 decades	279.4	2191.5	304.7	13.5%	14.3%

Source: Manorial accounts database.
Note: AGCR = Annual Gross Crop Receipt (see Chapter 2).

Chapter 4, each year certain percentages of crop receipts were sent to Norwich, re-invested in seeding, sold to local peasants and merchants, distributed among demesne animals and manorial *famuli* and carried over for the next year. It is the latter element that assumes particular significance here. As Table 6.4 indicates, the share of stored grain carried over for the next year was never significant. Before the Black Death it accounted for about 1.5 per cent of the total arable produce, rising in the post-1350 era to 8.1 per cent. In effect, the figure rose progressively from decade to decade and this rise is apparent particularly in the barley (both fresh and malted) sector, where the share of carryovers began rising significantly from the 1330s – that is, some two decades before the Black Death (Table 6.5). It would be erroneous, therefore, to connect this change to the new socio-economic reality brought about by the pestilence. Instead, it has to do with the increasing number of grain rents paid by local tenants in raw barley. The issue of grain rents, treated at greater length in Chapter 4, is most crucial for our understanding of storage dynamics.

Before the Black Death, food rents accounted for less than 2 per cent of the annual produce of barley. In the post-pestilence decades this figure rose to about 13 per cent. Accordingly, the relative share of annual carryovers of barley rose from 2 to some 14 per cent between the two periods. The compilers of the accounts were aware of the fact that the carryovers derived from the food rents. In many cases, the accounts state *et remanent de firma x quart' ordei* (and remain 10 quarters of barley from rent).

Space for grain: barns and granaries

Table 6.6
Pre-Black Death instances of excessive carryovers of grains (5 per cent or over) on Norwich Cathedral Priory demesnes (in quarters).

Demesne	Year	AGCR	Carryovers	As % of AGCR	Yields	Prices
Martham	1349–50	265	13.8	5.2%	unknown	1.44
Plumstead, Great	1295–6	482	25.8	5.4%	1.22	0.97
Sedgeford	1291–2	797	46.0	5.8%	unknown	1.00
Sedgeford	1349–50	518	32.6	6.3%	unknown	1.44
Hemsby	1334–5	1128	72.9	6.5%	0.81	0.93
Monks Granges	1334–5	172	11.3	6.5%	0.47	0.93
Monks Granges	1327–8	231	15.6	6.8%	1.07	1.20
Monks Granges	1309–10	245	18.2	7.4%	unknown	1.25
Denham	1299–1300	153	12.5	8.2%	1.01	0.87
North Elmham	1287–8	424	36.3	8.5%	unknown	0.57
Gateley	1287–8	145	12.7	8.8%	unknown	0.57
Monks Granges	1265–6	143	13.0	9.1%	unknown	0.89
Sedgeford	1333–4	885	85.8	9.7%	1.24	0.79
Monks Granges	1311–2	324	32.6	10.1%	0.79	0.88
Sedgeford	1278–9	658	75.5	11.5%	unknown	0.97
Hindringham	1327–8	455	56.2	12.3%	0.95	1.20
Hindringham	1349–50	340	42.1	12.4%	unknown	1.44
Taverham	1327–8	233	30.3	13.0%	1.06	1.20
Monks Granges	1331–2	170	23.3	13.7%	unknown	0.97
North Elmham	1288–9	293	73.3	25.0%	unknown	0.80
Thornham	1309–10	140	38.2	27.3%	unknown	1.25

Source: Manorial accounts database.
Notes: AGCR=Annual Gross Crop Receipt (see Chapter 4). Crop yields are indexed, demesne by demesne, on the period between 1261 and 1350, while prices are average Norfolk prices indexed on 1301–10, and advanced by a year (to allow harvests to make their impact on the market).

According to the 1415–16 account from Hindringham, 93.75 quarters of barley *de firma terre* were hoarded *contra annum futurum* (towards the next year).[44]

In other words, the proportion of annual carryovers was tightly correlated with the grain rents paid by local lessees. The low number of lessees before the 1330s meant that little could be carried over for the next year. So, for the pre-Black Death period, there were only 23 instances of crop carryovers exceeding 5 per cent of the AGCR (Table 6.6). Moreover, there seems to have been no correlation between failed harvests and the level of carryovers: crop yields could be high, normal or low in the years of relatively excessive carryovers. This indicates that the demesne officials did not view the granaries as a security measure against bad years or as a means of ensuring steady availability of food resources in case of potential scarcity or famine. Nor did they expect to make profits in years of high prices by speculating in hoarded grain. As Table 6.6 clearly shows, the rare instances of grain hoarding did not necessarily correspond with the years of bad harvests and, subsequently, of high grain prices in the following year. Unfortunately, there are only two extant rolls from the famine years of 1315–17, but neither of them indicates any attempts to profit from the

---

44. NRO, DCN 60/20/37.

increased prices by storing large amounts of crops in the hope of getting high cash returns in the subsequent year.[45]

The situation was altogether different after the Black Death. With the increased quantities of barley carryovers deriving from the grain rents, the demesne managers were able to maximise profits by selling malt in the summer – the 'hungry gap' period – when the prices were at their highest as a result of the depletion of grain resources.[46] Although in most cases the accounts did not specify the seasonality of crop sales, between the 1360s and the 1380s the rolls are full of detail in this regard. As these accounts indicate, in the summer the grain prices were approximately 40–50 per cent higher than at the beginning of the financial year.[47] The share of malted barley sold between approximately May and mid-July varied between 10 and 25 per cent of all annual malt sales. There is no doubt that, in some cases, the priory authorities profited not only from the 'hungry gap season' but also from some high-price years in general. The occurrence of such years was especially frequent in the first 25 years after the Black Death, before prices finally collapsed after 1376 and an era of prolonged deflation ensued. The grain prices were particularly high in 1363, 1364, 1365, 1368, 1370, 1373, 1375 and 1376.[48] In such circumstances, selling malt produced from hoarded barley would, undoubtedly, be a profitable venture. As we have seen in Chapter 4, over the entire period about 36 per cent of all barley was malted on the demesnes, mostly for the priory but also for the market. By contrast, very little barley was sold, and that which was was mostly spoiled grain (*bladum debile*) offered for reduced prices. Selling old barley in a malted form, on the other hand, had several advantages. First, it provided the customers with a processed ingredient ready for brewing. Second, the financial value of malt was usually 10–15 per cent higher than that of barley. Third, with improving living standards in the post-Black Death era malt was more widely demanded than fresh barley. Finally, if hoarded, old grain tended to produce finer bread and ale, and hence, was usually sold at a premium.[49]

All the same, however, there is no indication in the accounts that the hoarding of grain was a clearly considered disposal strategy of the priory authorities and their demesne managers. Rather, and particularly because of the increasing number of grain rents, it took them longer to clear out the crops they received and stored each year, and they were occasionally able to profit from this surplus simply because there was no alternative. And while the priory authorities and their demesne officials might profit from those situations when it was lucrative to sell the stored crops – usually in

---

45. The rolls in question are the 1314–15 one for Eaton (Bodleian Library, Norfolk Roll 25) and the 1315–16 one for Worstead (NRO, DCN 60/39/6).

46. For the discussion of the 'hungry-gap' season, see R.W. Frank, 'The "Hungry Gap", crop failure, and famine: the fourteenth-century agricultural crisis and *Piers Plowman*,' *The Yearbook of Langland Studies* 4 (1990), pp. 87–104.

47. NRO, Lest/IC/13–21; NRO, DCN 60/29/29a–33; NRO, Lest/IB/32–42; NRO, DCN 60/18/40–41; NRO, DCN 60/20/30–32.

48. Munro, *Phelps Brown and Hopkins 'basket of consumables'*, http://www.economics.utoronto.ca/munro5/ResearchData.html (accessed 11 October 2011).

49. S.L. Kaplan, *Provisioning Paris: merchants and millers in the grain and flour trade during the eighteenth century* (Ithaca, NY, 1984), pp. 50–51.

Space for grain: barns and granaries

Table 6.7
Annual carryovers of crops stored at the Great Granary, 1261–1536.

	Total granary incomings	Total carryovers	Total carryovers as % of all grain incomings	Wheat carryovers as % of all wheat incomings	Malted barley carryovers as % of all malted barley incomings
1261–70	2960.3	304.2	10.3%	10.0%	11.8%
1271–80	2575.3	223.8	8.7%	8.5%	10.0%
1281–90	3206.3	143.4	4.5%	3.0%	5.5%
1291–1300	3513.1	560.2	15.9%	13.7%	13.3%
1301–10	3237.0	314.1	9.7%	5.1%	10.7%
1311–20	3025.6	314.1	10.4%	5.3%	11.4%
1321–30	2646.9	93.8	3.5%	2.4%	4.6%
1331–40	2775.8	603.6	21.7%	6.9%	27.3%
1341–50	2689.8	487.3	18.1%	7.2%	19.2%
1351–60	1418.7	348.0	24.5%	13.7%	31.1%
1361–70	1487.7	327.1	22.0%	11.4%	31.2%
1371–80	1679.7	312.6	18.6%	11.1%	26.5%
1381–90	1471.8	292.8	19.9%	13.4%	31.1%
1391–1400	1331.3	272.8	20.5%	12.2%	35.6%
1401–10	1421.6	255.0	17.9%	14.2%	24.3%
1411–20	1361.7	238.1	17.5%	13.0%	22.8%
1421–30	1272.4	218.8	17.2%	9.2%	23.0%
1431–40	1276.1	209.5	16.4%	15.2%	21.0%
1441–50	1239.5	189.5	15.3%	17.1%	18.9%
1451–60	1403.9	179.4	12.8%	14.7%	15.6%
1461–70	1232.4	155.5	12.6%	17.6%	13.7%
1471–80	1668.6	133.1	8.0%	14.0%	6.7%
1481–90	1559.2	116.4	7.5%	10.9%	6.9%
1491–1500	1304.5	92.6	7.1%	16.5%	4.8%
1501–10	1454.9	127.9	8.8%	17.9%	6.2%
1511–20	1674.1	235.1	14.0%	5.7%	17.8%
1521–30	1071.7	75.4	7.0%	6.1%	8.6%
1531–6	808.3	49.1	6.1%	11.6%	5.0%
1261–1350	2958.9	338.3	11.4%	6.9%	12.6%
1351–1430	1430.6	283.2	19.8%	12.3%	28.2%
1431–1536	1335.8	142.1	10.5%	13.4%	11.4%

Source: NRO, DCN 1/1/1–108.

times of dearth – it is likely that higher proportions of carryovers also meant higher levels of spoilage and losses to insects and rodents. There is no doubt that the abiding concern of the priory authorities and their managers was to dispose of the stored crops as soon as possible, preferably through sales. This was achieved far more successfully before the Black Death than after.

How long would crops be stored in the barns? In most cases, the carryovers would be consumed or sold in the course of the next financial year. In some isolated instances, however, small quantities of grain were stored for more than two consecutive years. Thus, at Hindringham, 16 quarters of wheat reaped in 1421 were carried over to the financial year of 1423–4.[50] Similarly, at Monks Granges, one quarter of barley harvested in 1333 was hoarded to the financial year of 1335–6.[51] To distinguish between the carryovers of older and newer grains, the accounts speak of *vetus granum/bladum* and *novum granum/bladum*. Storing grain for a number of years was not unheard of in late medieval England: in some cases, grains were stored for up to three years, although contemporaries realised the potential hazards involved in over-storing (despite the potential to yield better flour and malt).[52]

What about the Great Granary? Did the priory authorities use it to profit from the high-price years resulting from failed harvests? A detailed analysis of the disposal patterns reveals that, over the entire period, about 15 per cent of all stored crops was carried over towards the next year (Table 6.7). Before the Black Death, about 7 per cent of wheat and 13 per cent of barley was stored in the granary for more than one year. Between the 1350s and 1430s the carryover rates rose to 12 and 28 per cent respectively. With the end of direct management in 1431, the wheat figures rose to 13 per cent but the malt ones fell to 11 per cent. In other words, the relative quantities of carried-over grains exceeded those kept in the manorial barns, at least in the pre-Black Death period. At the same time, however, it does not mean that the priory authorities used this carried-over grain to profit from periods of high prices. In fact, there are very few references to sales of grain from the Great Granary and in those few instances the quantities did not exceed several quarters. Instead, the carried-over grain seems to have been used as a security measure against dearth, especially in the pre-Black Death years. It was certainly true in the cases of the disastrous harvest failures of 1315, 1316 and 1321, when the amounts of grain carried over towards the next year drastically fell, indicating that the brethren tended to rely on the granary rather than the market in bad years. Thus, in 1315, grain carryovers fell to about 9 per cent of all the grain incoming; in 1316 the figure fell to merely 2 per cent; and they were as low in 1321, another year of a disastrous harvest. After the Black Death the share of carryovers went up, amounting, on average, to some 20 per cent of the annual grain incomings. The fact that the brethren always had a certain share of grain in reserve, possibly as an insurance measure against the deficits of bad years, meant that the annual supply of grain tended to exceed annual demand.

Grain storage mechanisms and depletion rates

It is important to consider the various entry and depletion mechanisms which guided the strategy of the officials overseeing the demesne barns and the Great Granary. Let us consider the demesne barns first. Obviously, the harvested crops did not remain there all year long. Rather, the amount stored immediately after the harvest would gradually dwindle away to a small fraction of the original quantity. Several components are to be distinguished here, as noted in Chapter 4. To begin with, a certain proportion of the AGCR was used as seed. Wheat, maslin and rye seed was stored for about one and a half or two months, from the harvest in August to the seeding of 'winter fields' in

---

50. NRO, DCN 60/20/38.
51. NRO, DCN 60/26/24, 25.
52. Claridge and Langdon, 'Storage in medieval England'.

Table 6.8
Estimated monthly depletion rates on Norwich Cathedral Priory crop storage facilities, c.1300–1500 (in quarters and percentage).

	Barns, c.1300		Barns, c.1400		Great Granary, c. 1300		Great Granary, c. 1400		Great Granary, c.1500	
September	6300.0	100.0%	4700.0	100.0%	2378.8	72.1%	866.8	61.9%	798.9	57.1%
October	4047.3	64.2%	3678.8	78.3%	2131.3	64.6%	770.0	55.0%	692.7	49.5%
November	3502.5	55.6%	3248.0	69.1%	1993.8	60.4%	735.0	52.5%	661.8	47.3%
December	3328.8	52.8%	3072.8	65.4%	1828.8	55.4%	686.0	49.0%	609.3	43.5%
January	3155.1	50.1%	2897.6	61.7%	1636.3	49.6%	623.0	44.5%	535.2	38.2%
February	2862.3	45.4%	2654.7	56.5%	1498.8	45.4%	588.0	42.0%	504.3	36.0%
March	2557.5	40.6%	2381.8	50.7%	1340.6	40.6%	542.5	38.7%	457.2	32.7%
April	2383.8	37.8%	2206.6	46.9%	1161.9	35.2%	486.5	34.7%	393.9	28.1%
May	2091.0	33.2%	1963.7	41.8%	962.5	29.2%	420.0	30.0%	314.4	22.5%
June	1040.3	16.5%	1134.3	24.1%	825.0	25.0%	385.0	27.5%	283.5	20.2%
July	866.6	13.8%	959.2	20.4%	660.0	20.0%	336.0	24.0%	231.0	16.5%
August	573.7	9.1%	716.3	15.2%	467.5	14.2%	273.0	19.5%	156.9	11.2%

Source: Accounts database; DCN 1/1/1–108.

the autumn. Legume seed was stored until late January, when it was sown. The spring crops (oats, barley and dredge – a mixture of oats and barley) would be stored for about six months and sown during April. Another component was grain allocated for the brethren's provision. Unfortunately the accounts do not specify whether wheat and malted barley were carted to the priory headquarters directly from the fields or whether they were transferred to and stored in the barns first, before being shipped to Norwich. Assuming that, at the very least, the majority of that part of the harvest that went to Norwich was transported during the harvest by hired carters, we may speculate that it was not stored in the barns for more than a month. Crops to be sold formed another part of the AGCR stored in the barns. Unfortunately, the accounts do not, in the vast majority of cases, specify *when* the crops were sold. Therefore, it is not known how long this component of the AGCR was held at the barns. In addition, a certain proportion of the AGCR was given to working and, in some cases, non-working animals as fodder. This was mainly oats and peas, with occasional allowances of oat bran, rye, beans and *pulmentum* (a mixture of oats and peas). Fodder was distributed all year round, but at variable rates. As some accounts indicate, about 20 per cent of all fodder was consumed during harvest, when the burden of work, and hence physical labour, was at its highest. With the exception of harvest time, the average monthly consumption rate of this component was 7.27 per cent. Further crop liveries were allowed to *famuli*. As the accounts indicate, the former were paid, in both cash and kind, in four equal instalments (Michaelmas, Christmas, Easter and Nativity of St John the Baptist). Additionally, further crop allowances were distributed among them during harvest. The harvest liveries accounted for about 28 per cent of the annual *famuli* allowances. Therefore, this component of the AGCR also dwindled in an uneven manner. The remainder of the AGCR was stored at the barns as carryover.

Since the relative share of each component of the AGCR varied across the period under study, the volume and the depletion rates of the stored AGCR fluctuated accordingly (Table 6.8). Around 1300, about 35 per cent of the AGCR was exhausted by Michaelmas as a result of large-scale dispatches of grain to Norwich and the use of winter seed corn. By Christmas, about half of the AGCR remained at the demesne barns. Around Easter (depending on its annually varying date), the demesne officials could expect to have about 37 per cent of the initial volume of crops still stored in the barns. This was followed by the 'hungry gap' period, when the stored resources were depleted considerably because of the use of spring seed corn. By early August, around the beginning of harvest, only about 9 per cent of the initial volume of the AGCR may have been stored in the barns. The depletion rates looked somewhat different a century later, however. Around Michaelmas, about 78 per cent of the initial AGCR was still stored in the barns. By Christmas, about 62 per cent of the annual grain supply was still in storage. The figure fell to about 47 per cent around Easter, and by harvest demesne storages contained about 15 per cent of the initial crop incomings. These changes in storage and use mirror the post-Black Death dynamics in crop disposal on the priory demesnes. As we have seen, after the pestilence and especially towards the end of the fourteenth century, much smaller amounts of grain, in both absolute and relative terms, were sent to the Norwich headquarters. On the other hand, the volume of annual carryovers rose owing to the increasing quantities of annual grain rents.

Estimating the depletion rates for the Great Granary is by far a trickier task for several reasons. First, its grain resources were brought in several times a year, whereas porterage of crops to the demesne barns was, for the most part, completed within the harvest period. Therefore, both incoming and outgoing patterns should be considered. Second, with the exception of several accounts, we are ignorant about the seasonal patterns of crop purchases, and our assumptions regarding the distribution of purchases, based on the patchy available evidence, which suggests four purchasing seasons a year, may well be insufficiently substantiated. On the other hand, it is certain that grain was consumed by the brethren at an equal rate over the year, as some late fifteenth-century rolls suggest.[53] In any event, the estimated depletion rates of the Great Granary around three benchmark points are shown in Table 6.8. The pace of depletion was somewhat slower *c.*1300 owing to a heavier reliance on demesne grain, all or most of which was shipped during and shortly after the harvest time. In other words, the greater the relative share of demesne grain the more grain was stored directly after the harvest, which, in turn, caused the stored supply to dwindle slower. The arrival of the grain from the demesnes tended to account for about 72 per cent of the total annual grain held by the brethren *c.*1300. A century later, when the relative share of market purchases rose, this figure stood at about 62 per cent, falling to about 57 per cent some 40 years before the Dissolution. One main difference between the barns and the Great Granary is the fact that the depletion rates of the former tended to be more aggressive and uneven, while those of the latter were smooth and even across the year.

Conclusions

Several conclusions arise from the discussion above. First, as the available evidence shows, both demesne barns and monastic granaries were sufficient storage facilities, with more than enough capacity to house the incoming grain. Second, late medieval storage facilities had two main functions. First and foremost, they provided immediate and practical storage for grain that was to be disposed of in the course of a single year. Second, as in the case of the Great Granary, they served as a space for hoarding, to avert the risk of bad harvests and, consequently, dearth and famine. Before the Black Death, however, this function seems to have been restricted to conventual granaries rather than demesne barns: as we have seen, before the pestilence the annual carryovers of grain stored at manorial granges were very small. After the plague, however, the levels of carryovers rose a great deal, in conjunction with the growing practice of parcel leasing in return for annual food farms paid in fresh barley. Third, both before and after the Black Death there is no evidence that the Norwich brethren or their demesne officials used their storage facilities to profit from high prices in dearth years by speculating in grain. This contradicts the assertion made by some scholars. Finally, as far as storage costs are concerned, these seem, for various reasons, to have been considerably lower than those recorded in the contemporary purveyance accounts. As expected, storage costs, both absolute and relative, did not remain fixed throughout the entire period. After the Black Death, and especially after 1376, when grain prices collapsed and real wages rose, storage costs rose a great deal. There is little doubt that the rising costs of grain storage was yet another factor which made direct demesne management cumbersome, ultimately contributing to the collapse of the *Gutsherrschaft* economy in the fifteenth century.

---

53. NRO, DCN 1/1/98.

Chapter 7

Grain into bread and ale: processing and consumption

Cathedral mills

Once the grain was brought into the granary it was ready to be processed. The first stage was the conversion of threshed grain into flour, which involved milling and sieving, one of the most widely used and important techniques of food processing in the Middle Ages.[1] Mills had an especially crucial role in medieval monasteries, whose communities, despite their position among higher social strata, were largely dependent on bread as a central staple prescribed by St Benedict of Nursia in his *Regula* in accordance with the precept of humility.[2] To what degree the Norwich monks actually observed Benedict's commandment is another issue, which will be dealt with below.

In the course of its days Norwich Cathedral Priory owned and operated a large number of mills, each having a different function and attached to a different obedientiary. They fall into three main groups. First, there were home mills, situated within the cathedral precinct and used for the grinding of grain stored at the Great Granary. The second group consisted of demesne mills, used for food processing and consumption on the demesne by manorial *famuli* and occasional guests. Finally, there were farm mills, which were appropriated to obedientiaries and leased out to better-off tenants. These included a mill at Trowse, belonging to the cellarer; a watermill at Ellingham and windmills at Keswick, Wicklewood and Attlebridge, all owned by the almoner; and a horsemill at Lakenham as well as a mill of uncertain type at Bracondale, both controlled by the chamberlain. For the purpose of the present study, however, it is necessary to focus on the first group, which consisted of a horsemill and a windmill situated within the cathedral precinct. On the basis of the existing evidence, both medieval and post-medieval, it is possible to reconstruct their *locus operandi*. The horsemill was situated beside the brewery and was sometimes referred to as 'the mill in the brewery' and 'the malt mill'. Horsemills, always much less numerous than the other types of mills, were often, as indeed in our case, associated with breweries and used for grinding malt.[3] The windmill was located at the western edge of Gardiner's

---

1. The most important works on mills and milling in late medieval England are: J. Langdon, 'Water-mills and windmills in the West Midlands, 1086–1500', *EcHR*, 44 (1991), pp. 424–44; D.L. Farmer, 'Millstones for medieval manors', *AHR*, 40 (1992), pp. 97–111; J. Langdon, 'Lordship and peasant consumerism in the milling industry of early fourteenth-century England', *P&P*, 145 (1994), pp. 3–46; J.H.A. Munro, 'Industrial energy from water-mills in the European economy, 5th to 18th centuries: the limitations of power', in S. Cavaciocchi (ed.), *Economia ed energia, seccoli XIII–XVIII, Atti delle 'Settimane di Studi' e altrie Convegni, Istituto Internazionale di Storia Economica, 'Francesco Datini da Prato'* (Florence, 2003), pp. 223–69; Langdon, *Mills in the medieval economy*.
2. R. Hanslik (ed.), *Benedicti Regula, Editio Altera Emendata*, Corpus Scriptorum Ecclesiasticorum Latinorum 75 (Vienna, 1977), Cap. 35.12 and 39.4.
3. Langdon, *Mills in the medieval economy*, pp. 125–6.

Meadows.⁴ The physical situation of the mills was most convenient, as they were placed within the cluster of the buildings all linked to food production and transportation, namely the bakery, brewery, granary, stables and boathouse (see Figure 6.1).⁵ This layout allowed efficient collaboration between monastic officials as well as reducing the costs of grain-based production, which related to the storing, moving, milling and processing of cereals. It should be noted that windmills had at least two advantages over watermills. First, windmills had a greater power and multure capacity. Secondly, they could be installed virtually anywhere, whereas watermills were confined to locations with a ready access to flowing water. However, not every day was windy enough to obtain results and this fact may have been especially an issue in Norfolk, a flat county with a relatively mild climate. It is, therefore, perhaps somewhat surprising that there was no watermill within the cathedral precinct, despite the fact that it contained a canal which flowed into the river Wensum.

The cathedral mills were supervised and operated by the cellarer. Surprisingly, and quite frustratingly, there is very little evidence for annual expenditure connected to mill maintenance. There are occasional references to repairs and horse and implement purchases, but these come mostly from late fifteenth-century accounts, while earlier rolls seem to have under-recorded or altogether omitted the mill-related expenses. Nevertheless, it is possible to reconstruct the approximate annual costs of mill upkeep on the basis of millers' wages and data on demesne and farm mills deriving from a vast number of manorial and obedientiary accounts. The annual wages of the millers were carefully recorded by the cellarer. As the accounts indicate, fluctuations in millers' stipends mirror the wages of workers in other areas. Before the Black Death, the wages amounted to about 5s a year, but this figure rose to 9s in 1351 and to 13s 3½d in 1387, remaining stable until 1440. Quite strikingly, from that year onwards, grain milling was at least partially performed by local bakers and brewers, while a miller's stipend fell to 4s a year. It is unclear what accounted for that functional change, but it is clear that the miller was no longer playing a meaningful part in victualling the brethren. After 1477 the office of miller disappears from the records altogether, and it seems that the keeping of the mill passed entirely into the hands of the bakers and brewers. Unlike the bakery and brewery, where there were usually two workers in each department, in addition to a number of young assistants, the priory had always employed one miller.

The mill expenses, which are rarely mentioned in the cellarer's accounts, can be inferred from various references to demesne and farm mills found in abundance in miscellaneous obedientiary and manorial rolls. The maintenance costs of the horsemill can be inferred from the chamberlain's rolls, which record annual expenses on the horsemill at Lakenham. As these rolls indicate, yearly maintenance costs for these

---

4. The physical location of the mill is attested in the 1532–3 account, according to which a new millstone was bought for the mill by the brewery. This certainly does not mean that the mill of the earlier period was the same one that was mentioned in the 1532–3 roll. See NRO, DCN 1/1/106. However, it is highly possible that the late medieval mill was located in the same place, namely by the brewery.

5. On the adjacent sites of bakery, brewery, granary and stable, see above, pp. 16–17. This idea has been already mentioned in Noble, 'Aspects of life', pp. 129–30.

mills appear to be in the region of about £2 a year, excluding the miller's stipend. In most cases, however, when no substantial repairs or constructions were required, annual expenditure would not exceed £1. Every once in a while the mill was demolished and a new one erected in the same place. Thus, at Lakenham at least five new mills are known to have been built between 1429 and 1510.[6] The construction of a new mill would cost anywhere between £7 and £28, depending on the size and materials used.[7] Windmills, free from dependence on horses, were seemingly cheaper to keep, as is implied by the almoner's accounts dealing with his windmills at Keswick, Wicklewood and Attlebridge. On average, the annual costs of a windmill were around 7s, while construction costs were similar to those of a horsemill.

Cathedral bakery and brewery

Unlike the Great Granary and the cathedral mills, each controlled by a single obedientiary, the monastic bakery and brewery were supervised by no fewer than three obedientiaries: the master of the cellar, the cellarer and the sacrist. The master of the cellar paid annual wages to the bakers and brewers, in addition to purchasing fuel, in the post-Black Death period. The cellarer was in charge of paying additional stipends to the bakers and brewers as well as providing all the necessary supplies, such as fuel, candles and working tools. The sacrist distributed further stipends to the bakers and brewers in the post-Black Death period, and he also spent meagre sums on bakers' clothes. The obedientiary accounts do not distinguish between bakery and brewery, and record their combined expenses under one heading '*pistrinum et bracinum*' (bakery and brewery). Hence, it is necessary here to consider both together.

The bakery and brewery were adjacent buildings standing next to the Great Granary, with the horsemill attached to the brewery (see Figures 2.2 and 6.1). The 1284 master of the cellar roll specifies that a new bake-house (*novum pistrinum*) was build at a cost of £8 5s 6½d.[8] The expenses included no fewer than 10,120 nails of different kinds (16s 3d), 18,000 tile pins (2s 7½d), 24,360 tiles (£2 15s 9d), an unspecified number of 'heap tiles' (2s 3.5d), iron rods (1d), the carting of the materials (4s 3d) and, finally, the wages of carpenters, masons, a tiller and a stone cutter (£4 4s 3d in total). In addition to occasional repairs and renovations, other expenses included annual purchases of fuel and implements, which were recorded in the master of the cellar's and the cellarer's rolls. Thus, in the 1320s about 10s was spent on candles for the bakery and brewery (presumably about 5s for each department). Over 20s was invested in various baking tools, including sieves, baker's peels, pans, knives, brewing scoops, pots and baskets. Clothes and canvases were also purchased, presumably for making dough. Finally, around 55s was spent on wood and faggots, and as much as £20 on fuel (turf).[9] In total, nearly £28 was spent on the bakery and brewery each

---

6. In 1429, 1439, 1467, 1475 and 1510. See NRO, DCN 1/5/55, 70, 97, 101, 132.
7. It should be noted, however, that elsewhere in the country the construction costs could have fallen outside this range. Thus, in 1409, at Ivinghoe (Oxon), it cost 108s 4d to produce a new horsemill. See Langdon, *Mills in the medieval economy*, p. 329.
8. NRO, DCN 1/1/11.
9. NRO, DCN 1/2/14a and 16.

year in the 1320s. After the Black Death, considerably smaller sums were allocated by the cellarer to the bakery and brewery. The master of the cellar had assumed virtually complete responsibility over these departments and it is hardly surprising that he had to increase his annual expenditure on them, particularly as regards fuel. Between 1351 and 1400, about £15 was spent on fuel on an annual basis. This figure fell in the course of the fifteenth century, which reflects the falling population of the priory and, therefore, its fuel requirements. Between 1451 and 1536, the annual expenditure on fuel materials amounted to about £8. For the most part, fuel came in the form of wood, underwood and faggots from the nearby woodlands of Postwick, Trowse, Eaton, Taverham, all providing alder wood, and, most importantly, Thorpe-by-Norwich. The latter had woodland extending to some 600 acres. In addition, the master of the cellar relied on the more distant manors of Hindolveston (elm, beech and willow), Plumstead (white poplar); and Gateley (beech).[10] Here, the expenses were mostly connected to the coppicing, cutting, chopping, binding and shipping of wood, all performed by the priory workers. In addition, some further wood and faggots were purchased at unspecified locations. Interestingly, charcoal was purchased for a smithy, rather than for the bakery and brewery.

The bakery and brewery were more expensive to operate than the granaries and mills. The daily demands made upon them required both the hiring of a permanent staff of two bakers and two brewers with their assistants and the spending of considerable sums on fuel and implements. The number of assistants varied over time. For instance, there were five servants in the bakery and brewery in 1356–7,[11] while in 1368–9 each had seven servants.[12] It is most likely that the 'servants' were, in fact, the bakers' and brewers' children. Examples of child labour among the *famuli* are noted in many late medieval accounts and they have been recently studied by John Langdon and his colleagues.[13]

In most cases, both the bakers and brewers were hired and paid by more than one obedientiary. Until the 1360s they were employed collectively by the master of the cellar and the cellarer. Between the 1360s and 1420s they were also paid wages by the sacrist. Each obedientiary contributed a different share to the total income of the workers. Thus, before the 1360s the master of the cellar was paying, on average, combined wages of 15s a year, while the cellarer was expending 32s a year. Between the 1360s and 1410s the combined wages of the bakers and brewers from the master

---

10. H. Beevor, 'Address [to the members of the Norfolk and Norwich Naturalists' Society]: Norfolk woodlands, from the evidence of contemporary chronicles', *Transactions of the Norfolk and Norwich Naturalists' Society*, 11 (1919–20 and 1923–4), pp. 487–508; Saunders, *Introduction*, p. 77; H.C. Darby, 'Domesday woodland in East Anglia', *Antiquity*, 8 (1934), pp. 211–15; H.C. Darby, *The Domesday geography of eastern England* (Cambridge, 1971), pp. 124–9; D.P. Dymond, *The Norfolk landscape* (London, 1985); G. Barnes, 'Woodlands in Norfolk: a landscape history', PhD thesis (University of East Anglia, 2003).
11. NRO, DCN 1/1/45.
12. NRO, DCN 1/1/51.
13. B.G. Bailey, M.E. Bernard, G. Carrier, C.L. Elliott, J. Langdon, N. Leishman, M. Mlynarz, O. Mykhed and L.C. Sidders, 'Coming of age and the family in medieval England', *Journal of Family History*, 33 (2008), pp. 50–55.

of the cellar and sacrist stood at about 20s a year, while the cellarer was paying almost twice as much. In the 1410s and 1420s, however, the sacrist's share fell to an average 1s 6d a year. This meant that the master of the cellar had to increase his share of the wages. Between the 1410s and 1470s, with the exception of the 1460s, his share was only slightly less than that of the cellarer. In the course of the fifteenth century, however, both the cellarer and sacrist became less and less involved in the bakery and brewery, the sacrist from the late 1420s and the cellarer from the 1470s. As a result, the main burden of their supervision was laid upon the shoulders of the master of the cellar.

The bakers and brewers received their annual salary in four equal instalments: the first was paid in the St Andrew term (30 November), the second in the Easter term, the third at the Nativity of St John the Baptist (24 June) and the fourth at Michaelmas (29 September).[14] Although in many cases the bakers and brewers received the same wages, there were some periods in which their stipends differed. For instance, between the 1400s and 1420s the brewers received 7s more wages from the master of the cellar than did the bakers. This gap persisted in the late fifteenth and the early sixteenth century, as Table 7.1 suggests. It should be noted, however, that wage differences within the same occupation depended upon the relative seniority of a worker. As a rule of thumb, a senior baker/brewer, known as a *magister pistrini/bracini*, received higher wages than a second baker/brewer, sometimes referred to as 'his servant' (*serviens suus*; not to be confused with the bakery/brewery assistants). From 1437 onwards the master of the cellar accounts specify the difference in wages between the head-baker/brewer and his junior colleague. On average, the masters' wages were about 20–25 per cent higher than those of their associates (22s and 16s for bakers and 33s and 26s for brewers, respectively, between 1437 and 1536). This gap between senior and junior employees was a commonplace in late medieval England and elsewhere in Europe. In many instances, urban masters were being paid twice as much as urban workers.[15]

Bearing in mind that the bakery and brewery had, in general, two workers apiece, we may now calculate the average annual income of each worker. As Table 7.1 shows, before the Black Death this stood at 15s 7¼d a year; between 1351 and 1430 it had risen to 24s 5d per worker; while between 1431 and 1536 it stood at 28s 7¼d per worker. Again, these are only average figures; in reality, as we have seen, the total wages varied not only across but also within the two occupations. A comparison of these figures with the living standards of the time may suggest at first sight that the bakers' and brewers' wages were particularly low. Given a working year of 270 days, the average daily pay was about three farthings per worker over the entire year before the Black Death and slightly more than a penny after the pestilence. These are strikingly low figures, compared with the sums of 3d and 1½d paid to a master mason and an ordinary building worker, respectively, before the Black Death. This sum would certainly be less than sufficient for year-long survival unless the workers were living on cheap bread only. Does it mean, then, that the bakers' assistants were hired as part-time workers and had to look for alternative means to earn their livings outside their work at the priory? Or does it mean that they were exploited by their monastic employers? It is possible that neither was the

---

14. NRO, DCN 1/1/13.
15. Munro, *Phelps Brown and Hopkins 'basket of consumables'*, http://www.economics.utoronto.ca/munro5/ResearchData.html (accessed 11 October 2011).

Table 7.1
Annual wages paid to the priory bakers and brewers, 1261–1536.

	Bakery	Brewery	Bakery	Brewery	Bakery and brewery	Total	Total annual income per worker
1261–70	16.3	13.1	16.0	16.0	0.0	61.4	15.4
1271–80	16.3	13.1	16.0	16.0	0.0	61.4	15.4
1281–90	17.0	13.7	16.0	16.0	0.0	62.7	15.7
1291–1300	15.0	11.9	16.0	16.0	0.0	58.8	14.7
1301–10	15.2	15.2	16.0	16.0	0.0	62.4	15.6
1311–20	16.0	16.0	16.0	16.0	0.0	64.0	16.0
1321–30	16.0	16.0	16.0	16.0	0.0	64.0	16.0
1331–40	16.0	16.0	16.0	16.0	0.0	64.0	16.0
1341–50	16.0	15.8	16.0	16.0	0.0	63.8	16.0
1351–60	10.3	10.3	15.5	15.5	0.0	51.5	12.9
1361–70	14.1	14.1	16.0	16.0	22.0	82.3	20.6
1371–80	14.2	14.2	16.0	16.0	19.0	79.4	19.8
1381–90	16.7	16.7	18.5	16.7	16.7	85.2	21.3
1391–1400	16.7	16.7	20.1	19.3	16.0	88.7	22.2
1401–10	26.4	41.0	21.7	21.7	30.0	140.8	35.2
1411–20	30.7	57.3	21.7	21.7	1.0	132.5	33.1
1421–30	31.4	45.0	21.1	21.1	2.0	120.6	30.1
1431–40	40.0	40.0	19.2	19.2	0.0	118.4	29.6
1441–50	33.5	36.8	20.0	20.0	0.0	110.3	27.6
1451–60	33.6	33.6	16.9	16.9	0.0	101.0	25.3
1461–70	33.6	33.6	17.5	4.0	0.0	88.7	22.2
1471–80	30.0	30.0	17.5	17.5	0.0	95.0	23.8
1481–90	48.0	60.0	0.0	0.0	0.0	108.0	27.0
1491–1500	53.3	60.0	0.0	0.0	0.0	113.3	28.3
1501–10	53.3	53.3	0.0	0.0	0.0	106.7	26.7
1511–20	40.0	106.5	0.0	0.0	0.0	146.5	36.6
1521–30	40.0	106.7	0.0	0.0	0.0	146.7	36.7
1531–6	46.7	80.0	0.0	0.0	0.0	126.7	31.7
Pre-1350 decades	16.0	14.5	16.0	16.0	0.0	62.5	15.6
1351–1430	20.1	26.9	18.8	18.5	13.3	97.6	24.4
1431–1536	41.1	58.2	8.3	7.1	0.0	114.7	28.7

Source: NRO, DCN 1/1/1–110; 1/2/1–115; 1/4/1–126.

case. The bakery and brewery assistants were classified as *famuli*, meaning servants living, together with their families, within the cathedral precinct and receiving their meals in the priory hall (*aula*) on a regular basis. In other words, these people were, in fact, free from the most basic daily concerns: food, drink and housing. Working for bed and board with a small additional stipend might have not been the worst option for a worker in the fourteenth century, especially prior to the Black Death.

Annual baking patterns

Each year the head baker received a certain amount of wheat, to be cleansed, milled, sieved, turned into dough and ultimately baked. As a rule, the *compotus pistoris*, the baker's account, was included within the *compotus granarii*. Between 1332 and 1343,

Table 7.2
The two increments of wheat, as reckoned by the master of the cellar,
1281–1343 (in quarters, in decennial means).

Decade	Before milling	After milling (1st increment)	Given to bakery	After sieving (2nd increment)
1281–1290	873.8	923.8	869.6	999.6
1291–1300	770.4	916.8	778.3	970.3
1301–1310	838.0	1001.3	866.7	1012.7
1311–1320	812.3	995.3	930.3	1054.0
1321–1330	725.4	836.3	808.0	1097.3
1331–1340	684.1	825.5	748.2	1060.0
1341–1343	695.5	824.0	783.8	1091.5
Average	771.4	903.3	826.4	1040.8

Source: NRO, DCN 1/1/6–28, 30–37, 39–40.
Note: Unfortunately, the pre-1281 accounts do not distinguish between the two kinds of increment and, as such, were excluded from the table.

however, we have separate accounts recorded on the dorse of each roll. Surprisingly, and frustratingly, between 1344 and 1495 no granary accounts were included in the master of the cellar rolls. As a result, we are left with a lacuna in the evidence of about 150 years' duration. Nevertheless, the post-1496 accounts provide important insights into baking and consumption patterns within the priory during its last decades.

The actual volume of grain reaching the bakery was, in reality, larger than that recorded by the bailiffs and master of the cellar in the manorial and granary accounts respectively. This should be ascribed to the difference between two measures, known as *incrementum*, which amounted to between 13 and 37 per cent of the total grain supply by volume. The first increment concerns the milling of the grain and represents the increase in the volume of grain when milled. On average, the grinding expanded the volume to 119 per cent of that of the original 'raw' grain. This agrees with John Langdon's findings and calculations regarding the grinding of grain based on the purveyance accounts.[16] The second increment is unclear, but might relate to the sieving and baking of the milled products, where the 'second increment', in fact, derives from the difference in volume between milled and sieved grain and loafs made of that grain. In other words, one would expect the volume of one loaf to be larger than the volume of flour that was required and used for its baking. In many cases, the accounts specify that a certain number of quarters were carried over to the next year in both bread and flour (*in pane et farina*) (Table 7.2).

Before the Black Death, the annual wheat supply was divided three ways: roughly speaking, half of the grain was converted into *panis militum* ('knights' bread') intended for the servants and workers, and the two remaining quarters were turned into *panis monachorum* (monks' bread) and *panis ponderis minoris* (lightweight bread intended for the *famuli*), respectively (Table 7.3). The late granary accounts do not, alas, specify the conversion of grain into different types of bread. At the same time,

---

16. Langdon, *Mills in the medieval economy*, Table 4.5 (p. 153). I am grateful to Prof. Langdon for his most valuable comments regarding the 'increment' problem.

Table 7.3
Distribution of wheat and maslin for baking bread (in quarters, in decennial means).

	Panis monachorum	Panis ponderis minoris	Panis militum	Total
1261–70	144.3	112.5	453.5	710.3
1271–80	201.3	190.2	463.4	854.9
1281–90	258.4	268.0	473.3	999.6
1291–1300	256.0	249.0	465.4	970.4
1301–10	260.5	295.1	457.1	1012.7
1311–20	243.8	262.0	548.3	1054.0
1321–30	241.8	279.3	576.1	1097.3
1331–40	233.5	248.9	577.6	1060.0
1341–3	232.9	253.7	604.9	1091.5
1495–1500				225.3
1501–10				261.8
1511–20				230.1
1521–30				233.1
1531–6				239.3
1261–1343	230.3	239.8	513.3	983.4
1495–1536				237.9

Source: NRO, DCN 1/1/6–28, 30–37, 39–40.

however, they indicate that some amounts of maslin were used in baking bread, presumably *panis militum*. Thus, between 1495 and 1510 maslin constituted 8 per cent of all baked bread, in the 1510s 36 per cent, in the 1520s 27 per cent and between 1531 and 1536 16 per cent. There is no evidence that maslin was ever used before the Black Death.

Panis monachorum

What were the attributes of each kind of bread? As the available evidence, both internal and external, suggests, the three types of bread differed from each other in terms of their contents, fineness and weight. *Panis monachorum*, sometimes referred to as *panis ponderis maioris* (heavyweight bread) and *panis albus* (white bread), was the single finest kind of bread baked at the priory. As its name suggests, it was consumed, for the most part, by the brethren. That the monks were entitled to the finest type of bread is attested in numerous monastic sources from various houses. High-quality brethren's bread is described in the documents of Canterbury Cathedral Priory (where it was known as *panis conventualis*),[17] Durham Cathedral Priory (*panis dominicus*),[18] Westminster Abbey (*panis albus, gastellum, micha* or *placenta*),[19] Ely Cathedral Priory

---

17. Canterbury Cathedral Archives, DCc/Granger 1–97 (various granger accounts).
18. Durham Cathedral Archives, granator's accounts; J.T. Fowler (ed.), *Extracts from the account rolls of the Abbey of Durham from the original mss* (Durham, 1898–1901), pp. 123 and 575.
19. Westminster Abbey Muniments, WAM 19155–19230 (various granger's accounts); mentioned in Harvey, *Living and dying*, p. 59.

(*panis conventualis*),[20] Glastonbury Abbey (*wastellum*),[21] Peterborough Abbey (*wastellum*),[22] Hereford Cathedral Priory (*panis conventualis*),[23] Beaulieu Abbey (*panis conventualis*),[24] the Abbey of Selby (*panis albus, panis monachalis*),[25] St Augustine's Abbey, Canterbury (*panis fratrum, choyns, gastellum*),[26] Osney Abbey (*michia*)[27] and Cirencester Abbey (*micha canonicalis*).[28] In other words, the terms *panis monachorum/monachalis/conventualis, panis albus, wastellum/ gastellum, panis fratrum, choyns* and *micha/michia* were synonymous and they all refered to high-quality white or wheat bread. According to the *Assisa Panis et Cervisie* (*Assize of Bread and Ale*, around 1256), wastel bread (interchangeable with our *panis monachorum*) was one of the finest breads, second only to *simnel* bread, consumed by the highest social classes.[29] It is worth noting that some monastic communities, such as that of Westminster Abbey, actually consumed *simnel*.[30] The iconographic evidence suggests that *wastel* was a small, round bread with a hole in the middle, resembling a doughnut or bagel.

The weight of wastel was dynamic, depending on price fluctuations, as is illustrated in various manuscripts and editions of the assize.[31] Similarly, the weight of *panis monachorum* differed from house to house. For instance, a (baked) loaf weighed 3.25lb troy (2.66lb avoirdupois) in Evesham,[32] 3lb troy (2.46lb avoirdupois) in Winchcomb (until 1306),[33] and 2.50lb troy (2.05lb avoirdupois) in Fécamp

---

20. Cambridge University Library, EDC 1/F/4/1–53.
21. Longleat House Muniments, MS 10643.
22. Northamptonshire Record Office, FM 265; FM 2889; PDC/AR/I3.
23. Hereford Cathedral Archives, R630–637c.
24. S.F. Hockey (ed.), *Account book of Beaulieu Abbey*, Camden Fourth Series 16 (London, 1975), pp. 290–91.
25. J.T. Fowler (ed.), *The Coucher book of Selby*, vol. II, The Yorkshire Archaeological and Topographical Association, Record Series 13 (Huddersfield, 1893), no. 1286.
26. E.M. Thompson (ed.), *Customary of the Benedictine Monasteries of Saint Augustine, Canterbury and Saint Peter, Westminster*, Henry Bradshaw Society 23 (London, 1902), pp. 160, 170, 396.
27. H.E. Salter (ed.), *Cartulary of Oseney Abbey*, vol. I (Oxford, 1929), p. 183 (no. 192).
28. M. Devine (ed.), *The cartulary of Cirencester Abbey, Gloucestershire*, vol. III (Oxford, 1977), p. 933 (no. 549).
29. The Assize described wastel as *[panis] albus et bene coctus*. Printed in *The statutes of the realm: printed by command of His Majesty King George the Third, in pursuance of an address of the House of Commons of Great Britain*, 11 vols (London, 1810–1828), vol. I, pp. 199–200.
30. Thompson, *Customary*, p. 98.
31. In addition to different printed editions of the Assize, based on various manuscripts, I have consulted an early fourteenth-century compilation of statutes deposited at the University of Toronto, Thomas Fisher Rare Books Library, MS. 1053. The Assize of Bread is copied on fols 138r–139r.
32. W. Dugdale, *Monasticon Anglicanum* (London, 1846), vol. II, p. 30.
33. D. Royce (ed.), *Landboc sive Registrum de Winchelcumba* (Exeter, 1892), vol. I, pp. 262–3.
34. D. Chadd (ed.), *The ordinal of the abbey of the Holy Trinity, Fécamp* (Fécamp, Musée de la Bénédictine, MS 186, Henry Bradshaw Society 111–12 (London, 1996–2002), p. 706.
35. Hockey, *Account book*, pp. 290–91.
36. Kershaw, *Bolton Priory*, pp. 132–3.

Grain into bread and ale: processing and consumption

Table 7.4
Bread: extraction rates, weight and calorific value, c.1300.

Kind of bread	Lb in quarter of wheat	Extraction rates	Flour weight after extraction (in lb)	Bread weight after baking	Lb in loaf	Loaves per quarter of wheat	Kcal per loaf
Panis monachorum	424.0	0.50	212.0	258.6	2.05	126.2	2554
Panis ponderis minoris	424.0	0.50	212.0	258.6	1.39	186.1	1732
Panis militum	424.0	0.85	360.4	439.7	2.05	214.5	2554
Average	424.0	0.62	261.5	319.0	1.83	175.6	2280

Source: NRO, DCN 1/1/1–28, 30–37, 39–40.

(Normandy),[34] Beaulieu Abbey (Hampshire),[35] Bolton Priory (Yorkshire)[36] and Westminster Abbey.[37] A weight of 2.05lb avoirdupois per loaf has been allowed for the purpose of estimating the overall number of loaves and their calorific value for three reasons. First, that was the weight in most monastic houses. Second, the customary of Norwich Cathedral Priory was largely based on that of Fécamp and it appears that the former may thus have adopted many usages and customs of the latter. Third, the Beaulieu book distinguishes between *magnum panis conventualis* weighing 2.50lb troy (2.05lb avoirdupois) and *parvum panis conventualis* weighing 1.70lb troy (1.39lb avoirdupois) each. As we shall see later, the latter must have corresponded to our *panis ponderis minoris*.

As we have seen, a quarter of wheat c.1300 weighed 424lb avoirdupois. Grain was converted into fine flour (*simula*) destined for monastic loaves through threshing, the removal of the germ and bran (leaving the endosperm only), milling and sieving. This conversion would result in a loss of about 50 per cent of the grain contents and of its calorific value, as the Beaulieu account book suggests: a quarter of wheat cleaned, milled and sieved yielded four bushels of either *simula* or *grutum* (second-rate flour).[38] In other words, milling and sieving one quarter of raw wheat would give about 212lb of *simula* by weight. It should be noted that the moisture content of medieval loaves may have been about 22 per cent (as opposed to modern bread, with a moisture content of 35–40 per cent).[39] This would increase the weight of flour, once baked, from 212lb to approximately 271.4lb avoirdupois per one quarter of wheat. Assuming that each loaf weighed 2.05lb avoirdupois, we arrive at the conclusion that one quarter of wheat, converted into fine flour, would have produced around 126.2 loaves of *panis monachorum*.

The calorific value of *panis monachorum* can also be approximately calculated without too much speculation. Each quarter of wheat weighing 424lb would render

---

37. Harvey, *Living and dying*, p. 59.
38. Hockey, *Account book*, pp. 290–91.
39. Campbell et al., *A medieval capital*, pp. 191–2.
40. Ibid.

around 644,480 kcal;[40] the fine flour extracted from this wheat would have rendered approximately 322,240 kcal and produced about 126.2 loaves; each loaf, therefore, would have rendered around 2554 calories. The weight and calorific value of *panis monachorum* and of the two other kinds of bread are given in Table 7.4.

Between 1261 and 1343 about 29,000 loaves of *panis monachorum* were produced at the priory bakery annually. About 79 per cent of its production was given to the monks as their daily bread. The remaining 20 per cent or so was distributed among various departments and persons, both within and without the priory. About 7 per cent was destined to be consumed in the guest hall, presumably by various visitors of high standing. The three cooks working in the priory kitchen consumed, apparently together with their family members, another 7 per cent. It is hardly surprising that the people responsible for producing fine food were presented with the finest kind of bread. Another 2 per cent was allowed for the almoner, who must have distributed the loaves among the poor. Another 4 per cent was allocated to the 'expenses of the Prior' (*expensis Prioris*) and distributed among the manorial tenants as a token of appreciation for hard work and as charity. Finally, a small part of the total (usually, less than 1 per cent) was given as livery to the *famuli* in addition to their regular supply of *panis ponderis minoris* (discussed below). The overall distribution of the bread, in quarters of grain and loaves, is shown in Table 7.5.

Panis ponderis minoris

It appears that the term *panis ponderis minoris* denotes not a type of bread, but its weight.[41] Contemporary sources indicate that this kind of bread was identical to *panis monachorum*, but of a lighter weight, a fact supported by several granary accounts from the 1280s which list *panis monachalis maioris et maioris ponderis*.[42] The fact that *panis monachorum* and *panis ponderis minoris* were the one and the same type is attested in several other monastic sources, such as the *Landboc* of Winchcomb Priory, which mentions *unum panem monachalem de antiquo pondere et alium panem minorem de eodem pastu* ('a monastic loaf of the ancient weight and another smaller loaf, made of the same dough').[43] The *de antiquo pondere* must have been understood as a regulated weight before wheat prices soared toward the end of the thirteenth century. Similarly, the Beaulieu book mentions *parvum* and *magnum panis conventualis* made from the same flour.[44] A 1289 deed from Little Dunmow Priory (Essex) mentions *duos panes albos minoris de pastu conventus*,[45] while a 1263–4

---

41. Thus, Hudson and Saunders identify this kind of bread with the *panis levatus* of the London *Liber Albus* and with *cocket* of the *Assize of Bread and Ale*, without actually justifying their identification. See W. Hudson, 'The camera roll of the Prior of Norwich in 1283, compiled by Bartholomew de Cotton', *Norfolk Archaeology*, 19 (1917), pp. 305–6; Saunders, *Introduction*, pp. 88–91.
42. NRO, DCN 1/16–8.
43. Royce, *Landboc sive Registrum de Winchelcumba*, vol. I, pp. 262–3.
44. Hockey, *Account book*, pp. 290–91.
45. R.E. Levy, 'The cartulary of Little Dunmowe Priory', MA dissertation (University of Virginia, 1971), no. 46.

Table 7.5
Annual allocation of *panis monachorum* bread, 1261–1343.

	Monks	Hall	Prior's expenses	Kitchen	Almoner	Servants' livery	Total
			In quarters of wheat				
1261–70	119.5	0.0	0.0	24.5	0.0	0.0	144.0
1271–80	169.0	4.1	5.5	22.4	0.1	0.0	201.2
1281–90	218.6	8.3	10.9	20.4	0.3	0.0	258.4
1291–1300	195.1	21.8	10.0	24.0	3.2	1.9	256.0
1301–10	200.2	24.5	5.9	19.6	5.3	5.2	260.5
1311–20	182.5	24.5	9.4	15.1	5.6	8.3	245.4
1321–30	191.8	15.5	9.3	19.0	6.0	0.1	241.8
1331–40	188.5	14.2	8.0	16.4	6.5	0.0	233.5
1341–3	187.0	13.1	10.0	15.7	6.5	0.6	232.9
Average	194.8	17.4	9.1	18.6	4.8	2.3	246.9

	Monks	Hall	Prior's expenses	Kitchen	Almoner	Servants' livery	Total
			In approximate loaf equivalent				
1261–70	15081	0	0	3092	0	0	18173
1271–80	21333	521	690	2832	16	0	25392
1281–90	27586	1041	1381	2572	32	0	32611
1291–1300	24620	2749	1262	3029	403	245	32307
1301–10	25264	3089	738	2471	663	652	32878
1311–20	23032	3092	1186	1909	704	1049	30972
1321–30	24199	1960	1179	2402	757	16	30513
1331–40	23790	1786	1003	2067	820	0	29466
1341–3	23599	1648	1266	1984	820	74	29392
Average	23167	1765	967	2484	468	226	29078

Source: NRO, DCN 1/1/1–28, 30–37, 39–40.

charter from Eynsham Abbey (Oxfordshire) describes the *panem album minoris ponderis* kept at the monastery cellar (*de celario nostro*).[46] In other words, both kinds of bread were made of the same dough. Various conventual houses had different names for *panis minoris monderis*. Thus, at Canterbury Cathedral Priory, it was known by its macaronic name *smallpayns*.[47] It should be noted, however, that in many cases late medieval monastic accounts did not distinguish between the two kinds of conventual bread.

The account book of Beaulieu shows that a loaf of *panis ponderis minoris* should have been lighter than one of *panis monachorum* by some 30 per cent. Since *panis ponderis minoris* was made from the same flour as the *panis monachorum* was, it presumably had the same extraction rate (of 50 per cent). Again, one quarter of grain would have produced 212lb avoirdupois of fine flour and about 258.6lb avoirdupois of

---

46. H.E. Salter (ed.), *Eynsham Cartulary*, vol. I (Oxford, 1907), pp. 231–2 (no. 335).
47. Canterbury Cathedral Archives, DCc/Granger/1–97 (various granger accounts).

Table 7.6
Annual allocation of *panis ponderis minoris* bread, 1261–1343.

	Cellar	In quarters of wheat Guests in hall	Famuli	Labourers	Prior's expenses	Total
1261–70	0.0	80.5	32.0	0.0	0.0	112.5
1271–80	5.7	151.9	32.3	0.0	0.3	190.2
1281–90	11.4	223.3	32.7	0.0	0.5	268.0
1291–1300	43.3	142.5	48.3	0.0	14.8	249.0
1301–10	41.7	189.1	56.7	1.0	6.6	295.1
1311–20	18.4	185.6	48.1	0.0	9.9	262.0
1321–30	30.7	162.8	71.5	0.0	14.4	279.3
1331–40	37.2	110.2	61.5	28.3	11.8	248.9
1341–3	28.2	107.6	59.2	45.1	13.6	253.7
Average	24.1	150.4	49.1	8.3	8.0	239.8

	Cellar	In approximate loaf equivalent Hall	Famuli	Labourers	Prior's expenses	Total
1261–70	0	14981	5955	0	0	20936
1271–80	1064	28273	6019	0	47	35403
1281–90	2129	41565	6083	0	93	49869
1291–1300	8066	26513	8997	0	2757	46333
1301–10	7758	35188	10546	186	1233	54911
1311–20	3427	34537	8956	0	1834	48754
1321–30	5711	30299	13300	0	2675	51986
1331–40	6914	20504	11436	5267	2198	46318
1341–3	5246	20017	11015	8398	2530	47205
Average	4479	27986	9145	1539	1485	44635

Source: NRO, DCN 1/1/1–28, 30–37, 39–40.

bread. The weight of a loaf of *panis ponderis minoris* was about 1.70lb troy (1.39lb avoirdupois), and thus one quarter of wheat would produce about 186 loaves.[48] If each loaf weighed 1.39lb avoirdupois, then the calorific value of each loaf may have been around 1732 kcal (Table 7.4).

As Table 7.6 estimates, each year the priory bakery produced close to about 45,000 loaves of *panis ponderis minoris*. This bread had two main destinations: the guest hall, presumably for consumption by the guests (about 60 per cent) and the servants living within the cathedral precinct (*servientibus in curia*), namely the *famuli* (about 20 per cent). The remaining 20 per cent went to the cellar and was occasionally distributed among the labourers (especially from c.1330 onwards) and manorial tenants visiting the priory on business trips.

---

48. Hockey, *Account book*, pp. 290–91. On different figures, see P.W. Hammond, *Food and feast in medieval England* (Stroud, 1993), pp. 63–79.

Panis militum

The term *panis militum* derives from a Norman misinterpretation of the Old English term *knihta hlaf* (*kniht*, here, was misunderstood as *miles*, 'knight', rather than *serviens*, 'servant'). This term lived to be witnessed in several post-Conquest documents. Some cellarer's accounts of Westminster Abbey mention *knytenlof*, the term evidently a later alteration of *knihtahlaf*.[49] In addition, a 1198 deed from Stoke-by-Clare Priory (Suffolk) mentions a bread called *sweinesloves* (deriving from 'swan', a synonym for *kniht*).[50] Curiously enough, the term *panis militum* has a continental counterpart which goes back to Carolingian times: *panis vasallorum*, which one encounters, *inter alia*, in the constitutions of Corbie Abbey as recorded by Abbot Adalhard in prescribing the distribution of one loaf of *panis vasallorum* among two paupers.[51]

Different monastic institutions referred to the servants' bread by different names. For instance, late medieval granator's accounts of Durham speak of *panis militaris*;[52] a 1269–70 account book from Beaulieu Abbey calls it *panis familie*,[53] while a fourteenth-century cartulary of Ramsey Abbey distinguishes between *panes monachorum* and *panes villarum*.[54] It should be noted, however, that some monastic documents use the term *panis servientum*, instead of *panis militum*, which reveals a better understanding of the original Old English term.[55] At Westminster Abbey, in addition to occasional references to *knytenlof*, the servant's bread was called *hogeman*, or *meynebread/lof*.[56] At Ely Cathedral Priory local servants and workers were consuming bread with the rather curious name *panis equorum* (horses' bread).[57] At Canterbury Cathedral two kinds of inferior bread were distributed among workers and servants: *feytys* and *plainpayn*.[58] Peterborough Abbey's labourers were given loaves known as *panis de turtes*.[59]

Although the granary accounts of Norwich Cathedral Priory do not provide any information about the nature of *panis militum*, a 1281 final concord from Norwich Cathedral Priory mentions *septem panes de illis panibus eorum qui vocatur albi panes et septem panes de illis panibus eorum qui vocantur panes militum* ('seven loaves of

---

49. Westminster Abbey Muniments, WAM 5908; Harvey, *Living and dying*, p. 171.
50. C. Harper-Bill and R. Mortimer (eds), *Stoke-by-Clare cartulary, BL Cotton Appx. XXI*, vol. I (Woodbridge, 1982), pp. 14–15 (no. 20).
51. K. Hallinger (ed.), *Adalhard, Statuta antiqua abbatiae Sancti Petri Corbeiensis* 1.3, Corpus Consuetudinum Monasticarum, vol. I (Sieburg, 1963), pp. 369.32–370.3.
52. Fowler, *Account rolls of the Abbey of Durham*, pp. 123 and 575.
53. Hockey, *Account book*, pp. 290–91.
54. W.H. Hart (ed.), *Cartularium Monasterii de Rameseia*, Rolls Series 79, vol. 3 (London, 1893), pp. 230–34.
55. For instance, see W.H. Hart (ed.), *Cartularium Monasterii de Rameseia*, Rolls Series 79, vol. 3 (London, 1893), no. 141.
56. Harvey, *Living and dying*, p. 171.
57. Cambridge University Library, EDC 1/F/4/1–53.
58. Canterbury Cathedral Archives, DCc/Granger/1–97 (various granger accounts).
59. Northamptonshire Record Office, FM 265; FM 2889; PDC/AR/I3.

those breads called "white breads" and seven loaves of those called "knights' breads"').[60] In other words, the 'knights'', or 'servants'' bread may have been of a darker colour. This supposition can be strengthened by the fact that high extraction rates (with about 85 per cent of the extracted part used in milling and baking) meant that bran was, in all likelihood, not removed from the grain, which, in turn, would result in the production of brown bread. As we have seen, some Westminster accounts refer to the servants' loaves, baked from a mixture of inferior wheat and rye flour, as *panes nigri* (black loaves).[61] At Canterbury Cathedral meagre amounts of rye were occasionally turned into bread for servants.[62] In the 1330s we witness some minor additions of rye and legumes to the bread; these, however, were always marginal components. Also, as we have seen, between 1495 and 1536 about 20 per cent of all bread was baked with maslin. These, however, were exceptions; in most cases, all types of bread baked at conventual houses were made of wheat.

Converting raw grain into flour of inferior quality (*farina*) suitable for making servants' bread required an extraction rate of about 85 per cent. Hence, a quarter of wheat containing 424lb avoirdupois would have produced around 360lb avoirdupois of inferior wheat flour. Since the flour constituted only 78 per cent of each loaf (and water the remainder), this flour would have produced about 440lb avoirdupois of bread, by weight. Determining the weight of each loaf is a more problematic task. The Beaulieu Book distinguishes between *parvum* and *magnum panis servientum*, weighing 2.5lb troy (2.05 avoirdupois) and 4lb troy (3.28lb avoirdupois), respectively. Our accounts, on the other hand, do not provide any clue regarding either the size or weight of loaves of *panis militum*. It would, nevertheless, be safer to assume that they correspond to the *parvum*, rather than the *magnum*, *panis servientium*, for had it weighed 3.28lb avoirdupois then one quarter of wheat would have produced about 134 loaves, each rendering around 4100 kcal. These seem to be rather unrealistic figures, given the fact that *c.*1300 the total number of priory workers exceeded the suggested number of loaves. Moreover, a daily allocation of a loaf worth some 4100 kcal per worker is an absurd figure. Hence, it would be safer to go with the lower figure – that is, with the estimation that each loaf of servants' bread weighed approximately 2.05lb avoirdupois.[63] One quarter of wheat would thus have produced about 215 loaves, each rendering approximately 2550 kcal. As Table 7.7 shows, *panis militum* was baked mostly for the workers of the priory, who received their bread in the priory hall. In addition, certain amounts of it were distributed as corrodies among the town's anchorites and as charity among the poor and prisoners incarcerated in the castle prison. This type of bread accounted for about half of the bread produced at the priory bakery.

---

60. B. Dodwell (ed.), *The charters of Norwich Cathedral Priory*, vol. 2 (London, 1985), no. 43.
61. Harvey, *Living and dying*, p. 171.
62. Thus, Canterbury Cathedral Archives, DCc/Granger/4 and 28.
63. Despite this reckoning, it should be noted that in many cases loaves baked for workers and peasants were bigger and heavier than those consumed by the lords. See Stone, 'Consumption of field crops', p. 14, citing the examples of harvest workers at Wisbech (=2.88lb each) and plowmen of Hinderclay (=3.58 lb each), both cases from the early fourteenth century.

Table 7.7
Annual allocation of *panis militum* bread, 1261–1343.

In quarters of wheat

	Cellar	Workers in the hall	Prior's expenses towards manors	Prisoners	Anchorites	Paupers	Horses	Livery to labourers within precinct	Total
1261–70	23.0	402.0	20.0	4.0	1.0	1.5	2.0	0.0	453.5
1271–80	41.3	373.2	31.9	6.0	1.5	2.3	3.4	5.1	464.6
1281–90	59.5	344.4	43.8	8.0	2.0	3.1	4.8	10.3	475.8
1291–1300	54.6	268.8	46.6	6.3	2.4	34.3	8.0	44.5	465.4
1301–10	24.9	328.8	28.8	5.8	2.5	9.8	8.7	47.9	457.2
1311–20	18.1	414.9	47.0	24.8	1.3	8.3	2.3	31.7	548.3
1321–30	19.4	398.5	52.1	10.6	0.0	8.8	30.4	56.3	576.2
1331–40	249.0	211.4	52.1	10.7	0.0	6.6	33.2	14.7	577.6
1341–3	227.8	231.5	62.7	8.6	0.0	10.0	37.4	26.9	604.9
Average	79.7	330.4	42.8	9.4	1.2	9.4	14.5	26.4	513.7

In approximate loaf equivalent

	Cellar	Workers in the hall	Prior's expenses towards manors	Prisoners	Anchorites	Paupers	Horses	Livery to labourers within precinct	Total
1261–70	4934	86229	4290	858	215	322	429	0	97276
1271–80	8848	80049	6837	1287	322	489	727	1103	99662
1281–90	12763	73868	9384	1716	429	657	1026	2205	102048
1291–1300	11710	57660	9988	1341	509	7360	1716	9539	99823
1301–10	5331	70517	6185	1247	536	2091	1868	10278	98053
1311–20	3888	89000	10073	5318	268	1770	483	6801	117600
1321–30	4169	85478	11167	2279	0	1877	6529	12079	123579
1331–40	53416	45335	11175	2298	0	1416	7121	3142	123903
1341–3	48872	49657	13453	1837	0	2145	8017	5778	129759
Average	17103	70866	9173	2020	253	2014	3102	5658	110189

Source: NRO, DCN 1/1/1–28, 30–37, 39–40.

Table 7.8
Bread consumption patterns across different groups, 1261–1343.

	Wheat quarters	Monks	Famuli	Labourers	Guests
1261–70	710.0	16.8%	4.5%	56.6%	11.3%
1271–80	856.1	19.7%	3.8%	44.2%	18.2%
1281–90	1002.2	21.8%	3.3%	35.4%	23.1%
1291–1300	970.3	20.1%	5.2%	32.3%	16.9%
1301–10	1012.8	19.8%	6.1%	37.3%	21.1%
1311–20	1055.7	17.3%	5.3%	42.3%	19.9%
1321–30	1097.3	17.5%	6.5%	41.4%	16.3%
1331–40	1060.0	17.8%	5.8%	24.0%	11.7%
1341–3	1091.5	17.1%	5.5%	27.8%	11.1%
Average	984.0	18.7%	5.2%	37.1%	16.7%

Source: NRO, DCN 1/1/1–28, 30–37, 39–40.

Bread consumption patterns

What were the annual consumption patterns across different groups of consumers living within the cathedral precinct? A close analysis of the accounts reveals that each group enjoyed a different share of the bread ration, in both absolute and relative terms (Table 7.8). Let us begin with the brethren. Before the 1320s the bread accounts distinguish between the two parts of the priory responsible for keeping and distributing the loafs among the brethren: the refectory and the cellar. From c.1320 onwards, however, the entire amount of bread given to the monks was stored in the cellar only. On average, the brethren consumed about 184 quarters of wheat on an annual basis: that is, about 19 per cent of the total wheat supply allocated to the baker and about 13 per cent of the total baked bread, perhaps equivalent to about 23,167 loaves of *panis monachorum*, which may be translated into approximately 59 million kcal. Given the fact that between c.1260 and the Black Death the number of the brethren rose from 60 to 67, it appears that each monk derived about 2600 kcal from his daily bread intake, although it is unlikely, as we shall later, that he would have consumed his daily bread ration in its entity. It is evident, nonetheless, that the total amounts of grain baked into the monks' bread, and, therefore, the *per capita* consumption of bread, increased between the 1260s and the 1280s.

The next group of bread consumers to be considered here is the *famuli*. Roughly speaking, the priory *famuli* received some 20 per cent of total *panis ponderis minoris*, representing about 5 per cent of all baked wheat. The estimations below will be based on the assumption that each loaf weighed about 1.39lb avoirdupois (1.70lb troy) and that the *famuli* population was fluctuating from decade to decade, as we have seen above. It appears that the *famuli* were allowed a much smaller intake of bread than the brethren: on average, they were allocated about 51 quarters of wheat, enough to bake approximately 9372 loaves, rendering close to about 9.3 million kcal a year. Assuming that between c.1261 and the Black Death there were, on average, 26 *famuli* living within the cathedral precinct, we arrive at the estimation that each *famulus* enjoyed no more than 1000 kcal on a daily basis. If not too removed from reality, this figure appears strikingly low, given the assumption that grain-based products may have contributed about 70 per cent to the calorific intake of non-monastic residents of the cathedral

Grain into bread and ale: processing and consumption

Cooks	Horses	Charity	Other	Total
3.5%	0.3%	0.9%	6.1%	100.0%
2.6%	0.4%	1.2%	9.9%	100.0%
2.0%	0.5%	1.3%	12.6%	100.0%
2.5%	0.8%	4.8%	17.4%	100.0%
1.9%	0.9%	2.3%	10.6%	100.0%
1.4%	0.2%	3.8%	9.7%	100.0%
1.7%	2.8%	2.3%	11.5%	100.0%
1.5%	3.1%	2.2%	33.8%	100.0%
1.4%	3.4%	2.3%	31.4%	100.0%
2.0%	1.5%	2.4%	16.5%	100.0%

precinct.[64] At the same time, the fact that the *famuli* were allowed bread of superior quality shows that they were undoubtedly valued more highly than the workers, who received mostly *panis militum*, namely bread made of inferior flour. It also demonstrates that the *famuli* were regarded as an integral part of the priory community.

The single largest proportion of *panis ponderis minoris* was allocated to the entertainment of guests (some 60 per cent of this type of bread, and about 17 per cent of all the baked loafs). The accounts refer to this allocation as *versus aulam* (for the [guest]-hall). Between the 1260s and 1343 about 164.4 quarters of wheat annually were baked into *panis ponderis minoris* to be distributed among the guests. This amount may have produced about 29,751 loafs. As Table 7.8 indicates, however, the amount of grain, and consequently of loaves, fluctuated from decade to decade. It is unclear, though, if the number of loaves distributed annually and daily is actually identical to the number of guests visiting the priory.

Priory labourers (*operatores*), hired by the priory authorities for various works and tasks, were yet another significant group of bread consumers. Their allowance was both in *panis ponderis minoris* and *panis militum*. The latter represented all or the majority of their bread diet (100 per cent before *c.*1330 and about 75 per cent between 1331 and 1343). From *c.*1330 onwards the priory authorities added certain amounts of *panis ponderis minoris* bread to the workers' diet. This development corresponds with the period of intensive renovation, expansion and building activities undertaken by the prior, and it is quite possible that he realised the importance of maintaining good terms with hired workers by supplying them with better food. On average, the labourers collectively consumed 365 quarters of wheat turned into, approximately, 78,063 loaves of both types of bread. This represented about 37 per cent of the total wheat supply and around 42 per cent of all the baked bread. As in case of other groups, the annual grain allocation varied from decade to decade. In the 1320s the annual amount of wheat converted into the two kinds of bread intended for the labourers' consumption reached its peak, at 455 quarters.

---

64. See above, Chapter 2.

Another group of bread consumers were the priory cooks. The average 19.7 quarters of grain allocated for *panis monachorum* to be distributed among the cooks in the kitchen (some 7.5 per cent of the total) would make about 2484 loaves capable of yielding, approximately, 6.34 million kcal on an annual basis. According to the cellarer's rolls, there were always three or four permanent cooks, along with several assistants (probably their own children), in the priory kitchen. Allowing for seven workers in the kitchen, we arrive at about 2488 kcal per cook per day. The fact that the cooks were fed with the finest kind of bread reveals that they were undoubtedly valued more highly than any other workers. After all, it was in the brethren's interests to please the cooks with high-quality food so that the latter would, in turn, please the monks with their culinary creations. As one historian of the priory stated, 'apart from the fact that it is always well to nurse those preparing food, these cooks were people of importance and apparently on an equal footing with the monks'.[65]

It is surprising to find priory horses among the regular daily recipients of bread. It is apparent that the priory horses, used mostly for riding, were kept better than the working horses of the demesnes. Thus, as the master of the cellar's accounts indicate, they were fed mostly on oats, as opposed to the manorial horses, which lived on hay and straw for the most part.[66] But provisioning the animals with processed food is even more striking, taking into account the time taken for baking and the loss of weight and calorific value after the extraction of chaff and bran. This was certainly an exceptional situation in late medieval England, where feeding horses with processed wheat, let alone with loaves, was by no means a commonplace.[67] The situation at Norwich Cathedral Priory was in fact completely contrary to that described in the Norfolk play *Mankind* (composed around 1470). In the dialogue between Mischief and Mercy, the former explains to Mercy that *Grain seruit bredibus, chaffe horsibus, straw fyrybusque* ('Grain serves for [the making of] loaves, chaff for [feeding the] horses, and straw for [kindling] fire').[68] There were cases, however, where horses were fed with a special horse-bread (*panis equinus*), made of beans, peas, bran and other coarse materials. Such a practice was common, for instance, at Durham Cathedral Priory in the late medieval period.[69] At Ely Cathedral Priory, both workers and horses were consuming *panis equorum*.[70] Our accounts indicate that before the 1320s the horses received meagre amounts of wheat loaves (about 5 quarters a year, collectively) and no bread was fed to them between 1314 and 1322 – that is, during the troublesome years of the Agrarian Crisis.[71] From the later 1320s onwards, however, we witness a sharp increase

---

65. Saunders, *Introduction*, p. 91.
66. The feeding of horses is discussed above, Chapter 5.
67. Campbell sites two fourteenth-century examples of using wheat as fodder. Both examples are from Norfolk (see Campbell, *English seigniorial agriculture*, p. 218, no. 89).
68. 'Mankind (Morality Play)', in Mark Eccles (ed.), *The macro plays*, Early English Text Society (Oxford, 1969), ll. 36–63. This is apparently a linguistic game, with Latin words and forms entering Middle English lexicon.
69. Durham Cathedral Archives, granator's accounts. See also Fowler, *Account rolls of the Abbey of Durham*, pp. 147, 160, 234, 252, 256, 527, 569, 577, 641, 722–4.
70. Cambridge University Library, EDC 1/F/4/1–53.
71. NRO, DCN 1/1/6–28.

in the amount of bread allocated to the horses, which stood at about 34 quarters a year. This amount was capable of producing about 7222 loaves annually and about 20 loaves daily, on average. It is clear, however, that these amounts were far from sufficient for meeting the calorific requirements of the animals. As we have seen, an average riding horse probably consumed about 20,000 kcal each day c.1300. It seems, then, that the loaves were given as an addition to regular daily oat fodder. Furthermore, it is evident that not every horse was fed with a loaf every day. For instance, during the 1310s, only about 483 loaves were produced from 2.3 quarters of wheat annually, enough to feed perhaps one horse each day on a regular basis. As we have seen, there were about 22 horses in the priory stables in the pre-Black Death period.[72] But then again, it is clear that in addition to cereals the horses were also offered hay and straw.

In addition to the aforementioned groups of bread consumers receiving their allowance on a daily basis, an additional group enjoyed the products of the priory bakery: corrodians. These fell into three main groups: paupers begging outside the gates of the cathedral, prisoners incarcerated in the castle prison and town anchorites secluded in their cells. Their fates will be discussed in the following chapter.

Two kinds of ale

As with bread, there were several kinds of ale, destined for consumers of different social groups.[73] Unfortunately, very few passages shed any light on the nature of these ale varieties. The 1281 final concord between the priory and Julian of Sedgeford establishes a weekly corrody of *quinque lagenas cervisie de illa cervisia eorum que vocatur cervisia aule* ('five gallons of ale from that ale called the "Hall's Ale"').[74] The 1283–4 granary roll has a memorandum note saying '*Memorandum quod isto anno partantur versus aulam cxui tunell(os) preter magnam lagenam de secunda cervisea quam quaerunt quolibet die*' ('Memorandum that in this year 136 tuns (of ale) were distributed to the hall, in addition to a large gallon of the secondary ale, which they request on any day').[75] The annual allowance of loaves, ale and pancakes on major feast days, mentioned in the sacrist's register, distinguishes between *cervisia bona* and *cervisia secunda*.[76] In other words, at least two sorts of ale were brewed at the priory: *cervisia bona*, monastic ale of a superior quality, and *cervisia aule/secunda*, interchangeable terms that signify ale of secondary quality, drunk in the guest hall.

---

72. See above, Chapter 2.
73. On varieties of ale/beer, its history and on the brewing process in the Middle Ages, see M. Nelson, *The barbarian's beverage: a history of beer in ancient Europe* (London, 2005); Bennett, *Ale, beer, and brewsters in England*, and R.W. Unger, *Beer in the Middle Ages and the Renaissance* (Philadelphia, PA, 2004). The brewing process is described, in great detail, in J. Brown, 'The malting industry', in G.E. Mingay (ed.), *The Agrarian History of England and Wales, vol. VI 1750–1850* (Cambridge, 1989), pp. 501–19; S. Hieronymus, *Brew like a monk: trappist, abbey and strong Belgian ales and how to brew them* (Boulder, CO, 2005).
74. Dodwell, *Charters of Norwich Cathedral Priory*, vol. 2, no. 43.
75. NRO, DCN 1/1/7. The 'C' stands for a long hundred here (=120).
76. NRO, DCN 40/11, fols 45r–45v.

It is unclear if only these two kinds of ale were actually brewed at the priory, but the distinction between the *bona cervisia/cervisia fratrum* and *secunda cervisia* was known since the early Middle Ages. For example, the first synod of Aachen of 816 decreed that where there was no wine the monks could drink a double measure of *cervisa bona*.[77] Similarly, Adalhard of Corbie, in his ancient statutes of the abbey, mentioned *cervisa fratrum*, to be distributed among the poor on certain days.[78] There are numerous examples from contemporary monastic sources that distinguish between *cervisia aule/secunda* and *cervisia conventualis/bona*.[79] Some sources also mention *melior servisia* and *posterior servisia*,[80] which probably correspond to our *cervisia bona* and *cervisia aule*. There were as many as four kinds of ale at Beaulieu Abbey: *bona/conventualis*, *mixta* (a mixture of *conventualis* and *secunda*), *secunda* (known as *lag*) and *tercia* (third-rate ale, also known as *Wilkin le Naket*). *Bona cervisia* was intended for the monks, aristocratic guests and master masons; *mixta* was distributed among the *conversi*, the lay brethren and *famuli*, and the two inferior kinds evidently went to workers of inferior status.[81] Similarly, Dunstable Priory (Bedfordshire) brewed three kinds of ale: *dominica cervisia* (lord's ale), *secunda cervisia* and *tercia cervisia*, otherwise known as *cervisia servientium vel carettariorum* (servants' or carters' ale).[82] These three kinds of ale are also known to have been brewed at Worcester Priory and Oseney Abbey (Oxfordshire).[83] The Norwich sources do not contain any similar information and all we can say with full confidence is that there were at least two varieties of ale: one brewed for the brethren and the other one for the *famuli* and workers.

It is unclear what the main difference was between ale enjoyed by the brethren and that drunk by the servants and labourers. The customary of the Benedictine Abbey of Eynsham in Oxfordshire (from after 1228/9) states that the brethren received fresh beer.[84] According to the customary of St Augustine's Abbey, Canterbury, 'sit bene

---

77. K. Hallinger (ed.), *Legislatio Aquisgranensis*, in Corpus Consuetudinum Monasticarum, vol. I (Sieburg, 1963), pp. 462–3; noted in M. Nelson, 'On a beautiful girl and some good barley beer', *Études Celtiques* 35 (2003), p. 258.
78. Hallinger, *Adalhard*, pp. 369.32–370.3.
79. For instance, W.H. Hale (ed.), *Registrum Prioratus Beate Marie Wigorniensis* (London, 1865), p. 130b; Salter, *Oseney Abbey*, vol. III, p. 82; Royce, *Landboc sive Registrum de Winchelcumba*, vol. I, pp. 298, 337, 340 and 348.
80. Just to name a few: Devine, *Cirencester Abbey*, vol. III, p. 933 (no. 402); Hockey, *Account book*, pp. 230–33; U. Rees (ed.), *The cartulary of Shrewsbury Abbey* (Aberystwyth, 1975), vol. 2, pp. 373–4 (no. 402b).
81. Hockey, *Account book*, pp. 230–33.
82. G.H. Fowler (ed.), *A digest of the charters preserved in the cartulary of the Priory of Dunstable*, Bedfordshire Historical Record Society 10 (Bedford, 1926), nos. 225, 227, 297, 299, 307, 332, 333, 467, 468, 469, 693, 906, 907, 908. The three kinds of ale brewed at Dunstable are noted in H.E. Hallam, 'The life of the people', in H.E. Hallam (ed.), *The Agrarian History of England and Wales*, vol. II 1042–1350 (Cambridge, 1988), p. 827 and Stone, 'Consumption of field crops', p. 16.
83. Hale, *Registrum*, p. 130b; Salter, *Oseney Abbey*, vol. III, p. 82.
84. A. Grasden (ed.), *The customary of the Benedictine abbey of Eynsham in Oxfordshire*, Corpus Consuetudinum Monasticarum, vol. II (Siegburg, 1963), pp. 187.

defecata, boni coloris, clara, bene granata et boni saporis' ('it should be well cleansed, have a good colour, be clear, possess grainy flavour and good taste').[85] The use of the expression *bene granata* might suggest that the monks' ale had a higher proportion of grain and a lower proportion of water compared with *cervisia secunda* and, consequently, could have been stronger than the latter. The possibility that *cervisia secunda* was weaker than *cervisia bona* is supported by a thirteenth-century continental source, the *Chronica Andrensis* of William of Andres (1177–after 1234). According to the 1198 entry, workers who built an infirmary for an abbey were paid not in money but in weak beer.[86] This continental source, however, might not necessarily reflect the situation in England.

It is equally possible that the difference between the two kinds of beer actually derived from the difference in malt with which they were brewed. Medieval English sources distinguish between *braseum capitale* and *braseum cursale/commune* – first and second grades of malt.[87] For instance, such a distinction was made in some *compotus* rolls of Worcester Cathedral Priory.[88] At Glastonbury Abbey, *braseum capitale* meant wheat malt.[89] The *braseum cursale/commune*, on the other hand, was a defective dark brown malt heated too severely to produce fine ale. If the only difference between the two varieties of ale was quality, it is possible that they were actually of more or less the same strength. In any event, any attempt to estimate the exact alcoholic strength and, consequently, the calorific value of medieval monastic ale could be speculative and misleading.

What is certain, however, is that both types of ale were made of barley malt; there is no evidence that oats were ever brewed and consumed as beer by the priory inhabitants. This was contrary to many other late medieval conventual houses, where different types of ale were made of different kinds of grain. Thus, at Canterbury Cathedral Priory, as well as at Durham Cathedral Priory, the inhabitants enjoyed both oat and barley ale.[90] Peterborough Abbey brewed two kinds of ale, one made of dredge and the other made of barley.[91] At Westminster Abbey, brewers produced three kinds of ale, brewed of barley, oats and dredge respectively.[92] The Ely Cathedral Priory brewers produced ale from wheat, barley and dredge.[93] The Hereford Cathedral

---

85. Thompson, *Customary*, p. 135.
86. I. Heller (ed.), *Willelmi Chronica Andrensis, Monumenta Germaniae Historica Scriptores*, vol. XXIV (Hanover, 1879), p. 724. I owe this reference to Max Nelson, of the University of Windsor.
87. For example, this distinction is made in the *forma compoti* (a 1298 guide to compiling annual bailiffs' accounts), printed in S.C. Ratcliff, A.J. Collins and B. Schofield (eds), *Legal and manorial formularies in memory of J.P. Gilson* (Oxford, 1933), pp. 38–9, and in the 1296–7 minister's account of the Earldom of Cornwall, printed in L.M. Migdley (ed.), *Ministers' accounts of the earldom of Cornwall*, vol. I (London, 1942), p. 13.
88. S.G. Hamilton (ed.), *Compotus rolls of Priory of Worcester* (Oxford, 1910), p. 73.
89. Longleat House Muniments, MS 10643.
90. Canterbury Cathedral Archives, DCc/Bartoner/1–106.
91. Northamptonshire Record Office, FM 265; FM 2889; PDC/AR/I3.
92. Westminster Abbey Muniments, granger's accounts, WAM 19155–19217.
93. Cambridge University Library, EDC 1/F/4/20–53.

canons drank both wheat and oat ale.[94] At St Paul's Cathedral, barley, wheat and oats were all used in brewing.[95] It was Glastonbury Abbey, however, that broke all the records in terms of ale versatility: its brewers were making ale from no less than four kinds of grain: wheat, oats, dredge and barley.[96] It should be noted that, in all cases, only small quantities of wheat were allocated to brewing. No evidence has come to light that any English monastic house was producing ale from rye, as was customary in late medieval Bavaria before the introduction of the *Reinheitsgebot* (German Beer Purity Law), between 1487 and 1516. In any event, the 'monoculturalism' of ale practised by Norwich Cathedral Priory can certainly be ascribed to the abundance of barley grown in Norfolk. Moreover, in virtually all instances dredge and oat ale were considered to be inferior types of drink and, as such, were allocated mostly to servants and labourers. In contrast, wheat ale, a rare thing in late medieval England, was normally associated with exceptionally wealthy households such as Glastonbury Abbey.

Our only information regarding late medieval brewing techniques in England comes from Walter of Bibbesworth's *Treatise* (*Le Tretiz*), composed in the mid-thirteenth century.[97] This treatise, dealing with the Norman French language as spoken in England, has a section on ale brewing which reveals that late medieval malting, with the exception that late medieval brewers did not have mechanical processing equipment at their disposal, was largely identical to the modern one.[98] Obviously, Walter's treatise, despite its significance, cannot shed any light on either the alcohol content or the energy value of late medieval ale. However, some recent practical experiments have suggested that late medieval ales may have had a higher food value than reported in modern scholarly estimates as a result of the mash temperature profile created by the addition of hot water using ladles. During the early phases of mashing using this method the temperatures are lower and therefore favour the creation of fermentable sugars. According to some experiments, such a mashing technique would have resulted in less alcohol and more sugar after fermentation.[99] On the other hand, this technique could have achieved the opposite: more alcohol and less sugar. Hence, this issue is rather too complicated and enigmatic to be resolved here. All we can say with a high degree of assurance is that late medieval monastic ale was weaker, and consequently had less energy, than most modern beers.

---

94. Hereford Cathedral Archives, R630–637c.
95. W.H. Hale (ed.), *The Domesday of St Paul's of the year MCCXII*, Camden Society Old Series 69 (London, 1858), p. l.
96. Longleat House Muniments, MS 10643.
97. A. Owen (ed.), *Walter of Bibbesworth, Le Traité de Walter de Bibbesworth sur la langue francaise* (Paris, 1929); W. Rothwell (ed.), *Walter de Bibbesworth: Le Tretiz*, Anglo-Norman Text Society Plain Texts Series 6 (London, 1990).
98. Rothwell, *Walter de Bibbesworth*, ll. 459–512.
99. I am grateful to Mr Henry Davis, Chief Operating Officer of Applied Plasmonics and an experimental brewer, for being kind enough to share some valuable and profound knowledge of brewing techniques (pers. comm., 11 May 2007).

Table 7.9
The increment of barley malt, as reckoned by the master of the cellar,
1261–1343 (in decennial means).

	Before milling	After milling (increment)	Given to brewery
1261–70	1817.6	1873.6	1681.0
1271–80	1859.1	1887.1	1757.2
1281–90	1900.7	1900.7	1833.3
1291–1300	2094.7	2248.9	1972.0
1301–10	2313.6	2403.1	1908.0
1311–20	1912.4	2003.3	1726.7
1321–30	1826.5	1890.0	1650.0
1331–40	1832.4	1916.7	1430.5
1341–3	1677.1	1714.2	1403.3
Average	1936.8	2011.0	1703.4

Source: NRO, DCN 1/1/1–28, 30–37, 39–40.

Annual brewing patterns

Annual brewing patterns were similar to those related to baking. The vast majority of malt was given to the brewer to be converted into drink, and meagre proportions were granted to other people, the bishop and the king's retinue among them. As in the case of bread, we have to account for the increment in volume arising from the grinding of malt, which increases its volume by about 4 per cent (Table 7.9).

On average, about 80 per cent of the total malt supply in the granary was allocated to the brewer. The total amount of malt used for brewing varied from year to year. For example, as many as 2260 quarters of malt were brewed in 1299–1300, while in 1335–6 only 1320 quarters were converted into ale. The remainder was, for the most part, stored at the granary to be carried over to the next year. Occasionally, small quantities of malt were given as gifts. In 1299–1300, 1309–10 and 1313–14 the prior granted to John Salmon, bishop of Norwich (1299–1325) 12, 10 and 5 quarters of malt respectively.[100] In 1309–10 the priory provided Edward II with 20 quarters of malt, possibly in exchange for an exemption from military service required from all lords in his writ from 18 June 1310.[101] According to Edward's *Vita*, many ecclesiastical magnates received the exemption having paid the king large sums of money.[102] It is equally possible, however, that the 20 quarters of malt were contributed for the provisioning of Edward's garrisons on their way to Scotland.

Turning malt into ale: gallons and calories

Malting increases the volume of barley by 14 per cent and lowers its density, reducing its weight by 25 per cent. As Bruce Campbell and his colleagues have estimated, a

---

100. NRO, DCN 1/1/15, 21, 23.
101. NRO, DCN 1/1/21.
102. W.R. Childs (ed. and tr.), *Vita Edwardi Secundi* (Oxford, 2005), pp. 20–21.

quarter of malted barley containing approximately 468,715 kcal (14 per cent more than a quarter of raw barley) would have produced about 400 pints (50 gallons) of strong or 765 pints (95.6 gallons) of weak ale. Each pint of ale contained about 320 or 160 kcal, depending on its strength.[103] Hence, one quarter of malt would have produced between 122,380 and 168,000 kcal, which is approximately 30 per cent of the original calorific value of raw barley (malting and brewing together resulted in a reduction of calorific content of about 70 per cent). Again, as stated above, these estimations are somewhat speculative, but they should not be too removed from reality because they accord with some late medieval evidence.[104] It should be noted that medieval ale was usually measured in larger quantities than the pint: 8 pints made 1 gallon (*galo, lagena*); 32 gallons made up 1 barrel (*barrillum*); and 240 gallons (in the late thirteenth century) or 252 gallons (in the early modern period) made up 1 tun, or cask (*tunnelum, doleum*).[105]

Our sources do not directly specify the number of gallons distributed each day among the brethren and servants. In this regard a piece of information whose importance cannot be overstated comes from the marginal memorandum entries in the 1282–3 and 1283–4 accounts, which states that the recipients of *cervisia secunda*, namely the vast majority of the priory population, received a gallon of ale each day. It is only reasonable to interpret this as meaning that a gallon of ale was allowed for each person, not for the whole lay community. This was a common practice in various monastic houses, including Beaulieu, Bolton and Dunstable priories, as well as St Paul's Cathedral.[106] The 1282–3 and 1283–4 rolls also specify that, in addition to the daily gallon of ale, the workers were allowed 122 and 136 tuns of ale, respectively, throughout the year.[107]

This, in turn, sheds light on the nature of the ale produced at the priory. Between 1282 and 1284 the priory brewer received 1815 quarters of malt each year, an amount capable of yielding either about 173,539 gallons (723 tuns) of weak or 90,750 gallons (378 tuns) of strong ale. In the early 1280s there were approximately 60 brethren and 220 labourers and servants residing within the precinct. A daily allowance of a gallon per person suggests that, each year, the non-monastic population of the priory consumed approximately 0.92 tuns (220 gallons) on a daily basis and 333.7 tuns (80,135 gallons) on an annual basis. To this amount we should add another 122 tuns – those mentioned in the rolls – which were allowed in addition to the daily gallon. This would make some 455.7 tuns, or 109,368 gallons, in total. It would require 1143.8 quarters of malted barley to produce this amount of weak ale and 2187.4 quarters of malted barley to brew the same amount of strong ale. This amount, therefore, even though it does not include the ale drunk by the brethren and highly valued guests,

---

103. Campbell *et al.*, *A medieval capital*, p. 34, note 59.
104. Stone, 'Consumption of field crops', p. 16.
105. Hockey, *Account book*, p. 229 (for late thirteenth century); R.D. Connor (ed.), *Weights and measures of England* (London, 1987), pp. 21–2 (for early modern period).
106. Hockey, *Account book*, pp. 230–33; Kershaw, *Bolton Priory*, pp. 132–3; Kershaw and Smith, *Bolton Priory Compotus*, pp. 163, 473, 492; Fowler, *Digest*, nos 225, 227, 297, 299, 307, 332, 333, 467, 468, 469, 693, 906, 907, 908; Hale, *Domesday of St Paul's*, pp. 165–75.
107. NRO, DCN 1/1/6–7.

already exceeds the possible limit of strong ale, which could not have yielded more than 378.1 tuns a year between 1282 and 1284 (deriving from 1815 quarters of malted barley given to the brewery). Hence, it is presumably the case that the ale made for the non-monastic population was weak ale that corresponded to our *cervisia secunda*. If this calculation is not too far removed from reality, it appears that in the early 1280s 455.7 tuns (109,368 gallons) of weak ale, made of approximately 1143.8 quarters of grain, would have constituted about 63 per cent of total ale brewed in the same year (that is, out of about 723.3 tuns). If this pattern remained more or less consistent in the pre-Black Death period, and if our identification of *cervisia secunda* with weak ale is correct, then we may assume that weak ale represented about 63 per cent of all brewed ale in the priory.

The remaining malt (37 per cent, or so, representing 671.6 quarters) was converted into *cervisia bona*, or monastic ale. It is most likely that *cervisia bona* was stronger than c*ervisia secunda*, in terms of its alcoholic and calorific content. If we were to assume that the *cervisia bona* was strong ale, yielding approximately 50 gallons per quarter of malted barley, while each gallon contained 3360 kcal, we would, then, arrive at around 139.9 tuns, equal to 33,578 gallons of ale. This amount was enough to produce about 92 gallons of strong ale each day, an amount well exceeding the number of brethren. It is clear, however, that the brethren were not the only consumers of *cervisia bona*. From time to time, other priory residents, as well as occasional guests, were entertained with the fine ale. In addition, the priory workers were allowed, communally, certain amounts of *cervisia bona* during major feasts. According to the sacrist's register, they received (communally) four gallons at Christmas, Easter (including the Octaves), Pentecost, Circumcision, Epiphany, Purification of BMV, Day of Ascension, Holy Trinity, Nativity of St John, Dedication of the Church, All Saints, Michaelmas and the Anniversary of Bishop Herbert Losinga (23 July). They were given the same amount also during annual synods at Easter and Michaelmas. Furthermore, two gallons of monastic ale were distributed among the labourers twice a year, during a *lectio divina* said by the cellarer. In addition, they were given one gallon of fine ale each day within the two-week period before Christmas (*contra Natale per quindenam*), as well as during the three-week period before Easter and the two-week period before the Nativity of St John. Finally, the sacrist's carpenter received a gallon of *cervisia bona* each day, which underlines his importance in the eyes of the priory authorities.[108] All this amounts to an additional 505 gallons, or some 2.10 tuns, of the best ale.

But even if we were to assume that the brethren were allowed one gallon of *cervisia bona* on a daily basis, it is most unlikely that such a gargantuan allowance was consumed in its entirety. Drinking one gallon of strong ale a day, containing 3360 kcal, in addition to all other meals, would have meant a daily ingestion of about 6000 kcal: an exceedingly high figure, even by monastic and aristocratic standards of the time. It is hard to imagine that a daily calorific intake of ale per brother exceeded that of a lay resident (1280 kcal per person) and such a conservative estimate sits well with estimates of other food components (Table 7.13). It is, therefore, apparent that each monk must have consumed less than half of his daily ale allowance. Annual brewing and overall distribution patterns are represented in Table 7.10.

---

108. NRO, DCN 40/11/fols 45r–45v.

Table 7.10

Estimated levels of ale brewing at Norwich Cathedral Priory, 1261–1343 and 1495–1536 (in decennial means).

	Cervisia bona	Cervisia secunda	Approximate gallons of cervisia bona	Approximate gallons of cervisia secunda	Tuns	Kcal in ale	Potential consumers
1261–70	622	1,059	31,099	101,243	551	234,082,343	363
1271–80	650	1,107	32,508	105,831	576	244,688,459	380
1281–90	678	1,155	33,917	110,418	601	255,294,576	396
1291–1300	730	1,242	36,482	118,770	647	274,604,628	426
1301–10	706	1,202	35,298	114,915	626	265,692,511	412
1311–20	639	1,088	31,943	103,994	566	240,441,975	373
1321–30	611	1,040	30,525	99,376	541	229,765,536	357
1331–40	529	901	26,463	86,153	469	199,192,795	309
1341–3	519	884	25,962	84,520	460	195,416,285	303
1495–1500	211	359	10,545	34,330	187	79,373,549	123
1501–10	237	403	11,840	38,546	210	89,121,178	138
1511–20	167	284	8,339	27,148	148	62,767,767	97
1521–30	176	299	8,788	28,608	156	66,144,624	103
1531–6	201	342	10,030	32,655	178	75,500,607	117
Pre-Black Death decades	630	1,073	31,513	102,592	559	237,201,186	368
1495–1536	198	337	9,908	32,257	176	74,581,545	116

Source: NRO, DCN 1/1/1–28, 30–37, 39–40, 98–108.
Notes: The number of potential consumers has been calculated on the assumption that each consumer would have received a gallon of ale a day.

It is rather unfortunate that not a single account between 1344 and 1495 indicates the annual disposal of ale among the priory inhabitants. The total amount of malt allocated for brewing fell drastically after the Black Death, and it appears that the figures for 1495–1536 are considerably lower than they were in the late fourteenth century. It should be borne in mind that, despite an incipient demographic recovery in the early Tudor era, the monastic population in general experienced stagnation and, eventually, decline in the early sixteenth century.[109] Moreover, not only were the monks and nuns in decline, but so too were their servants and the house's other inhabitants. This is reflected well in the post-1495 rolls. During the last decades of the priory's life, about 535 quarters of malt were brewed into ale each year, yielding around 213 tuns rendering some 82,161 kcal: enough to sustain no more than some 140 drinkers, if we continue to allow a daily gallon per person. As discussed above in Chapter 2, the amounts of grain baked and brewed have been used by me, perhaps unwisely, as a rough guide to the late fifteenth- and early sixteenth-century lay population of the priory.

The amounts of ale drunk on a daily basis might appear surprising to a modern drinker. It should be remembered, however, that the ale produced at Norwich Cathedral Priory was considerably weaker than modern beer. Its alcoholic strength must have been no more than about 2 per cent, and probably even less than that, compared with around 5 per cent for modern beer. Hence, drinking eight pints of the weaker ale would not have intoxicated a late medieval drinker as much as the same quantity of modern beer would. On the other hand, in Langland's *Piers Plowman* a glutton collapses after drinking a gallon of ale.[110] The historical validity of this allegoric description, however, lies outside the scope of the present work.

Grain consumption in a comparative perspective

Do the baking and brewing patterns of Norwich Cathedral Priory reflect those of other conventual houses? A glimpse into other houses' granator accounts may be revealing (Table 7.11).

There can be little doubt that Norwich Cathedral Priory was one of the most conspicuous consumers of grain-based products among late medieval conventual houses, in both absolute and *per capita* terms. In the pre-Black Death era it was second only to Peterborough Abbey, one of the largest monastic communities in the country, which expended almost 3800 quarters of grain on bread and ale to be shared between the convent and the abbot. Canterbury Cathedral Priory and Westminster Abbey, whose overall population may have been around the size of Norwich Cathedral Priory, converted around 2150 quarters into food and drink. Other houses were less generous. Thus, Ely Cathedral Priory, a house to about 70 brethren and an unknown number of lay residents and workers, allocated just over 1700 quarters of grain to be baked and brewed. Similar figures are found at St Paul's Cathedral, whose total population, however, may have been smaller than that of Ely: in 1286, its religious

---

109. For the most up-to-date survey of late medieval English monasticism, see M. Heale (ed. and tr.) *Monasticism in late medieval England* (Manchester, 2009), Introduction.
110. A.V.C. Schmidt (ed.), *William Langland, Piers Plowman* (Oxford, 1992), pp. 53–4.
111. Hale, *Domesday of St Paul's*, p. l.

Table 7.11
Annual baking and brewing patterns at select late medieval conventual houses.

	Wheat + rye supply	Baked	Total malt supply	Brewed	Baked as % of all wheat + rye supply	Conventual bread as % of all bread	Brewed as % of all supply	Monastic/ canonical population
1260–1350								
Norwich Cathedral Priory	1040.8	938.5	2011.0	1703.4	90.2%	24.5%	84.7%	63
Canterbury Cathedral Priory	1116.7	913.8	1289.5	1233.7	81.8%	42.1%	95.7%	70
Westminster Abbey	763.0	545.8	1704.0	1614.1	71.5%		94.7%	55
Peterborough Abbey	1404.6	1391.9	2451.0	2388.0	99.1%	35.8%	97.4%	80
Hereford Cathedral	913.0	847.2	108.5	104.4	92.8%		96.2%	15
Ely Cathedral Priory	642.3	543.8	1544.4	1083.0	84.7%		70.1%	70
Bolton Priory	451.5	404.8	2558.8	683.9	89.7%	56.0%	26.7%	20
St Paul's Cathedral	720.0	545.0	1070.0	1070.0	75.7%		100.0%	30
1350–1420								
Canterbury Cathedral Priory	862.0	764.8	1581.1	1252.8	88.7%	41.5%	79.2%	70
Westminster Abbey	458.9	380.9	2087.5	1254.4	83.0%		60.1%	50
Peterborough Abbey	1072.0	559.8	1600.9	1404.7	52.2%	48.6%	87.7%	70
Glastonbury Abbey	1191.9	1159.3	1491.4	1110.0	97.3%	60.5%	74.4%	50
Hereford Cathedral	364.3	357.3	127.4	122.4	98.1%		94.3%	12
Ely Cathedral Priory	504.1	424.1	838.5	712.5	84.1%		85.0%	35
1470–1536								
Norwich Cathedral Priory	296.8	237.9	780.3	535.6	80.1%		68.6%	40
Hereford Cathedral	403.6	210.8	121.4	89.4	52.2%		99.6%	7
Ely Cathedral Priory	375.3	280.0	657.6	567.0	74.6%		86.2%	30

Sources: Canterbury Cathedral Archives, Granger 4–37, 70–76, 89–95, Bartoner 4–34, 52–66; Westminster Abbey Muniments WAM 19155–19217; W.H. Hale (ed.), *Domesday of St Paul's of the Year MCCXII*, Camden Society Old Series 69 (London, 1858), pp. xlviii–li; Northamptonshire Record Office, Fitzwilliam 2389 and PDC AR/I/9; Longleat House, MS 10643; Hereford Cathedral Archives, R630–R637c; Cambridge University Library, EDC EDC 1/F/4/1–53 and I.M. Kershaw and D.M. Smith (eds.), *The Bolton Priory Compotus, 1286–1325*, The Yorkshire Archaeological Society 154 (1999–2000) (Woodbridge, 2000).

Note: For Norwich Cathedral Priory, wheat, rye and malt supply is calculated after the increments.

portion consisted of 30 canons.[111] Smaller communities, such as Bolton Priory and Hereford Cathedral, distributed much smaller quantities to their bakers and brewers. The strikingly low figures for Hereford Cathedral can be ascribed to the itinerant life of its canons, who resided within the precinct only part-time. After the pestilence, the figures, naturally, went down. At Ely Cathedral Priory and Westminster Abbey they fell by 30 and 25 per cent respectively, and at Ely and Hereford Cathedral the overall amounts of grain allocated for baking and brewing fell by half. At Canterbury Cathedral Priory, on the other hand, the overall figures c.1400 were only slightly lower than before the pestilence. This reflected the fact that that its monastic population actually exceeded its pre-Black Death levels by 1390.

Before the Black Death about 40 per cent of all bread was distributed among monks/canons, although the figures varied from house to house. Thus, at Norwich Cathedral Priory conventual bread accounted for about a quarter of all the baked bread, while elsewhere the figure tended to be higher. Thus, at Bolton Priory as much as about 56 per cent of all bread was distributed among the canons between 1297 and 1319, even though the latter did not represent more than about 10 per cent of the priory's population.

Bread and ale consumption in a wider perspective

Cereal products, namely bread and ale, constituted only a part of the daily monastic diet. Despite the omnipresent threat of the eternal damnation that gluttony could earn a sinner, and contrary to the mandate of St Benedict's *Rule*, calling for abstention from excessive eating, Norwich monks consumed food in heroic proportions. Their overall calorific intake exceeded by far the normal requirements of an adult male, let alone a non-working one. Our main information on non-cereal food consumed by the monks comes from larder accounts, sometimes called kitchen accounts (*compoti de coquina*), incorporated into cellarer's accounts. Unfortunately, there are no surviving accounts pre-dating 1319.[112] The biggest challenge, however, is the converting of carcasses of animals and lasts of fishes into numbers and their calorific equivalent. Skeletal analyses of medieval animal remains suggest that medieval domestic animals and fish differed in size from their modern descendants.[113] Barbara Harvey's figures for the diet of Westminster monks, as well as numerous zooarchaeological reports and McCance and Widdowson's *The Composition of Foods*[114], have been used to allow the conversion of raw carcasses and products into their approximate weights and calorific

---

112. The first surviving account of 1318–19 is, in fact, an early eighteenth-century copy made by a local Norwich historian and antiquary (1686–1728), John Kirkpatrick (NRO, DCN 125/6).

113. M.L. Ryder, 'The animal remains found at Kirkstall Abbey', *AHR*, 7 (1959), pp. 1–5; M.L. Ryder, 'Livestock remains from four medieval sites in Yorkshire', *AHR*, 9 (1961), pp. 105–10; M.L. Ryder, 'The animal remains from Petergate, York, 1957–1958', *Yorkshire Archaeological Journal*, 42/4 (1971), pp. 418–28; M. Prestwich, 'Victualling estimates for English garrisons in Scotland during the early fourteenth century', *English Historical Review*, 82 (1967), pp. 536–43; Kershaw, *Bolton Priory*, pp. 157–8; Stouff, *Ravitaillement et alimentation*, pp. 186–9 and 301–15; A.J.S. Gibson, 'The size and weight of cattle and sheep in early modern Scotland', *AHR*, 36 (1988), pp. 162–71; Harvey, *Living and dying*, pp. 226–30.

114. Food Standards Agency, *McCance and Widdowson's The Composition of Foods*, 6th edn (Cambridge, 2002).

equivalent. Using the 1329–30 larder account as our guideline, we may attempt to undertake this difficult task.

Let us begin with meat. In 1329–30 the priory purchased 93 carcasses of oxen for beef. Allowing about 240.2lb for edible meat per carcass of ox, with each carcass yielding, approximately, 307,303 kcal, we arrive at about 28.6 million kcal deriving from beef. In addition, the cellarer purchased 186 carcasses of ovids (*bidentes*) for mutton.[115] Allowing about 24.2lb for edible meat per carcass of a mature ovid, we may estimate that each carcass may have yielded about 36,524 kcal. In turn, 186 carcasses would have rendered approximately 6.8 million kcal.[116] In other words, in that year, the total calorific value of meat cooked for the brethren may have been in the region of 31 million kcal. If the entire amount of beef and mutton was indeed offered to the brethren then it appears that a monk received, on average, some 1494 kcal deriving from meat on a daily basis. It should be noted, however, that after the Black Death, with the addition of pork, geese and rabbits to the meat portfolio, the calculations become even more complicated.

Fish, especially herring, was bought and consumed in large quantities. In 1327–8 the priory acquired 15 lasts of herring. With each last containing 12,000 fish,[117] the total number of herring may have been around 180,000. Archaeological findings show that the average size of medieval fish was larger than that of modern ones,[118] and that the edible part of a herring weighed about 0.28lb per fish.[119] This would render about 53.4 million kcal a year and thus every monk could have potentially received about 2258 kcal deriving from about eight fish on a daily basis. After the Black Death the fish menu was considerably diversified with the addition of salmon, ling, eels, cod, sprats, sturgeons and roach. This, in turns, adds much complication to our estimates.

To these products we should add meagre amounts of dairy produce, mostly cheese. In 1329–30 the cellarer spent £2 2s on cheese, enough to buy about 969.2lb of this product rendering, approximately, 732,884 kcal. This would contribute about 31 kcal per monk on a daily basis. We may also add small numbers of hens and eggs rendered by the estates. Before the Black Death the manors sent 190 hens and 1080 eggs, which would have added approximately 20 and 3.71 kcal respectively on a daily basis.[120] It is likely that the eggs were used for baking rather than consumed directly. Additionally, tiny amounts of honey, dried fruits and spices were purchased on an annual basis, but their calorific contribution was extremely small.

If we rely on our sources and add to these non-farinaceous products one loaf of monastic bread yielding about 2554 kcal and one gallon of monastic ale rendering

---

115. NRO, DCN 1/2/14a.
116. Harvey, *Living and dying*, p. 228. This is, however, only an average figure. It is clear that wethers (castrated rams) would weigh more than rams and ewes.
117. 31st Edward I (1302), printed in *The statutes of the realm*, vol. I.
118. A. Wheeler, 'Fish bone', in H. Clarke and A. Carter (eds), *Excavations in King's Lynn, 1963–1970*, Society for Medieval Archaeology monograph series vii (London, 1977), pp. 403–8; A. Wheeler and A. Jones, 'Fish remains', in A. Rogerson (ed.), *Excavations on Fuller's Hill, Great Yarmouth*, East Anglian Archaeology 2 (Norwich, 1976), pp. 208–26.
119. Harvey, *Living and dying*, p. 226.
120. Calculated on the basis of NRO, DCN 60/18/9–41 and NRO, DCN 60/20/7–30.

Table 7.12
Estimated calorific values allowed to an average Norwich monk on a daily basis, 1329–30.

	Bread	Ale	Meat	Fish	Dairy	Total
All year, average	2554	1280	1494	2258	31	7617
Outside Advent and Lent	2554	1280	1769	2258	35	7895
Advent	2554	1280	0	2258	31	6123
Lent	2554	1280	0	2258	0	6092
All year, average	33.5%	16.8%	19.6%	29.6%	0.4%	100.0%
Outside Advent and Lent	32.3%	16.2%	22.4%	28.6%	0.4%	100.0%
Advent	41.7%	20.9%	0.0%	36.9%	0.5%	100.0%
Lent	41.9%	21.0%	0.0%	37.1%	0.0%	100.0%

Source: NRO, DCN 1/2/16.

about 1280 kcal, totalling 3834 kcal, we may estimate, perhaps quite crudely, that in 1329–30 a Norwich monk was offered daily food worth perhaps as much as 7600 kcal. However, the amount of food and calories consumed varied from period to period and from day to day. For instance, the monks were forbidden to eat meat during Advent (four weeks before Christmas) and the 'Long Lent' periods (seven weeks before Easter Sunday). In addition, they were required to 'fast' three days a week (Wednesday, Friday and Saturday) – that is, to live on fish and cereal products only.[121] Hence, they could eat meat only 118.25 days a year, outside Advent, Lent and the weekly fasting periods. Table 7.12 summarises the structure of daily monastic diet over the three periods.

The surprisingly large proportions described above seem to have been a norm for a medieval monastic community in late medieval England. Late fifteenth-century dietary accounts from Westminster Abbey show similar trends: bread accounted for 41.5 per cent (Advent), 45 per cent (Lent) and 35 per cent (on a regular day) of the diet; ale and wine constituted 30, 32.5 and 25 per cent, respectively; fish represented 17, 18 and 6 per cent; meat, when allowed, accounted for 17 per cent; and finally, eggs contributed around 5 per cent. Outside Advent and Lent, an average Westminster monk received an equivalent of as much as c.6210 kcal, while on a day when meat was allowed his daily allowance might be as high as c.7375 kcal. During Lent, the average value was around c.4870 a day.[122] The main difference between Westminster and Norwich, it seems, was not so much proportions as components. While the latter relied heavily on fish, which constituted around 30 per cent of the energy intake of the monks, the former consumed fish in much smaller quantities and replaced it, to a great degree, with meat. In this regard, the Norwich brethren observed St Benedict's commandment to abstain from meat more closely than did their fellow-monks from Westminster.

The overall figures did not vary much over the period, as show in Table 7.13. It was, rather, the different components of the brethren's diet that shifted over time. Thus, over the entire period there was a gradual fall in fish consumption, whose share fell from almost 30 per cent in the 1320s to just 9 per cent towards the end of the priory's

---

121. Harvey, *Living and dying*, pp. 38–41.
122. Ibid., pp. 34–71.

Table 7.13
Estimated calorific values allowed to an average Norwich monk on a daily basis, 1327–1530.

	Bread	Ale	Meat	Fish	Dairy	Total	Consumed calories
1327–30	2554	1280	1802	2358	31	8025	4012
1361–70	2554	1280	3318	2055	66	9272	4636
1401–10	2554	1280	2531	1909	67	8341	4170
1441–50	2554	1280	1950	1021	38	6843	3421
1481–90	2554	1280	2225	1293	60	7412	3706
1521–30	2554	1280	3561	731	63	8188	4094
Average	2554	1280	2565	1561	54	8013	4007

Source: NRO, DCN 1/2/14a–98.

existence. At the same time there was a pronounced increase in meat intake, so that it accounted for almost half of all the consumed calories.

So far we have discussed daily allowances of food. But how much of it did the Norwich monks actually consume? Certainly, 7600 kcal is an astonishing figure, which by far exceeds the recommended calorific intake for male consumers: around 2500 kcal a day for a man neither performing excessive physical labour nor suffering from a disabling disease. The consumption of such large amounts by the monks, who led a passive and contemplative way of life, would cause not only obesity but also some lethal symptoms, such as overdeveloped adiposity. In other words, the daily intake of over 7600 kcal could have led to very high mortality rates among the brethren. But did they really consume the entire amount of food available to them on a daily basis? The practice of passing leftovers to servants and paupers was widespread in late medieval monasticism, as is illustrated in late fifteenth-century evidence from Westminster Abbey studied by Barbara Harvey. The Westminster sources indicate that a monk would consume only about 55 to 60 per cent of his allowance. The remainder was left to the servants, workers and paupers.[123] These estimations left a Westminster monk with around 3730 kcal on an average day. Subtracting 40 per cent from the Norwich allowance of c.7600 kcal leaves some 4500 kcal. In addition, we may subtract an additional 10 per cent for waste and tasting in the course of food preparation. This reduced the figure to about 3800 kcal, which accords with Harvey's estimation. This energy intake, though not as quite excessive as 7600 kcal, is still large for sedentary male consumers, since it exceeds the suggested 2500 kcal recommended for active men. Recent archaeopathalogical studies suggest that medieval English monks certainly tended towards obesity. Philippa Patrick's work suggests that omnipresent signs of osteoarthritis detected on the skeletons of medieval London monks reveal that the latter could well have consumed over 4500 kcal on regular, non-fasting days.[124] The archaeological data accords well with the written sources from both Westminster and Norwich, but a more profound, full-scale study of monastic obesity is yet to be undertaken.

---

123. Ibid., pp. 67–70.
124. Patrick, 'Creaking in the Cloisters'; Patrick, 'An archaeology of overindulgence'; Patrick, '"Greed, gluttony and intemperance"?'.

Chapter 8

Economics of charity: grain alms as poor relief

Apart from providing food products for their own community, Norwich Cathedral Priory authorities distributed limited amounts of grain to non-resident recipients in the form of alms. This was a common practice in western monasticism throughout the Middle Ages.[1] As far as Norwich Cathedral Priory is concerned, we can speak about three distinctive groups of alm recipients: the urban hermits and anchorites secluded in their cells; prisoners incarcerated in the castle prison, located within walking distance of the cathedral; and the town's paupers, who formed by far the largest group enjoying grain alms. Food charity was profitable for both parties: it provided the needy with food while helping the monks to fulfil the Benedictine ideal of charity.

Hermits and anchorites

It is impossible to establish the hermit population of Norwich town before the Black Death. The information, which entirely derives from non-monastic sources, is scarce and problematic. First, some hermits appear only in a single document and, as a result, we are unable to determine the chronology of their lives in the town. In other words, if a hermit appears in a document from 1300, we cannot be certain that he was still alive, or practised eremitism, say, five years later. Second, we are ignorant about the total number of hermits and anchorites. For instance, if a certain source mentions four hermits at the same time, it does not mean that there were *only* four hermits present at Norwich in the given year. The surviving evidence, imperfect as it might be, suggests that there was *at least* one anchorite in 1244, four in 1247 and 1250, two or three in 1287–8 and two in 1304–5 and 1312–13.[2] A will from 1313 mentions four recluses.[3] The last non-cathedral document to mention anchorites was a will of Catherine, an anchorite of St Margaret Newbridge, dated 22 February 1315. Catherine left her Norwich messuage to be sold and ordered its revenue to be distributed 'for her soul' (*pro mea anima*), presumably among the poor.[4] There are also a number of undated deeds and wills from the thirteenth century that mention recluses of Norwich.[5] Between 1315 and 1393/4, the year when Julian of Norwich first appears in the

---

1. On Westminster corrodies and alms, consult B. Harvey, *Living and dying in England, 1100–1540: the monastic experience* (Oxford, 1993), pp. 179–209 and 238–51.
2. W. Rye (ed.), *A short calendar of the deeds relating to Norwich enrolled in the court rolls of the city, 1285–1306* (Norwich, 1903), pp. 100 and 103; R.M. Clay, *The hermits and anchorites of England* (London, 1914), pp. 232–7; Tanner, *The church*, p. 58; R. Gilchrist and M. Oliva, *Religious women in medieval East Anglia* (Norwich, 1993), pp. 97–9.
3. British Library, MS Add. Charter 15527.
4. NRO, NCR Case 1/7/9.
5. NRO, PHI 249/3, 577x3; Clay, *Hermits and anchorites*, p. 235.

records,[6] no document mentions a single recluse living in the town, however. Hermits are also attested in our bread accounts recorded on the dorse of the cellarer's rolls. Each year they recorded a certain number of loaves of *panis militum* distributed among the 'anchorites/anchors/recluses within the town' (*anachoritis/reclusis in villa*). Interestingly enough, the recluses disappear from the bread accounts around roughly the same time that they disappear from other contemporary sources. The last roll to mention the distribution of bread among them was that of 1315–16. No anchorites are mentioned from the next surviving roll (1318–19). This might suggest their temporary disappearance from the town, at least until c.1394. The reasons for their disappearance are unclear, but might have been related to the severe famine of 1315–17, which may have weakened the townsfolk badly.

Some rolls also specify that the recluses used to receive their loaves as a custom (*de constuetudine*).[7] From this we might conclude that the priory had a long tradition of giving bread to the anchorites and hermits. Before c.1291–2, the customary amount of grain turned into loaves for recluses was two quarters; from c.1294–5 onwards, the priory allocated two and a half quarters of wheat. Unfortunately, the accounts do not specify whether the loaves were given once a year on a specific day, or throughout the year. Two quarters and two and half quarters of grain would have produced around 429 and 536 loaves of *panis militum* respectively, if we assume that a quarter of flour, at the extraction rate of 85 per cent, would have made around 214.5 loaves.[8] Keeping in mind the fact that the recluses consumed many fewer calories than their non-reclusive counterparts, we might speculate that this number of loaves could have sustained two hermits throughout the entire year. Hermits lived on vegetarian foods, chiefly cereal products, vegetables, fruit and milk. Some recluses had only bread and water on certain days. In addition, they normally took only one meal each day, at midday outside Lent and not until Vespers (6 p.m.) during Lent.[9]

The giving of grain alms to hermits by the monastic authorities seems to have been a widespread practice in late medieval England.[10] For instance, somewhere between 1127 and 1134 Westminster Abbey established the perpetual corrody (monastic allowance) of bread, ale, mead and wine for three anchorites of Kilburn.[11] Around 1235 a similar corrody was established at St Alban's Abbey to feed a local anchorite.[12] Towards the end of Henry III's reign the authorities of Blyth Priory granted annual liveries

---

6. NRO, PRCC, Register Harsyk (Norwich Consistory Court Probate Records, 1381–1408), fol. 194 v. The document in question is a will of Roger Reed, rector of St Michael's Coslany in Norwich, dated 20 March 1393 or 1394. The will is mentioned in E. Colledge and J. Walsh (eds), *A book of showings to the anchoress Julian of Norwich* (Toronto, 1978), p. 33, and in N. Watson and J. Jenkins (eds), *The writings of Julian of Norwich* (University Park, PA, 2006), p. 431.
7. NRO, DCN 1/1/6–8.
8. For conversion of raw grain into loaves, see above, Chapter 7.
9. Clay, *Hermits and anchorites*, pp. 101–5.
10. A.K. Warren, *Anchorites and their patrons in medieval England* (Berkeley, CA, 1985), pp. 45–50.
11. Harvey, *Living and dying*, pp. 239–40.
12. H.T. Riley (ed.), *Gesta Abbatum Monasterii Sancti Albani*, Rolls Series 28/4, vol. 1 (London, 1867), p. 305.

(*liberations*) of one conventual loaf, a gallon of conventual wine and some food from the kitchen to be granted on a daily basis to Joanna the anchoress.[13] Sometime before 1285 the livery of two loaves of white bread (*liberation albi panis*) and two flagons (*juste*) of ale was granted to recluses of Worcester, presumably two in number.[14]

Prisoners in the castle prison

Distributing bread among the incarcerated in the castle prison was yet another aspect of 'food charity' practised by the priory authorities.[15] The amount of grain allocated to be converted into *panis militum* for the prisoners varied from year to year. For instance, the roll of 1298–9 allocates only three quarters, while that of 1315–16 indicates that as many as 33.25 quarters were turned into bread for the incarcerated.[16] There were also years when no bread was given to the prisoners at all.[17] These, however, may have been rare instances and the general rule appears to be that the brethren took care of felons awaiting their trial. On average, the priory allocated eight quarters of wheat (around 1716 loaves) in the 1280s; 6.25 quarters (around 1341 loaves) in the 1290s; 5.81 quarters (around 1246 loaves) in the 1300s; as much as 24.79 quarters (around 5317 loaves) in the 1310s; 10.63 quarters (around 2280 loaves) in the 1320s; 10.71 quarters (around 2297 loaves) in the 1330s and 8.56 quarters (around 1836 loaves) between 1341 and 1343. Generally speaking, with the exception of the 1310s, the prisoners' bread amounted to between 1 and 2 per cent of all the *panis militum* baked at the priory bakery.

Were these amounts enough to feed the felons? In order to answer this question we have to juxtapose the quantity of bread with the number of inmates held at the castle prison. For the purpose of this exercise, let us focus on the period between 1308 and 1316. Our information regarding the number of prisoners and their penal conditions derives from two sources: jail delivery rolls[18] and the king's rolls – close, patent and

---

13. R.T. Timson (ed.), *The cartulary of Blyth Priory* (London, 1973), p. 508.
14. Hale, *Registrum Prioratus Beate Marie Wigorniensis*, pp. 120b and 124b.
15. On crime, jail delivery, imprisonment and the penal system of late medieval England, consult R.B. Pugh, *Imprisonment in medieval England* (Cambridge, 1968); B.A. Hanawalt, *Crime and conflict in English communities, 1300–1348* (Cambridge, MA, 1979); J. Bellamy, *Crime and public order in England in the later Middle Ages* (London, 1978); T.R. Gurr, 'Historical trends in violent crime: a critical review of the evidence', *Crime and Justice: An Annual Review of Research*, 3 (1981), pp. 295–353; M. Eisner, 'Long-term historical trends in violent crime', *Crime and Justice: A Review of Research*, 30 (2003), pp. 83–242. On internal conditions of prisons and prison life in *trecento* Italy, see G. Geltner, *Medieval prisons: a social history* (Princeton, NJ, 2008).
16. NRO, DCN 1/1/14 and 1/1/25.
17. NRO, DCN 1/1/12 (1294–5) and 1/1/19 (1308–9).
18. Norfolk jail delivery rolls are printed in B. Hanawalt (ed.), *Crime in East Anglia in the fourteenth century: Norfolk gaol delivery rolls, 1307–1316*, Norfolk Record Society 44 (Norwich, 1976) (the edition of The National Archives (TNA) JUST 3/48). Other relevant Norfolk Delivery Rolls are: TNA, JUST 3/47/1 (1294–5), JUST 3/47/2 (1295), JUST 3/47/3 (1299–1302), JUST 3/49/1 (1313, 1316–1324), JUST 3/49/2 (1332–4), JUST 3/49/3 (1333), JUST 3/50/1 (1332–3), JUST 3/50/2 (1335–9).

fine.[19] Determining the number of prison inmates is rather a problematic task, as the jail delivery rolls tell us about the number of prisoners held in the castle only at the time of the circuit justices' visits. The rolls indicate that there were 'high' and 'low' incarceration seasons. For example, there was only one inmate on 21 January 1314, while during the delivery on 7 June 1316 there were as many as 189. As a rule, the justices visited the prison three times a year in order to try the prisoners, either for indictment or acquittal. After each delivery, the castle prison was 'purged', partially or completely, of felons. Taking into account 'high seasons' only, it appears that, on average, about 30 per cent of total (suspected) felons returned to the prison for either further investigations or for the king's pardon; about 50 per cent were acquitted; some 13 per cent were indicted and consequently executed by hanging; around 3 per cent were released on bail or manucaption; a further 3 per cent were handed over to the bishop because of their clerical status; and usually under 1 per cent managed to get away, either by paying a fine or by breaking from the prison. In other words, the number of inmates fell drastically after the delivery was carried out and felons were either released or hanged. However, we know nothing about the frequency of incarceration – that is, how many felons would be thrown into the prison on, say, a weekly or monthly basis – and hence we are ignorant, in most cases, about the length of most incarcerations; we only know when felons were released or executed. As a result, we cannot calculate the number of inmates on a daily basis; all we can do is

---

19. The relevant commissions regarding Norwich Castle Prison appear in the fine rolls: *Calendar of the Fine Rolls* (CFR) *Vol. I, Edward I, AD 1272–1307* (London: HMSO, 1911), pp. 116, 157, 165, 264, 326 and 501; *CFR Vol. II, Edward II, AD 1307–1319* (London: HMSO, 1912), pp. 141 and 259; in the close rolls: *Calendar of the Close Rolls* (CCR), *Edward I, Vol. II, AD 1279–1288* (London: HMSO, 1902), pp. 73, 151, 215, 311, 323, 334, 446 and 509; *CCR, Edward I, Vol. III, AD 1288–1296* (London: HMSO, 1904), pp. 12, 17, 70, 75, 174, 222, 373, and 414; *CCR, Edward I, Vol. IV, AD 1296–1302* (London: HMSO, 1906), pp. 458, 523, 533, 548; *CCR, Edward I, Vol. IV, AD 1302–1307* (London: HMSO, 1908), pp. 24, 49, 57, 117, 136, 148, 151, 163, 187 and 385; *CCR, Edward II, Vol. I, AD 1307–1313* (London: HMSO, 1892), pp. 190, 191, 208 and 510; *CCR, Edward II, Vol. II, AD 1313–1318* (London: HMSO, 1893), pp. 34, 35, 55, 251, 284, 555 and 556; *CCR, Edward II, Vol. III, AD 1318–1323* (London: HMSO, 1895), pp. 6, 224, 386 and 388; *CCR, Edward II, Vol. IV, AD 1323–1327* (London: HMSO, 1898), p. 114; *CCR, Edward III, Vol. I, AD 1327–1330* (London: HMSO, 1896), pp. 11, 282, 299, 300, 455 and 456; *CCR, Edward III, Vol. II, AD 1330–1333* (London: HMSO, 1898), pp. 106, 313 and 375; *CCR, Edward III, Vol. III, AD 1333–1337* (London: HMSO, 1898), pp. 2, 26, 37, 62 and 390; *CCR, Edward III, Vol. V, AD 1339–1341* (London: HMSO, 1901), pp. 355 and 369; and in the patent rolls: *Calendar of the Patent Rolls* (CPR), *Edward I, Vol. I, AD 1272–1281* (London: HMSO, 1901), pp. 141, 338, 339, 341 and 344; *CPR, Edward I, Vol. II, AD 1281–1292* (London: HMSO, 1893), pp. 23, 88, 254, 260, 284, 288, 332 and 336; *CPR, Edward I, Vol. III, AD 1292–1301* (London: HMSO, 1895), pp. 11, 20, 25, 54, 82, 110, 112, 113, 116, 141 159, 160, 165, 191, 192, 215, 218, 238, 254, 257, 258, 319, 374, 375, 379, 381 and 440; *CPR, Edward I, Vol. IV, AD 1301–1307* (London: HMSO, 1898), pp. 8, 54, 379, 445, 491 and 510; *CPR, Edward II, Vol. I, AD 1307–1313* (London: HMSO, 1894), pp. 144, 194, 211, 227, 341 and 381; *CPR, Edward II, Vol. II, AD 1313–1317* (London: HMSO, 1898), pp. 153, 218, 246, 452, 493 and 503; *CPR, Edward II, Vol. III, AD 1317–1321* (London: HMSO, 1903), pp. 467, 489, 512, 539, 677 and 701; *CPR, Edward II, Vol. IV, AD 1321–1324* (London: HMSO, 1904), p. 248; *CPR, Edward II, Vol. V, AD 1324–1327* (London: HMSO, 1904), pp. 154 and 158; *CPR, Edward III, AD 1327–1330* (London: HMSO, 1891), pp. 182, 272, 388 and 551.

Table 8.1
Number of prisoners at Norwich Castle and the amounts of bread distributed among them, 1308–16.

Year	Male prisoners	Female prisoners	Quarters of wheat	Estimated loaves	Loaves per inmate
1308–9	35	10	0.0	0	0
1309–10	33	7	5.0	1073	27
1310–11	45	9	8.0	1716	32
1313–14	12	0	26.0	5577	452
1314–15	27	7	21.3	4558	133
1315–16	102	37	33.3	7132	51
Average	42.3	11.7	15.6	3342.6	115.8

Sources: B.A. Hanawalt (ed.), *Crime in East Anglia in the fourteenth century: Norfolk gaol delivery rolls, 1307–1316*, Norfolk Record Society 44 (Norwich, 1976); DNC 1/1/19–25.

estimate the average number of prisoners on an annual basis. Since the bread accounts cover each year from Michaelmas to Michaelmas, each prison year has been adjusted accordingly by calculating the average number of prisoners between the two Michaelmases (namely, between the delivery closest to Michaelmas of the previous year and that closest to Michaelmas of the following year) (Table 8.1).

As Table 8.1 indicates, the amount of bread sent to the castle was far from sufficient to feed each inmate on a daily basis. The only exception was 1313–14, when the number of felons in the prison was low and it is quite possible that the priory authorities could have provided every prisoner with his daily bread. During the troublesome year of 1315–16, when the number of inmates reached an unprecedented peak, the priory allocated an exceptionally large amount of bread to be distributed among them. Nevertheless, the distributed loaves were insufficient to feed every mouth and many prisoners undoubtedly starved as a result of the widespread famine. The high number of felons kept in the prison during 1315–16 reflects, undoubtedly, the exceptionally high volume of crime that took place across England and most of Europe during the famine years.[20] During the crisis years we find more and more felons accused of plundering barns and granaries and stealing supplies of grain, chiefly wheat and malt. Between 26 November 1315 and 15 March 1316 14 robbers of grain were taken to the castle prison (10.14 per cent of total felons incarcerated there), while between 15 March and 7 June 1316 as many as 41 people suspected of stealing grain and malt were imprisoned (an astonishing 21.69 per cent of all felons).[21] These are certainly high figures compared with previous years, when grain robbers constituted a maximum of 6 per cent of total felons incarcerated in the prison.[22] Indeed, some

---

20. On the connection between crime rates and chaotic times in the fourteenth century, see B.A. Hanawalt, 'Economic influences on the pattern of crime in England, 1300–1348', *American Journal of Legal History*, 18/4 (1974), pp. 281–97; B.A. Hanawalt, 'The peasant family and crime in fourteenth-century England', *Journal of British Studies*, 13 (1974), pp. 1–18; Hanawalt, *Crime and conflict*, pp. 238–60; Gurr, 'Historical trends in violent crime'.
21. Figure calculated from Hanawalt, *Crime in East Anglia*, pp. 79–116.
22. Calculated from ibid., pp. 23–76.

entries in the delivery rolls specify that it was hunger and want (*fames et inopia*) that prompted the felons to plunder barns and steal cereals. The Great Famine must have inflicted exceptionally hard suffering upon the incarcerated. As John of Trokelowe, a contemporary Suffolk chronicler reports, there were cases of cannibalism among prison inmates.[23]

It should be noted, however, that some entries clearly indicate the inmates' hardships during 'normal' years. There are numerous examples of prisoners becoming the victims of the arbitrary rule of the prison guards and the king's justices. For instance, a certain Richard of Sapling, who was accused of abjuration of the realm, and spent at least eight years in the prison, served part of his sentence in the castle tower. The tower was exposed to pouring rain, which destroyed the charter of pardon granted by Edward I to Richard. The justices failed to test the authenticity of the charter, because of its ruined condition, and asked the chancellor of the king to search for a copy of the document and send it to the castle. As a result, Richard became a victim of royal bureaucracy and ended up suffering long-term imprisonment.[24] A certain Welshman, Rhys ap Rhys ap Mereduk, presumably a war prisoner or traitor, appears to have spent about 30 years in the prison (between *c.*1305 and 1335), and it is likely that he ended his life there.[25] Another felon, John Bonde, indicted as a burglar and sentenced to be hanged, complained that the constable of the castle forced him to act as an informer under various tortures inflicted in the lowest room of the prison.[26] Some prisoners, such as John of St Olav and James Syffe, did not even live to hear their sentence.[27] Some prisoners who refused to accept a jury trial were returned to the prison and put on a special severe diet and living conditions to force them to plead. Two particular conditions are mentioned in the rolls: *ad dietam* (torture by penal starvation) and *peine forte et dure* (torture by putting a board on a prisoner's body and piling weights on it until he/she consented to answer to the charge). Several pregnant women sentenced to death by hanging were returned to their cells to await execution, which was to occur shortly after they delivered their babies.[28] Unlike modern jails, medieval prisons did not distinguish between sexes or ages. Men and women, young and old were kept at the same cells. Unfortunately, our delivery accounts do not, as a rule, specify the age of the convicted. There are some exceptions to this rule, however. For example, a certain William Junior of Walesby

---

23. H.T. Riley (ed.), *Johannis de Trokelowe Monachi Annales*, Rolls Series 28C (London, 1866), p. 95.
24. The case of Richard of Sapling appears in Hanawalt, *Crime in East Anglia*, pp. 28, 29 and 64. Richard claimed to have a charter of pardon issued by Edward I on 16 January 1307; however, he was still found among the imprisoned felons on 4 July 1314 and it is unclear what was his fate afterwards.
25. *CCR, Edward II, Vol. I, AD 1307–1313* (London: HMSO, 1892), p. 191; *CCR, Edward II, Vol. IV, AD 1323–1327* (London: HMSO, 1898), p. 114; *CCR, Edward III, Vol. I, AD 1327–1330* (London: HMSO, 1896), pp. 11, 282, 299, 300, 455 and 456; *CCR, Edward III, Vol. II, AD 1330–1333* (London: HMSO, 1898), p. 106 and 375; *CCR, Edward III, Vol. III, AD 1333–1337* (London: HMSO, 1898), pp. 2, 26, 37 and 390.
26. Hanawalt, *Crime in East Anglia*, pp. 39–40.
27. Ibid., pp. 81–2 and 91.
28. Ibid., pp. 25, 71, 92 and 93.

could not be indicted because he appeared to have been less than ten years old.[29] Similarly, the castle authorities did not distinguish between laymen and clergy. Thus, our rolls are full of clerks suspected of and indicted for various felonies, varying from harbouring criminals to homicide. Out of 92 felons tried on 19 June 1315, 9 were clerks (that is, almost 10 per cent).[30] Unlike the laymen, however, the clerks could refuse to acknowledge their sentence and demand to be judged at the bishop's court.

These are but a few examples of hardships experienced by the castle prison inmates. The priory authorities were undoubtedly aware of the harsh conditions in which prisoners were kept, and attempted to ease their suffering by providing them with their most basic necessity: bread. The distribution of loaves among the felons must be considered a charitable activity *par excellence*, as prescribed by the *Rule* of St Benedict.

Almoner's soup kitchen for Norwich paupers

The most numerous group of needy people fed by the brethren were urban paupers. They received their charity from two obedientiaries: the master of the cellar and the almoner. The distribution of loaves by the former represented purely a symbolic, liturgical act, occurring once a year, on Maundy Thursday. The particulars of this act are described in detail in the priory customary, composed between 1258 and 1265. The customary specified, *inter alia*, that each pauper was to be given a quarter of a loaf, and that 80 paupers were to be welcomed into the guest hall, where they would be fed by the brethren. The remaining poor had, presumably, to wait outside the hall. On average, on each Maundy Thursday about 6.6 quarters of wheat were converted into the paupers' bread – enough to produce about 1422 loaves, to be distributed among some 5688 hungry mouths.

It was the almoner's support, however, on which the paupers could count on a daily basis. Before *c.*1300 the almoner made extensive purchases of crops to be turned into bread, ale and pottage for the poor. After *c.*1300, however, no more crop purchases were made. Instead, the almoner started drawing upon his landed property in order to supply the paupers with food, relying on 12 appropriated estates and tithe-paying churches providing his department with grain, kept at the almoner's granary. Unfortunately, the almoner's rolls, as a rule, did not include granary accounts on their dorse and there are only four surviving rolls mentioning the return and disposal of crops received from the manors and appropriated churches as tithes (the accounts for 1310–11, 1339–40, 1345–6 and 1353–4).[31] Consequently, and as opposed to the master of the cellar's rolls, we cannot establish any firm statistical analysis regarding the almoner's granary, let alone reconstruct seeding and harvesting patterns practised on the almoner's manors.

Although the fragmentary nature of the evidence does not allow us to reconstruct the full picture of grain supply and disposal within the almoner's granary, one thing is clear: its structure and function were different from those of both the Great Granary and the granary of the master of the cellar. The grain supplies stored in the almoner's granary were not intended for domestic consumption within the cathedral community.

---

29. Ibid., p. 108.
30. Ibid., pp. 69–76.
31. NRO, DCN 1/6/9, 12, 13 and 17.

Since wheat was the grain of the higher echelons of society, it is hardly surprising that the almoner's granary, specialising in grain distribution among the poor, was strongly rye-biased. Furthermore, the almoner's granary stored much smaller quantities of cereals than did the monastic granary.

Now let us look more closely at the grain distributed among the poor. The surviving granary accounts of the almoner distinguish between wheat, given annually on Bishop Herbert de Losinga's anniversary (23 July) and amounting to no more than 10 per cent of the total distributed grain, and other grains and legumes (rye, peas and barley), which were distributed throughout the year (Tables 8.2 and 8.3). The distribution trends show that the priory authorities clearly preferred to provide the paupers with rye as the principal bread grain and barley as a drinking cereal. It is unclear whether the poor were provided with raw grains or with actual loafs and beverages. We might argue that the consumption of wheat bread carried a festive connotation for the poor, for they could enjoy this usually unaffordable staple during two feasts only: Herbert's anniversary and Maundy Thursday. The distribution and consumption of rye bread, on the other hand, was an everyday reality. Peas, presumably turned into pottage, represented nearly 10 per cent of the charity distributed in 1310–11 and about a quarter in 1339–40 and 1345–6. Neither wheat nor peas were given to the poor in 1353–4. In estimating calorific equivalents, we learn that Norwich Cathedral Priory was generous in its charitable activities among the town's paupers. Thus, in 1339–40 and 1345–6 around 27 quarters of wheat were spent on the poor, enough to feed about 5800 persons with a loaf of *panis militum* each (Table 8.3). According to the almoner's roll, the entire amount was distributed on a single day, the anniversary of Herbert. These are certainly high figures, given the fact that the estimated population of Norwich c.1339–40 was around 25,000, or possibly higher.[32] In other words, the amount of wheat allocated to the poor was capable of feeding some 20 to 25 per cent of the (estimated) total population of the town. This does not mean, however, that about a quarter of the townsfolk ran to Ethelbert Gate to receive the loaves on Herbert's anniversary. It is highly unlikely that as much as a quarter of the population were paupers living on alms; according to various taxations and assessments, Norwich was one of the wealthiest towns in fourteenth-century England.[33] It is possible that the poor in question were, in fact, tenants from surrounding villages, or perhaps the priory manors, who knew of the charitable activities of their lords and, hence, made their way to the town.

Charitable works connected to food distribution at major feasts and anniversaries were a commonplace in various monasteries of late medieval England. For instance, the monks of Battle Abbey used to entertain the town's poor with wine on the anniversary of Master Hugh de Mortimer,[34] while the brethren of Evesham Abbey distributed loaves on the

---

32. Rutledge, 'Immigration and population growth'; Rutledge, 'Economic life'. Norwich had a population of approximately 25,000 by 1333 and it is likely that the town continued expanding until the Black Death. Hollingsworth suggested that there might have been as many as 41,000 inhabitants by 1348; however, his dubious methodology makes this figure rather suspicious and possibly somewhat exaggerated (T.H. Hollingworth, *Historical demography* (London, 1969), pp. 363–4). It is unlikely that the town's population was any higher than, say, 32,000 people by 1348.
33. A. Dyer, 'Appendix. Ranking lists of English medieval towns', in D.M. Palliser (ed.), *The Cambridge urban history of Britain*, vol. 1 (Cambridge, 2000), pp. 754–5.
34. This is stated in a 1278–9 cellarer's account (printed in E. Searle (ed.), *The cellarers' rolls of Battle Abbey, 1275–1513*, Sussex Record Society 65 (Lewes, 1967), p. 44).

Table 8.2
The AGCR stored at the almoner's granary, c.1310–1354.

	1310–11	1339–40	1345–6	1353–4
Wheat	50.6	63.6	75.0	13.0
Rye	173.5	69.3	97.9	30.0
Peas	47.3	116.3	132.5	30.0
Oats	88.8	33.4	37.4	4.1
Barley	42.0	21.5	29.6	0.0
Malt	304.1	375.7	332.0	84.3
Total	706.3	679.8	704.4	161.4
Financial value (in £)	193.9	186.6	193.4	44.3
Given to poor (as % of AGCR)	54.9%	58.2%	52.2%	22.5%

Source: NRO, DCN 1/6/9, 12, 13 and 17.

Commemoration of All Persons, on Maundy Thursday and on any funeral day.[35] The monks of Durham Priory commemorated the person of William of Durham (d. 1249), a reputed founder of University College, Oxford and a rector of Wearmouth. In addition, they fed the paupers with loaves at nine feasts between All Saints (31 October) and the Nativity of St John the Baptist.[36] A similar situation pertained at late medieval Peterborough Abbey, where the brethren supported the local poor with food and clothes.[37]

Outside Maundy Thursday and Herbert Losinga's anniversary, the paupers enjoyed free meals served by the almoner throughout the year. In 1310–11 163.3 quarters of rye, 37.1 quarters of peas and 169 quarters of barley producing over 33,000 loaves, about 28,500 portions of pottage and over 216,000 gallons of weak ale were allocated to the poor. The overall composition of food charity varied from year to year. Thus, in 1339–40 the amount of rye fell to 66.6 quarters (fewer than 14,000 loaves), while the proportions of peas and barley rose to 92.8 and 209.3 quarters, producing some 71,200 pottage plates and 268,000 gallons of ale respectively. In 1353–4, shortly after the pestilence, which had decimated the local population, the almoner distributed only 16.3 quarters of rye, which would have made just over 3300 loaves, and 20 quarters of barley, enough to brew some 25,600 gallons of weak ale.

How many paupers could have potentially been fed, on a daily basis, outside Herbert Losinga's anniversary? The numbers of loaves, plates of pottages and gallons of ales should not be equated with the numbers of paupers; after all, it is highly implausible that each pauper would receive food worth approximately 4600 kcal on a daily basis. Perhaps a more realistic allowance would be about 2000 kcal *per capita*. It appears that the produced food was capable of feeding over 500 paupers on a daily basis in the pre-Black Death period. These are, obviously, only average figures. In reality, the number of paupers fed each day must have been higher than that, given the fact that the charity season lasted for slightly under 150 days, from early spring to mid-summer, when the grain prices

---

35. W. Dugdale, *Monasticon Anglicanum* (London, 1846), vol. II, p. 29.
36. Fowler, *Account rolls of the Abbey of Durham*, pp. 484 and 531.
37. J. Greatrex (ed.), *Account rolls of the obedientiaries of Peterborough* (Northampton, 1984), p. 14.

Table 8.3
Annual distribution of crops among the paupers, its calorific equivalent and hypothetical amount of people it was capable of feeding, c.1310–54.

	1310–11			1339–40			1345–6			1353–4		
	Quarters	Loaves/ plates/ gallons	Kcal (millions)	Quarters	Loaves/ plates/ gallons	Kcal (millions)	Quarters	Loaves/ plates/ gallons	Kcal (millions)	Quarters	Loaves/ plates/ gallons	Kcal (millions)
Wheat	18.3	3915	10.0	27.0	5792	14.8	27.5	5899	15.1	0.0	0	0.0
Rye	163.3	33,642	86.1	66.6	13,725	35.1	82.5	16,995	43.5	16.3	3348	8.6
Peas	37.1	28,512	23.2	92.8	71,232	57.9	92.0	70,656	57.4	0.0	0	0.0
Malt	169.0	216,320	276.9	209.3	267,920	342.9	166.0	212,480	272.0	20.0	25,600	32.8
Total	387.7		396.1	395.7		450.7	368.0		387.9	36.3	28,948	41.3
Poor capable of feeding, daily basis	530			598			512			57		
Poor capable of feeding, during the charity season	1304			1472			1259			140		

Source: NRO, DCN 1/6/9, 12, 13 and 17.
Notes: Quarters of rye were converted into loaves, assuming the extraction rates of 0.85. The numbers of pottage plates were estimated on the basis of the assumption that each plate was about 10oz, as indicated in some late medieval sources. See Hammond.

were at their highest, as some earlier almoner's accounts indicate.[38] If we are to assume that no food was distributed outside the charity season, then it appears that the daily number of paupers enjoying the almoner's soup kitchen may have been around 1350. These are, naturally, hypothetical figures, which, however, may be not too far removed from truth, and certainly reflect the pre-Black Death reality. The 1353–4 account, indicating much lower figures, is reflective of the immediate aftermath of the pestilence. Unfortunately, the later accounts of the almoner do not contain details of this charity and we thus remain in ignorance of the dynamics of the post-Black Death soup kitchen.

Grain alms in a wider context, theological and social

Care for the imprisoned and paupers played an important part in the fulfilment of the medieval Christian concept of the seven corporal works of mercy: feeding the hungry; giving drink to the thirsty; sheltering the homeless; clothing the naked; visiting the sick; visiting prisoners; and burying the dead. This concept derived from the description of the Last Judgement (Matthew 25:31–46). For example, Beatus of Liébana (d. 798), stated that whoever does not fast, pray, distribute his property among the poor, visit the sick and imprisoned, dress the naked and wash guests' feet cannot see the majesty of God.[39] The association of the incarcerated with other people in need is also found in Rather of Verona's (c.890–974) *Praeloquia*.[40] Jean Beleth (d. *c.*1182) distinguished between six charitable activities (*sex opera misericordie*): feeding the hungry, letting the thirsty drink, visiting the sick, dressing the naked, hosting the poor and pilgrims and attending the incarcerated.[41] A short time after Beleth's death, we find the same in a sermon of Gerard Iterius, abbot of Grandmont (1188–98).[42] Beleth and Gerard were followed by Guillaume Durand (1237–96) and Ramon Llull (1232/3–1315/16), two influential theologians of their age.[43] This concept is also found in the Western liturgy, in a private Carolingian prayer composed *c.*850, which has been for a long time falsely ascribed to Alcuin of York. The prayer in question implores God to appear favourable

---

38. In 1280, the charity activities began on Ash Wednesday, in the beginning of Lent, and continued well into the summer, down to the Feast of Mary Magdalene (22 July), the anniversary of Bishop Herbert Losinga (23 July) or *Ad Vincula* (1 August). See NRO, DCN 1/4/4–8.

39. B. Löfstedt (ed.), *Beati Liebanensis et Eterii Oxomensis Adversus Elipandum Libri Duo*, Corpus Christianorum Continuatio Mediaevalis 59 (Turnhout, 1984), p. 72.

40. B. Bischoff (ed.), *Ratherii Veronensis Praeloquiorum Libri VI*, Corpus Christianorum Continuatio Mediaevalis 41A (Turnhout, 1984), p. 130.

41. H. Douteil (ed.), *Johannis Beleth Summa de Ecclesiasticis Officiis*, Corpus Christianorum Continuatio Mediaevalis 41A (Turnhout, 1976), p. 142.

42. J. Becquet (ed.), *Scriptores Ordinis Grandimontensis*, Corpus Christianorum Continuatio Mediaevalis 8 (Turnhout, 1968), p. 399.

43. A. Davril and T.M. Thibodeau (eds), *Guillelmi Duranti Rationale Divinorum Officiorum V–VI*, Corpus Christianorum Continuatio Mediaevalis 140A (Turnhout, 1998), p. 215; F. Domínguez Reboiras and A. Soria Flores (eds), *Raimundi Lulli Opera Latina. Summa Sermonum in Civitate Maioricensi Annis MCCCXII–MCCCXIII Composita*, Corpus Christianorum Continuatio Mediaevalis 76 (Turnhout, 1987), pp. 468–9; A. Soria Flores, F. Domínguez Reboiras and M. Senellart (eds), *Raimundi Lulli Opera Latina. Summa Sermonum in Civitate Maioricensi Anno MCCCXIII Composita*, Corpus Christianorum Continuatio Mediaevalis 80 (Turnhout, 1991), p. 143.

to 'widows, orphans, captives, penitents, sick, suffering, sailours, pilgrims, imprisoned and to those placed in whatever necessities and miseries'.[44] The reluctance of the clergy to keep up with this mandate and visit prisoners is reflected in a sermon of Thomas of Chobham (d. c.1233/6), who complained that no preachers of his day preached to prisoners, who needed consolation and spiritual guidance.[45]

Apart from a manifestation of charity, the distribution of bread among prisoners can also be interpreted as an aspect of *imitatio Christi*. First, it alludes to the Miracle of the Loaves and Fishes, with Jesus feeding 4000 men with seven loaves (Matthew 15:32–38). Second, it alludes to Jesus' attachment to and activities among sinners. In Matthew 9:9–10 Jesus ate together with 'sinners and tax collectors'; in Matthew 11:19 he was called 'a friend of tax collectors and sinners' (*publicanorum et peccatorum amicus*); in Matthew 21:31–32, he promises that the tax collectors and harlots who believed in him would go into the kingdom of God before the priests of the Temple; finally, he was crucified with felons (*latrones*).

During the 1270s and 1280s the distribution of bread among the prisoners seems to have carried yet another connotation: the mandate of love and forgiveness prescribed by Jesus to his disciples. After the riot of 1272, when Norwich's citizens sacked the cathedral and killed some monks, the castle prison was filled with attackers of the church. While some were sentenced to death and some pardoned, others were confined in the prison. A close roll from 26 March 1287 (almost 15 years after the riot) mentions seven citizens of Norwich still kept in the prison on account of their participation in the attack.[46]

It was precisely to these theological roots and foundations that late medieval charity, both religious and lay, was connected. In order to appreciate the significance and the extent of the grain alms established by the priory authorities, we need to consider the more general context of urban charity and piety in fourteenth-century Norwich, in particular, and in England, in general. Unfortunately, because of the nature and extent of available documentation, scholars have tended to deal with later periods, chiefly the fifteenth and sixteenth centuries.[47] The major sources for their

---

44. 'Propitiare … viduis, orphanis, captives, poenitentibus, infirmis, afflictis, navigantibus, itinerantibus, incarcerates, et in quibuscunque necessitatibus atque miseriis constitutis.' *B. Flacci Albini seu Alcuini Opera*, Patrologia Latina 101, col. 488C. The prayer constitutes a part of a larger liturgical work of Pseudo-Alcuin, known as *De Usu Psalmorum*.

45. 'Est iterum alius defectus magnus in predicatoribus, quod numquam predicant incarceratis, cum sepe multi carceres pleni sint captiuis qui maxime indigent consolatione et magno consilio animarum, et in articulo tante necessitatis non habent predicatorem qui eos instruat, cum multi forte inter eos sint in odio fraterno, parati congredi in duello cum fratribus, parati etiam periurare pro peccatis super quibus accusantur'. F. Morenzoni (ed.), *Thomas de Chobham, Summa de Arte Praedicandi*, Corpus Christianorum Continuatio Mediaevalis 82 (Turnhout, 1988), p. 88.

46. CCR, *Edward I, Vol. II, AD 1279–1288* (London: HMSO, 1902), p. 446.

47. W.K. Jordan, *Philanthropy in England, 1480–1660* (London, 1959); W.K. Jordan, *The charities of London* (London, 1960); J.A.F. Thomson, 'Piety and charity in late medieval London', *Journal of Ecclesiastical History*, 16 (1965), pp. 178–95; S.L. Thrupp, *The merchant class of medieval London, 1300–1500* (Ann Arbor, MI, 1962), pp. 174–80; Tanner, *The church*; M.K. McIntosh, 'Local responses to the poor in late medieval and Tudor England', *Continuity and Change*, 3 (1988), pp. 209–45; B.R. McRee, 'Charity and gild solidarity in late medieval England', *Journal of British Studies*, 32 (1993), pp. 195–225.

studies are late medieval and early modern private wills probated in urban consistory courts. Although appearing in the late Anglo-Saxon period, wills become truly plentiful only in the decades following the Black Death and it is only from then that a quantitative analysis based on solid statistical data is possible. This holds true also for fourteenth-century Norwich: between *c.*1314 and 1339 only some 60 wills have survived copied and enrolled into what became later known as 'City Court Rolls' and a few more are extant elsewhere, in their original form.[48] Between 1340 and 1370 no wills survive either in original or copied/enrolled form. The earliest comprehensive register of enrolled wills, probated at Norwich Consistory Court and known as 'Heydon's Register', contains over 600 wills compiled between 1370 and 1383.[49] These two registers will serve as our guidelines to understanding the phenomenon of charity in fourteenth-century Norfolk.

There are obvious traps in using these sources. First, there is the 30-year gap between registers. Second, because of its fragmentary nature, the 1314–39 register might not reflect the entire picture. Third, Heydon's register was compiled some 30 years after the last priory granary roll and after the shock of the plague. Hence, it is probable that it reflects a reality completely different from that of the pre-Black Death era. Nevertheless, these are the only available sources for measuring the piety of Norwich citizens in the fourteenth century. Because of the voluminous nature of Heydon's register, a four-year span only, between 1370 and 1373 inclusive, was examined.

Only 14 testators (11 men and 3 women), out of a total of 60 (23.33 per cent), left alms to the poor between 1314 and 1339. In most cases, the testators stipulated that part of their property be sold and distributed among the paupers. Heydon's register shows higher proportions of testators bequeathing charitably: 6 testators out of a total of 16 in 1370 (37.50 per cent); 16 out of a total of 33 in 1371 (48.48 per cent); 6 out of a total of 23 in 1372 (26.09 per cent) and 13 out of a total of 33 in 1373 (39.39 per cent).[50] Most testators bequeathed alms in the form of money, but some also left grain to be distributed among the paupers. For example, William de Inthburgh, rector of Salle, bequeathed three quarters of wheat, five quarters of malt and six quarters of oats.[51] Similarly, John Palmere de Benham left seven bushels of 'whatever kind of grain' (*de aliquo genere bladi*).[52] A parson named William Ely commanded that one quarter of wheat be baked into bread and distributed among the poor (*unum quarterium frumenti ut fiat in panem*).[53] Only one testator, John de Reppes, left alms to the prisoners in Norwich Castle prison, in the form of five shillings.[54] The number of bequests to prisoners, however, increased during the fifteenth and into the sixteenth century, as Norman Tanner has shown in his study of Norwich piety in the fifteenth and sixteenth centuries. For instance, between 1490 and 1517, 22 per cent of lay and 27

---

48. NRO, NCR Cases 1/1–1/13.
49. NRO, PRCC, Register Heydon (1370–83).
50. NRO, PRCC, Register Heydon (1370–83), fols 1r–41r.
51. NRO, PRCC, Register Heydon (1370–83), fol. 12r.
52. NRO, PRCC, Register Heydon (1370–83), fol. 32r.
53. NRO, PRCC, Register Heydon (1370–83), fol. 33v.
54. NRO, PRCC, Register Heydon (1370–83), fol. 32r.

per cent of clerical testators left bequests to the prisoners in the castle prison and the Guild Hall.[55] J.A.F. Thompson gives similar figures for late medieval London.[56] The evidence from late medieval Yorkshire shows even higher figures: up to 60.70 per cent of total bequests left between 1389 and 1398 had charitable intentions.[57] Similar figures are reported in late medieval Hull.[58] As far as the late medieval English aristocracy is concerned, about one in three wills left money for alms.[59]

It was in this context that the almoner of Norwich Cathedral Priory practised his extensive charitable activities. The problem of the poor was widely recognised in late medieval English society, and helping paupers, by giving either money or food, was both considered a moral duty of every able Christian and one of the most recognisable forms of piety. The distribution of grain among the anchorites, prisoners and poor by the priory authorities embodies, to a great extent, the care for the needy so typical of late medieval society. After all, Norwich Cathedral Priory was both a religious institution and a wealthy temporal lord and, as such, it could not have been indifferent towards people in need. And, above all, the brethren could not evade the fulfilment of their moral obligation which supposedly earned them entrance to Heaven.

Conclusions

The provisioning of grain was not limited to the priory community. Although the primary concern of the priory authorities was, understandably, to feed their own community, they did not ignore the needy people of their town: the hermits and anchorites, prisoners incarcerated in the prison and paupers. The anchorites disappear from the granary rolls by 1316–18, as they disappear from other town records around the same time. Perhaps their sudden disappearance can be explained by their physical extinction after the troublesome years of 1314–17. Examining the jail delivery rolls of Norwich Castle, we learn about the conditions in which prisoners were kept and the arbitrary rule and abuse which might be inflicted on them by their guards. The brethren must have been aware of their hardships and did what they could to support them until their sentence was proclaimed. This was especially true during the 1315–16 season, when the prison was unusually full of felons as crime rates rose during the anarchy created by the Great Famine and sheep epizootics.

The largest amount of grain allocated for charitable purposes, however, went to the paupers. Here we can distinguish between two types of distribution. One, with a ritual or liturgical character, was made on Maundy Thursday, in accordance with Jesus'

---

55. Tanner, *The church*, pp. 222–3.
56. Thomson, 'Piety and charity', p. 185.
57. P.H. Cullum, '"And hir name was Charite": charitable giving by and for women in late medieval Yorkshire', in P.J.P. Goldberg (ed.), *Women in medieval English society* (Stroud, 1997), pp. 182–221, esp. p. 184. Between 1440 and 1459, however, the figure fell to 40.60 per cent (ibid., p. 184).
58. P. Heath, 'Urban piety in the later Middle Ages: the evidence of Hull wills', in B. Dobson (ed.), *Church, politics and patronage* (Gloucester, 1984), p. 224.
59. J.T. Rosenthal, *The purchase of paradise: gift giving and the aristocracy, 1307–1485* (London, 1972), p. 103.

mandate to his apostles. The other, also driven by religious principles but more work-a-day in nature, was the distribution by the almoner, apparently assisted by other brethren and *famuli*, of hundreds of loaves, plates of pottage and pints of ale every day. With a certain degree of reservation, we may see this as a primitive form of poor relief, administered by the Church long before this responsibility passed into the hands of state with the Elizabethan Poor Laws of 1597–1601. Theologically speaking, the paupers and prisoners were considered to be a part of the same group of 'people in need' and helping them constituted two of the corporal works of mercy. Finally, charitable grain distribution by the brethren should be seen in a wider context of late medieval charity. To that end, surviving wills from fourteenth-century Norfolk have been examined and compared with analogous data from other parts of the country. The analysis of the bequests revealed that caring for paupers and prisoners was an important phenomenon in late medieval England which often took the form of the distribution of grain. It was regarded as a moral obligation of an able Christian, which earned him a 'passport to Paradise'.

Conclusion: Seigniorial conservativism as an economic strategy

This book has addressed several interrelated issues all connected to larger meaningful questions relating to the late medieval economy. Some of these issues have been the subjects of scholarly debate for many decades now. Others, on the other hand, remain unexplored. The first and, arguably, the largest issue is the dichotomy between commercialisation and seigniorial autarky, both before and after the Black Death. In the world of a commercialising and marketising economy many landlords, and especially conventual institutions, preferred to preserve the existing order rather than switching to the new alternative. This order was favourable in the eyes of the Norwich Cathedral Priory authorities, as well as in those of other manorial lords, in the context of instability and crisis in the late thirteenth and early fourteenth century. The 'dual' provisioning strategy, making use of both demesne and market grain, was an effective measure of security against various vagaries of nature that resulted in unexpected harvest failures and, consequently, fluctuating grain markets. As we have seen, in many cases crop yields varied not only across years, but also across places within the same harvest year. This meant that one of the dual channels could have failed in any given year. At the same time, however, we should not exaggerate the importance of local markets, and in particular before the Black Death. The share of crops purchased at local markets did not exceed 20 per cent of the annual receipt before the pestilence, but even when the *Gutsherrschaft* economy was no longer attractive and all the demesnes were leased out for good in 1431, the priory authorities were not yet ready to entrust the daily provisioning of their household entirely to the market. To a certain degree, this reliance on two channels distantly mirrors the modern economic concept of risk aversion through the diversification of portfolios.

The relationship between demesne, markets and lords is tied to a larger and no less meaningful topic addressed in this study: the perseverance of the *Gutsherrschaft* economy and the reasons for its decline and eventual demise in the early fifteenth century. Two not necessarily contradictory models have been offered in order to explain this phenomenon: a Ricardian-demographic model stressing the real factors and a monetary theory focusing on the behaviour of prices and real wages in the post-Black Death reality. It seems that the case of Norwich Cathedral Priory and, seemingly, other conventual lords too, fully supports the second model. In particular, the combination of relatively high crop prices and low agricultural wages in the pre-Black Death era made direct demesne management a highly attractive and desirable option, while after the pestilence, and especially from the late 1370s onwards, when the relationship between prices and real wages reversed, keeping and managing the demesnes directly became an increasingly heavy burden upon the shoulders of the lords. In both periods, the relationship between prices and wages had an immense impact on production, transportation and storage costs, the three most essential elements affecting food supply in the pre-industrial world. Thus, before the pestilence, to produce a unit of grain on the demesne was about 60 per cent cheaper than to purchase the same unit at local markets. After the Black Death production costs rose, and were especially high in the 1380s and the 1420s. During the final ten years of the *Gutsherrschaft* era, the ratio between production costs and market prices of one unit of grain rose to 1.45. It was precisely in this context that the priory authorities decided to give up direct management of their demesnes for good. The abandonment of direct cultivation and switch to leasing considerably increased the annual manorial revenue of the priory. The same can be said about transportation costs: in the pre-Black Death period, when the real wages of agricultural workers were notoriously low, it made much economic sense for the Norwich brethren to rely on the cheap labour of the manorial carters to transport portions of annual harvests to the Great Granary. Once wages rose in the 1370s, however, it became more and more costly to rely on their services; instead, it became increasingly convenient to make use of the priory's 'great boat' (*magna navis*), to ship grain, rendered as annual food farms, from the leased demesnes situated on the Yare river. Finally, farming out the demesnes meant eliminating the burden of grain storage at demesne barns, the costs of which were rising after the Black Death.

The issue of grain storage within the seigniorial context, hitherto much understudied, is closely related to the strategies and choices undertaken by the priory authorities in the context of both the *Gutsherrschaft* and *Grundherrschaft* economies. As a close study of the demesne and obedientiary accounts reveals, after the Black Death the priory authorities indeed used their storage facilities to carry over a grain surplus from year to year. This strategy can be seen as a risk-averse policy against potential harvest failures, high prices and dearth. What is striking here, however, is the fact that the priory does not seem to have used its grain storage facilities to profit from 'hungry gap' seasons or high-price years. In other words, the priory authorities and their demesne officials seem to have treated the barns and granaries as practical space from which grain could be, first and foremost, fed to the brethren, rather than sold at markets. This reveals that the Norwich brethren were, in fact, quite 'conservative' landlords, not acting in a particularly 'commercial' or entrepreneurial way.

This economic conservativism on the part of the priory should by no means be equated with 'irrationality', 'inefficiency' or 'backwardness', however. In fact, it seems to have been, in many cases, the most profitable strategy for the priory authorities. In the era of socio-economic and environmental instability in the first half of the fourteenth century it was much more rewarding, if not 'rational', to hold on to the most valuable asset the brethren possessed – their landed estates, which provided them with a cheap annual food supply – rather than moving to allegedly more 'progressive' commercial methods of household economy. But even when it was no longer profitable to rely upon direct management of the demesnes, the priory authorities could only afford to partially 'commercialise' their economy. Although the relative share of the grain deriving from sales did indeed increase, at least one half of the total supply still came from the leased demesnes in the form of annual food farms. The Black Death may have solved the problems of overpopulation and pressure on land resources, which, in turn, may have improved the performance of local grain markets and the volume of their goods, but it did not resolve the potential hazards connected to unexpected natural disasters. In other words, it would have still have been somewhat dangerous to give up the direct grain supply in favour of a complete reliance on local markets, as far as grain provisioning of the brethren is concerned.

Another crucial issue addressed in this study is the ambiguous relationship between nature and institutions. Roughly, and perhaps grossly oversimplifying, one can summarise the debate over economic growth in pre-industrial Europe as having taken place between 'institutionalists' and 'environmentalists'. To a certain degree, each camp seems to assign perhaps too much weight to what it believes to have been the primary mover of economic development. In reality, the situation was more complex. It is impossible to study the pre-industrial economy, and late medieval economic development in particular, when the two factors are divorced from each other. Rather, they seem to have clearly complemented each other. Thus, we have seen that price movement was a highly complex phenomenon tied to both institutional and environmental forces, at times acting together. The geography of crop cultivation on the priory estates was dictated equally by institutional and ecological factors. The structure of grain provisioning and its chronological dynamics were shaped by both monetary and natural forces. And, above all, the choice between the *Gutsherrschaft* and *Grundherrschaft* economies that the priory authorities had to face cannot be fully appreciated without considering both sides of the coin.

In addition to the production aspect, this study looks also upon both the consumption side of the story. Although the monastic rolls were compiled by and for the brethren, they reveal the consumption patterns of several social strata within late medieval English society. First, we have seen that the brethren, being the equivalent of aristocratic consumers, ate and drank in truly heroic quantities, although it is clear that they would not have consumed the entire plate placed before them each day. Grain products, consisting of white bread and barley ale, may have constituted about half of their daily ration outside the major fasting times, while the other half would have come from fish and meat. By contrast, very few dairy-based products were consumed by them, which, naturally, deprived them of an important source of protein and calcium. Despite the presence of a garden supervised by a permanent official, neither fruit nor vegetables were included in the monks' diet, meaning that they were also deprived of sources of many important vitamins.[1] This stood in sharp contrast with the daily menu of the paupers, fed at the priory soup kitchen, which included loaves of coarser, yet much healthier, whole rye bread and legume-based pottage. The dichotomy between the 'fat monk' and the 'slim pauper' is also supported by recent archaeological and palaeopathological findings.

Finally, the almoner's soup kitchen operated within a wider framework of late medieval charity. This phenomenon may be regarded as a primitive form of poor relief administered by the Church long before the concept of social security passed into the hands of the state. Clearly, Norwich Cathedral Priory is not to be credited with the invention of this form of charity: food and alms distribution by the Church goes back to its earliest days. It is not until our period, however, that we can relate this concept to the wider economic world. In other words, thanks to the detailed information of the almoner's accounts, we can quantify the *extent* of grain charity. Charitable works were integral to the late medieval economy, all the more so within its religious sector. Giving alms and food was by no means considered a 'loss', but rather an efficient investment in the afterlife. The interaction between religion and economy is truly a fascinating topic, whose many manifestations are yet to be thoroughly studied; food distribution among the poor is just one such aspect. Norwich Cathedral Priory was by no means the only

---

1. The fact that vegetables were deemed to be the food of poorer elements and, as such, consumed mostly by the latter, is discussed in C. Dyer, 'Gardens and garden produce in the later Middle Ages', in C.M. Woolgar, D. Serjeantson and T. Waldron (eds), *Food in medieval England: diet and nutrition* (Oxford, 2006), pp. 27–40.

Conclusion

late medieval house practising food charity – there is an abundance of excellent evidence from other monastic and ecclesiastical institutions, chiefly associated with the office of almoner and his annual accounts.[2] In addition, the wealth of material from various hospitals is waiting to be thoroughly explored by scholars. The plenitude and the degree of survival of statistical material from late medieval England is without parallel elsewhere in Europe, and its numerous archives and repositories are a true paradise (or, perhaps, a 'Klondike') for the economic historian of the pre-industrial era.

---

2. Canterbury Cathedral Archives, DCc/Almoner/1–60 (1269–1438); Westminster Abbey Cathedral, WAM 18962–19154, 31777, 31860 and 50733 (1269–1539) and Worcester Cathedral Archives, C170–212 (1341–1507). One should also mention a much thinner coverage of almoner's accounts from Ely Cathedral Priory, running, with many gaps, between 1327 and 1475 (Cambridge University Library, EDC 1/F1/1–14).

Appendix: Transportation costs, requirements and speed estimates[1]

Inland transportation costs (iTC) can be estimated once the following variables are known: (1) the share of the harvest crops dispatched to Norwich; (2) carters' wages or stipends (cW), paid both during and outside the harvest time; (3) the length of harvest periods (Lh), during which most grain must have been shipped to Norwich; (4) the approximate length of the carting period outside harvest time (which may be deduced from carters' stipends) (Lc); (5) annual fodder expenses on horses (Fe) during the carting process (whose length has been deduced from (3) and (4)); (6) costs of horse shoeing (hS); (7) costs of cart repairs (cR). Once the variables are known, the approximate transportation costs of inland carting of grain (iTC) can be established:

$$iTC = cW + Fe + hS + cR$$

The following example, taken from the 1273–4 account roll of Newton-by-Norwich, may be instructive. We know that 63 per cent of all harvest issue was sent to Norwich, while the remaining 37 per cent was stored at local barns, to be invested in seed, consumed or sold later. In that year, the total wages paid to the carters stood at 55.46 shillings (53.8 shillings during and just 1.66 shillings outside the harvest period). However, the harvest carters did not spend the entire period of their employment period carrying the grain to Norwich. Nor was the entire amount of harvested crops dispatched to the priory. Here, we may subtract about 5 per cent of the time (and hence, wages) ((53.8 / 100 x 5) = 2.69) and multiply the result by a factor of 0.37 to allow for porterage costs – that is, the costs of carting the crops from the fields to the barns. Therefore, the harvest time carting costs from the fields to Norwich stood at 52.8 shillings (53.8 – (2.69 x 0.37) = 52.8). Adding the harvest time wages to the stipend paid outside the harvest time gives an estimated cW of 52.8 + 1.66 = 54.46 shillings. In that year the harvest, and hence the carting activities during this period, lasted for 38 days.

Calculating the carting period outside harvest time is trickier. It is known that two carters, paid 10d each, were employed outside the harvest period. Allowing daily wages of 1.25–1.35d per carter and taking the average of the low and high estimates, this suggests that each carter had to cart for about 7.7 days. We may therefore assign the figure of 7.7 days as an approximate length of the carting period outside harvest time (Lh).

In the course of that year the demesne officials allocated 45 quarters of oats to 13 horses (an average of 3.46 quarters of oats per animal). No other crops are known to have been distributed among the demesne horses in that year. It should be borne in mind, however, that crop fodder resources were not distributed evenly over the year.

---

1. I am indebted to Kenneth MacKenzie of McGill University for his careful reading of this appendix and for offering a number of valuable suggestions.

Bread and Ale for the Brethren

There is a handful of references to the fact that horses consumed larger quantities of oats (and other fodder crops), during harvest time, when they were hauling heavy carts. On average, about 20 per cent of the annual crop fodder resources was consumed during harvest. Using the same figure for carting days outside the harvest period, we can estimate that, during the total 45.7 carting days, the horses would have consumed about 10.82 quarters of oat (about 9 quarters in harvest, lasting 38 days, and a further 1.82 during the course of the remaining 7.7 carting days). In order to convert this amount into its financial equivalent, we need to know the price of oats, preferably at the local level. Unfortunately, no oats were sold at Newton that year, so we have to turn to the neighbouring markets. One quarter of oats was selling for 2s 1d in Norwich and its surrounding hinterland and it is highly likely that the prices at Newton, itself located close to the town, were not much different. Hence, in 1273–4 the feeding expenses for horses (Fe) were 22.51 shillings (10.82 x 2.08).

In the demesne accounts, the costs of shoeing are either included in the section *custos carrecte*, or, in some cases, are listed under the separate heading *ferrura equorum*. In 1273–4 no horse was shod, and therefore, no costs were incurred within this sector. Various expenses connected to cart repairs (cR) are listed under the rubric *custos carrecte*. During that year, 22.92 shillings was spent on various materials and works in this sector.

Joining the variables altogether, we arrive at the following figure:

$$iTC = 54.46 + 22.54 + 0 + 22.92 = 99.9 \ (99s\ 11d,\ or,\ nearly\ £5)$$

This figure alone, however, appears meaningless if it is not considered in relation to the quantities of grain (wheat and malted barley) sent to Norwich. In that year the demesne officials sent 19 quarters of wheat and 175 quarters of malted barley to the priory. In other words, it cost around 0.51 shillings (or sixpence) to transport one quarter of grain from Newton to the priory headquarters. This is by no means a representative figure. The costs varied within demesnes depending on annual expenses and across the demesnes depending on the quantities of grain dispatched and the physical distance to Norwich.

Carting transportation capacities and requirements

The basic guideline in estimating the requirements of inland transportation is the assumption that (1) most demesne carts were pulled by three horses; (2) the maximum weight of each cartload was either 3 quarters of wheat or 4.24 quarters of malted barley. The approximate number of carts required to transport the demesne grain to Norwich, without using the same cart more than once, can be calculated using the following formula:

$$nC = [(tW / 3) + (tMB / 4.24)]$$

where nC stands for the number of cartloads, tW for total transported wheat and tMB for total transported malted barley. The approximate number of horses (nH) required to perform the transportation task, without using the same horse more than once, can be inferred from multiplying nC by 3:

Appendix

$nH = nC \times 3$

Obviously, the demesnes did not have enough carts and horses to avoid multiple trips. In other words, in most cases more than one trip using the same carts and horses was required. The actual number of carting trips (nCT) depended on (1) the total number of horses required to cart the grain supply without undertaking multiple trips (nH, calculated above); (2) the total number of demesne horses (nDH) available for carting. Thus:

$nCT = nH / nDH$

Maritime transportation capacities and requirements

Although there is no evidence that the priory authorities used the services of their boatmen in transporting the demesne grain to the Great Granary before 1391, it is instructive to estimate the maritime transportation requirements, had the priory authorities chosen to rely on this option, before that date.

Our basic assumption here is that the priory authorities would have used their great boat (*magna navis*), constructed in 1320–21. Judging from the master of the cellar accounts, this ship could carry as much as 200 quarters of malted barley on three voyages – that is, it had a carrying capacity of either 45 quarters of wheat or 66 quarters of malted barley (equal to, approximately, 18 tons). To calculate the approximate number of boat trips (nBT) required to carry the grain by water, we need to divide the amounts of dispatched wheat (tW, given in quarters) by 45 (maximum wheat capacity of the boat, in quarters) and the amounts of the shipped malt (tM, given in quarters) by 66 (maximum malted barley capacity of the boat, in quarters). Both results are to be added, thus:

$nBT = (tW / 45) + (tM / 66)$

Route lengths (in miles), inland and river, between the demesnes and the cathedral precincts in Norwich

In order to calculate the approximate difference in speed between the inland and river transportation it is necessary to establish the route lengths, both overland and maritime, between the demesnes and the cathedral precincts (Table A.1). It was impossible, however, to carry the grain supply exclusively by river: even those manors located in proximity to rivers (such as Eaton, Gateley, Newton, North Elmham, Great Plumstead and Taverham), would have required grain to be carted from their fields to the watercourse. Thus, it would be, perhaps, more accurate to speak about 'mixed routes', rather than 'river routes'. Moreover, the manors of Catton, Denham, Monks Granges and Worstead were practically inaccessible by river.

Transportation speed estimates, by carts and boats

Estimates of transportation speed are derived from the following assumptions: (1) the average speed of one horse-drawn cart would have been around 3.25 miles an hour; (2) a fully loaded cart was unlikely to have traversed more than 20 miles a day (and

Bread and Ale for the Brethren

Table A.1
Mixed and inland routes from the demesnes to the priory precincts (in miles).

Demesne	Mixed route	Inland route	Mixed route as % of inland route
Catton	n/a	3.3	n/a
Denham	n/a	31.8	n/a
Eaton	9.3	3	310.0%
Gateley	29.6	30.8	100.0%
Gnatingdon	52.2	59.5	90.0%
Hemsby	34.4	28	120.0%
Hindolveston	32	30	110.0%
Hindringham	40.1	37	110.0%
Martham	37	24.6	150.0%
Monks Granges	n/a	1.6	n/a
Newton	2.8	2.1	130.0%
North Elmham	30.1	27.1	110.0%
Plumstead, Great	6.9	8.2	80.0%
Sedgeford	51.7	58.3	90.0%
Taverham	8.7	8.7	100.0%
Thornham	52.7	60.3	90.0%
Worstead	n/a	23	n/a

Note: the 'mixed' routes were calculated with the aid of *Google Maps* application (http://maps.google.co.uk/), accessed at various points in late 2010 and early 2011.

thus, was unlikely to have actively carted for more than six hours a day); (3) the boat's speed is around 2 knots (2.30 mph), in fair, non-windy weather;[2] (4) the boat, unlike horses, did not require rest and, hence, daily trips by river were likely to have been longer than by land (I have allowed eight hours a day). Carting speed (CS) can be estimated using the following formulae:

Cart-hours required to cart the total amount of wheat per mile:

$CHw = [(tW / 3) \times (1 / 3.25)]$
(where 3 stands for the carrying capacity of wheat (in quarters) per cart, while 3.25 stands for an estimated carting speed per cart)

Cart-hours required to cart the total amount of malt per mile:

$CHmb = [(tMB / 4.24) \times (1 / 3.25)]$
(where 4.24 stands for the carrying capacity of malted barley (in quarters) per cart and 3.25 stands for an estimated carting speed per cart)

Cart-hours required to cart the total amount of all grain, door to door:

---

2. Perhaps this is a somewhat conservative estimate, compared to other data: see McGrail, *Ancient boats*, pp. 262–4.

Appendix

$CHtg = [(CHw + CHmb) \times \text{distance (in miles) from the demesnes to the priory}]$

Total number of hours to perform the door-to-door carting of the total amount of all grain:

$tHC = (CHtg / \text{number of available carts})$

Total number of days to perform the door-to-door carting of the total amount of all grain:

$tDC = (tHC / 6)$ (where 6 stands for the maximum carting hours a day per cart)

The calculations above, however, account only for the one-way trip, namely from the demesnes to the cathedral precincts. Invariably, more than one (return) trip would be required to cart the entire amount of grain to the priory. To account for the return trips, a multiplier of 2 is required. Therefore:

Total number of hours to perform the door-to-door carting of the total amount of all grain, including the return trips:

$tHC \times 2$

Total number of days to perform the door-to-door carting of the total amount of all grain, including the return trips:

$tDC \times 2$

For instance, in the 1300s Gnatingdon dispatched about two quarters of wheat and 43 quarters of malted barley. Carting the total amount of wheat and malted barley would have required approximately 3.33 cart-hours per mile (0.21 for wheat and 3.12 for malt). The distance between Gnatingdon and the cathedral precincts was 59.54 miles by road. It would take about 200 cart-hours for one horse-cart to transport the full amount from Gnatingdon to the priory, door to door. However, it is known that Gnatingdon kept, on average, between 10 and 11 horses in that decade, capable of hauling some 3.5 carts. With all horses and carts employed it would take some 114 hours to carry that amount, door to door (including the return journeys). Converting the hours into days by dividing the hours by six (the estimated daily working hours of one cart), we arrive at about 19 cart-days.

Similarly, boating speed (BS) can be estimated using the related formulae:

Boat-hours required to transport the total amount of wheat per mile:

$BHw = [(tW / 45) \times (1 / 2.3)]$
(where 45 stands for the carrying capacity of wheat (in quarters) per boat, while 2.3 stands for the estimated sailing speed per boat)

Boat-hours required to transport the total amount of malted barley per mile:

$BHmb = [(tW / 66.7) \times (1 / 2.3)]$
(where 66.7 stands for the carrying capacity of malted barley (in quarters) per boat, while 2.3 stands for the estimated sailing speed per boat)

Boat-hours required to ship the total amount of grain, door to door:

$BHtg = [(BHw + BHmb) \times distance\ (in\ mileage)\ from\ the\ demesnes\ to\ the\ priory]$

Total number of hours to perform the door-to-door shipping of the total amount of grain by boat(s):

$tHB = (BHtg / number\ of\ available\ boats)$

Total number of days to perform the door-to-door shipping of the total amount of grain by boat(s):

$tDB = (tHB / 8)$
(where 8 stands for the maximum shipping hours a day per boat)

Again, to allow for the return trips, a multiplier of 2 is required when calculating tHB and tDB.

However, as we have seen, a 'pure' boat transporting scenario would not be possible, in the majority of cases, since most demesnes were not located on riverbanks. Therefore, a mixed scenario, of carting by road and then river shipping, would have been required, were the priory officials willing to employ boats and boatmen in transporting the grain supplies. To calculate the speed of the 'mixed transportation' it is necessary to know the distance of each demesne from the closest navigable river bank and then the distance from that point to the cathedral precincts by river. Calculating the length of both the inland and river parts of the trip can easily be done with the assistance of the Google Maps application. Once the mileage of both the road and river legs is calculated, the approximate speed of the 'mixed delivery scenario' may be estimated by adding the speed of the inland leg to that of the river one. For instance, in order to ship the grain from Hindolveston to Norwich, relying on this scenario, it would be necessary first to cart it for 4.37 miles and then ship it for 27.5 miles by river. To estimate the speed of this scenario, we need to add tHC (the total amount of hours to cart the grain from the demesne to the river) to tHB (the total amount of hours to carry the grain from the embarkation point to the cathedral precincts by boat). In the case of Hindolveston, the result is 124.1 hours (tHC = 7.2 and tHB = 116.9); in other words, it would take about 124 hours to deliver the entire amount of grain, door to door, using both the carting and boating services and accounting for the return trips of each cart.

Bibliography

Manuscript sources

Demesne account rolls

The account rolls used in this study come from a much larger corpus of demesne accounts, identified, digitised and tabulated by the author for future projects. As of September 2011 the database of accounts, tentatively named *MAME* (Manorial Accounts of Medieval England), consists of over 28,000 accounts covering 2319 demesnes all over England and parts of Wales from 1208 to 1535. Because of the vast nature of the database, individual shelfmarks of each account cannot be listed here. However, many sources are referred to in the footnotes of this book, especially those for Chapter 4. Since the study focuses on a single estate, the relevant accounts of Norwich Cathedral Priory demesnes are listed below, demesne by demesne. For the most part, these accounts are deposited at the Norfolk Record Office (NRO), Norwich.

(Old) Catton: NRO, DCN 60/4/1–43.
Denham: NRO, DCN 60/7/1–7.
Eaton: NRO, DCN 60/8/1–28; Bodleian Library, Norfolk Rolls, 20–33.
Gateley: NRO, DCN 60/13/1–26a.
Gnatingdon: NRO, DCN 60/14/1–24; Lest/IC/1–41.
Hemsby: NRO, DCN 60/15/1–16.
Hindolveston: NRO, DCN 60/18/1–61.
Hindringham: NRO, DCN 60/20/1–39.
Martham: NRO, DCN 60/23/1–25; NNAS 5890 20 D1; NNAS 5892 20 D1; NNAS 6894 20 D1; NNAS 5898–5903 20 D1; NNAS 5904–5918 20 D2.
Melton: NRO, DCN 60/25/1–3.
Monks Granges: NRO, DCN 60/26/1–25.
Newton-by-Norwich: NRO, DCN 60/28/1–6.
North Elmham: NRO, DCN 60/10/1–26.
(Great) Plumstead: NRO, DCN 60/29/1–46a.
Scratby: NRO, DCN 60/30/1–12.
Sedgeford: NRO, DCN 60/33/1–30; Lest/IB/16–64.
Taverham: NRO, DCN 60/35/1–52.
Thornham: NRO, DCN 60/37/1–21.
Worstead: NRO, DCN 60/39/1–26.
Grouped accounts: NRO, DCN 62/1–2.

Extents

The 'Stowe Survey', or the '*Terrarium Prioratus*', of the priory's manors (1275–92): British Library, MS Stowe 936 (the main portion of the Stowe Survey); Add. MS 57973 (the remaining portion of the Stowe Survey).
British Library, MS Cotton Claudius C.XI (a 1251 extent of Bishop of Ely's manors).

Norwich Priory obedientiary account rolls (all at the NRO)

Almoner's account rolls: DCN 1/6/1–138.
Cellarer's account rolls: DCN 125/6; 1/2/1–102.
Chamberlain's account rolls: DCN 1/5/1–151.

Communar's and pitancer's account rolls: DCN 1/12/1–112.

Gardiner's account rolls: DCN 1/11/1–33.
Hostilar's account rolls: DCN 1/7/1–148.
Infirmar's account rolls: DCN 1/10/1–110.
Master of the cellar's account rolls: DCN 1/1/1–108.
Precentor's account rolls: DCN 1/9/1–98.
Refectorer's account rolls: DCN 1/8/1–119.
Sacrist's account rolls: DCN 1/4/1–125.
St Leonard's Cell, Thorpe: DCN 2/3.
Status obedientiatorum: DCN 1/13/1–6.

Other conventual houses' obedientiary rolls

Canterbury Cathedral Priory, granger's and bartoner's accounts: Canterbury Cathedral Archives, DCc/Granger 4–37, 70–76, 89–95, Bartoner 4–34, 52–66.
Ely Cathedral Priory, granator's accounts: Cambridge University Library, EDC 1/F/4/1–53.
Durham Cathedral Priory, granator's accounts: Granator Rolls, 1296–1402.
Glastonbury Abbey, granary account: Longleat House Muniments, MS 10643.
Hereford Cathedral, canons' bakehouse accounts: Hereford Cathedral Archives, R630–R637c.
Peterborough Cathedral Priory, granary accounts: Northamptonshire Record Office, Fitzwilliam 2389 and PDC/AR/I/9.
Westminster Abbey, granger's accounts: Westminster Abbey Muniments, WAM 19155–19217.

Norwich Cathedral registers (at the NRO)

Chamberlain's Register: DCN 40/6.
The First Register of Norwich Priory: DCN 40/1.
Sacrist's Register: DCN 40/11.

Visitations to the Priory

Visitation of 1304 by Robert, archbishop of Canterbury: DCN 42/1/5.
Visitation of 1308 by John Salmon, bishop of Norwich: DCN 92/1.
Visitation of 1319 by John Salmon, bishop of Norwich: DCN 92/2.

Private deeds and wills from Norwich

British Library, Add. MS Charter 15527 (a 1313 will from Norwich).
NRO, NCR Case 1/1–13 (City Court Rolls, enrolled deeds and wills).
NRO, PHI 249/3 577x3 (an undated will).
NRO, PRCC, Register Heydon (Norwich Consistory Court Probate Records, 1370–83).
NRO, PRCC, Register Harsyk (Norwich Consistory Court Probate Records, 1381–1408).
NRO, PRCC, Register Goldwell 7/12 (Norwich Consistory Court Probate Records, 1472–99).

Other sources

The National Archives, Kew Gardens, E 368/105 (the 1332–3 *Memoranda Roll of the Exchequer*).

Printed sources

Allen, R.C. and Weisdorf, J.L., 'The working year of English day labourer, c. 1300–1830' (University of Oxford Working Paper, 2010), available: http://graduateinstitute.ch/webdav/site/international_history_politics/users/stefano_ugolini/public/papers/Weisdorf.pdf

Aloisio, M., 'A test case for regional market integration? The grain trade between Malta and Sicily in the late Middle Ages', in L. Armstrong, I. Elbl and M.M. Elbl (eds), *Money, markets and trade in late medieval Europe: essays in honour of John H.A. Munro* (Leiden, 2007), pp. 297–309.

Atherton, I., 'The close', in I. Atherton, E.C. Fernie and C. Harper-Bill (eds), *Norwich Cathedral: church, city and diocese, 1096–1996* (London, 1996), pp. 634–64.

Ault, W.O., *Open-field farming in medieval England: a study of village by-laws* (New York, 1972).

Ayers, B., 'Archaeological evidence for trade in Norwich from the 12th to the 17th centuries', in M. Gläser (ed.), *Lübecker Kolloquium zur Stadtarchäologie im Hanseraum, II: Der Handel* (Lübeck, 1999), pp. 25–35.

Backhouse, J. *Medieval rural life in the Luttrell Psalter* (Toronto, 2000).

Bailey, B.G., Bernard, M.E., Carrier, G., Elliott, C.L., Langdon, J., Leishman, N., Mlynarz, M., Mykhed, O. and Sidders, L.C., 'Coming of age and the family in medieval England', *Journal of Family History*, 33 (2008), pp. 41–60.

Bailey, M., '*Per Impetum Maris*: natural disaster and economic decline in eastern England, 1275–1350', in B.M.S. Campbell (ed.), *Before the Black Death: studies in the 'crisis' of the early fourteenth century* (Manchester, 1991), pp. 184–208.

Barnes, G., 'Woodlands in Norfolk: a landscape history', PhD thesis (University of East Anglia, Norwich, 2003).

Bateman, V.N., 'The evolution of markets in early modern Europe, 1350–1800: a study of wheat prices', *EcHR*, 64 (2011), pp. 447–71.

Becquet, J. (ed.), *Scriptores Ordinis Grandimontensis*, Corpus Christianorum Continuatio Mediaevalis 8 (Turnhout, 1968).

Beevor, H., 'Address [to the members of the Norfolk and Norwich Naturalists' Society]: Norfolk woodlands, from the evidence of contemporary chronicles', *Transactions of the Norfolk and Norwich Naturalists' Society*, 11 (1919–20 and 1923–4), pp. 487–508.

Bekar, C.T. and Reed, C.G., 'Open fields, risk and land divisibility', *Explorations in Economic History*, 40/3 (2003), pp. 308–25.

Bellamy, J., *Crime and public order in England in the later Middle Ages* (London, 1978).

Bennett, J.M., *Ale, beer, and brewsters in England: women's work in a changing world, 1300–1600* (Oxford, 1996).

Biddick, K., *The other economy: pastoral husbandry on a medieval estate* (Berkeley, CA, 1989).

Bischoff, B. (ed.), *Ratherii Veronensis Praeloquiorum Libri VI*, Corpus Christianorum Continuatio Mediaevalis 41A (Turnhout, 1984).

B. Flacci Albini seu Alcuini Opera, Patrologia Latina 101.

Blanchard, I.S.W., 'Economic change in Derbyshire in the late Middle Ages', PhD thesis (London School of Economics, 1967).

Brady, N.D.K., 'The sacred barn: barn-building in southern England, 1100–1550: a study of grain storage technology and its cultural context', PhD thesis (Cornell University, 1996).

Brenner, R., 'Agrarian class structure and economic development in pre-industrial Europe', *P&P*, 70 (1976), pp. 30–74, reprinted in T.H. Aston and C.H.E. Philpin (eds), *The Brenner debate: agrarian class structure and economic development in pre-industrial Europe* (Cambridge, 1985), pp. 10–63.

Bridbury, A.R., 'The Black Death', *EcHR*, 26 (1973), pp. 557–92.

Briggs, C., *Credit and village society in fourteenth-century England* (Oxford, 2009).

Briggs, D.E., Stevens, R., Young, T.W. and Hough, J.S., *Malting and brewing science: malt and sweet wort*, 2nd edn (Bury St Edmunds, 1981).

Britnell, R.H., *Britain and Ireland, 1050–1530: economy and society* (Oxford, 2004).
—, 'Avantagium Mercatoris: a custom in medieval English trade', *Nottingham Medieval Studies*, 24 (1980), pp. 37–50.
—, 'The marketing of grain in England, 1250–1350', available: http://www.dur.ac.uk/r.h.britnell/articles/Grainframe.htm (last accessed May 2011).
—, 'Town life', in R. Horrox and M. Ormrod (eds), *A social history of England, 1200–1500* (Cambridge, 2006).
—, and Campbell, B.M.S. (eds), *A commercializing economy: England 1086 to c.1300* (Manchester, 1995).
Broadberry, S., Campbell, B., Klein, A., Overton, M. and van Leeuwen, B., 'British economic growth, 1270–1870' (working paper, 2010), available: http://www2.warwick.ac.uk/fac/soc/economics/staff/academic/broadberry/wp/britishgdplongrun8a.pdf (accessed 11 October 2011).
Brown, J., 'The malting industry', in G.E. Mingay (ed.), *The agrarian history of England and Wales, vol. VI 1750–1850* (Cambridge, 1989), pp. 501–19.
Campbell, B.M.S., *English seigniorial agriculture 1250–1450* (Cambridge, 2000).
—, 'The agrarian problem in the early fourteenth century', *P&P*, 188 (2005), pp. 3–70.
—, 'Agricultural progress in medieval England: some evidence from eastern Norfolk', *EcHR*, 36 (1983), pp. 26–46.
—, 'Agriculture in Kent in the High Middle Ages', in S. Sweetinburgh (ed.), *Later medieval Kent 1220–1540* (Woodbridge, 2010), pp. 25–53.
—, 'Arable productivity in medieval England: some evidence from Norfolk', *JEH*, 43 (1983), pp. 379–404.
—, 'Commercial dairy production on medieval English demesnes: the case of Norfolk', *Anthropozoologica*, 16 (1992), pp. 107–18.
—, 'Four famines and a pestilence: harvest, price, and wage variations in England, 13th to 19th centuries', in B. Liljewall, I.A. Flygare, U. Lange, L. Ljunggren and J. Söderberg (eds), *Agrarhistoria på många sätt; 28 studier om manniskan och jorden. Festskrift till Janken Myrdal på hans 60-årsdag* (Stockholm, 2009), pp. 23–56.
—, 'Matching supply to demand: crop production and disposal by English demesnes in the century of the Black Death', *JEH*, 57/4 (1997), pp. 827–58.
—, 'Nature as historical protagonist: environment and society in pre-industrial England' (the 2008 Tawney Memorial Lecture), *EcHR*, 63/2 (2010), pp. 281–314.
—, 'Population pressure, inheritance and the land market in a fourteenth century peasant community', in R.M. Smith (ed.), *Land, kinship and life-cycle* (Cambridge, 1984), pp. 87–134.
—, 'A unique estate and a unique source: the Winchester Pipe Rolls in perspective', in R.H. Britnell (ed.), *The Winchester Pipe Rolls and medieval English society* (Woodbridge, 2003), pp. 21–43.
—, and Bartley, K., *England on the eve of the Black Death: an atlas of lay lordship and wealth, 1300–1349* (Manchester, 2006).
—, Galloway, J.A., Keene, D. and Murphy, M., *A medieval capital and its grain supply: agrarian production and distribution in the London region, c.1300* (London, 1993).
Chadd, D. (ed.), *The ordinal of the abbey of the Holy Trinity, Fécamp (Fécamp, Musée de la Bénédictine, MS 186)*, Henry Bradshaw Society 111–12 (London, 1996–2002).
Childs, W.R. (ed. and tr.), *Vita Edwardi Secundi* (Oxford, 2005).
Claridge, J. and Langdon, J., 'Storage in medieval England: the evidence from purveyance accounts', *EcHR*, forthcoming (the early view version is available at http://www.blackwellpublishing.com/journal.asp?ref=0013-0117).
Clark, G., 'The long march of history: farm wages, population, and economic growth, England, 1209–1869', *EcHR*, 60/1 (2007), pp. 97–135.
—, 'Markets and economic growth: the grain market of medieval England' (University of California, Davis, working paper, 2001), available: http://www.econ.ucdavis.edu/faculty/gclark/210a/readings/market99.pdf.
Clay, R.M., *The hermits and anchorites of England* (London, 1914).

Colledge, E. and Walsh, J. (eds), *A book of showings to the anchoress Julian of Norwich* (Toronto, 1978).

Connor, R.D. (ed.), *Weights and measures of England* (London, 1987).

Coulton, G.G., *Five centuries of religion*, vol. III (Cambridge, 1936).

Cullum, P.H., '"And hir name was Charite": charitable giving by and for women in late medieval Yorkshire', in P.J.P. Goldberg (ed.), *Women in medieval English society* (Stroud, 1997), pp. 182–221.

Darby, H.C., *The Domesday geography of eastern England* (Cambridge, 1971).

—, 'Domesday woodland in East Anglia', *Antiquity*, 8 (1934), pp. 211–15.

Davril, A. and Thibodeau, T.M. (eds), *Guillelmi Duranti Rationale Divinorum Officiorum V–VI*, Corpus Christianorum Continuatio Mediaevalis 140A (Turnhout, 1998).

Devine, M. (ed.), *The cartulary of Cirencester Abbey, Gloucestershire*, vol. III (Oxford, 1977).

DeWindt, A.R. and DeWindt, E.B., *Ramsey: the lives of an English fenland town, 1200–1600* (Washington, 2006).

Dijkman, J., *Shaping medieval markets: the organization of commodity markets in Holland, c.1200–c.1450* (Leiden, 2011).

Dobson, B., 'The monks of Canterbury in the later Middle Ages, 1220–1540', in P. Collinson, N. Ramsay and M. Sparks (eds), *A History of Canterbury Cathedral* (Oxford, 1995), pp. 69–153.

Dobson, R.B., *Durham Priory, 1400–1450* (Cambridge, 1973).

Dodds, B., *Peasants and production in the medieval north-east: the evidence from tithes, 1270–1536* (Woodbridge, 2007).

Dodwell, B., 'The free peasantry of East Anglia in Domesday', *Norfolk Archaeology*, 27 (1941), pp. 145–57.

—, 'The monastic community', in I. Atherton, E.C. Fernie and C. Harper-Bill (eds), *Norwich Cathedral: church, city and diocese, 1096–1996* (London, 1996), pp. 231–54.

—, 'William Bauchun and his connection with the Cathedral Priory at Norwich', *Norfolk Archaeology*, 36 (1975), pp. 113–16.

— (ed.), *The charters of Norwich Cathedral Priory*, vol. 2 (London, 1985).

Domínguez Reboiras, F. and Soria Flores, A. (eds), *Raimundi Lulli Opera Latina. Summa Sermonum in Civitate Maioricensi Annis MCCCXII–MCCCXIII Composita*, Corpus Christianorum Continuatio Mediaevalis 76 (Turnhout, 1987).

Douteil, H. (ed.), *Johannis Beleth Summa de Ecclesiasticis Officiis*, Corpus Christianorum Continuatio Mediaevalis 41A (Turnhout, 1976).

DuBoulay, F.R.H., *The lordship of Canterbury: an essay on medieval society* (London, 1966).

—, 'Who were farming the English demesnes at the end of the Middle Ages?', *EHR*, 17/3 (1965), pp. 443–55.

Dugdale, W., *Monasticon Anglicanum*, vol. II (London, 1846).

Dunn, P., 'Trade', in C. Rawcliffe and R. Wilson (eds), *Medieval Norwich* (London, 2004), pp. 213–34.

Dyer, A., 'Appendix. Ranking lists of English medieval towns', in D.M. Palliser (ed.), *The Cambridge urban history of Britain*, vol. 1 (Cambridge, 2000), pp. 754–5.

Dyer, C., *Lords and peasants in a changing society* (Cambridge, 1980).

—, *Standards of living in the later Middle Ages: social change in England, c.1200–1520* (Cambridge, 1989).

—, 'Changes in diet in the late Middle Ages: the case of harvest workers', *AHR*, 36 (1988), pp. 21–37.

—, 'Gardens and garden produce in the later Middle Ages', in C.M. Woolgar, D. Serjeantson and T. Waldron (eds), *Food in Medieval England: diet and nutrition* (Oxford, 2006), pp. 27–40.

Dymond, D.P., *The Norfolk landscape* (London, 1985).

Eccles, M. (ed.), *The macro plays*, Early English Text Society (Oxford, 1969).

Ecclestone, M., 'Dairy production on the Glastonbury Abbey demesnes, 1258–1334', MA thesis (University of Bristol, 1996).

Eisner, M., 'Long-term historical trends in violent crime', *Crime and Justice: A Review of Research*, 30 (2003), pp. 83–242.

Elton, H., *Warfare in Roman Europe, AD 350–425* (Oxford, 1996).

Farmer, D.L., 'The *Famuli* in the later Middle Ages', in R.H. Britnell and J. Hatcher (eds), *Progress and problems in medieval England: essays in honour of Edwards Miller* (Cambridge, 1996), pp. 207–36.

—, 'Marketing the produce of the countryside, 1200–1500', in E. Miller (ed.) *The Agrarian History of England and Wales, vol. III 1348–1500* (Cambridge, 1991), pp. 324–430.

—, 'Millstones for medieval manors', *AHR*, 40 (1992), pp. 97–111.

—, 'Prices and wages', in H.E. Hallam (ed.), *The Agrarian History of England and Wales, vol. II 1042–1350* (Cambridge, 1988), pp. 716–817.

Fenoaltea, S., 'Risk, transactions costs, and the organization of medieval agriculture', *Explorations in Economic History*, 13 (1976), pp. 129–51.

Ferrie, E. and Whittingham, A.B. (eds), *Communar rolls of Norwich Cathedral Priory*, Norfolk Record Society 41 (Norwich, 1974).

Food Standards Agency, *McCance and Widdowson's the composition of foods*, 6th edn (Cambridge, 2002).

Fowler, G.H. (ed.), *A digest of the charters preserved in the cartulary of the Priory of Dunstable*, Bedfordshire Historical Record Society 10 (Bedford, 1926).

Fowler, J.T. (ed.), *The Coucher book of Selby*, vol. II, The Yorkshire Archaeological and Topographical Association, Record Series 13 (Huddersfield, 1893).

—, *Extracts from the account rolls of the Abbey of Durham from the original mss* (Durham, 1898–1901).

Frank, R.W., 'The "Hungry Gap", crop failure, and famine: the fourteenth-century agricultural crisis and *Piers Plowman*', *The Yearbook of Langland Studies* 4 (1990), pp. 87–104.

Galloway, J.A. (ed.), *Trade, urban hinterlands and market integration c.1300–1600*, Centre for Metropolitan History, Working Papers Series, No. 3 (London, 2000).

Geltner, G., *Medieval prisons: a social history* (Princeton, NJ, 2008).

Gibson, A.J.S., 'The size and weight of cattle and sheep in early modern Scotland', *AHR*, 36 (1988), pp. 162–71.

Gilchrist, R., *Norwich Cathedral close: the evolution of the English cathedral landscape* (Woodbridge, 2005).

— and Oliva, M., *Religious women in medieval East Anglia* (Norwich, 1993).

Goodburn, D.M., 'Reused medieval ship planks from Westminster, England, possibly derived from a vessel built in the cog style', *International Journal of Nautical Archaeology*, 26/1 (1997), pp. 26–38.

Gottfried, R.S., 'Population, plague and the sweating sickness: demographic movements in late-fifteenth century England', *Journal of British Studies*, 17/1 (1977), pp. 12–37.

Grantham, G., 'What's space got to do with it? Distance and agricultural productivity before the Railway Age' (McGill University Working Paper, 2010), available: http://ideas.repec.org/p/mcl/mclwop/2010-04.html.

Grasden, A. (ed.), *The customary of the Benedictine abbey of Eynsham in Oxfordshire*, Corpus Consuetudinum Monasticarum, vol. II (Siegburg, 1963).

Greatrex, J., 'St. Swithun's Priory in the later Middle Ages', in J. Crook (ed.), *Winchester Cathedral: nine hundred years* (Chichester, 1993), pp. 139–66.

— (ed.), *Account rolls of the obedientiaries of Peterborough* (Northampton, 1984).

Grigg, D., *The dynamics of agricultural change: the historical experience* (London, 1982).

Gurr, T.R., 'Historical trends in violent crime: a critical review of the evidence', *Crime and Justice: An Annual Review of Research*, 3 (1981), pp. 295–353.

Hagen, W.W., 'How mighty the junkers? Peasant rents and seigniorial profits in sixteenth-century Brandenburg', *P&P*, 108 (1985), pp. 80–116.

Hale, W.H. (ed.), *The Domesday of St Paul's of the Year MCCXII*, Camden Society Old Series 69 (London, 1858).

— (ed.), *Registrum Prioratus Beate Marie Wigorniensis* (London, 1865).

Hallam, H.E., 'The climate of eastern England, 1250–1350', *AHR*, 32 (1984), pp. 124–32.

—, 'The life of the people', in H.E. Hallam (ed.), *The agrarian history of England and Wales, vol. II 1042–1350* (Cambridge, 1988), pp. 815–57.

Hallinger, K. (ed.), *Adalhard, Statuta antiqua abbatiae Sancti Petri Corbeiensis*, Corpus Consuetudinum Monasticarum, vol. I (Sieburg, 1963).

Hamilton, S.G. (ed.), *Compotus rolls of Priory of Worcester* (Oxford, 1910).

Hammond, P.W., *Food and feast in medieval England* (Stroud, 1993).

Hanawalt, B.A., *Crime and conflict in English communities, 1300–1348* (Cambridge, MA, 1979).

—, 'Economic influences on the pattern of crime in England, 1300–1348', *American Journal of Legal History*, 18/4 (1974), pp. 281–97.

—, 'The peasant family and crime in fourteenth-century England', *Journal of British Studies*, 13 (1974), pp. 1–18.

— (ed.), *Crime in East Anglia in the fourteenth century: Norfolk gaol delivery rolls, 1307–1316*, Norfolk Record Society 44 (Norwich, 1976).

Hanslik, R. (ed.), *Benedicti Regula, Editio Altera Emendata*, Corpus Scriptorum Ecclesiasticorum Latinorum 75 (Vienna, 1977).

Hare, J., 'The bishop and prior: demesne agriculture in medieval Hampshire', *AHR*, 54/1 (2006), pp. 187–212.

Harper-Bill, C. and Mortimer, R. (eds), *Stoke-by-Clare cartulary, BL Cotton Appx. XXI*, vol. I (Woodbridge, 1982).

Hart, W.H. (ed.), *Cartularium Monasterii de Rameseia*, Rolls Series 79, vol. 3 (London, 1893).

Harvey, B., *Living and dying in England, 1100–1540: the monastic experience* (Oxford, 1993).

—, *The obedientiaries of Westminster Abbey and their financial records, c.1275–1540* (Woodbridge, 2002).

—, *Westminster Abbey and its estates in the Middle Ages* (Oxford, 1977).

— and Oeppen, J., 'Patterns of morbidity in late medieval England: a sample from Westminster Abbey', *EcHR*, 54/2 (2001), pp. 215–39.

Harvey, P.D.A., 'The English inflation of 1180–1220', *P&P*, 61 (1973), pp. 3–30.

Hatcher, J., 'Mortality in the fifteenth century: some new evidence', *EcHR*, 39 (1986), pp. 19–38.

—, Piper, A.J. and Stone, D., 'Monastic mortality: Durham Priory, 1395–1529', *EcHR*, 59/4 (2006), pp. 667–87.

Haverfield, H., 'Romano-British remains [in Norfolk]', in H.A. Doubleday (ed.), *A history of Norfolk*, vol. 1, The Victoria County History of England (London, 1901), pp. 279–324.

Heale, M. (ed. and tr.), *Monasticism in late medieval England* (Manchester, 2009).

Heath, P., 'Urban piety in the later Middle Ages: the evidence of Hull wills', in B. Dobson (ed.), *Church, politics and patronage* (Gloucester, 1984), pp. 209–34.

Heller, I. (ed.), *Willelmi Chronica Andrensis*, Monumenta Germaniae Historica Scriptores, vol. XXIV (Hanover, 1879).

Hieronymus, S., *Brew like a monk: trappist, abbey and strong Belgian ales and how to brew them* (Boulder, CO, 2005).

Hockey, S.F. (ed.), *Account book of Beaulieu Abbey*, Camden Fourth Series 16 (London, 1975).

Hollingworth, T.H., *Historical demography* (London, 1969).

Hudson, W., 'The camera roll of the Prior of Norwich in 1283, compiled by Bartholomew de Cotton', *Norfolk Archaeology*, 19 (1917), pp. 268–313.

Hybel, N., 'The grain trade in Northern Europe before 1350', *EcHR*, 55 (2002), pp. 219–47.

Jessopp, A. (ed.), *Visitations of the diocese of Norwich, 1492–1532*, Royal Historical Society, Camden 2nd Series 43 (London, 1888).

Jordan, W.C., *The great famine: northern Europe in the early fourteenth century* (Princeton, NJ, 1996).

Jordan, W.K., *The charities of London* (London, 1960).

—, *Philanthropy in England, 1480–1660* (London, 1959).

Kaplan, S.L., *Provisioning Paris: merchants and millers in the grain and flour trade during the eighteenth century* (Ithaca, NY, 1984).

Keene, D. (ed.), *Survey of medieval Winchester*, 2 vols (Oxford, 1985).

Keil, I.J.E., 'Estates of Glastonbury Abbey in the later Middle Ages', PhD thesis (University of Bristol, 1964).

Kershaw, I.M., *Bolton Priory: the economy of a northern monastery, 1286–1325* (Oxford, 1973).

—, 'The great famine and agrarian crisis in England, 1315–1322', *P&P*, 59 (1973), pp. 3–50.

— and Smith, D.M. (eds), *The Bolton Priory compotus, 1286–1325*, Yorkshire Archaeological Society 154 (1999–2000) (Woodbridge, 2000).

King, A., 'The merchant class and borough finances in late medieval Norwich', DPhil thesis (University of Oxford, 1989).

Kitsikopoulos, H., 'Manorial estates as business firms: the relevance of economic rent in determining crop choices in London's hinterland, c.1300', *AHR*, 56 (2008), pp. 142–66.

—, 'Urban demand and agrarian productivity in pre-plague England: reassessing the relevancy of Von Thunen's Model', *Agricultural History*, 77/3 (2003), pp. 482–522.

Komlos, J. and Landes, R., 'Anachronistic economics: grain storage in medieval England', *EcHR*, 44 (1991), pp. 36–45.

Landers, J., *The field and the forge: population, production, and power in the pre-industrial west* (Oxford, 2003).

Langdon, J., *Horses, oxen and technological innovation: the use of draught animals in English farming from 1066 to 1500* (Cambridge, 1986).

—, *Mills in the medieval economy: England, 1300–1540* (Oxford, 2004).

—, 'The economics of horses and oxen in medieval England', *AHR*, 30 (1982), pp. 31–40.

—, 'Lordship and peasant consumerism in the milling industry of early fourteenth-century England', *P&P*, 145 (1994), pp. 3–46.

—, 'Water-mills and windmills in the West Midlands, 1086–1500', *EcHR*, 44 (1991), pp. 424–44.

Latimer, P., 'The English inflation of 1180–1220 reconsidered', *P&P*, 171 (2011), pp. 3–29.

Levy, R.E., 'The cartulary of Little Dunmowe Priory', MA dissertation (University of Virginia, 1971).

Liger, L., *Le nouvelle maison rustique* (Paris, 1755).

Löfstedt, B. (ed.), *Beati Liebanensis et Eterii Oxomensis Adversus Elipandum Libri Duo*, Corpus Christianorum Continuatio Mediaevalis 59 (Turnhout, 1984).

Lomas, R.A., 'The Priory of Durham and its demesnes in the fourteenth and fifteenth centuries', *EHR*, 31/3 (1978), pp. 339–53.

Lyons, P.A. (ed.), *Two compoti of the Lancashire and Cheshire manors of Henry de Lacy, Earl of Lincoln*, Chetham Society 122 (Manchester, 1884).

McCloskey, D., 'English open fields as behavior towards risk', *Research in Economic History*, 1 (1976), pp. 124–71.

—, 'The persistence of English common fields', in W.N. Parker and E.L. Jones (eds), *European peasants and their markets: essays in agrarian economic history* (Princeton, NJ, 1975), pp. 93–120.

McGrail, S., *Ancient boats in north-west Europe: the archaeology of water transport to AD 1500* (London, 1987).

McIntosh, M.K., 'Local responses to the poor in late medieval and Tudor England', *Continuity and Change*, 3 (1988), pp. 209–45.

McRee, B.R., 'Charity and gild solidarity in late medieval England', *Journal of British Studies*, 32 (1993), pp. 195–225.

Masschaele, J., 'Transport costs in medieval England', *EcHR*, 46 (1993), pp. 266–79.

Mate, M., 'High prices in early fourteenth century England: causes and consequences', *EcHR*, 28 (1975), pp. 1–16.

Migdley, L.M. (ed.), *Ministers' accounts of the earldom of Cornwall*, vol. I (London, 1942).

Miller, E., *The abbey and bishopric of Ely: the social history of an ecclesiastical estate from the tenth century to the early fourteenth century* (Cambridge, 1951).

— and Hatcher, J., *Medieval England: towns, commerce and crafts, 1086–1348* (London, 1995).

Morenzoni, F. (ed.), *Thomas de Chobham, Summa de Arte Praedicandi*, Corpus Christianorum Continuatio Mediaevalis 82 (Turnhout, 1988).

Morimoto, N., *The sheep farming of Norwich Cathedral Priory in the 13th and 14th centuries*, Discussion Paper No. 2, Institute of Industrial Sciences, Nagoya Gakuin University (Seto City, 1977).

Munro, J.H.A., 'Before and after the Black Death: money, prices and wages in fourteenth-century England', in T. Dahlerup and P. Ingesman (eds), *New approaches to the history of late medieval and early modern Europe: selected proceedings of two international conferences at the Royal Danish Academy of Sciences and Letters in Copenhagen in 1997 and 1999*, Historisk-filosofiske Meddelelser, no. 104 (Copenhagen, 2009), pp. 335–64.

—, 'The coinages and monetary policies of Henry VIII (r. 1509–1547): contrasts between defensive and aggressive debasements', University of Toronto Working Paper no. 417 (MUNRO: no. 40), November 2010.

—, 'From *Gutsherrschaft* to *Grundherrschaft*: demographic, monetary and political-fiscal factors', in M. Bailey and S. Rigby (eds), *Town and countryside in the age of the Black Death: essays in honour of John Hatcher* (Turnhout, 2011).

—, 'Industrial energy from water-mills in the European economy, 5th to 18th centuries: the limitations of power', in S. Cavaciocchi (ed.), *Economia ed energia, seccoli XIII–XVIII, Atti delle 'Settimane di Studi' e altrie Convegni, Istituto Internazionale di Storia Economica, 'Francesco Datini da Prato'* (Florence, 2003), pp. 223–69.

—, 'The "new institutional economics" and the changing fortunes of fairs in medieval and early modern Europe: the textile trades, warfare and transaction costs', *Vierteljahrschrift für Sozial- und Wirtschaftgeschichte*, 88/1 (2001), pp. 1–47.

—, 'Wage stickiness, monetary changes, and real incomes in late medieval England and the Low Countries, 1300–1500: did money matter?' *Research in Economic History*, 21 (2002), pp. 185–287.

Muskett, J.J. and White, C.H.E., 'Church goods in Suffolk', *East Anglian*, New Series, 1 (1885–6), pp. 24–7.

Nelson, M., *The barbarian's beverage: a history of beer in ancient Europe* (London, 2005).

Nelson, M., 'On a beautiful girl and some good barley beer', *Études Celtiques*, 35 (2003), pp. 257–9.

Newfield, T.P., 'A cattle panzootic in early fourteenth-century Europe', *AHR*, 57 (2009), pp. 155–90.

Nicholas, D., 'Commercial credit and central place function in thirteenth-century Ypres', in L. Armstrong, I. Elbl and M.M. Elbl (eds), *Money, markets and trade in late medieval Europe: essays in honour of John H.A. Munro* (Leiden, 2007), pp. 310–48.

Nightingale, P., 'The growth of London in the medieval economy', in R.H. Britnell and J. Hatcher (eds), *Progress and problems in medieval England* (Cambridge, 1996), pp. 89–106.

—, 'Norwich, London, and the regional integration of Norfolk's economy in the first half of the fourteenth century', in J.A. Galloway (ed.), *Trade, urban hinterlands and market integration c.1300–1600*, Centre for Metropolitan History, Working Papers Series, No. 3 (London, 2000), pp. 83–101.

—, 'Some new evidence of crises and trends of mortality in late medieval England', *P&P*, 187/1 (2005), pp. 33–68.

Noble, C., 'Aspects of life at Norwich Cathedral Priory in the late medieval period', PhD thesis (University of East Anglia, 2001).

— (ed.), *Farming and gardening in late medieval Norfolk*, Norfolk Record Society 61 (Norwich, 1997).

Oakley, A., 'Rochester Priory, 1185–1540', in N. Yates and P.A. Welsby (eds), *Faith and fabric: a history of Rochester Cathedral, 604–1994* (Woodbridge, 1996), pp. 29–55.

Ogilvie, S., *Institutions and European trade: merchant guilds, 1000–1800* (Cambridge, 2011).

Oliva, M., *The convent and the community in late medieval England* (Woodbridge, 1998).

Oschinsky, D. (ed.), *Walter of Henley and other treatises on estate management and accounting* (Oxford, 1971).

Owen, A. (ed.), *Walter of Bibbesworth, Le Traité de Walter de Bibbesworth sur la langue francaise*

(Paris, 1929).

Palliser, D. (ed.), *The Cambridge urban history of Britain*, vol. I (Cambridge, 2000).

Patrick, P., 'An archaeology of overindulgence', *Archaeological Review from Cambridge*, 20/2 (2005), pp. 98–117.

—, 'Creaking in the cloisters: observations on prevalence and distribution of osteoarthritis in monks from medieval London', in G. Helmig, B. Scholkmann and M. Untermann (eds), *Centre, region, periphery: medieval Europe, Basel 2002* (Basel, 2002), pp. 89–93.

—, '"Greed, gluttony and intemperance"? Testing the stereotype of the "obese medieval monk"', PhD thesis (University College London, 2005).

Prestwich, M., 'Edward I's monetary policies and their consequences', *EcHR*, 22 (1969), pp. 406–16.

—, 'Victualling estimates for English garrisons in Scotland during the early fourteenth century', *English Historical Review*, 82 (1967), pp. 536–43.

Pribyl, K. and Pfister, C., 'The beginning of the grain harvest in Norfolk as a proxy for mean April–July temperatures, c.1270 AD–1430 AD', *Geophysical Research Abstracts*, 11 (2009), p. 784.

Postan, M.M., *The famulus: the estate labourer in the XIIth and XIIIth centuries* (Cambridge, 1954).

Pugh, R.B., *Imprisonment in medieval England* (Cambridge, 1968).

Raftis, J.A., *The estates of Ramsey Abbey: a study in economic growth and organization* (Toronto, 1957).

—, 'The structure of commutation in a fourteenth-century village', in T.A. Sandquist and M.R. Powicke (eds), *Essays in medieval history presented to Bertie Wilkinson* (Toronto, 1969), pp. 282–300.

Ratcliff, S.C., Collins, A.J. and Schofield, B. (eds), *Legal and manorial formularies in memory of J.P. Gilson* (Oxford, 1933).

Rees, U. (ed.), *The cartulary of Shrewsbury Abbey* (Aberystwyth, 1975).

Rigg, A.G., '"Descriptio Northfolchie": a critical edition', in A. Bihrer and E. Stein (eds), *Nova de Veteribus: Mittel- und neulateinische Studien für Paul G. Schmidt* (Munich and Leipzig, 2004), pp. 577–94.

Riley, H.T. (ed.), *Gesta Abbatum Monasterii Sancti Albani*, Rolls Series 28/4 (London, 1867).

— (ed.), *Johannis de Trokelowe Monachi Annales*, Rolls Series 28C (London, 1866).

Rogers, J., 'The palaeopathology of joint disease', in M. Cox and S. Mays (eds), *Human osteology and archaeology and forensic science* (London, 2000), pp. 163–82.

— and Waldron, T., 'DISH and the monastic way of life', *International Journal of Osteoarchaeology*, 11 (2001), pp. 357–65.

Rose, M., 'The vault bosses', in I. Atherton, E.C. Fernie and C. Harper-Bill (eds), *Norwich Cathedral: church, city and diocese, 1096–1996* (London, 1996), pp. 363–78.

Rosenthal, J.T., *The purchase of paradise: gift giving and the aristocracy, 1307–1485* (London, 1972).

Rothwell, W. (ed.), *Walter de Bibbesworth: Le Tretiz*, Anglo-Norman Text Society Plain Texts Series 6 (London, 1990).

Royce, D. (ed.), *Landboc sive Registrum de Winchelcumba* (Exeter, 1892).

Rutledge, E., 'Economic life', in C. Rawcliffe and R. Wilson (eds), *Medieval Norwich* (London, 2004), pp. 157–88.

—, 'Immigration and population growth in early fourteenth-century Norwich: evidence from the tithing roll', *Urban History Yearbook 1988* (Cambridge, 1988), pp. 15–30.

Ryder, M.L., 'The animal remains found at Kirkstall Abbey', *AHR*, 7 (1959), pp. 1–5.

—, 'The animal remains from Petergate, York, 1957–1958', *Yorkshire Archaeological Journal*, 42/4 (1971), pp. 418–28.

—, 'Livestock remains from four medieval sites in Yorkshire', *AHR*, 9 (1961), pp. 105–10.

Rye, W. (ed.), *A short calendar of the deeds relating to Norwich enrolled in the court rolls of the city, 1285–1306* (Norwich, 1903).

Salter, H.E., *Eynsham cartulary*, vol. I (Oxford, 1907).

— (ed.), *Cartulary of Oseney Abbey*, vol. I (Oxford, 1929).

Saunders, H.W., *An introduction to the rolls of Norwich Cathedral Priory* (Norwich, 1930).

— (ed.), *The first register of Norwich Cathedral Priory*, Norfolk Record Society 11 (Norwich, 1939).

Schmidt, A.V.C. (ed.), *William Langland, Piers Plowman* (Oxford, 1992).

Searle, E. (ed.), *The cellarers' rolls of Battle Abbey, 1275–1513*, Sussex Record Society 65 (Lewes, 1967).

Slavin, P., 'Between death and survival: Norfolk cattle, c.1280–1370', *Fons Luminis*, 1 (2008), pp. 53–7.

—, 'Feeding the brethren: grain provisioning of Norwich Cathedral Priory, c.1280–1370', PhD thesis (University of Toronto, 2008).

—, 'The fifth rider of the apocalypse: the great cattle plague in England and Wales and its economic consequences, 1319–1350', in S. Cavaciocchi (ed.), *Le interazioni fra economia e ambiente biologico nell'Europa preindustriale, secc. XIII–XVIII. Proceedings of the 41st Study-Week of the Fondazione Istituto Internazionale di Storia Economica 'F. Datini'* (Firenze, 2010), pp. 165–79.

—, 'Food security, safety, and crises', in K. Albala (ed.), *A cultural history of food: vol. 3: the Renaissance 1300–1600* (London, 2011), pp. 63–82.

—, 'The great bovine pestilence and its economic and environmental consequences in England and Wales, 1318–50', *EcHR*, forthcoming (the early view is available at http://onlinelibrary.wiley.com/journal/10.1111/(ISSN)1468-0289/earlyview).

Smil, V., *Energy in world history* (Boulder, CO, 1994).

Smith, R.A.L., *Canterbury Cathedral Priory* (Cambridge, 1943).

Smith, R.M., 'Human resources', in G. Astill and A. Grant (eds), *The countryside of medieval England* (Oxford, 1992), pp. 188–212.

Soria Flores, A., Domínguez Reboiras, F. and Senellart, M. (eds), *Raimundi Lulli Opera Latina. Summa Sermonum in Civitate Maioricensi Anno MCCCXIII Composita*, Corpus Christianorum Continuatio Mediaevalis 80 (Turnhout, 1991).

Spector, T.D., 'The fat on the joint: osteoarthritis and obesity', *Journal of Rheumatology*, 17 (1990), pp. 357–65.

Spufford, P., *Money and its use in medieval Europe* (Cambridge, 1988).

The statutes of the realm: printed by command of His Majesty King George the Third, in pursuance of an address of the House of Commons of Great Britain, 11 vols (London, 1810–1828).

Stone, D., 'The consumption of field crops in late medieval England', in C.M. Woolgar, D. Serjeantson and T. Waldron (eds), *Food in medieval England: diet and nutrition* (Oxford, 2006).

Stouff, F., *Ravitaillement et alimentation en Provence aux XIVe et XVe siècles* (Paris, 1970).

Swanson, R.N., 'A universal levy: tithes and economic agency', in B. Dodds and R.H. Britnell (eds), *Agriculture and rural society after the Black Death: common themes and regional variances* (Hatfield, 2008), pp. 104–12.

Tanner, N.P., *The church in late medieval Norwich* (Toronto, 1984).

Thompson, E.M. (ed.), *Customary of the Benedictine monasteries of Saint Augustine, Canterbury and Saint Peter, Westminster*, Henry Bradshaw Society 23 (London, 1902).

Thomson, J.A.F., 'Piety and charity in late medieval London', *Journal of Ecclesiastical History*, 16 (1965), pp. 178–95.

Thrupp, S.L., *The merchant class of medieval London, 1300–1500* (Ann Arbor, MI, 1962).

Thünen, J.H., von, *Der isolierte Staat in Beziehung auf Landwirtschaft und Nationalökonomie* (Berlin, 1910).

—, tr. Carla M. Wartenberg, *Isolated state: an English edition of Der isolierte Staat* (Oxford, 1966).

Timson, R.T. (ed.), *The cartulary of Blyth Priory* (London, 1973).

Trivellato, F., *The familiarity of strangers: the Sephardic diaspora, Livorno and cross-cultural trade in the early modern period* (New Haven, CT, 2009).

Unger, R.W., *Beer in the Middle Ages and the Renaissance* (Philadelphia, PA, 2004).

—, 'Thresholds for market integration in the Low Countries and England in the fifteenth century', in L. Armstrong, I. Elbl and M.M. Elbl (eds), *Money, markets and trade in late medieval Europe: essays in honour of John H.A. Munro* (Leiden, 2007), pp. 349–81.

Virgoe, R., 'The estates of Norwich Cathedral Priory', in I. Atherton, E.C. Fernie and C. Harper-Bill (eds), *Norwich Cathedral: church, city and diocese, 1096–1996* (London, 1996), pp. 339–59.

Waldron, T., 'DISH at Merton Priory: evidence for a "new" occupational disease?' *British Medical Journal*, 291 (1985), pp. 1762–3.

Warren, A.K., *Anchorites and their patrons in medieval England* (Berkeley, CA, 1985).

Watson, N. and Jenkins, J. (eds), *The writings of Julian of Norwich* (University Park, PA, 2006).

Wheeler, A., 'Fish bone', in H. Clarke and A. Carter (eds), *Excavations in King's Lynn, 1963–1970*, Society for Medieval Archaeology monograph series vii (London, 1977), pp. 403–8.

— and Jones, A., 'Fish remains', in A. Rogerson (ed.), *Excavations on Fuller's Hill, Great Yarmouth*, East Anglian Archaeology 2 (Norwich, 1976), pp. 208–26.

Whittingham, A.B., 'The development of the close since the Reformation', in G.A. Metters (ed.), *The parliamentary survey of dean and chapter properties in and around Norwich in 1649*, Norfolk Record Society 51 (Norwich, 1985), pp. 102–20.

—, 'The monastic buildings of Norwich Cathedral', *Archaeology Journal*, 106 (1949), pp. 86–7.

Online databases

Campbell, B.M.S, Three centuries of English crops yields, 1211–1491, http://www.cropyields.ac.uk.

Letters, S. Gazetteer of markets and fairs in England and Wales, http://www.history.ac.uk/cmh/gaz/gazweb2.html.

Munro, J.H.A., John Munro's database of coinage output in England (http://www.economics.utoronto.ca/munro5/MoneyCoinage.htm).

—, John Munro's revised tabulations of David Farmer's series of English 'national' agrarian wages, http://www.economics.utoronto.ca/munro5/ResearchData.html.

—, John Munro's revisions of the Phelps Brown and Hopkins 'basket of consumables' commodity price series and craftsmen's wage series, 1264–1700, http://www.economics.utoronto.ca/munro5/ResearchData.html.

Soilscapes: soils dataset covering England and Wales, Cranfield University-based project, http://www.landis.org.uk/soilscapes/.

Index

Abingdon Abbey (Berkshire) 10
accounts, manorial (demesne) 23, 54, 69, 73, 82–5, 94, 99, 112, 120–4, 126, 128, 130, 132, 136
accounts, monastic (obedientiary) 12, 14, 18, 26, 37–8, 134, 141–4, 146, 150–1, 153–4, 156–8, 161, 164, 167, 169, 171, 174, 177–80, 183, 189–91
accounts, purveyance 119, 125, 146
accounts, sheriffs' 112, 118
Adalhard of Corbie 153, 160
AGCR (Annual Gross Crop Receipt)
    disposal of, on Norwich Priory demesnes 69–75, 77
    disposal of, on other estates 75–7
    farms, share of 69
    harvest, share of 69
    purchases, share of 69
    tithes, share of 69
Alcuin of York 183
ale
    for brethren 159–60
    brewing patters 163
    brewing rates 164–7
    calorific value of 164–5
    consumption patterns 163–9
    distribution among the poor 181–2
    grains for 161–2
    kinds of 159–62
    for lay residents of Norwich Priory 160–1
    names of 160–1
arable
    composition of
        on Canterbury Cathedral estates 53–4
        in Norfolk 53–7
        on Norwich Priory demesnes 50–3
        in other regions 54–7
    contraction of 51–4
    production levels 67
    relative shift to pastoralism 53
    see also barley, beans, crops, dredge, grains, legumes, oats, peas, *pulmentum*, rye, wheat, yields
Assize of Bread and Ale (*c*.1256) 148
autarky, seigniorial 1–7, 188–9
avantagium mercatoris 26, 73

bakers
    manorial 92
    at Norwich Priory
        assistants of 144–5
        employments terms 143–5
        families of 143
        masters 144
        numbers 143
        also serving as millers 141
        wages of 103, 144–5
    in towns 3
    see also bakery, bread, brewers, *famuli*
bakery 11, 126, 141–6, 150, 152, 154, 159, 175
Baltic 4
barley
    baked into bread 56
    barns for 120
    cultivation 53–7
    disposal 70–4
    fields, leased 81–3
    malting 72
    prices of 40–1
    as principal drinking grain 72
    rent payment in 132–4
    share of 54–5, 57–8
    as specialism of Norfolk agriculture 53–7
    spring grown (commonly) 56
    stored 131, 137–8
    straw-to-grain ratio 125
    tithes payment in 21, 69, 71, 179
    winter grown (uncommonly) 56
    yields 24
    see also ale, crop farms, malt
barns (manorial)
    for each individual crop 120
    for hay 120
    layout of 120–2
    maintenance costs of 122–6
    size of 121–2
    stone 121
    storage capacity 122
    thefts from 177
    tithe 120
    wooden 121
    works of 122
    see also granary, storage
beans
    carryovers of 64
    as fodder crop 138, 158
    see also fodder, legumes
Beatus of Liébana 183
Beaulieu Abbey (Hampshire) 148–51, 153–4, 160, 164
Bedfordshire 56
beef consumption 170, see also meat consumption
Beeston (Norfolk) 31
Bircham (Norfolk) 65
Bishop of Norwich
    de jure head of Norwich Cathedral Priory 10
    influence in Norfolk 33

Black Death of 1348–51
  and decline of demesne economy 6, 23, 37, 53
  and demographic decline 46
  and monastic population in England 9
  and Norwich Cathedral Priory population xv–i, 2, 7–9, 12
Blofield (Norfolk) 31
boatmen
  employment terms of 103–5
  at Norwich Priory 103–5
  wages 103
boats
  archaeology of 87–8
  carrying capacities 88, 111, 195
  kinds of 84–5
  maintenance costs 111
  manorial 85
  of Norwich Priory 84
  numbers of 84
  size of 88
  speed of 195–8
  see also, boatmen, Great Boat (*Magna Navis*), transportation
Bolton Priory (North Riding, Yorkshire) 14, 21, 31–2, 38–9, 74–5, 77, 149, 164, 168–9
Boston (Lincolnshire) 4
bread
  baked for horses 153, 155, 157–9
  baking patterns 145–7
  consumption by poor masses 179–83
  consumption by Priory cooks 157–8
  consumption by Priory guests 152, 156–7
  made of rye, for poor 180
  monastic, various names of 147–8, 150–1, 153–4
  panis militum 153–6
  panis monachorum 150–3
  panis ponderis minoris 147–50
  see also bakers, bakery
brewers
  manorial 92
  at Norwich Priory
    assistants of 144–5
    employment terms of 143–5
    families of 143
    masters 144
    numbers of 143
    also serving as millers 141
    wages of 103, 144–5
  in towns 3
  see also ale, bakery, bread, brewers, brewing, *famuli*
brewery 11, 72, 126, 140–5, 163, 165
brewing, in Norwich Priory 159–69
  in other conventual houses 167–9
  process, late-medieval 162

see also ale, brewers, brewery
Bristol 1
Britnell, Richard H. 1–2, 26, 45, 73
Broads, the (Norfolk) 84, 87
Bromholm (Norfolk) 27
Bury St Edmunds Abbey (Suffolk) 10, 48, 53, 74–5, 77, 97, 101

calorific requirements estimates
  for demesne horses 86
  for hermits 174
  for late-medieval monks 15, 172
  for late-medieval Provencal nobles 15
  for Norwich brethren 15, 169–72
  for Norwich paupers 181–3
  for Norwich Priory horses 18–9
  for Norwich Priory population 18
  for Westminster brethren 15, 171
  see also ale, bread, food consumption, horses
Cambridgeshire 40–1, 44–5, 48, 54–6, 75, 83
Campbell, Bruce M.S. 3–5, 15, 18, 39, 43, 56, 60, 63, 72, 101, 112, 158, 163
Canterbury Cathedral Priory
  ale consumption at 161, 167
  alms distribution at 191
  bread consumption at 147–8, 151, 153–4, 167–9
  demesne economy of 5, 48, 52–5, 74–5, 77, 100–1
  grain supply of 21–3
  population 10, 12, 167–9
capons 75
carryovers, stored at barns and granaries 22, 69, 120, 129, 132–6, 138–9
carters
  manorial
    assistants 94
    customary 88–92
    employment terms 94–6
    fed *en route* to Norwich 113, 155
    hired, among harvest workers 92–103
    masters 94
    numbers 98–9
    socio-economic status 88–92
    wages 94–7
  at Norwich Priory
    assistants 103
    assisting manorial carters 94
    employment terms 103–5
    master 103
    wages 103
  on other estates 100
  see also cartloads, carts, carting, cartloads, *famuli*
carting
  capacities 105–6

Index

costs and savings 109–112
customary dues 88–92
equipment 87, 98–9, 107, 109, 111–12
seasonality 98, 102–3
speed 116–17, 196–8
strategies 105–115
cartloads 105–6, 109, 194
carts 84, 91–2, 98–9, 105–7, 109, 111–12, 116–17, 194–5, 197
cattle pestilence (Great Bovine Pestilence of 1319-20) 51, 85
Catton, Old (Norfolk) 51, 55, 59, 63, 65, 72, 195–6
Celtic Fringe 6
chaff 75, 158
charity, as Christian virtue 173, 175, 183–7
Chronica Andrensis of William of Andres 161
Clark, Gregory 119–20, 130
cod, consumption of 170
commercialisation xv, 1–4, 66, 72–3, 77, 83, 119, *see also* trade in grain, urbanisation
conservativism, economic of late-medieval religious lords xv–i, 9, 23, 83, 188–9
conventual houses
  estates of 75, 77, 81
  food and drink consumption at 148–51, 154, 160–1, 167–9
  grain supply of 4–5, 21, 23, 25, 33
  conservativism of xv–i, 4, 188
  population 14, 33
cooks
  manorial 92
  at Norwich Priory
    as privileged workers 157–8
    numbers 150
    wages 103–4
  in towns 3
  see also famuli
Corbie Abbey, France (Picardy) 153, 160
cornmongers xv, 3–4
corrodians, corrodies 10, 154, 159, 173–4
cows 53
credit
  carting 84
  grain xv, 2–4
crime in Norfolk 177–8
crops
  acreage 48–57
  consumption on the demesne 102
  disposal of 69–77
  gifts of 22, 69, 71, 75, 163
  farms of (food rents) 5,7, 19, 21–3, 26–9, 35, 37, 49, 51, 69, 75, 79, 81–3, 88, 105, 116, 118, 139, 189
  fed to animals 61, 73, 85–7, 109, 113, 118, 138, 158– 9, 193–4
  harvests of 21–2, 24–5, 36, 39, 42–4, 66, 69, 71, 74–7, 79, 83–4, 88, 92–102, 105,
    109, 111, 120, 124–5, 130, 133, 136, 138–9, 188
  prices of xv, 3,6, 7, 18, 20, 22, 35, 37, 38, 39–47, 51, 56–7, 61, 73, 76–7, 79, 81, 83, 87, 91–2, 98, 109, 118–20, 125, 130, 133–4, 136, 139, 148, 150, 181, 188–90, 194
  production costs of 6, 76–81, 83, 188
  purchase of 15–47, 69, 73, 75, 79, 111, 118
  sale of 15–47, 65–7, 69, 71–4, 77, 119, 128, 132, 134–6, 138, 189
  seeding 24, 51, 53, 55–7, 59–60, 62–3, 71–72, 74, 77, 132, 136, 138, 179
  specialisation 57–69
  storage xv–i, 4, 37, 79, 119–141, 188–9
  tithes 19, 21, 30–1, 69, 71, 75–6, 179
  trade in, *see* purchase and sale of
  transportation of xv, 3, 45, 60–1, 65–6, 72, 79, 105–18, 124–5, 138, 141, 188–9, 193–8
  yields 24, 39, 42–3, 47, 71, 79, 133, 136, 149, 158, 164–6, 167, 170, 188
  see also ale, barley, beans, bread, dredge, fodder, food, malt, maslin, rye, oats, peas, *pulmentum*, wheat
Crowland Abbey (Cambridgeshire) 74–5, 77
Cumberland 54
Customary
  of Norwich Priory 149, 179
  of other monastic houses 148–9, 160, 165

dairy products xvi, 88, 170–2, 190
debasement 39, 44, *see also* crops, prices, wages
deflation 39, 43, 98, 109, 134, *see also* crops, prices, wages
demesne
  acreage 48–57
  contraction of 51–4
  expansion of 50–1
  famuli 73, 79, 84–5, 87–8, 92–104, 107, 109, 112, 115–16, 118, 124, 132, 138
  farmers 5, 7, 21, 26, 29–33, 37, 75, 81–2, 88, 111, 116, 125
  leasing of 5, 7, 21–2, 32, 35, 51, 53–4, 69, 81–3, 85, 88, 105, 111
  see also Grundherrschaft, Gutsherrschaft, manorialism
Denham (Suffolk) 48, 51, 60, 63–6, 89, 97, 102, 117, 133, 195
Derbyshire 55
Descriptio Northfolchie 57
Dissolution of the Monasteries xv–i, 7, 10, 14, 19, 127–8, 130, 139
diversified portfolio, concept of 24–5, 188
dredge (barley–oat mixture) 54, 62, 138, 161–2
Dunningsworth (Suffolk) 56

213

Dunstable Priory (Bedfordshire) 160, 164
Durham (county) 54
Durham Cathedral Priory (Durham)
    ale consumption at 161
    alms distribution at 181, 191
    bread consumption at 147, 153, 158
    demesne economy 53, 101
    grain supply 5, 21, 23
    population 10
Dyer, Christopher 15, 121, 190

Earsham (Norfolk) 55
Eaton (Norfolk) 43, 51, 55, 57, 59–60, 63–6, 84–5, 89–92, 97, 100, 107, 112–17, 134, 143, 195–6
eel, consumption of 170
eggs
    consumption 170–1
    demesne production 90
Ely, Bishop of 48, 107
Ely Cathedral Priory
    ale consumption at 161, 168–9
    alms distribution at 191
    bread consumption at 147, 153, 158, 168–9
    demesne economy 32
    grain supply 21, 23
    population 10, 167
Enford (Wiltshire) 56
Evesham Abbey (Worcestershire) 148, 180
Eynsham Abbey (Oxfordshire) 151, 160

famuli
    manorial 73, 79, 84–5, 87–8, 92–104, 107, 109, 112, 115–16, 118, 124, 132, 138
    of Norwich Priory 11–12, 15, 145–6, 150, 152, 156–7, 160, 187
Farmer, David 94, 97, 100
Fécamp Abbey, France (Normandy) 148–9
felons, at Norwich Castle
    age of 178–9
    bread distribution among 175, 177
    clerics among 176
    conditions 178–9
    gender of 177–8
    and Great Famine 177–8
    numbers of 177–8
    sentences 176
fish, consumption xvi, 169–72, 190
flour 136, 140, 146, 149–51, 154, 157, 174, *see also grutum*, mills, *simula*
fodder
    calories 86
    components 19, 61, 86–7
    consumed by horses 18–19, 85–6, 106, 113, 118, 138, 194
    costs of 108–9, 193–4
    crops 64, 73, 86–7, 138, 158–9, 194, *see also* grass, hay, legumes, oats, straw
food charity
    commanded by Norwich citizens in their wills 184–7
    among hermits 173–5
    among Norwich paupers 179–83
    at other conventual houses 180–1
    among prisoners in Norwich Castle 175–9
    see also charity, food distribution, soup kitchen, paupers, wills
food consumption patterns
    by Norwich Priory brethren 169–72
    by Westminster Abbey brethren 172
forum frumenti (wheat market in Norwich) 27, 29
France, wars with 3, 39, 42, 44, 112
fruits and vegetables
    consumption by hermits 174
    consumption by peasants 190
    cultivation of 61
    non-consumption by Norwich brethren xvi, 170, 190
fuel 11, 61, 88, 91–2, 104, 142–3

Gateley (Norfolk) 30, 51, 55, 59–60, 63–6, 71, 89, 94, 97, 102, 117, 133, 143, 195–6
geese, consumption of 170
Gerard Iterius 183
Germany 4, 45
Gidingheythe (Norfolk) 91–2
Gilbert de Clare, Earl of Gloucester 49
Glastonbury Abbey
    ale consumption at 161–2, 168
    bread consumption at 148, 168
    demesne economy 49, 74–5, 77, 100–1, 118
    grain supply of 21, 23, 77
    population 10
Gloucester 1
Gluttony, sin of 169
Gnatingdon (Norfolk) 51, 57, 59–60, 65, 72, 82, 89, 97, 102, 107, 117, 120, 196
grain, *see* crops
Granary
    almoner's 126, 130, 179–81
    Great 104–5, 115, 126–30, 135–40, 142, 179, 189, 195
grass 18–9, 65, 85–7, 90
Great Boat (*Magna Navis*) 87–8, 111, 115–16, 189, 195
Great European Famine of 1315–22 xiv, 4, 39, 46, 79, 178, 186
Great Hospital of Norwich 31, 33
Great Yarmouth (Norfolk) 27, 51, 65, 73, 88, 105
Grundherrschaft
    decline of 6
    definition of 6
    in early-modern Eastern Germany 6
    as economic strategy 188–9

Index

rise of 6, 7, 22–3, 30, 37, 51, 54, 69, 71, 75, 77, 79, 81, 83, 88, 98, 111, 139, 188
see also, demesne, *Gutsherrschaft*, manorialism
grutum (second-rate flour) 149
Guillaume Durand 183
Gutsherrschaft
  decline of 7, 22–3, 30, 37, 51, 54, 69, 71, 75, 77, 79, 81, 83, 88, 98, 111, 139, 188
  definition of 6
  in early-modern Eastern Germany 6
  as economic strategy 188–9
  rise of 6–7
  see also, demesne, *Grundherrschaft*, manorialism
Guy Beauchamps, Earl of Warwick 49

Hanseatic League 46
harvest
  carting 92–103
  disposal of 69–77
  famuli 100–3
  length of 93–6
  storage of 122–6, 136–9
  see also AGCR, yields
Harvey, Barbara 15, 169, 172
hay 19, 61, 85–6, 90, 92, 113, 120, 158–9, see also fodder, grass, horses, straw
Hemsby (Norfolk) 28, 51, 59, 65–6, 72, 81–2, 88, 102, 105, 107, 109, 111, 116–17, 133, 196
Henry de Lacy, Earl of Lincoln 55
hens
  consumption of 170
  on demesnes 75, 90–1
Herbert de Losinga 165, 180, 181–3
Hereford Cathedral
  ale consumption of 161–2, 168–9
  bread consumption of 148, 168–9
  grain supply of 21, 23, 38
  population of 39, 169
hermits in Norwich
  decline of 173–4
  food consumption patterns 174
  grain distribution among 174–5
  numbers of 173
herring, consumption of 170
Heythe (Norfolk) 49, 59
Highclere (Hampshire) 56
Hindolveston (Norfolk) 51, 59–60, 63–6, 82, 89, 91–2, 97, 100, 107, 117, 121, 143, 196
Hindringham (Norfolk) 30–1, 39, 43, 51, 59, 65, 82, 89–92, 97, 100, 107, 117, 121–2, 133, 135, 196
hinterland 4, 27–8, 45–6, 49, 51, 60–1, 63–5, 69, 194, see also Von Thünen
hoarding of crops 130–6
Holywell (Oxfordshire) 96

honey, consumption of 170
horses
  calorific requirements 18, 86
  carting with 85–7, 98–9, 102, 105–9
  fodder consumption patterns of 85–7
  manorial 85–7, 105–9
  medieval, size 86
  numbers 18, 86
  ploughing with 77, 84–5, 115
  for riding 18
  see also carters, carting, cartload, carts, fodder
Horsford (Norfolk) 31
Hoxne (Suffolk) 27–8, 31, 33
Hull (East Riding, Yorkshire) 4, 186
Huntingdonshire 48, 56, 107

institutions, economic significance of 26, 32–3, 44, 63, 83, 189
Isabella de Fortibus 55

Jean Beleth 183
John Brend, merchant 29–30
John Gladman 46
John of Trokelowe 178
Julian of Norwich 173–4
Julian of Sedgeford 159

Kempstone (Norfolk) 28
Kent 48, 55, 75
King's Lynn (Norfolk) 27, 65, 73

labour
  customary 88–92, 97–8, 100, 104, 116, 118, 124
  hired 12, 84, 88, 92–105, 112, 116, 118, 120–1, 138, 143–4, 157
  payment in cash 96–100
  payment in credit 98
  payment in kind 97–8
Lancashire 2, 54–5
Langdon, John 85, 119, 124, 143, 146
legumes
  baked into bread 154
  baked into pottage 180, 190
  barns for 120, 138
  carryovers of 64
  consumed by poor xvi, 154, 180, 190
  cultivation 54–5, 60–2, 63–4
  disposal 66, 69, 71, 73
  as fodder crops 18, 85, 87, 138, 158
  marketed 3, 66, 73, 88
  prices of 40–1
  share of 59–60, 62
  see also beans, fodder, peas, pottage, *pulmentum*
Lincolnshire 2, 54, 56, 83

ling (fish) consumption of 170
livestock
    husbandry 50–3, 61–2, 64, 85, 105
    prices 7
    see also pastoralism
London xv, 1, 3, 15, 18, 38, 45, 60–1, 172, 186
Low Countries 45–6
lumber, used for construction 88, 121
Luttrell Psalter 99

malt
    barn for 120, 131
    brewing capacities 163–5, 168
    carryovers of 135–6
    conversion from barley 71–2
    extraction rates 72
    increment of 163
    kinds 161
    marketed 56–7, 134, 136
    mill for 140
    prices of 40–1, 40–5
    purchased 30–1, 34–7
    production in Norfolk 48, 56
    quality 56, 161
    sent to Norwich 84, 88, 90–2, 105, 107, 109, 111–12, 116, 138
    stored 120, 126, 131, 135
    supplied by the demesnes 35, 62, 66, 70, 72, 84, 88
    supplied by farmers 37, 82
    transportation costs 112–13
    weight and volume 72
Mankind, Norfolk play 158
manorialism
    decline of 7, 22–3, 30, 37, 51, 54, 69, 71, 75, 77, 79, 81, 83, 88, 98, 111, 139, 188
    definition of 6
    as economic strategy 188–9
    in early-modern Eastern Germany 6
    rise of 6–7
    see also, demesne, *Gutsherrschaft*, *Grundherrschaft*
market integration 2, 44–6
markets for grain
    in England 2
    extent of 26–9
    formal 2
    informal 3
    network of 3, 5, 73
    in Norfolk 2
    in Norwich 27, 29
    numbers of 2, 26–9
    prices at 39–44
    transaction frequency and seasonality 36–9
    see also cornmongers, *forum frumenti*, merchants, trade in grain

Martham (Norfolk) 39, 43, 51, 59–60, 63, 65–6, 81–2, 88–92, 94, 97, 100, 105, 111, 116–17, 124, 133, 196
maslin (wheat–rye mixture) xvi, 30, 34–5, 40–1, 54, 56, 60, 62, 72–3, 82, 120, 131, 136, 147, 154
meat, consumption at Norwich Priory 170–2
meat, consumption at Westminster Abbey 172, see also beef consumption, mutton consumption
Meaux Abbey (East Riding, Yorkshire) 9
merchants, grain
    in London xv, 3–4
    networks of 31
    of Norfolk 29–31
    of Norwich 29–31
    reputation of 29–36
    social status of 29–31
    trust in and between 32–4
    see also cornmongers, markets for grain, trade in grain
Merton College, Oxford
    estates 75, 96, 101
    grain supply of 74–5, 77
millers
    employment terms 141
    numbers of 141
    replaced by bakers and brewers 141
    wages of 141–2
    see also *famuli*
mills
    manorial
        farms of 140
        maintenance costs 141–2
        numbers of 140
        types of 140
    within the Cathedral precincts
        location of 140–1
        maintenance costs 141–2
        numbers of 140
        types of 140
minting 42–4, see also debasement, deflation, prices
Monks Granges (Norfolk) 49, 51, 59–60, 63, 65, 81, 89, 94, 97, 117, 121, 124, 133, 136, 195–6
mortality, monastic 7–9
Munro, John H.A. 6–7
mutton, consumption of 170, see also meat consumption

Nature, as historical protagonist 24, 44, 63, 83, 94, 188
Newcastle 45
Newton-by-Norwich (Norfolk) 57, 59–60, 63, 65, 81–2, 84, 89, 97, 102, 107, 111, 115, 117, 120, 193–6

Index

Norfolk
    agriculture 54–6
    altitude 65
    as a barley county 54–7
    commercialisation 2, 56
    customs and traditions 57
    dairy farming in 47
    ecology of 57
    free peasantry of 100
    geology of 57
    landlords 5, 48–9, 53,
    malt production in 47, 56–7
    markets 2, 26
    population density 46, 56
    population growth 46
    rivers 65
    soil types 64–5
North Elmham (Norfolk) 30–1, 51, 59–60, 63, 66, 69, 71–2, 81–2, 89, 98–9, 107, 111, 113–15, 117, 133, 195–6
Northampton 1
Norwich
    grain trade 3, 21–2, 26
    hermits in 173–5
    hinterland 4, 27–8, 45–6, 49, 51, 60–1, 63–5, 69, 194
    paupers in 179–83
    population of 1, 180
Norwich Castle 175–9, *see also* felons
Norwich Cathedral Priory
    bakery 11, 126, 141–6, 150, 152, 154, 159, 175
    Black Death in xv–i, 2, 7–9, 12
    brethren xv–i, 6–15, 18–9, 21–3, 25–6, 32–3, 51, 53, 60, 66, 69, 71, 72, 81–3, 85, 102, 109, 111–12, 116, 118–19, 126, 136, 138–9, 141, 147, 156, 158, 160, 164–5, 167, 170–2, 175, 179–81, 186–7, 189–90
    brewery 11, 72, 126, 140–5, 163, 165
    canal 14, 141
    dietary requirements of 169–72
    famuli 11–12, 15, 145–6, 150, 152, 156–7, 160, 187
    food consumption patterns at 167–72
    grain requirements of 15–1
    Great Granary 104–5, 115, 126–30, 135–40, 142, 179, 189, 195
    guest-hall 11, 92, 150, 157, 159, 179
    guests 11–12, 84, 113, 140, 152, 156–7, 160, 164–5, 183
    horses 18
    labourers 11–12, 14, 103–4, 152–3, 155–7, 160, 162, 164–5
    landed estates 48–57
    meadows around 19
    mills 140–2

oats
    barns for 120, 181
    brewed into ale, at other houses 161–2
    carryovers of 131
    cultivation 54–5, 63–4
    disposal of 73
    distributed among poor 185
    food farms, paid in 82
    geography of 66, 69
    growth tolerance 64–5
    as horse fodder 18–19, 73, 85–7, 106–7, 109, 112–15, 158–9, 193–4
    marketed 73
    prices of 40–1, 61
    purchased 30–1, 34–7
    sent to Norwich Priory 71
    share of 54–5, 60, 62, 66
    stored 137–8, 181
    straw-to-grain ratio of 125
    volume of 61
    yields 24
obedientiaries
    almoner xvi, 11, 31, 126, 130, 140, 142, 150–1, 179–81, 183, 186–7, 190–1
    cellarer 11, 19, 31, 103, 104, 140–4, 153, 158, 165, 169–70, 174
    chamberlain 11, 140–1
    communar 8, 11–12
    gardener 11
    infirmerer 11
    master of the cellar 8, 11–12, 14, 26, 31, 37–8, 84–5, 88, 103–4, 105, 128–30, 142–4, 146, 158, 163, 179, 195
    pitancer 11–12
        precentor 11
        refectorer 11
        sacrist 11–12, 31, 126, 142–4, 159, 165
    population of 8–14
    precinct 12, 14, 16–19, 28, 72, 88, 124, 127–8, 130, 140–1, 145, 152, 155–7, 164, 169, 195–8
    Registrum Primum of 8
    revenue of 48, 78–9, 81
    soup kitchen xvi, 179–83, 190
    stables 18–19, 84, 126, 141, 159
Oseney Abbey (Oxfordshire) 160
oxen
    fed with crops 73
    meat of, consumption 170
    perished in Great Bovine Pestilence 85
    replaced with horses 53
    see also Great Bovine Pestilence
Oxfordshire 56, 75, 96, 151, 160

pastoralism
    before Black Death 51–3
    relative shift to after Black Death 53

pasturage 61, 64, 82, 86–7, see also fodder, hay, horses, straw
peas
　baked into bread 154
　baked into pottage 180, 190
　barns for 120, 138
　carryovers of 64, 131
　consumed by poor xvi, 154, 180, 190
　cultivation 54–5, 60–2, 63–4
　disposal 66, 69, 71, 73
　as fodder crops 18, 85, 87, 138, 158
　marketed 3, 66, 73, 88
　prices of 40–1
　share of 59–60, 62
　stored 137–8
　straw-to-grain ratio 125
　yields 24
　see also fodder, legumes, pottage
Peterborough Abbey (Cambridgeshire)
　ale consumption at 148, 153, 167–8
　alms distribution at 181
　Black Death at 9
　bread consumption at 161, 167–8
　estates of 48, 74, 75
　grain supply of 5, 21, 23, 77
　population of 9–10
pigs 75, see also pork
plough-drivers, ploughmen 94, 102
ploughing 77, 84–5, 90, 94, 102
Plumstead, Great (Norfolk) 24, 30–1, 43, 51, 59–60, 81–2, 84, 89, 94, 97, 102–3, 105, 111, 115–17, 133, 143, 195–6
Poland 4
poor relief
　under Elizabeth I 187
　late-medieval 184–6, 190–1
　in Norwich 184
　by Norwich Cathedral Priory 173–87, 190–1
pork, consumption of 170, see also meat consumption
Postwick (Norfolk) 31, 143
prices
　crops xv–i, 2–3, 6–7, 18, 20, 22, 35, 37–47, 51, 57, 79, 81, 83, 87, 91–2, 94, 96, 98–100, 118–20, 130, 133–4, 136, 139, 150, 181, 188–9, 194,
　livestock 7
Prior's Barton (Hampshire) 56
pulmentum (oat–legume mixture) 87, 138

rabbits, consumption of 170
Ramon Llull 183
Ramsey (Huntingdonshire) 1
Ramsey Abbey (Huntingdonshire)
　bread consumption at 153
　estates of 5, 74, 75, 77, 101
　grain supply of 21, 48, 74

Rather of Verona 183
Reinheitsgebot (German Beer Purity Law) 162
Rhys ap Rhys ap Mereduk, Welsh war prisoner, kept in Norwich Castle prison 178
Ricardian demographic model 6, 42, 188
risk aversion xv, 4, 24–5, 32–3, 119, 130, 139, 188–9
roach, consumption of 170
Rule of St Benedict 179
Rutland 56, 75
rye
　baked into bread xvi, 154, 168, 180–2, 190
　barns for 120, 138
　carryovers of 64, 131
　consumed by poor xvi, 154, 180–2, 190
　cultivation 54–5, 57, 60–2, 63–4
　disposal 66, 69, 71, 73
　fed to animals 73, 87
　food farms, paid in 82
　geography of 66, 69
　growth tolerance 64–5
　marketed 72–3, 88
　prices of 40–1
　purchased 34
　sent to Norwich Priory 71
　share of 54, 57, 59–60, 62
　stored 131, 136
　straw-to-grain ratio 125
　yields 24
　see also bread

salmon, consumption of 170
Scotland, war with 3, 112, 163, 169
Sedgeford (Norfolk) 7, 43, 57, 59–60, 73, 81, 85, 89, 92, 96–8, 102, 107, 113, 117, 121–2, 133, 159, 196
servants, see famuli
sheep 73, 87, 186, see also livestock, mutton
shipping
　advantages over carting 115–16
　costs 195–8
　speed 116–17, 195–8
　by various boats 84–5, 88, 111, 195
　see also boats
Shropshire 55
Sicily 4, 45
simula (first-rate flour) 149
soup kitchen, at Norwich Priory xvi, 179–83, 190
sprats, consumption of 170
St Augustine's Abbey, Canterbury 148, 160
St Benet at Holm, Abbey of (Norfolk) 5, 55
St Paul's Cathedral, London
　ale consumption at 162, 164
　bread consumption at 168
　grain supply of 5, 21
　population 167
Stoke-by-Clare Priory (Norfolk) 153

Index

storage
   costs
      late-medieval 122–6, 128–30,
        in 2010 (in UK) 125
   depletion rates 136–9
   mechanisms 136–9
   scholarly debate about 119–20
   see also barns, Great Granary, hoarding of crops
straw 19, 61, 85–7, 125, 158–9, *see also* fodder, hay, horses
sturgeon, consumption of 170
Suffolk 27–8, 30, 33, 48, 51, 54–6, 75, 83, 153, 178
Sussex 75

Tasburgh (Norfolk) 31
Taverham (Norfolk) 24, 39, 51, 59–60, 63–6, 81, 83–85, 89, 97, 102, 105, 107, 111, 115–17, 120–1, 133, 143, 195–6
Templar Knights 49
Thomas Brewe, merchant of Norwich 30, 32
Thomas of Chobham 184
Thornham (Norfolk) 51, 59–60, 64–5, 81, 89, 102, 133, 196
threshers, threshing
   manorial 76, 90, 97,
   at Norwich Priory 123–5, 128–9, 140
Thünen, Johann-Heinrich von 60–1, 66, 69, 83
towns
   conventual houses in 4–6
   economic decline after Black Death
   grain requirements 3
   grain trade 3–4, 15–47
   hinterland 4, 27–8, 45–6, 49, 51, 60–1, 63–5, 69, 194
   markets, proliferation of 2
   population growth 1–2, 180
trade in grain 3–4, 15–47, 65–7, 69, 71–4, 77, 119, 128, 132, 134–6, 138, 189
transportation
   costs and savings 109–112, 195–8
   inland (with carts) 105–12, 116–7
   speed 116–17, 196–8
   strategy 105–15
   by water (with boats) 115–17, 196–8
   see also boatmen, boats, carters, carts, shipping
Trowse (Norfolk) 140, 143
Tuddenham (Norfolk) 31

urbanisation 1–4, *see also* London, Norwich, towns, trade in grain

wage-earners 91
wages
   manorial *famuli* of 20, 22, 76, 94, 96–7, 103, 107–9, 124, 193
   Norwich Priory *famuli* of 103–5, 128, 130, 141–5
   real
      and Great Famine 3
      low-to-medium before 1376 3, 79, 83,
      high after 1376 xv, 18, 22, 59–60, 87, 98, 118, 128, 139, 188–9
   stickiness 6
Wales 6, 9, 55
Walter of Bibbesworth 162
Walter of Henley 115
Welsh Marches 6
Wensum River (Norfolk) 115, 141
West Walton (Norfolk) 56
Westley (Suffolk) 56
Westminster Abbey (Middlesex)
   ale consumption 161, 167–9
   alms distribution 174, 191
   Black Death in 9
   bread consumption 147–9, 153–4, 167–9
   estates of 48, 53, 74, 75, 101
   famuli of 12, 101
   food consumption 15, 170–2
   grain supply of xv, 5, 21, 23, 77
   monastic obesity, evidence on 15, 170–2
   population of 9–10, 12, 14
   see also Harvey, Barbara
Westonzoyland (Somerset) 56
Weybourne Hall (Norfolk) 27
wheat
   baked into bread xvi, 3, 56, 145–59, 168–9, 174–5, 177, 179–82, 185
   barns for 120
   brewed into ale 161–2
   carryovers of 64, 131
   cultivation 54–5, 57, 60–2, 63–4
   disposal 66, 69–73
   fed to animals 73, 87
   food farms, paid in 82
   geography of 61–6, 69
   growth intolerance 64–5
   malted 161
   marketed 72–3, 88
   prices of 40–5
   purchased 30–1, 34–8
   sent to Norwich Priory 84, 91, 105, 109, 112–13, 194–7
   share of 54, 57–60, 62
   stored 131, 136
   straw-to-grain ratio 125
   supply of towns with 3–4
   transportation costs 112–13
   yields 24

see also bread
Wiggenhall (Norfolk) 56
Wighton (Norfolk) 28, 31
wills, charitable bequests in 183–7, *see also* food charity
Winchcombe Abbey (Gloucestershire) 150
Winchester 1, 45
Winchester, Bishop of 5, 49, 97, 100–1
Winchester Cathedral Priory 10, 48, 74–5, 77
winnowers
    manorial 76, 97
    at Norwich Priory
        wages 104, 128
        see also famuli
Worcester, Bishop of 48, 53, 97

Worcester Cathedral Priory
    ale consumption at 160–1
    alms distribution at 175, 191
    estates 48, 53, 101
Worcestershire 75
Worstead (Norfolk) 51, 55, 59, 65, 72, 98–9, 102, 134, 195–6

Yare River (Norfolk) 84, 111, 115, 189
yields, *see* crops, harvest
York 1
Yorkshire 9, 54, 75, 148–9, 186
Yorkshire Dales (North Riding, Yorkshire) 75, *see also* Bolton Priory